INTERNATIONAL
RULES

INTERNATIONAL
RULES

Approaches from
International Law and
International Relations

Edited by

ROBERT J. BECK

ANTHONY CLARK AREND

ROBERT D. VANDER LUGT

New York   Oxford
OXFORD UNIVERSITY PRESS
1996

Oxford University Press

Oxford   New York
Athens   Auckland   Bangkok   Bombay
Calcutta   Cape Town   Dar es Salaam   Delhi
Florence   Hong Kong   Istanbul   Karachi
Kuala Lumpur   Madras   Madrid   Melbourne
Mexico City   Nairobi   Paris   Singapore
Taipei   Tokyo   Toronto

and associated companies in
Berlin   Ibadan

Copyright © 1996 by Oxford University Press, Inc.

Published by Oxford University Press, Inc.
198 Madison Avenue, New York, NY 10016

Library of Congress Cataloging-in-Publication Data
Beck, Robert J., 1961–
International Rules : approaches from
international law and international relations /
edited by
Robert J. Beck, Anthony Clark Arend, Robert D. Vander Lugt.
p.   cm.
Includes bibliographical references.

ISBN 978-0-19-508539-6 ISBN 978-0-19-508540-2 (pbk.)

1. International law.   I. Arend, Anthony C.   II. Vander Lugt,
Robert D.   III. Title.
JX3091.B43   1996
341'.1—dc20   95-9258   CIP

6 8 9 7 5
Printed in the United States of America
on acid-free paper

Ad Majorem Dei Gloriam

Preface

This book seeks to further existing interdisciplinary dialogue between scholars of International Law and International Relations. For nearly three hundred years, scholars commonly examined international phenomena through the lens of international law. Even during much of the twentieth century, international legal approaches were popularly so employed. After World War II, however, the study of international law essentially became alienated from that of political science. Indeed, only recently have scholars of International Law and International Relations made conspicuous efforts to end this estrangement. We wish to foster this nascent trend by providing a cross-disciplinary tool for research and teaching. With the Cold War's end, the time for such collaboration would seem especially propitious.

As its title suggests, our book concerns itself with approaches to international rules. Virtually each word in our title invites some further explanation.

First, we are interested in the study of *rules*. This word connotes a variety of things to a variety of different scholars. Stephen Krasner, for example, defines rules as "specific prescriptions or proscriptions for action."[1] Friedrich Kratochwil designates as a rule "a type of directive that simplif[ies] choice-situations by drawing attention to factors which an actor has to take into account."[2] For Robert Keohane, "rules of a regime are difficult to distinguish from its norms; at the margin, they merge into one another. Rules are, however, more specific: they indicate in more detail the specific rights and obligations of members. Rules can be altered more easily than principles or norms, since there may be more than one set of rules that can attain a given set of purposes."[3] Finally, Oran Young contends that at the core of every regime is "a cluster of norms and rules," "well-defined guides to action or standards setting forth actions that members are expected to perform (or to refrain from performing) under appropriate circumstances."[4] Without embracing or articulating a specific definition of rules ourselves, we have nevertheless included works that evince a particular notion of international "rules." Some of the authors, such as Grotius, Hart, and Kennedy, speak specifically of *legal* rules; others, such as Krasner and Keohane, use the word "rule" to refer to a host of different types of rules. But what unites all the writings included in this volume is that each focuses prominently on rules.

Second, this book concentrates on *international* rules. All the selections address rules at the international level. We have, therefore, not included works concerned with rules in general or law in general unless those works exhibit self-conscious attention to the international dimension. As a consequence, some classic writings about rules have not been included because they lacked a sufficiently "international" quality or were composed in a pre-Westphalian setting. For example, even though Thomas Aquinas represents one of the most important figures of the natural law approach, we have not included excerpts from the *Summa Theologiae* because his work predates the emergence of the modern international system.

Third, our book deals with *approaches* to international rules. We use "approach" here in its conventional sense—as a particular school of thought within a single broader discipline. Each approach addressed in this volume has been generally understood by scholars as constituting a discrete strand of thought. Not all these approaches seek to accomplish the same scholarly ends. Some, like Legal Positivism, are more doctrinally oriented; others, like the Classical Realist approach, seek to explain behavior; still others, like the New Haven School, are both prescriptive and descriptive. Similarly, some of the approaches are extremely well elaborated; others are less so. Nevertheless, each approach offers its own distinctive treatment of "international rules."

In selecting the texts for inclusion in this anthology we have been guided by five main principles.

First, we have sought to identify the most significant authors from the most important approaches. Accordingly, we have included works by such prominent individuals as Hugo Grotius, H. L. A. Hart, Robert Keohane, Stephen Krasner, David Kennedy, Hilary Charlesworth, Christine Chinkin, and Shelly Wright. For some approaches we have included more than one selection if we believed that different perspectives existed within the broader approach.

Second, we have included only works by authors writing within a given approach, not critiques of that approach per se. Limitations of space rendered it unfeasible to include pieces that constituted merely replies to or critiques of the various approaches. Frequently, however, our selected writers provide critiques of other approaches in the course of explaining their own. Joseph Grieco, for example, critiques the Institutionalists while setting out his Structural Realist approach.

Third, whenever possible we have included *complete* articles or complete sections of books. Frequently editors will delete portions of articles or book chapters to make their selected excerpts tighter and to allow room for more selections. We have deliberately eschewed this approach. Instead, we have included what might be called "stand-alone works" that allow the author to speak as the author so chooses.

Fourth, space considerations have precluded inclusion of some seminal works of extraordinary length. Myres McDougal and David Kennedy, for example, have written several important but very long law review articles. Rather than including one of these articles—some of which exceed one hundred printed pages—we have attempted to include shorter, representative works. We have, however, included reference to lengthier writings in chapter bibliographies.

Fifth, because we are addressing a particular body of literature in the International Relations and International Law disciplines, we have limited our selections to approaches that some might describe as "western." We might have assembled a collection of works reflecting the diversity of global viewpoints on international rules, but that would have been to engage in a valuable but *different* intellectual dialogue. Moreover, to have included merely one "developing world" or "socialist" work, as spatial considerations would have dictated, would have vastly oversimplified or risked caricature.

We have organized this book into ten chapters, eight of which feature selections from a specific approach to "international rules." Each of these eight chapters begins with a focus essay explaining the particular approach. Each concludes with bibliographies of other works within the approach.

Chapter 1 is entitled "International Law and International Relations: The Prospects for Interdisciplinary Collaboration." It addresses two principal questions: Where lie the most promising opportunities for collaboration between International Law and International Relations? and What constitute the most significant obstacles to sustained and robust interdisciplinary collaboration?

Chapter 2 begins the examination of different approaches with a selection from the Natural Law school, one of the oldest approaches to law. For a Natural Law thinker, law has a metaphysical source. Law comes not from consent but from higher principles of right and wrong. Even today the Natural Law tradition can be seen in modern just war theory, international human rights law, and international legal issues relating to development.

Chapter 3 contains works of the approach that developed after Natural Law—Legal Positivism. To a Positivist, law is created through consent. Positivism has been the most predominant approach to international legal rules for the past several centuries. There are, however, a variety of perspectives within Positivism with different views about whether "international law" is really "law."

Chapter 4 contains selections on the first approach that seriously challenged the usefulness of international law—Classical Realism. To a Classical Realist, law reflects underlying power relationships in the world. It does not exert a significant independent influence on state behavior.

Chapter 5 examines the so-called New Haven School of International Law. This approach is also known as the "McDougal–Lasswell" approach, as a "configurative jurisprudence," and as a "policy-oriented jurisprudence." This approach seeks to examine international law in a broader context. Law, in fact, is not a set of rules but rather a process. The New Haven approach is self-consciously interdisciplinary, seeking to incorporate insights from a variety of social sciences.

Chapter 6 includes a selection from the Structural Realist approach. This International Relations school represents an elaboration and modification of Classical Realism. It is currently one of the most prominent approaches to International Relations. Scholars from this school focus on the structure of the international system—its anarchical nature. At present there is an important contemporary dialogue between these scholars and "neoliberal institutionalists" on the role of international institutions and international rules.

Chapter 7 contains selections from Institutional Approaches. While many different Institutional perspectives exist, what unites them is a concern for rules. Institutionalists take rules and institutions seriously. They must therefore respond to the skepticism of the Classical and Structural Realists.

Chapter 8 explores the self-styled "New Stream" of international legal scholarship. This approach views law as discourse and tends to focus on the structure of legal rhetoric and argument, not on its substance. New Stream scholars draw heavily upon critical theory in either the modernist or postmodernist traditions.

Chapter 9 contains the most comprehensive article to date reflecting "feminist voices" on international law. Feminists view the contemporary international legal system as inherently gendered. International law is masculine in its orientation and operates to the detriment of women. As the Feminists note, there is no *one* approach; there are many Feminist "voices."

Finally, Chapter 10, "Toward an Understanding of International Legal Rules," seeks to integrate the insights of many of the approaches contained in this volume and to elaborate further our own approach to international legal rules.

We wish to emphasize that our anthology is designed to be a useful point of departure for interdisciplinary study of international rules. It is far from the last word on the subject. Our intent is to take further steps along a journey that has recently begun. If we can stimulate continued interdisciplinary research and teaching, we will have accomplished our purpose.

Charlottesville, Virginia   R. J. B.
Washington, D.C.   A. C. A.
Springfield, Virginia   R. D. V. L.
September 1995

Notes

1. Stephen D. Krasner, "Structural Causes and Regime Consequences: Regimes as Intervening Variables," in Stephen D. Krasner, ed., *International Regimes* (Ithaca, N.Y.: Cornell University Press, 1983), p. 2.

2. Friedrich V. Kratochwil, *Rules, Norms, and Decisions: On the Conditions of Practical and Legal Reasoning in International Relations and Domestic Affairs* (Cambridge: Cambridge University Press, 1989), p. 72.

3. Robert O. Keohane, *After Hegemony* (Princeton, N.J.: Princeton University Press, 1984), p. 58.

4. Oran R. Young, *International Cooperation: Building Regimes for Natural Resources and the Environment* (Ithaca, N.Y.: Cornell University Press, 1989), p. 16.

Acknowledgments

This book has its roots in a graduate seminar first taught in the University of Virginia's Department of Government and Foreign Affairs. As Robert Beck prepared to teach a course on international rules, he sought the assistance of his regular collaborator, Anthony Clark Arend of Georgetown University. Together, we were unable to find a single compilation that included works dating from the modern international system's origins through the post–Cold War period. Nor could we find a single text self-consciously embracing scholarship from both the International Relations and International Law disciplines. As a consequence, we set out to draw together readings for the seminar that satisfied both these criteria.

With our original collection as a foundation, Beck twice offered an international rules seminar at Virginia, and Arend twice the equivalent course at Georgetown. Our classroom experiences proved invaluable and convinced us of the necessity of a single book with an interdisciplinary focus. Accordingly, we decided to prepare this anthology with Robert Vander Lugt, drawing on insights gleaned from our classroom experiences. Vander Lugt was a law student at the University of Virginia when he participated in Beck's first course. He is now an attorney with an international law firm in the District of Columbia.

Over the past several years, our project has significantly benefited from the advice and encouragement of many colleagues in International Law and International Relations. These include Francis A. Boyle, Hilary Charlesworth, John King Gamble, Michael J. Glennon, Joseph Grieco, Lowell S. Gustafson, Stephan Haggard, Louis Henkin, Mark W. Janis, Christopher Joyner, David W. Kennedy, Robert O. Keohane, Stephen D. Krasner, Friedrich Kratochwil, John Norton Moore, Myres S. McDougal, John F. Murphy, Nicholas Onuf, W. Michael Reisman, Oscar Schachter,

Anne-Marie Slaughter, Michael Joseph Smith, Barbara Stark, Kenneth N. Waltz, and Alexander Wendt. We also appreciate the comments of Larry Taulbee, who comprehensively reviewed our project when we presented it at the 1995 International Studies Association Annual Meeting. For their careful readings of chapter 1 and constructive suggestions, Robert Beck wishes particularly to thank John S. Duffield, Lawrence LeBlanc, Michael Schechter, Herman Schwartz, and Alexander Wendt. Anthony Clark Arend is especially grateful to Robert J. Lieber, Charles E. Pirtle, and Nigel Purvis for similarly valuable assistance on chapter 10.

The selection of works for inclusion here was done jointly by the three editors. Beck and Arend collaborated on the editing and preparation of the selected works for publication. Beck compiled the supplemental bibliographies. Proofreading assistance was provided by Kevin Markland, Elizabeth Martell, Sally Roever, and Ruth Vander Lugt. Finally, with the guidance of Beck and Arend, Vander Lugt drafted most of the focus essays.

Contents

INTERNATIONAL RULES

1

International Law and International Relations: The Prospects for Interdisciplinary Collaboration

ROBERT J. BECK

[T]he student of law and the student of politics . . . purport to be looking at the same world from the vantage point of important disciplines. It seems unfortunate, indeed destructive, that they should not, at the least, hear each other.

So submitted Louis Henkin in his classic study, *How Nations Behave: Law and Foreign Policy.*[1] The present volume is animated by the spirit of interdisciplinary collaboration called for by Henkin, and more recently by Kenneth Abbott, Robert Keohane, Anne-Marie Slaughter, and Oran Young.[2] For too long, International Relations (IR) scholars have simply dismissed international law as either irrelevant or epiphenomenal: in general, "law" has been left, rather unceremoniously, to the lawyers.[3] International Law (IL) scholars, meanwhile, have typically returned the favor, ignoring routinely the work of political scientists on international rules and institutions.[4] Such pervasive academic insularity must not be allowed to continue, however. As law professor Slaughter has cogently argued, "Just as constitutional lawyers study political theory, and political theorists inquire into the nature and substance of constitutions, so too should two disciplines that study the laws of state behavior seek to learn from one another."[5]

Toward this end, chapter 1 focuses on two principal questions. First, where lie the most promising opportunities for collaboration between International Law and International Relations? And second, what constitute the most significant obstacles to sustained and productive interdisciplinary collaboration? To address these questions, the chapter opens with a characterization of the International Law and International Relations disciplines. Next it illustrates specific IR and IL approaches to international rules by reviewing their responses to four significant issues. With the necessary groundwork in place, it concludes with an assessment of the problems and prospects of cooperation between the disciplines.

The Disciplines

Any discussion of scholarly collaboration between International Relations and International Law should commence with an elementary but vital acknowledgement: both disciplines are thoroughly heterogeneous.[6] Whether or not they explicitly focus on international rules, for example, contemporary IR scholars embrace differing ontologies, proceed from divergent epistemological assumptions, and employ a wide array of methods. Postmodernists vie today with Weberian social scientists,[7] cognitivists with rational choice model builders. Such *intradisciplinary* variety, moreover, has increasingly described International Law, as Feminist and New Stream scholars have joined debates with New Haven School members, Legal Positivists, and Naturalists about law's character, structure, and substance. If the prospects for interdisciplinary learning are to be maximized, therefore, the collaborative enterprise must be informed by a genuine appreciation of the profound diversities of International Law and International Relations. As this book seeks clearly to demonstrate, there is more to IR than rationalistic[8] studies of regimes, more to IL than Legal Positivist analyses of doctrine and state practice.[9]

To this general observation, three caveats must be added. First, the *disciplinary* borders between IL and IR are not always clearly or easily demarcatable, and thus will remain contestable.[10] Second, within the same academic discipline, the dividing lines may at times become obscured *between different scholarly approaches*. Within International Relations, for example, many Classical Realists, Structural Realists (or "Neorealists"), and Institutionalists share certain prominent epistemological and methodological affinities. So, too, do a number of Feminist and New Stream students of International Law. Finally, even *within the same scholarly approach* of a single discipline, a broad spectrum of perspectives may exist. International Relations' Institutionalists, for instance, can be grouped into "Rationalistic" and "Sociological" (or "Reflective") camps, and those groups can be further subdivided. Similarly, within International Law, the Lasswell-McDougal "configurative jurisprudence" approach has been employed by scholars as distinct as W. Michael Reisman and Richard A. Falk, a broad array of publicists have been dubbed Legal Positivists, and many different Feminist "voices" have been expressed.[11] Ultimately, scholars from both IR and IL either may personally reject efforts by others to categorize them by approach or may effectively elude such categorization because of the unique natures of their works.[12] To be sure, whenever labels are used, the danger exists that they will obscure more than they illuminate.

Despite the diversities of IR and IL and the inherent limitations of any taxonomical exercise, it is nevertheless possible to adduce some useful generalizations about the two disciplines and to propose a scheme for classifying their respective approaches to international rules. From the outset, it should be noted that both International Relations and International Law began as largely state-centered disciplines, but that each has come increasingly to appreciate the significance of non-state actors and phenomena. Indeed, some International Law and International Relations scholars now even find the very notions of state-centric analysis and state sovereignty problematic. Second, both disciplines have traditionally shared some of the same core interests, including interests in international peace and cooperation. To posit such common disciplinary concerns, of course, is not to suggest that the various IR and IL approaches similarly construe them or respond to them. Nor is it to deny the existence of prominent scholarly outliers in each discipline. Third, the scholarship of both IR and IL features a substantial amount of description per se. Such description typically focuses on patterns of state practice and on the formal structures of international institutions and rules, though it is only rarely undertaken as an end in itself.[13] Finally, both disciplines' principal approaches to international rules can be mapped on to the same two conceptual divides: an empiricist-critical divide reflecting the approach's basic method; and an explanatory-prescriptive divide reflecting the approach's primary objective or animus. As a consequence, all the major approaches to rules of both disciplines can be situated, if with some inevitable imprecision, within a single two-by-two matrix.[14]

Before seeking to place specific approaches on this matrix, however, further elaboration is necessary. What, for example, does the empiricist-critical divide entail? Those IR and IL approaches to international rules that can be labeled empiricist lie within the "positivist" tradition of social science.[15] They assume both that some form of objective knowledge is realizable[16] and that the natural and social worlds are not fundamentally different.[17] As a consequence, an "empiricist" is one who holds that knowledge of the social world and its rules can reliably be derived from "empirical testing of propositions or hypotheses against evidence or facts."[18]

IR and IL approaches whose method is critical, in contradistinction, reject the notion that the social world is amenable to the same essential research process as the natural world, that international politics can be studied like particle physics.[19] Emphasizing discourse and the importance of "intersubjective meaning," the critical study of international rules is thus often interpretive, hermeneutical, not "scientific" in the traditional sense.[20] It is grounded in an assumption of historical contingency, in the view that behavioral regularities observable in the social world do not exist independently of place and time.[21] As a consequence, critical scholarship tends to be skeptical of the prospects for objective knowledge. Not all critical scholars of international rules are equally pessimistic, however, as both postmodernists *and* modernists may employ critical methods.[22]

What of the explanatory-prescriptive divide? Those approaches to international rules whose purpose is primarily explanatory seek to discover *why* and/or *how* such rules are originated, structured, evolve, and influence state action. Explanatory scholarship strives, then, for more than accurate description per se. Some approaches—typically those that are empiricist in method—attempt principally to derive causal explanations for rule-related outcomes or events. Other approaches, often those critical in method, endeavor to understand whence rules have come and what they mean.[23]

Prescriptive approaches, meanwhile, embrace two distinct projects. First, some prescriptive scholars deliberately limit their task to the accurate characterization of existing doctrine: the formal rules by which states are bound, those with which states should by legal obligation comply. Second, other prescriptive scholars strive not only to ascertain doctrine but also to endorse or to propose changes of existing international rules. Appeals to such criteria as "justice," "equality," and "human dignity" dominate their work. Prescriptive scholarship, in sum, is fundamentally concerned with either what "by law" state behavior should be, or with what international rules governing state behavior should be. The divide between prescriptive and explanatory approaches, therefore, can reasonably be described as an "ought" versus "is" dichotomy.[24]

On the basis of this classification scheme (Figure 1), where are the various approaches to international rules represented in this volume to be placed? In the empiricist/explanatory quadrant of the matrix three approaches can confidently be located: Classical Realist, Structural Realist, and Rationalistic Institutionalist. All these IR approaches seek to devise meaningful social scientific generalizations about state behavior. According to IR scholar Oran R. Young: "We want a body of [such] generalizations, and furthermore we would like even better to be able to embed those generalizations in models—intellectual constructs from which we could derive the various individual generalizations."[25] Though their appreciations of international rules' nature and significance vary substantially, these three approaches share a common empiricist orientation and a common scholarly aim, the explanation of state conduct.

Three approaches, similarly, can be positioned in the empiricist/ prescriptive quadrant: Natural Law, Legal Positivist, and New Haven School ("NHS," "Lasswell-McDougal," or "configurative jurisprudence"). The Natural Law approach's prescriptive character is manifest, but an empiricist label might at first seem problematic insofar as Naturalist scholars posit a transempirical source of rules. Two of Naturalism's defining attributes, however, support its empiricist classification: first, the approach assumes that objective knowledge can be attained through a process requiring human observation; and second, it rejects as misplaced the distinction between the natural and social realms, insisting that human society is a thoroughly natural phenomenon. Though not as scientifically self-conscious as, for example, Rationalistic Institutionalism, the Natural Law

PRIMARY OBJECTIVE

	EXPLANATORY Why? How?	PRESCRIPTIVE What is obligatory? What should be obligatory?
EMPIRICIST	Classical Realist Structural Realist Rationalistic Institutionalist	*Natural Law* *Legal Positivist* *New Haven School*
METHOD		
CRITICAL	Sociological Institutionalist *New Stream*	*Feminist Legal*

Legal approaches to international rules are italicized.

Figure 1.

approach nonetheless fits the empiricist category as here described. By contrast, the New Haven School's "scientific" heritage, and hence its empiricist orientation, is deep-rooted, but its categorization as predominantly prescriptive is open to challenge. Certainly, the NHS approach features an important explanatory dimension: it seeks accurately to depict the social context within which international (legal) rules exist and the social process by which they are constituted. The New Haven School's primary impetus, however, has arguably remained prescriptive: the disciples of Lasswell and McDougal's "policy-oriented" jurisprudence have repeatedly and explicitly expressed their purpose in terms of promoting "a world public order of human dignity."[26] Finally, placement of the Legal Positivist approach within the empiricist/prescriptive quadrant will not likely provoke controversy given Legal Positivism's unambiguously empiricist assumptions and its signal objective of ascertaining doctrine, the formal rules by which states are bound. Legal Positivism's prescriptive agenda is narrower than that of the Naturalists and New Haven scholars, of course, for it refuses to embrace a specific teleology.

In the critical/explanatory quadrant, both the Sociological Institutionalist and New Stream approaches merit placement. New Stream IL scholarship deliberately and explicitly eschews the prescriptive enterprise. Instead, it seeks by critical means—deconstructive analysis of international legal discourse—to reveal international law's incoherence, restricted intellectual structure (liberal ideology), indeterminacy, and self-validating authority. The New Stream pursues limited "critical knowledge," exposing "the hidden ideological structure and political choices underlying international law."[27] IR's Sociological Institutionalists (labeled "Reflective Institutionalists" by Keohane) use critical, in general interpretivist, means to address "why" and "how" questions.[28] With the New Stream scholars,

Sociological Institutionalists share an appreciation of the historical/cultural context of international rules and an emphasis on the "web of intersubjective meanings" that constitutes human consciousness.[29]

A substantial portion of the Feminist IL literature, finally, can be assigned to the critical/prescriptive quadrant. Because Feminist international legal scholarship is self-consciously diverse and inclusive, it eludes ready classification. Nevertheless, many of its most prominent works thus far have proved avowedly critical in method, and these can therefore reasonably be described as such. One may still debate, however, whether the aim of critical Feminist IL has been primarily prescriptive or explanatory. Scholars like Hilary Charlesworth, Christine Chinkin, and Shelley Wright have remained, of course, keenly interested in the task of uncovering the "thoroughly gendered" nature of the international legal system and its rules. Nevertheless, their work and that of others has regularly extended beyond such exposition, evincing specific international legal rule preferences and thereby distinguishing itself from the strictly explanatory New Stream. Moreover, the desire to change "biased" rules as well as the procedures by which international rules per se are made, to effect a "feminist transformation of international law," seems fundamentally to have inspired Feminist IL scholarship, whether critical or otherwise.[30]

Approaches to International Rules

One efficient means of further characterizing the principal International Relations and International Law approaches to international rules is to review how they and others[31] respond to questions of mutual concern. Such a strategy is employed here because it permits a simultaneous highlighting of substantive avenues for potential cross-disciplinary debate and learning. Specifically, the responses by IR and IL scholars to four prominent questions are considered. Though all four questions are to varying degrees associated, for analytical purposes each is addressed separately.

What Relationship Exists (Should Exist) between International Rules and Morality?

An issue of manifest concern to constituents of both disciplines, but especially to prescriptive scholars, is that of morality's relationship to international rules. This exceptionally broad question necessarily entails multiple lines of inquiry, including the following: What moral quality, if any, imbues international rules? Toward what moral ends[32] should international rules be directed? Do moral considerations and associated perceptions of "obligation"[33] actually influence behavior related to international rules (e.g., rule creation and enforcement)? If so, how? Should they be permitted to do so?

The most "natural" IL respondents to the morality question may well be the Natural Law scholars. The first prominent International Law thinkers, of course, were Naturalists: Francisco de Vitoria and Francisco Suarez. So, too, was the publicist most often considered "the father of international law," Hugo Grotius.[34] Beyond their primary assumptions of law's metaphysical source and its capacity to be apprehended by human reason, what unites the Naturalists is their abiding appreciation of the "sources of obligation" question[35] and their serious treatment of it.[36] Natural Law scholarship is significant, as well, for its regular attention to transnational, justice-related issues.[37]

Feminist scholars have emerged recently within the International Law discipline to embrace spiritedly such justice concerns as well, if not always formally so. Charlesworth, Chinkin, and Wright,[38] for instance, have challenged the allegedly "objective" and "neutral" operation and nature of international law and its context:

> [B]oth the structures of international lawmaking and the content of the rules of international law privilege men; if women's interests are acknowledged at all, they are marginalized. International law is a thoroughly gendered system.[39]

Though their argument eschews direct appeals to ethics or justice per se, it nevertheless expresses objectives that are manifestly value based, for example: "*genuine equality* between the sexes,"[40] the *inclusion* of "different voice[s], both female *and* non-European," in the discourse of law and politics,[41] and "*balanced representation* in international organizations."[42]

A third strand of the IL discipline prominently to have engaged questions of "norms and values"[43] is the New Haven School, or "configurative jurisprudence," inaugurated by Harold Lasswell and Myres McDougal. This approach proposes as its goal "a world public order of human dignity," views international law as serving social ends and values, and candidly espouses a social engineering mission. Because of its postulation of human "goals" and "values," the New Haven School has been characterized by Oscar Schachter as "natural law thinking without theology or metaphysics."[44]

Contributing in particular to the question of obligation are the Legal Positivists[45] John Austin,[46] Hans Kelsen,[47] and H.L.A. Hart.[48] For Austin, "law properly so-called" is constituted by a sovereign's command; where law exists, human conduct is rendered in some sense nonoptional, or *obligatory*. Because international law rules are not obligated by sovereign coercion, Austin concludes, they are not "law" but merely "positive international morality." Kelsen, though building on Austin's coercive order conceptions of law and obligation, nevertheless concludes that international law is "law," albeit primitive law based on the legal technique of self-help. In Kelsen's view, "states must eventually evolve from their present non-coercive primitivism to become a genuine, organized community in which 'real' obligations are enforced by judges and a police force deployed by a supranational executive."[49] Hart, in an important insight that distinguishes him from his Legal Positivist colleagues, differentiates the notions of "being obliged" by coercion from "having an obligation," before developing his own "concept of law" based on primary and secondary rules.[50] Notwithstanding their distinct views of obligation, however, Legal Positivists are united in accepting the fundamental if controversial premise that positive law is a realm separate from morality.[51]

Finally, IL's New Stream scholarship led by David Kennedy will likely prompt vigorous debate by its aggressive challenge of mainstream thinking on rules and morality. The approach denies, for example, the objectivity of international law's rules, as well as the human capacity to assess the substantive validity and desirability of those rules. The New Stream utterly rejects, moreover, the conceptual utility of "sovereignty," a notion suffused with moral overtones. The principle has been routinely construed, for instance, as representing a legal impediment to humanitarian intervention.

International Relations scholars have also broached the issue of the nexus between international rules and morality, though recently from a standpoint typically more explanatory than prescriptive or strictly descriptive.[52] Opinions vary widely within the discipline about the degree to which moral considerations actually influence international rule-associated behavior, and about whether, and how, the "moral factor" should be introduced into explanatory models of state behavior.[53]

Some writers, including Sociological Institutionalists, view moral considerations as at times significantly affecting such behavior, and hence as worthy of serious scholarly treatment. Andrew Hurrell, for example, argues that international rules like those on human rights, armed conquest, and territorial annexation "depend on a common moral awareness that works directly, if still in fragile and uneven ways, on the minds and emotions of individuals within states."[54] Similarly, Ethan Nadelmann submits that "despite the inattentions of most international relations scholars, . . . moral and emotional factors related to neither political nor economic advantage . . . can and do play important roles" in the evolution of international regimes.[55]

Rationalistic Institutionalists and Structural Realists, by contrast, tend to exclude moral factors altogether from their analyses of state action, to subsume such factors under the rubrics of "reputation" and "reciprocity," or to relax somewhat their basic assumption of rational egoism. Illustrative of this third trend is Robert O. Keohane's *After Hegemony*. Here, in a chapter on "bounded rationality and self-interest," Keohane briefly discusses "the moralistic overlay of world politics" in which government leaders "proclaim their adherence" to international principles and rules.[56] Although Keohane proposes that one can explain such behavior "on purely self-interested grounds," he judges that such an explanation is "probably too cynical." Moralists "sometimes gain high office," Keohane concedes, and the requirements of public justification may cause some government officials "to take on some of the beliefs that they profess."[57]

Profoundly concerned about the presence of "moralists" in high government office, surely, are many of IR's Classical Realists. George F. Kennan, for example, maintains in a 1951 lecture that the "legalistic-moralistic approach to international problems" constituted the "most serious fault" in past U.S. foreign policy. This approach, Kennan asserts, is characterized by the misplaced "belief that it should be possible to suppress the chaotic and dangerous aspirations of governments in the international field by the acceptance of some system of legal rules and restraints."[58] Not only does the approach suffer many inherent "theoretical deficiencies," Kennan argues, but also a "greater deficiency": "the carrying-over into the affairs of states of the concepts of right and wrong, the assumption that state behavior is a fit subject for moral judgment."[59] Kennan shares this last conviction, if little else, with the New Stream scholars.[60]

The Classical Realists should not be caricatured, however, as dismissing altogether the roles that are (or should be) played in international politics by moral and legal considerations.[61] In *Politics Among Nations,* for instance, Hans Morgenthau acknowledges that "moral rules do not permit certain policies to be considered [by statesmen] at all," that "certain things are not being done on moral grounds, even though it would be expedient to do them," and that "in most instances" international law has been "scrupulously observed."[62] Raymond Aron, moreover, concedes in *Peace and War* that "even in the relations between states, respect for ideas, aspirations to higher values and concern for obligation have been manifested. Rarely have collectivities acted as if they would stop at nothing with regard to one another."[63]

Why Do Actors Comply with International Rules?

Closely related to the "moral question," though not coextensive with it,[64] is the problem of compliance.[65] In his celebrated 1990 book, *The Power of Legitimacy among Nations,* Thomas Franck poses this question: "Why do powerful nations obey powerless rules?"[66] Students of both International Relations and International Law have begun in earnest to address variations of this "compliance" question, and it would appear to constitute an area where significant gains can be jointly achieved. "By drawing [here] on insights and perspectives from scholars in both fields," Anne-Marie Slaughter writes, "it should be possible to formulate a set of questions to which both sides can contribute factual information and theoretical insight. The results of inquiries from both perspectives," she concludes, "could then be synthesized in a common framework that would highlight the overlap of both disciplines and the comparative advantage of each."[67]

One of the earlier IR students of compliance was the Institutionalist Oran Young. In his 1979 book *Compliance and Public Authority,* Young examined "compliance with behavioral prescriptions" through an explicitly *multidisciplinary* lens. In his bibliographic note there Young maintained that because "materials pertaining to this problem are scattered widely through a variety of differentiable fields, . . . any systematic consideration of compliance can hardly proceed without taking account of the ways in which it has been approached in a number of separate disciplines."[68] Robert Keohane, another eminent Institutionalist, is currently engaged in a comprehensive study of U.S. compliance with "inconvenient [international] commitments." Here, Keohane intends to test the explanatory power of five hypotheses drawn from both the Institutionalist and Realist literatures of International Relations.[69] A third Institutionalist, John S. Duffield, has recently employed regime theory to explain why alliance members comply with rules governing conventional force levels. Duffield identifies and elaborates two categories of "mutually reinforcing" sources of compliance, external and internal, based on differing assumptions about the nature of states.[70]

International Law scholars across a broad disciplinary spectrum have also grappled with the compliance phenomenon. Franck, for example, posits in *The Power of Legitimacy* that an international rule's capacity to induce compliance is not dependent on the existence of an Austinian coercive authority. Instead, he submits, a rule's ability "to exert compliance pull" depends on state perceptions of that rule's *legitimacy*, a property that varies with four factors: determinacy; symbolic validation, ritual, and pedigree; coherence; and adherence. Abram and Antonia Chayes, meanwhile, argue in a series of works[71] that treaty compliance provisions less effectively "enforce" compliance than they structure processes and specify venues for the resolution of disputes.[72] In stark contrast to these more mainstream scholars and consistent with elements of New Stream analysis, Nigel Purvis proposes his own "anthropological theory" to explain international law's "authority" in terms of its "cultural self-validation."[73]

Other IL writers of the past half century who have contributed important insights to the literature of rule compliance include the Legal Positivist H.L.A. Hart;[74] his dialogue partner and Naturalist, Lon L. Fuller;[75] the World Order scholar Richard Falk;[76] and various practitioners of the Lasswell-McDougal jurisprudence.[77] On this last group's significance, for instance, Oran Young observes: "The policy-oriented work of the 'New Haven School' has taught me that it is often hazardous to think about compliance in simple dichotomous terms."[78]

What Influence Do Domestic Political Factors Exert on Behavior Related to International Rules?

Yet another question of increasing interest to both IR and IL scholars, one closely linked to the morality and compliance questions, is that of domestic politics' influence on international rule-related behavior. Although the majority of IR and IL scholars may well continue largely to ignore it, writers from both disciplines have recently lamented the insufficient attention the domestic factor has thus far received.[79] In a 1993 article, for example, Anne-Marie Slaughter argues that mainstream IR's and IL's common model of state behavior is unfortunately a "'black box' or 'billiard ball' . . . in which states are regarded as identical in form and function and opaque with regard to domestic regime type and state–society relations."[80] Robert Keohane advanced a similar theme in a prominent 1988 address: "As formulated to date, both rationalistic and . . . reflective approaches [to international institutions and rules] share a common blind spot: neither pays sufficient attention to domestic politics."[81] And in a 1992 presentation before the American Society of International Law, Kenneth W. Abbott contended that "the ultimate aim" of a joint IL-IR discipline should be "to integrate the domestic and international arenas as fully as possible."[82]

Important work on the influence of domestic factors is proceeding now in both disciplines. In her effort to open the black box, for example, Slaughter has sketched the outlines of a new "Liberal Agenda."[83] This theory proceeds from three core assumptions: that individuals and privately constituted groups, the members of domestic society, constitute the principal actors in politics; that all governments represent some segment of domestic society, whose interests are in turn reflected in state policy; and that the behavior of states reflects the nature and configuration of state preferences.[84]

Keohane is addressing the domestic dimension in another way, including it as the fifth of five compliance hypotheses he is testing: "Institutional enmeshment increases the probability of compliance."[85] The phenomenon of institutional enmeshment obtains "when domestic decision making with respect to an international commitment is affected by the institutional arrangements established in the course of making or maintaining that commitment." A state's commitment, Keohane explains, "affects not only the state's legal freedom of action, but also the political process by which it decides what course to follow."[86]

Finally, in his 1993 essay "Bringing the Second Image (Back) In," Institutionalist Michael Zurn explores the domestic sources of regime formation. Here he outlines the qualities of a regime-conducive foreign policy, then develops hypotheses about the relationship between domestic politics variables and other unit properties and about the pursuit of a regime-conducive foreign policy.[87]

Such recent work on domestic politics and international rules is not the only significant inquiry to have been proposed or conducted, however. Indeed, one of the signal qualities of the Lasswell-McDougal jurisprudence has been its appreciation of the complex "process of authoritative decision-making" that constitutes the law. McDougal and Lasswell assert, for example, that in comparing "systems of public order," many questions related to decision-maker "authority" must be addressed, of which many have a manifest domestic politics aspect:

> Who are regarded as authoritative decision-makers and by what processes are they established and identified as authoritative? What is the degree of

community participation in such processes of establishment and identification? Are decision-makers in the various authority functions distinguished from parties to the interactions regulated? . . . How, in sum,
must such [governance] structures be appraised in terms of such fundamental *continua* as democracy—despotism, centralism—decentralization, concentration—deconcentration, pluralism—monopolization, and
regimentation—individuation?[88]

Such concerns, *inter alia,* would seem now to be echoed by the emergent
"Liberal Paradigm."

How Are International Rules Formulated?

Overlapping the three already identified, a fourth question of mutual
concern to IR and IL and ripe for interdisciplinary attention is that of how
international rules originate. By what specific mechanisms do such rules
come into existence? Does rule creation reflect merely the international
system's configuration of power? What role, if any, do gender and ideology
play? How central are individuals and groups to the international "legislative" process? And of what consequence for rule development per se are
basic considerations of morality?

Significant contributors to the interdisciplinary enterprise here can be
the critical Feminist IL scholars. Charlesworth, Chinkin, and Wright, for
example, argue that contemporary "international legal structures and
principles" represent merely "international men's law."[89] That law results
inevitably from a rule-creating *process* from which women and women's
experiences are excluded, and from a normative *structure* that "has allowed issues of particular concern to women to be either ignored or
undermined."[90] They contend, for instance, that women's voices have
been denied expression in "those bodies with special functions regarding
the creation and progressive development of international law," with only
one woman ever sitting as International Court of Justice judge and none
ever serving as International Law Commission member.[91] In addition,
they assert that the intellectual structure within which "certain principles
of international law" are defined "rests on and reproduces" a mistaken
"public/private distinction." This false dichotomy, central to liberal theory, has been built into international legal discourse, thereby "privileg[ing]
the male world view and support[ing] male dominance in the international
legal order."[92] Given the skewed process and structure through which
international rules are formulated, such rules necessarily fail adequately to
address women's experiences and to protect distinctly women's rights.[93]

The views of the New Stream thinkers about international rule creation resemble in some important respects those of many critical Feminists. New Stream scholars submit, for example, that "traditional international legal reasoning operates within a restricted intellectual *structure*."
This predominant, western liberal ideological structure renders international law "narrow-minded" and receptive to "only some goals and val-

ues." As a consequence, "some arguments qualify as international legal arguments but others do not, and international law rules out some conceptions of international life altogether."[94] Proponents of the New Stream approach are far less concerned than many Feminists, however, about the actual historical process of rule creation. Because the New Stream rejects objective epistemology, "a determinate or historical understanding of law's origin or authority" is precluded.[95] Nevertheless, New Stream devotees hold that international law's rules are the product of "a particular type of discourse about international social life," of a "conversation" defined by liberal ideology's inherent contradictions.[96]

An alternative perspective on the question of law's creation is provided by the New Haven School's elaborate conceptual framework. Lasswell and McDougal were arguably the first students of international law to concentrate on the dynamic social process in which international legal rules originate and evolve. For appliers of their "configurative jurisprudence," a "decision" constitutes "the means whereby individual confrontations involving competing claims about the distribution of values are settled," and "law" is merely the record established by a succession of such decisions over time, provided those decisions are "authoritative" and "effective." Every "claim" regarding the allocation of values, therefore, can be viewed as a law-creating effort: "If a claim is successful in the sense that an authoritative and effective decision ensues that conforms to its demands, the claim becomes, *ipso facto,* an element of the law of the social system in question." Conversely, if the claim fails in these terms, it lacks the status of "law," at least until a similar claim yields an authoritative and effective decision.[97]

IR's Classical and Structural Realists, like IL's Feminist, New Stream, and New Haven School scholars, emphasize the integral role of power in the rule-creation process. In their view, international rules and institutions fundamentally reflect the configuration of power in the international system, and "specific [rule-based] arrangements come into existence when those possessing sufficient power take the necessary steps to create them."[98] The Structural Realist Robert Gilpin maintains, for example, that "[a]lthough the rights and rules governing interstate behavior are to varying degrees based on consensus and mutual interest, the *primary foundation* of rights and rules is in the power and interests of the dominant groups or states in a social system." Modern "international law," according to Gilpin, "was imposed on the world by Western civilization, and it reflects the values and interests of Western civilization."[99] Similarly, "the rules of a liberal international economic order" were created and enforced by two successive hegemonic powers, Great Britain and the United States.[100]

In seeking to explain the dynamics or absence of "state cooperation," Realists argue that states are motivated principally by a desire to ensure their own survival,[101] that the fundamental goal of states is to prevent other states "from achieving advances in their relative capabilities," and that "state positionality may [therefore] constrain the willingness of states to cooperate."[102] Implicit in these Realist premises is a presumption that state calculations of "relative gains" will suffuse, and therefore regularly undermine, efforts to establish international rules and institutions.

Significantly more optimistic than the Realists about the prospects for international rule development, in particular for that without a hegemon, are Rationalistic Institutionalists like Robert Keohane.[103] Though his *After Hegemony* focuses primarily on the question of whether international cooperation can persist without hegemonic dominance, Keohane also offers there an account of regime creation in microeconomic terms. "Whether a hegemon exists or not," he submits, "international regimes depend on the existence of patterns of common or complementary interests that are perceived or capable of being perceived by political actors."[104] According to his "functional" approach, regimes (of which rules constitute a core element) are devised by utilitarian states to address the problem of political "market failure," to "overcome the deficiencies that make it impossible to consummate . . . mutually beneficial agreements." The "anticipated effects" of these regimes, Keohane proposes, "explain their causes."[105] International regimes "rarely emerge from chaos," furthermore, but are "built on one another." As a consequence, scholars should "think as much about the evolution of regimes as about their creation *ex nihilo*."[106]

Institutionalists of the less rationalistic/economistic variety stress the significance of individual persons and groups for the establishment of international rules.[107] Oran Young, for instance, argues that individual leadership constitutes "a critical determinant of success or failure in the processes of institutional bargaining that dominate efforts to form international regimes or . . . institutional arrangements," the essence of which are international rules. In an effort to "bring the individual back in," Young differentiates three forms of individual leadership: structural, entrepreneurial, and intellectual.[108] In a more narrowly focused argument, Andrew Hurrell submits that international rules "do not develop as a result of the direct interplay of state interests or because of the functional benefits which they provide." Instead, Hurrell contends, "they depend on a common moral awareness" within the minds and emotions of individual persons.[109]

Ethan Nadelmann similarly underscores the influence of moral considerations upon rule formation, though he accords greater importance to state economic and security interests than does Hurrell. Nadelmann maintains that "transnational moral entrepreneurs" have contributed notably to the process of establishing international prohibition regimes. These nongovernmental transnational organizations, he contends, "mobilize popular opinion and public support both within their host country and abroad; they stimulate and assist in the creation of like-minded organizations in other countries; and they play a significant role in elevating their objective beyond its identification with the national interests of their government."[110]

Employing a different vocabulary, Peter M. Haas and his collaborators[111] advance an argument in some respects reminiscent of Nadelmann's.[112] "Epistemic communities," they suggest, can assume significant roles in the international policy coordination process and, more specifically, in the development of international rules. These "networks of knowledge-based experts"[113] play a part, for example, in "articulating the cause-and-effect relationships of complex problems, helping states identify their interests, framing the issues for collective debate, proposing specific policies, and identifying salient points for negotiation."[114]

The Problems and Prospects for Collaboration

In his 1992 address before the American Society of International Law, Kenneth Abbott proffered a "very optimistic" assessment of the potential for disciplinary cooperation between International Law and International Relations. The law professor maintained then that "IL and the new approaches of IR" were "so neatly complementary" that the two "could enrich each other tremendously across a wide range of intellectual activities." Indeed, Abbott predicted the possible "emergence of a new joint discipline" that might be dubbed "the study of organized international cooperation." Over the long term, he concluded, this new field might "transcend its constituent disciplines," much the same way that the "law and economics" movement had done.[115]

Abbott's intentionally optimistic forecast may nevertheless have been unduly sanguine. At least two significant impediments could hinder or even completely frustrate sustained IR-IL cooperation, both of which may be associated with what Oran Young has aptly dubbed a "two cultures problem."[116] This infelicitous circumstance has persisted for nearly half a century and is unlikely soon or easily to be transcended.

One conspicuous hindrance to collaboration is the general tendency of the "two cultures" to "ask different questions and to expect different answers."[117] To be sure, similar core interests in such areas as international peace and cooperation have historically inspired the mainstream scholarship of both IR and IL. And as has been shown, there are other, more specific substantive areas of mutual scholarly interest, which researchers from both disciplines have already begun to explore. Nevertheless, this exploration has not yet been regularly undertaken, nor has it typically assumed a deliberately interdisciplinary aspect. Furthermore, and of far greater concern, a pronounced gap exists between the predominantly explanatory aspirations of the IR scholarship devoted to international rules and the predilection of most modern IL scholarship for prescribing doctrine.

This divergence of intellectual foci, of "why is/how is?" from "what is/what ought to be obligatory?" questions, was clearly exhibited at a workshop for lawyers and political scientists convened in 1992 by the American Society of International Law (ASIL) and the Academic Council on the United Nations System (ACUNS). Here, at least in the program's first days, many of the IL participants seemed either amused or annoyed by their IR colleagues' reverence for properly labeled dependent and independent variables. The IR participants, meanwhile, appeared generally frustrated at the lawyers' preoccupation with accurately characterizing the substance of the law and not with identifying its causal relationships to specific behaviors. Such reactions were probably inevitable given the different ends toward which legal and political science educations are directed: advocacy and analysis, respectively. Though the members of each group ultimately gained some appreciation for the concerns of the other group, that appreciation was cultivated only over two weeks of intensive classes, research, colloquia, and informal discussions. Given the number and diversity of its participants, the ACUNS/ASIL summer 1992 workshop arguably represented a microcosm of the larger IR and IL communities. Accordingly, the experience of that international, interdisciplinary program suggests that the explanatory-prescriptive divide is not altogether unbridgeable.

A second symptom of the two cultures problem, and hence a further challenge to cross-disciplinary dialogue and debate, is the entrenched practices of the two disciplines. Scholars from each group, for example, tend to publish almost exclusively in the journals of their own disciplines—and with good reason. The American scholar of International Relations who publishes in a student-edited law review, the most common IL venue, may well find that work largely ignored by professional colleagues and even disregarded altogether at tenure or promotion time; unfortunately, the International Law scholar who places work in an IR periodical may risk a similar fate. A second related practice of the two cultures is to maintain separate professional associations and scholarly conferences,[118] whose mere existence greatly challenges aspiring interdisciplinarians. Of the American Political Science Association's thirty-two special topical "sections," for instance, not one is devoted to "International Law," "International Institutions," or "International Organization." Finally, by their training and socialization, the members of the two cultures thoroughly ensconce themselves in "different language communities."[119] As a consequence, such vitally important words as "regime," "positivism," "system," and "theory" have quite different connotations for international lawyers and political scientists. Other essential concepts like *opinio juris,* epistemic community, *jus cogens,* soft law, *rebus sic stantibus,* and hegemonic stability are generally meaningful for scholars only of one discipline or the other. Until a common vocabulary emerges or a substantial number of scholars from each culture learn both disciplinary languages, no broad and sustained cross-disciplinary dialogue can reasonably be expected.

Even so, what benefits might be gleaned by the two cultures from their collaboration? At least three significant gains could be jointly realized. First, each discipline could borrow constructively from the other's existing conceptual lexicon. Scholars of all disciplines share an unfortunate propensity to reinvent the wheel because of their ignorance of concepts that have already been routinely and fruitfully employed elsewhere. Even modest cross-disciplinary cooperation could help reduce this counterproductive phenomenon's incidence within IR and IL.[120] IR scholars studying the evolution of international rules, for example, might usefully apply IL's distinctions between *lex lata* and *lex ferenda* as well as those between customary state practice informed by *opinio juris* and that not so informed. Second, each discipline could make effective use of the other's analytical and research tools. IR's literatures on "international regimes," "game theory," "relative gains," and "hegemonic stability," for instance, have already been tapped by a few adventurous IL scholars.[121] IL's extensive corpus on treaty interpretation methods, in a similar fashion, could likely be wielded by IR students of rule creation, evolution, and compliance. Finally, each discipline could profitably draw upon the vast array of descriptive materials generated by the other. International Law, for example, could "bring to the table a wealth of data, on legal practices and procedures, [on] primary rules of conduct, [and on] secondary rules of law formation, interpretation and application . . . , most of it at a level of detail that IR has so far rarely addressed."[122]

But who are the most apt interdisciplinarians? The greatest natural affinities seem likely to exist between approaches to international rules that share the same basic objective and method. Thus, IL's New Stream and IR's Sociological Institutionalist approaches, both of which employ critical means for largely explanatory purposes, appear strong candidates for cross-disciplinary dialogue and learning. Indeed, the work of such "International Relations" scholars as Friedrich Kratochwil and Nicholas Onuf can arguably be characterized as straddling the critical/explanatory literatures of International Law and International Relations.[123] Further collaboration can probably be effected, as well, across the explanatory-prescriptive divide between IR and IL approaches of an empiricist methodological orientation. The research of IL scholars like Abbott, in fact, has already drawn upon that of Rationalistic Institutionalists like Keohane.[124] The New Haven School literature, similarly, may offer important insights to both Rationalistic and Sociological Institutionalists. Finally, of whatever their particular approaches, those International Relations and International Law scholars addressing the same substantive issues may find the works of their colleagues of "the other discipline" stimulating points of departure. Only four such common questions have been reviewed here, though other important ones surely exist. For example, is there a significant difference[125] between legal and nonlegal rules? How can international rules optimally be designed to fulfill their desired ends? And of what importance is the distinction that has been drawn[126] between "regulative" and "constitutive" rules?

Ultimately, vigorous cooperation between the two cultures will not be brought about unless disciplinary inertia is mastered. As with many things in life, security and convenience lie in the familiar, risk and exertion in change. Scholars will not likely overcome the inertia hurdle by the forces of intellectual valor and hard work alone. Rather, reward structures in both disciplines must be modified to foster cross-disciplinary work, those few fluent in both the IL and IR discourses must be appropriately supported,[127] and the venues for spoken and written presentation of research must be increased and liberalized. In addition, opportunities for joint projects will surely need to be expanded, existing curricula altered, and many prominent scholars across the disciplines genuinely convinced that collaborative ventures are worthwhile. Such profound changes will not readily be effected, of course, but the attendant rewards could prove abundant.

Notes

1. Louis Henkin, *How Nations Behave: Law and Foreign Policy* (New York: Praeger, 1968), p. 6. Noted Kenneth Abbott in 1992: "It has been difficult to tell for the last twenty years that the two disciplines [of International Law and International Relations; see note 3] were even talking about the same world." Kenneth W. Abbott, "International Law and International Relations Theory: Building Bridges —Elements of a Joint Discipline," *Proceedings of the American Society of International Law* 86 (1992): 167.

2. Recent discussions about the prospect and desirability of interdisciplinary collaboration include Kenneth W. Abbott, "Modern International Relations Theory: A Prospectus for International Lawyers," *Yale Journal of International Law* 14 (1989): 335–411; Abbott, "Building Bridges," pp. 167–72; Anne-Marie Slaughter Burley, "International Law and International Relations Theory: A Dual Agenda," *American Journal of International Law* 87 (1993): 205–39; Robert O. Keohane, "Compliance with International Commitments: Politics Within a Framework of Law," *Proceedings of the American Society of International Law* 86 (1992): 176–80; Oran R. Young, "International Law and International Relations Theory: Building Bridges—Remarks," *Proceedings of the American Society of International Law* 86 (1992): 172–75; and J. Martin Rochester, "The Rise and Fall of International Organization as a Field of Study," *International Organization* 40 (1986): 777–813. Upon these works this chapter substantially draws.

As a convention, this chapter will refer in the text to "Anne-Marie Slaughter," the Harvard Law professor's preferred designation. She has published in the past under "Anne-Marie Burley" and "Anne-Marie Slaughter Burley."

3. In this chapter, "International Law" and "International Relations" are capitalized when they denote scholarly disciplines; the terms are not capitalized when they denote phenomena.

4. Prominent exceptions include Kenneth Abbott, "Modern International Relations Theory"; Francis Boyle, *World Politics and International Law* (Durham, N.C.: Duke University Press, 1985); and Morton A. Kaplan and Nicholas deB. Katzenbach, *The Political Foundations of International Law* (New York: Wiley, 1961).

5. Burley, "International Law and International Relations Theory," p. 205. Cf. Boyle, *World Politics and International Law*, p. 60.

6. See, e.g., Young, "Building Bridges," p. 174.

7. On a "Weberian approach to 'objectivity' in social science," see Robert O. Keohane, "The Analysis of International Regimes: Towards a European-

American Research Programme," in Volker Rittberger, ed., *Regime Theory and International Relations* (Oxford: Oxford University Press, 1993), pp. 24–26.

8. The term *rationalistic* is Keohane's. See Robert O. Keohane, "International Institutions: Two Approaches," *International Studies Quarterly* 32 (1988): 379–96.

9. In "Modern International Relations Theory"—an article explicitly designed to promote interdisciplinary ties and published in a prominent International Law venue—Abbott depicted "modern IR theory" as "regime theory and related theories of international cooperation" (p. 338). Readers unfamiliar with the International Relations literature might well conclude from this characterization that "cooperation studies," especially rationalistic-economistic ones, constitute the entire contemporary IR discipline. In fact, cooperation studies represent only one strand of the discipline, albeit a very important one.

10. Various critical approaches to international rules, for instance, would seem arguably to straddle the International Law and International Relations disciplines. Similarly, the "International Society" scholarship to which Martin Wight, Hedley Bull, Thomas M. Franck, and others, have contributed is not readily situated within one discipline or the other. Arguably, the International Society scholars can be characterized as Sociological Institutionalists.

On the International Society tradition, see Andrew Hurrell's essay reprinted in this volume: "International Society and the Study of Regimes: A Reflective Approach," in Volker Rittberger, ed., *Regime Theory and International Relations,* pp. 49–72. On the relationship between regime studies and the "English school," see Tony Evans and Peter Wilson, "Regime Theory and the English School of International Relations: A Comparison," *Millenium: Journal of International Studies* 21 (1992): 329–51. Prominent recent International Society works include Hedley Bull, *The Anarchical Society* (New York: Columbia University Press, 1977); Hedley Bull and Adam Watson, eds., *The Expansion of International Society* (New York: Oxford University Press, 1985); Adam Watson, *The Evolution of International Society: A Comparative Analysis* (New York: Routledge, 1992); Barry Buzan, "From International System to International Society: Structural Realism and Regime Theory Meet the English School," *International Organization* 47 (1993): 327–52; Barry Buzan, Charles Jones, and Richard Little, *The Logic of Anarchy: Neorealism to Structural Realism: New Directions in World Politics* (New York: Columbia University Press, 1993); and Martin Shaw, "Global Society and Global Responsibility: The Theoretical, Historical and Political Limits of 'International Society,'" *Millenium* 21 (1992): 421–34. Though not of the English School per se, Thomas Franck's *The Power of Legitimacy Among Nations* (New York: Oxford University Press, 1990) arguably fits within the International Society approach as well.

11. On the varieties of Feminist scholarship, see Fernando R. Tesón, "Feminism and International Law: A Reply," *Virginia Journal of International Law* 33 (1993): 647–84.

12. Indeed, scholars may even resist being categorized by discipline.

13. Abbott, "Building Bridges," p. 168.

14. The author is indebted to Herman Schwartz for this insight.

15. Though scholars typically oppose "positivist" to "critical," "empiricist" will be employed here to avoid the confusion of social science "positivism" with "Legal Positivism."

16. Keohane, "Analysis of International Regimes," pp. 24–26.

17. Mark Neufeld, "Interpretation and the 'Science' of International Relations," *Review of International Studies* 19 (1993): 40.

18. This is how Viotti and Kauppi have defined "positivist." Paul R. Viotti and Mark V. Kauppi, eds., *International Relations Theory: Realism, Pluralism, Globalism,* 2nd ed. (New York: Macmillan, 1993), p. 591.

19. Friedrich Kratochwil, for example, has derided IR for its "physics envy."

20. On interpretive study in IR, see Neufeld, "Interpretation and the 'Science' of International Relations," pp. 39–61; Richard Price, "Interpretation and Disciplinary Orthodoxy in International Relations," *Review of International Studies* 20 (1994): 201–4; and Alexander Wendt, "Constructing International Politics," *International Security* 20 (1995), pp. 71–81.

21. Neufeld, "Interpretation and the 'Science' of International Relations," p. 43.

22. In contrast to IR's "postmodern critical theorists," however, IR's modern critical theorists "endorse the scientific project of falsifying theories against evidence." Wendt, "Constructing International Politics," p. 75.

23. See Price, "Interpretation and Disciplinary Orthodoxy in International Relations," pp. 202–4.

24. Prescriptive scholars often employ some explanation, of course, while explanatory scholars at times explicitly endorse specific policy prescriptions. Moreover, some explanatory approaches have implicit normative standpoints within them. For example, the scholarship that seeks to problematize the taken-for-granted institutions of social life arguably contains within it an inherently transformative normative standpoint. Author's correspondence with Alexander Wendt. Similarly, "there is an implicit moral concern in the work of [rationalistic] regime theorists, centered around the assumption that the understanding and promotion of cooperation has an intrinsic value." Hurrell, "International Society and the Study of Regimes," p. 67.

25. Young, "Building Bridges," p. 174.

26. Frederick S. Tipson, "The Lasswell-McDougal Enterprise: Toward a World Public Order of Human Dignity," *Virginia Journal of International Law* 14 (1974); 536.

27. See Nigel Purvis, "Critical Legal Studies in Public International Law," *Harvard International Law Journal* 32 (1991): 122–23.

28. The label "Sociological Institutionalist" will be used here instead of "Reflective Institutionalist" for two principal reasons: first, to juxtapose the sociological orientation of those scholars Keohane labeled "Reflectivist" with the "economic" orientation of the "Rationalists"; and second, to employ a term more acceptable to those Institutionalists not of the Rationalist camp. Alexander Wendt, for example, has noted that the label "Reflectivist" (1) would not typically be used by those scholars it seeks to describe; (2) suggests that "Reflectivists" are subjectivists in their explanatory orientation, when they are in fact structuralists; and (3) conflates modern and postmodern "Reflectivists." Wendt's correspondence with author. See also Wendt, "Constructing International Politics."

29. See Price, "Interpretation and Disciplinary Orthodoxy in International Relations," pp. 201–2; and Purvis, "Critical Legal Studies in Public International Law," pp. 121–22.

30. Hilary Charlesworth, Christine Chinkin, and Shelley Wright, "Feminist Approaches to International Law," *American Journal of International Law* 85 (1991): 644. One of the "twin aims" of "the feminist project" has been to "challeng[e] the existing norms" (p. 643).

31. One approach to international rules discussed here but not included in this volume is the Liberal one advocated by Slaughter. The International Society school of Hedley Bull, Thomas Franck, and other scholars arguably constitutes one variation of the Sociological Institutionalist approach.

32. Slaughter has lamented that although "[i]nternational ethics is an obvious area of overlap for international political theorists and international lawyers," the field "has suffered a fate similar to that of international law in international relations theory." Burley, "International Law and International Relations Theory," p. 224. Slaughter's appraisal of the status of "international ethics" studies may be a bit too pessimistic, but her portrayal of the domain as one ripe for collaboration is nevertheless compelling.

33. Responding to Abbott's 1992 ASIL remarks, Oran R. Young observed that in seeking to promote interdisciplinary collaboration, one must identify subjects with characteristics rendering them "unusually conducive" and "unusually attractive" to such an activity. One area explicitly recognized by Young then was "the question of 'sources of obligation.'" The International Relations professor explained: "Why is it that an actor acquires and feels some sense of obligation to conform its behavior to the dictates or requirements of a regime or an institution? There are a number of reasons, and for the most part we have conflated them. For example, I think that there are differences in being obligated to do something because of a moral reason, a normative reason and a legal reason." Though Young did not distinguish here or elaborate further on these "streams of obligation," he nevertheless proposed that interdisciplinary collaboration might help to explain the ways in which the three streams interacted. Young, "Building Bridges," p. 175.

34. Arthur Nussbaum, *A Concise History of the Law of Nations* (New York: Macmillan, 1947), p. 107. Brierly rejects the title. J. L. Brierly, *The Law of Nations,* 6th ed. (Oxford: Oxford University Press, 1963), p. 28.

35. On the obligation question, see especially Francisco Suarez, *De Legibus* (1612); Samuel Pufendorf, *De Jure Naturae et Gentium* (1672); and Hugo Grotius, *De Jure Belli Ac Pacis* (1625).

36. Franck observes:

When both the national and international systems of dominance, governance, or order were based on similar divine or natural-order rationales, . . . questions [about obligation] were addressed to both national and international systems, if only because, in the two fields of inquiry, the respective phenomena of social behavior could not be separated neatly. The same "natural" or divine validation which was believed to authorize national governance also validated the rules of interstate behavior. God's writ, or the natural order of things, was no respecter of the puny lines drawn by men on maps.

The Power of Legitimacy, pp. 6–7.

37. However, the Naturalist Alberico Gentili "was perhaps the first writer to make a definite separation of international law from theology and ethics and to treat it as a branch of jurisprudence." Brierly, *The Law of Nations,* p. 26.

38. For a critique, see Tesón, "Feminism and International Law."

39. Charlesworth, Chinkin, and Wright, "Feminist Approaches to International Law," pp. 614–15.

40. Ibid., p. 644.

41. Ibid., p. 619.

42. Ibid.

43. See Oran R. Young, "International Law and Social Science: The Contributions of Myres S. McDougal," *American Journal of International Law* 66 (1972): 72–76.

44. Remarks by Oscar Schachter, "McDougal's Theory and Approach to International Law," *Proceedings of the American Society of International Law* 79 (1985): 266–73.

45. See also Oscar Schachter, "Towards a Theory of International Obligation," *Virginia Journal of International Law* 8 (1968): 300–322. Whether Schachter should be considered a Legal Positivist is arguable.

46. John Austin, *The Province of Jurisprudence Determined* (1832).

47. Hans Kelsen, *General Theory of Law and the State,* Anders Wedberg, trans. (Cambridge, Mass.: Harvard University Press, 1945); and *The Pure Theory of Law* (Berkeley: University of California Press, 1967).

48. H.L.A. Hart, *The Concept of Law* (Oxford: Oxford University Press, 1961).

49. Franck, *The Power of Legitimacy,* p. 196.

50. See especially Hart, *The Concept of Law,* pp. 79–88.

51. On international law's relationship to morality, e.g., see Hart, *The Concept of Law,* pp. 221–26. See also John Austin, *The Province of Jurisprudence Determined and The Uses of the Study of Jurisprudence* (London: Weidenfeld and Nicolson, 1954), p. 185.

52. Important works with a significant ethical dimension, however, include Stanley Hoffmann, *Duties Beyond Borders* (Syracuse, N.Y.: Syracuse University Press, 1981); Chris Brown, *International Relations Theory: New Normative Approaches* (New York: Columbia University Press, 1992); Michael Walzer, *Just and Unjust Wars* (New York: Basis Books, 1977); Terry Nardin, "Realism, Cosmopolitanism, and the Rules of Law," *Proceedings of the American Society of International Law* 81 (1987): 416–20; Michael W. Doyle, "Kant, Liberal Legacies, and Foreign Affairs," *Philosophy and Public Affairs* 12 (1983): 205–35, 323–53; and Michael W. Doyle, "Liberalism and World Politics," *American Political Science Review* 80 (1986): 1151–69.

53. James Lee Ray has observed, however: "the differences between these schools of thought in the field of international politics, although admittedly sharp in some respects, are relatively subtle when it comes to the role of ethical considerations and moral constraints." Ray, "The Abolition of Slavery and the End of International War," *International Organization* 43 (1989): 420.

54. Hurrell, "International Society and the Study of Regimes," pp. 65–66. Reacting to the Austinian notion of obligation, Hurrell contends: "Once states see themselves as having a long-term interest in participating in an international legal system, then the idea of obligation and the normativity of rules can be given concrete form and can acquire a degree of distance from the immediate interests or preferences of states. Within this society, law exists but is no longer seen to depend on the command of the sovereign." Instead, it becomes "the symbol of the idea of being bound and voluntarily accepting a sense of obligation." Law, in Hurrell's view, is "not based on external sanctions or the threat of them but is based rather on the existence of shared interests, of shared values, and of patterned expectations" (p. 60).

55. Ethan A. Nadelmann, "Global Prohibition Regimes: The Evolution of Norms in International Society," *International Organization* 44 (1990): 480. See

also Janice E. Thomson, "State Practices, International Norms, and the Decline of Mercenarism," *International Studies Quarterly* 34 (1990): 23–47; Robert H. Jackson, "Quasi-States, Dual Regimes, and Neoclassical Theory: International Jurisprudence and the Third World," *International Organization* 41 (1987): 519–49; and Ray, "The Abolition of Slavery."

56. All citations from Robert O. Keohane, *After Hegemony: Cooperation and Discord in the World Political Economy* (Princeton, N.J.: Princeton University Press, 1984), p. 127.

57. In Keohane's most recent work, notably, he is testing the hypothesis that compliance with inconvenient commitments "Will vary as a function of the degree to which justifications of noncompliance are consistent with the *normative views* held by U.S. foreign policy elites." Keohane, "Compliance with International Commitments," p. 179. Emphasis added.

58. George F. Kennan, *American Diplomacy, 1900–1950,* expanded ed. (Chicago: University of Chicago Press, 1984), p. 95.

59. Ibid., p. 100.

60. While proceeding from a number of realist assumptions, Robert Keohane rejects this view, however. See *After Hegemony,* pp. 243–59.

61. As James Lee Ray has observed: "Ultimately, realists, radicals, idealists, and interdependence/regime analysts all concede that while self-interested behavior predominates, behavior inspired by norms and ethical standards or constrained by moral values is by no means absent." Ray, "The Abolition of Slavery," p. 420. See also Joel H. Rosenthal, "Rethinking the Moral Dimensions of Foreign Policy," in Charles W. Kegley, Jr., ed., *Controversies in International Relations Theory: Realism and the Neoliberal Challenge* (New York: St. Martin's, 1995), pp. 317–29.

62. Hans J. Morgenthau, *Politics Among Nations,* 6th ed. (New York: Knopf, 1985), pp. 249, 295.

63. Raymond Aron, *Peace and War: A Theory of International Relations* (New York: Praeger, 1967), p. 609.

64. "Moral considerations" represent only one of multiple explanations that have been proffered for rule-associated behavior, a broad category of activities that includes, in addition to rule compliance, rule creation and rule enforcement. Many scholars, moreover, suggest that moral notions such as those of justice should not be considered in analyses of compliance. Thomas Franck, for example, deliberately excludes justice from his discussion of the "factors making for legitimacy," and hence for international rule compliance. Franck, *The Power of Legitimacy,* pp. 208–46.

On the link between obligation and compliance, see John Finnis, *Natural Law and Natural Rights* (Oxford: Clarendon Press, 1980), pp. 297–98.

65. Early prominent treatments of this question include Abram Chayes, "An Inquiry into the Workings of Arms Control Agreements," *Harvard Law Review* 85 (1972): 905–69; Roger Fisher, "Constructing Rules that Affect Governments," in Donald G. Brennan, ed., *Arms Control, Disarmament, and National Security* (New York: George Braziller, 1961); Roger Fisher, *Improving Compliance with International Law* (Charlottesville: University Press of Virginia, 1981); Henkin, *How Nations Behave,* pp. 45–64; and Oran R. Young, *Compliance and Public Authority: A Theory with International Applications* (Baltimore: Johns Hopkins University Press, 1979).

Recent studies include Abram Chayes and Antonia Chayes, "On Compliance," *International Organization* 47 (1993): 175–205; Antonia Chayes and

Abram Chayes, "From Law Enforcement to Dispute Settlement: A New Approach to Arms Control Verification and Compliance," *International Security* 14 (1990): 147–64; Franck, *The Power of Legitimacy;* Keohane, *After Hegemony,* pp. 98–106, 237–40; Keohane, "Compliance with International Commitments," 176–80; Robert O. Keohane, "U.S. Compliance with Commitments," ACUNS/ASIL Summer Workshop, Dartmouth College, Hanover, N.H., 1992; Friedrich Kratochwil, *Rules, Norms and Decision: On the Conditions of Practical and Legal Reasoning in International Relations and Domestic Affairs* (Cambridge: Cambridge University Press, 1989); and Oran R. Young, *International Cooperation: Building Regimes for Natural Resources and the Environment* (Ithaca, N.Y.: Cornell University Press, 1989), pp. 70–80.

John Duffield provides a useful review of compliance approaches in "International Regimes and Alliance Behavior: Explaining NATO Conventional Force Levels," *International Organization* 46 (1992): 819–55.

66. Franck, *The Power of Legitimacy,* p. 3.

67. Burley, "International Law and International Relations Theory," p. 224.

68. Young, *Compliance and Public Authority,* p. 148. Young's *International Cooperation* also addresses the compliance question.

69. Keohane, "Compliance with International Commitments."

70. Duffield, "International Regimes and Alliance Behavior," pp. 834–40.

71. See, e.g., "On Compliance"; "From Law Enforcement to Dispute Settlement"; and "Regime Architecture: Elements and Principles," in Janne E. Nolan, ed., *Global Engagement: Cooperation and Security in the 21st Century* (Washington, D.C.: Brookings Institution, 1994), pp. 65–130.

72. Burley, "International Law and International Relations Theory," pp. 223–24.

73. Purvis, "Critical Legal Studies in Public International Law," pp. 109–13.

Purvis responds here to the challenge posed by Franck that the New Stream present "a theory that can illuminate more generally the occurrence of voluntary normative compliance . . . in the absence of coercion." Thomas Franck, "Legitimacy in the International System," *American Journal of International Law* 82 (1988): 705. Purvis concedes that "very few CLS [i.e., New Stream] academics have attempted to address this issue." Purvis, "Critical Legal Studies," p. 110.

74. Hart, *The Concept of Law.*

75. Lon L. Fuller, *The Morality of Law,* rev. ed. (New Haven, Conn.: Yale University Press, 1969).

76. See, e.g., Richard Falk, *The Status of Law in International Society* (Princeton, N.J.: Princeton University Press, 1970).

77. See, e.g., Myres S. McDougal et al., *Studies in World Public Order* (New Haven, Conn.: Yale University Press, 1960).

78. Young, *Compliance and Public Authority,* p. 150.

79. Stephan Haggard and Beth A. Simmons, "Theories of International Regimes," *International Organization* 41 (1987): 491–517. See also Hurrell, "International Society and the Study of Regimes," pp. 69–71.

Ironically, as early as 1963 the problem of overlooking the domestic factor was noted. Stanley Hoffmann argued then that

> foreign policy is not totally determined and dominated by the international competition or system. Indeed, the system itself is the outcome of a number of developments many of which originate from the component

units. Any "systemic" study of international law that tries to explain the legal order of a given system exclusively in terms of the number of main units or of the kinds of alignments characteristic of the system, neglects such important considerations as the impact of domestic practices and beliefs. . . .

"The Study of International Law and the Theory of International Relations," *Proceedings of the American Society of International Law* (1963): 28–29.

80. Burley, "International Law and International Relations Theory," p. 226. Such a model, in her view, fails to take account of "increasing evidence of the importance and impact of so many factors excluded from the reigning model: individuals, corporations, nongovernmental organizations of every stripe, political and economic ideology, ideas, interests, identities and interdependence" (p. 227).

81. Keohane, "International Institutions: Two Approaches," p. 392.

82. "Domestic interest groups and bureaucracies, for example, have tremendous influence on the form and extent of a state's international obligations and on compliance with those obligations; while international commitments have strong internal effects: environmental agreements may increase costs for polluters; trade agreements may help governments restrain groups seeking protection; agreements in legal form may mobilize lawyers in support of compliance, and so on." Abbott, "Building Bridges," p. 171.

83. Burley, "International Law and International Relations Theory." See also Burley, "Law and the Liberal Paradigm in International Relations Theory," *Proceedings of the American Society of International Law* 86 (1992): 180–85.

84. Burley, "International Law and International Relations Theory," pp. 227–28.

85. Keohane, "Compliance with International Commitments," p. 180.

86. Ibid., p. 179. Cf. Hurrell, "International Society and the Study of Regimes," pp. 70–71.

87. Michael Zurn, "Bringing the Second Image (Back) In: About the Domestic Sources of Regime Formation," in Volker Rittberger, ed., *Regime Theory*, pp. 282–314. Cf. Oran R. Young, "Political Leadership and Regime Formation: On the Development of Institutions in International Society," *International Organization* 45 (1991): 285.

88. Myres S. McDougal and Harold D. Lasswell, "The Identification and Appraisal of Diverse Systems of Public Order," *American Journal of International Law* 53 (1959): 16. Their preoccupation with "democratic values" was manifest from Lasswell and McDougal's initial proposal to reform legal education. See Harold Lasswell and Myres S. McDougal, "Legal Education and Public Policy: Professional Training in the Public Interest," *Yale Law Journal* 52 (1943): 203–95.

89. Charlesworth, Chinkin, and Wright, "Feminist Approaches to International Law," p. 644.

90. Ibid., p. 625.

91. Ibid., pp. 623–24. In 1995, Rosalyn Higgins became the second woman to serve on the ICJ.

92. Ibid., p. 627.

93. Moreover, because "distinctive women's experiences . . . are factored out," the IL discipline cannot lay claim to "universal validity," Ibid., p. 616.

94. Purvis, "Critical Legal Studies," p. 98.

95. Ibid., p. 115.

96. Ibid.

97. Oran R. Young, "International Law and Social Science: The Contributions of Myres S. McDougal," *American Journal of International Law* 66 (1972): 62.

98. This description is provided by Oran R. Young, "The Politics of International Regime Formation: Managing Natural Resources and the Environment," *International Organization* 43 (1989): 350.

99. Robert Gilpin, *War and Change in World Politics* (Cambridge: Cambridge University Press, 1981), pp. 35, 36. Emphasis added.

100. Ibid., pp. 144–45.

101. States, according to Kenneth Waltz, "are unitary actors who, at a minimum, seek their own preservation and, at a maximum, drive for universal domination." Waltz, *Theory of International Politics* (New York: Random House, 1979), p. 118.

102. Joseph M. Grieco, "Anarchy and the Limits of Cooperation: A Realist Critique of the Newest Liberal Institutionalism," *International Organization* 42 (1988): 498, 499.

103. See, e.g., Robert O. Keohane, "The Demand for International Regimes," *International Organization* 36 (1982): 325–55; and Keohane, *After Hegemony*. For a discussion of Keohane's approach, see Young, *International Cooperation*, pp. 199–202.

104. Keohane, *After Hegemony*, p. 78.

105. Ibid., p. 83. Keohane concedes that functional explanations are "generally *post hoc* in nature" and that "the functional argument as applied to our subject-matter must rest on the premise of rational anticipation. Unless actors can be assumed to anticipate the effects of their behavior, effects cannot reasonably explain causes, and understanding the functions of international regimes will not help to explain their occurrence" (pp. 80, 82).

106. Ibid., p. 79. The "intricate connection between the operation of old regimes and the creation of new ones means that a functional analysis of regimes . . . is crucial for understanding not only why regimes are created and maintained, but also how they evolve over time."

107. While regarding "demand for agreements" as "exogenous," Keohane acknowledges the role of individuals in the rule-creation process: "[D]emand for agreements . . . may be influenced by . . . the perceptions that leaders of governments have about their interests in agreement or nonagreement. These perceptions will, in turn, be influenced by domestic politics, ideology and other factors not encompassed by a systemic, constraint choice approach." "The Demand for International Regimes," p. 337.

108. Young, "Political Leadership and Regime Formation," p. 281. "The structural leader *translates power resources into bargaining leverage* in an effort to bring pressure to bear on others to assent to the terms of proposed constitutional contracts. The entrepreneurial leader makes use of *negotiating skill* to frame the issues at stake, devise mutually acceptable formulas, and broker the interests of key players in building support for these formulas. The intellectual leader, by contrast, relies on the *power of ideas* to shape the thinking of the principals in processes of institutional bargaining" (p. 307). Emphasis added. Young also discusses the role of leadership in *International Cooperation,* pp. 201–2.

109. Hurrell, "International Society and the Study of Regimes," pp. 65–66.

110. Nadelmann, "Global Prohibition Regimes," p. 482.

111. See Peter M. Haas, ed., *Knowledge, Power and International Policy Coordination*, a special issue of *International Organization* 46 (1992).

112. Haas strives to differentiate "epistemic communities" from other groups, however. Peter M. Haas, "Introduction: Epistemic Communities and International Policy Coordination," *International Organization* 46 (1992): 16–20.

113. "An epistemic community is a network of professionals with recognized expertise and competence in a particular domain and an authoritative claim to policy-relevant knowledge within that domain or issue area." Members of a given epistemic community have a shared set of normative and principled beliefs, shared causal beliefs, shared notions of validity, and a common policy enterprise. Ibid., p. 3.

114. Ibid., p. 2.

115. Abbott, "Building Bridges," p. 168.

116. This section is heavily indebted to Young, "Building Bridges," pp. 173–75, and to the author's experiences at the 1992 ACUNS/ASIL Summer Workshop at Dartmouth College, Hanover, N.H.

117. Young, "Building Bridges," p. 174.

118. Abbott, "Modern International Relations Theory," p. 337. The International Studies Association, however, has retained a generally multidisciplinary character.

119. Young, "Building Bridges," p. 175. See also Burley, "International Law and International Relations Theory," p. 205.

120. The "regime," for example, has with some justification been characterized as an International Law notion rediscovered by International Relations. See, e.g., Burley, "International Law and International Relations Theory." IR scholars should be acknowledged as having elaborated and extended the regime concept, however.

121. See, e.g., William B. T. Mock, "Game Theory, Signalling, and International Legal Relations," *George Washington Journal of International Law and Economics* 26 (1992): 34–59; Miguel Montaña-Mora, "International Law and International Relations Cheek to Cheek: An International Law/International Relations Perspective on the US/EC Agricultural Export Subsidies Dispute," *North Carolina Journal of International Law and Commercial Regulation* 19 (1993): 1–60; Burley, "International Law and International Relations Theory"; Kenneth W. Abbott, "Trust but Verify: The Production of Information in Arms Control Treaties and Other International Agreements," *Cornell International Law Journal* 26 (1993): 26–58; Abbott, "Modern International Relations Theory"; and Kenneth W. Abbott and Duncan Snidal, "Mesoinstitutions in International Politics," paper presented at 1995 International Studies Association Convention, Chicago, Ill.

122. Abbott, "Building Bridges," p. 169.

123. Onuf's recent work includes "Review of David Kennedy's *International Legal Structure*," in *American Journal of International Law* 83 (1989): 630–40; "Review of Martti Koskenniemi's *From Apology to Utopia*," in *American Journal of International Law* 84 (1990): 771–75; and *World of Our Making: Rules and Rule in Social Theory and International Relations* (Columbia: University of South Carolina Press, 1989). Three recent publications by Kratochwil are Friedrich Kratochwil and John G. Ruggie, "International Organization: A State of the Art on the Art of the State," *International Organization* 40 (1986): 753–75; Kratochwil,

Rules, Norms, and Decisions; and Kratochwil, "Contract and Regimes: Do Issue Specificity and Variations of Formality Matter?" in Rittberger, ed., *Regime Theory and International Relations,* pp. 73–93.

124. See, e.g., Abbott, "Modern International Relations Theory."

125. See, e.g., Kratochwil, "Contract and Regimes"; Hurrell, "International Society and the Study of Regimes," pp. 58–61, 66; and Anthony Clark Arend's essay in this volume.

126. See, e.g., Michael N. Barnett, "The United Nations and Global Security: The Norm Is Mightier than the Sword," *Ethics and International Affairs* 9 (1995): 37–54.

127. Young, "Building Bridges," p. 175.

Selected Bibliography

Works on Legal and Social Scientific Theory

Allott, Philip. *Eunomia: New Order for a New World* (1990).

Berman, Harold J. *Law and Revolution: The Formation of the Western Legal Tradition* (1983).

Boyle, Francis A. *World Politics and International Law* (1985).

———. *The Future of International Law and American Foreign Policy* (1989).

Brierly, J. L. "The Origins of International Law," in Brierly, *The Law of Nations* (1963), pp. 1–40.

D'Amato, Anthony. *International Law Anthology* (1994).

Ehrlich, Thomas. "The Development of International Law as a Science," *Recueil des Cours* 105 (1962).

Falk, Richard A., Saul H. Mendlovitz, and Friedrich V. Kratochwil, eds. *International Law: A Contemporary Perspective* (1985).

Ferguson, Yale H., and Richard W. Mansbach. *The Elusive Quest: Theory and International Politics* (1988).

Kaplan, Morton A., and Nicholas DeB. Katzenbach. *The Political Foundations of International Law* (1961).

Koskenniemi, Martti, ed. *International Law* (1992).

Kuhn, Thomas S. *The Structure of Scientific Revolutions* (1962).

Lakatos, Imre. "Falsification and the Methodology of Scientific Research Programmes," in I. Lakatos and Alan Musgrave, eds., *Criticism and the Growth of Knowledge* (1970).

Macdonald, Ronald St. J., and Douglas M. Johnston, eds. *The Structure and Process of International Law: Essays in Legal Philosophy, Doctrine and Theory* (1983).

McDougal, Myres S., Harold D. Lasswell, and W. Michael Reisman. "Theories About International Law: Prologue to a Configurative Jurisprudence," *Virginia Journal of International Law* 8 (1968): 188–299.

Nussbaum, Arthur. *A Concise History of the Law of Nations* (1947).

Onuf, Nicholas. "International Legal Order as an Idea," *American Journal of International Law* 73 (1979): 244–66.

———, ed. *Lawmaking in the Global Community* (1982).

Schiffer, W. *The Legal Community of Mankind* (1954).

Schwarzenberger, Georg. *A Manual of International Law,* 4th ed. (1960).

Steiner, H., and Detlev Vagts. *Transnational Legal Problems,* 2nd ed. (1976).

Viotti, Paul R. and Mark V. Kauppi. *International Relations Theory: Realism, Pluralism, Globalism,* 2nd ed. (1993).

Recent Literature Reviews

Abbott, Kenneth W. "Modern International Relations Theory: A Prospectus for International Lawyers," *Yale Journal of International Law* 14 (1989): 335–411.

Bull, Hedley. "International Law and International Order," in Bull, *The Anarchical Society: A Study of Order in World Politics* (1977), pp. 127–61.

Burley, Anne-Marie. "Law and the Liberal Paradigm in International Relations Theory," *Proceedings of the American Society of International Law* 86 (1992): 180–85.

Buzan, Barry. "From International System to International Society: Structural Realism and Regime Theory Meet the English School," *International Organization* 47 (1993): 327–52.

Evans, Tony, and Peter Wilson. "Regime Theory and the English School of International Relations: A Comparison," *Millenium* 21 (1992): 329–51.

George, Robert P. "Recent Criticism of Natural Law Theory," *University of Chicago Law Review* (1988): 1371–1430.

Haggard, Stephan, and Beth A. Simmons. "Theories of International Regimes," *International Organization* 41 (1987): 491–517.

Higgins, Rosalyn. "Integration of Authority and Control: Trends in the Literature of International Law and International Relations," in W. Michael Reisman and Burns Weston, eds., *Toward World Order* (1976).

Kennedy, David, and Chris Tennant. "New Approaches to International Law: A Bibliography," *Harvard Journal of International Law* 35 (1994): 417–60.

Keohane, Robert O. "Theory of World Politics: Structural Realism and Beyond," in Ada W. Finifter, ed., *Political Science: The State of the Discipline* (1983): pp. 503–40.

Kratochwil, Friedrich, and John G. Ruggie. "International Organization: A State of the Art on the Art of the State," *International Organization* 40 (1986): 753–75.

Milner, Helen. "International Theories of Cooperation Among Nations: Strengths and Weaknesses," *World Politics* 44 (1992): 466–96.

Morison, W. L. "The Schools Revisited," in Ronald St. J. Macdonald and Douglas M. Johnston, eds., *The Structure and Process of International Law: Essays in Legal Philosophy, Doctrine and Theory* (1983), pp. 131–76.

Powell, Robert. "Anarchy in International Relations Theory: The Neorealist-Neoliberal Debate," *International Organization* 48 (1994): 313–44.

Rochester, J. Martin. "The Rise and Fall of International Organization as a Field of Study," *International Organization* 40 (1986): 777–813.

Trimble, Phillip R. "International Law, World Order, and Critical Legal Studies," *Stanford Law Review* 42 (1990): 811–45.

Wendt, Alexander. "Constructing International Politics," *International Security* 20 (1995): 71–81.

Young, Oran R. "International Regimes: Toward a New Theory of Institutions," *World Politics* 39 (1986): 104–22.

Interdisciplinary Works

Abbott, Kenneth W. "International Law and International Relations Theory: Building Bridges—Elements of a Joint Discipline," *Proceedings of the American Society of International Law* 86 (1992): 167–72.

Abbott, Kenneth W., and Duncan Snidal. "Mesoinstitutions in International Politics," paper presented at the 1995 International Studies Association Convention.

Burley, Anne-Marie Slaughter. "International Law and International Relations Theory: A Dual Agenda," *American Journal of International Law* 87 (1993): 205–39.

————. "Law and the Liberal Paradigm in International Relations Theory," *Proceedings of the American Society of International Law* 86 (1992): 180–85.

Dorsey, Gray L. "Bridging the Gap Between Political Scientists and Lawyers— Remarks," *Proceedings of the American Society of International Law* 81 (1987): 381–83.

Gould, Wesley L. "Bridging the Gap Between Political Scientists and Lawyers— Remarks," *Proceedings of the American Society of International Law* 81 (1987): 383–85.

Hoffmann, Stanley. "The Study of International Law and the Theory of International Relations," *Proceedings of the American Society of International Law* 57 (1963): 26–35.

Joyner, Christopher C. "Crossing the Great Divide: Views of a Political Scientist Wandering in the World of International Law," *Proceedings of the American Society of International Law* 81 (1987): 385–91.

Keohane, Robert O. "Compliance with International Commitments: Politics Within a Framework of Law," *Proceedings of the American Society of International Law* 86 (1992): 176–80.

Montaña-Mora, Miguel. "International Law and International Relations Cheek to Cheek: An International Law/International Relations Perspective on the U.S./EC Agricultural Export Subsidies Dispute," *North Carolina Journal of International Law and Commercial Regulation* 19 (1993): 1–60.

Starr, Harvey. "International Law and International Order," in Charles W. Kegley, Jr., *Controversies in International Relations Theory: Realism and the Neoliberal Challenge* (1995), pp. 299–315.

Young, Oran R. "International Law and International Relations Theory: Building Bridges—Remarks," *Proceedings of the American Society of International Law* 86 (1992): 172–75.

2

Natural Law

Of the many approaches to the study of international rules, Natural Law boasts the lengthiest intellectual tradition. Indeed, Naturalism predates by many centuries the emergence of states, and thus the advent of "international" scholarship per se. Naturalists submit that the "law" consists of principles of right and wrong that transcend time, place, political system, religion, and culture. This law can be apprehended by human reason and remains eternally and universally valid, notwithstanding human legislative enactments ("positive law").

The ancient Greeks, in particular the Stoics, are generally credited with originating Natural Law thinking. Nonetheless, natural law gained far greater prominence during the Roman period. It was then that Marcus Tullius Cicero defined true law as "right reason in agreement with nature." Also during Cicero's time, a legal development parallel to natural law (*jus naturale*) was reinforcing natural law's cogency. Roman magistrates known as *praetores peregrini* had been developing since the third century B.C. the "law of peoples," the *jus gentium*, to resolve disputes between non-Roman persons throughout the empire. The *jus gentium* drew in part upon Greek, Phoenician, and Babylonian law principles. The Romans' ability to formulate a single body of positive law applicable to differing peoples appeared to confirm the existence of natural law.[1]

During the Middle Ages, Thomas Aquinas elaborated a view of law that was quintessentially Naturalist. He divided law into four "kinds": *lex aeterna,* eternal law known only to God; *lex divina,* the law of God known by humans through revelation; *lex naturalis,* the participation of rational creatures in the eternal law; and *lex humana,* positive law enacted by human beings. Aquinas distinguished *jus gentium* from other forms of positive law. Its innate rationality, suggested by its tenet's commonality to all peoples, linked it to the natural law. This close analogy between the *jus gentium,* a precursor to international law, and natural law laid the foundations for international law's Naturalist origins.

When the emergence of the Westphalian system of states in the seventeenth century made possible a truly "international" law, natural law conceptions guided the early thinkers. The scholastics of the Spanish "Golden Age" were perhaps the first to treat international rules as a focus of inquiry distinct from domestic rules.[2]

Francisco de Vitoria (1483–1546), for example, employed natural law arguments to evaluate the treatment of indigenous American peoples by the Spanish crown. In his famous public lecture, *De Indis Recenter Inventis,* Father Vitoria suggested that principles derived from nature bind states in their external relations. Notwithstanding the behavior of sovereigns then, Vitoria reasoned that duties of "natural society and communication" constrained both the "Indians" and the Spanish crown in their relations with one another. In a second relectio, Vitoria adduced the first significant modern treatment of the law of war, *De Jure Belli Hispanorum in Barbaros.*

Francisco Suarez (1548–1617), a Spanish Jesuit, built upon the work of Vitoria to establish a more elaborate theory of the *jus gentium.* In a departure from the Romans, Suarez characterized *jus gentium* as an intermediary normative order between natural law, as a rule of pure reason, and the civil law by which human states govern themselves. A justly famous excerpt from his work, *De Officiis,* expressed this relationship:

> The human race though divided into different nations and states, still has a certain unity, not only as a species but, as it were, politically and morally as is indicated by the precept of mutual love and charity which extends to all, even to strangers of any nation whatsoever. Therefore, though each perfect polity, republic, or kingdom is in itself a perfect community, consisting of its members, nevertheless each of these communities, inasmuch as it is related to the human race, is in a sense also a member of this universal society. Never, indeed, are these communities, singly, so self-sufficient unto themselves as not to need a certain mutual aid and association and communication, sometimes for their welfare and advantage, sometimes because of a moral necessity or indigence, as experience shows. For this reason they need a law by which they are guided and rightly ordered in respect to communication and association. To a great extent this is done by natural reason but not so sufficiently and directly everywhere. Hence, certain special rules could be established by the customs of these nations.

Suarez's work on the norms governing international behavior indeed focuses "to a great extent" on the role of natural reason, which Suarez continued to consider the primary source of the law governing nations.

Dutch jurist and statesman Hugo Grotius (1583–1642), identified by many scholars as the father of modern international law, was influenced by the Spanish Naturalists. Though Grotius specifically recognized the practice of states as an alternative source of international law, he, too, considered natural law to constitute the greater part of any law governing state conduct, for "outside of the sphere of the law of nature, which is also commonly called the law of nations, there is hardly any law common to all nations."[3] Grotius was eclectic in his use of scriptural, naturalist, and positive sources of deriving legal principles, and has been revered by some commentators for extricating law from theology and from "vague" natural law tenets.

Grotius's prologue to his *De Jure Belli ac Pacis,* reprinted here, provides a glimpse into the complexity and nuance of his approach. He notes a distinction between the law of nations, which is based on the mutual consent of states, and the law of nature, which proceeds from the essential traits implanted in humans. Despite this distinction, Grotius often speaks of the law of nature and the law of nations as if the two impose identical obligations on states—as if, notwithstanding their different sources, the law of nature and the law of nations speak to states with one voice. Like other natural lawyers, Grotius values reason or "well-tempered judgement" as a tool for discerning the content of the law from the nature of things. This eclectic Naturalism proved difficult for others to maintain, however, and after Grotius the study of international law became more conspicuously divided between Naturalists and Legal Positivists.

Though there exists a wide variety of natural law perspectives to the study of international rules, perhaps the purest example of Naturalism is that represented by Samuel Pufendorf (1632–1694). The character of Pufendorf's Naturalist approach may well reflect the period in which the German law professor worked. By the late seventeenth century, the positivist notion of international law's basis in state consent began seriously to challenge the naturalist view. In contrast to the positivists, Pufendorf held in his *Elements of Universal Jurisprudence* that no "law of nations" existed apart from the natural law that governed individuals. This natural law was readily applicable to nations that "have coalesced into one moral person."

Although the influence of Natural Law thinking about international rules has appeared substantially to have waned in the past two centuries, Naturalism continues to play a notable contemporary role. The approach is well evidenced in the realm of human rights law; it also undergirds much of the modern work on "just war." Moreover, many scholars have viewed the Nuremberg War Crimes Trials, which condemned "crimes against humanity" and "crimes against peace," as demonstrating Naturalism's longevity. To be sure, many of the more recent approaches to international rules—the New Haven School, the New Stream, and elements of Feminist scholarship—have reflected Natural Law's legacy.

Notes

1. Lee MacDonald, *Western Political Theory* vol. 1 (New York: Harcourt, Brace, Jovanovich, 1968), p. 98.

2. Alfred Verdross and Heribert Franz Koeck, "Natural Law: The Tradition

of Universal Reason and Authority," in Ronald St. J. Macdonald and Douglas M. Johnston, eds., *The Structure and Process of International Law: Essays in Legal Philosophy, Doctrine and Theory* (The Hague: Martinus Nijhoff, 1983), p. 19.

3. Hugo Grotius, *De Jure Belli ac Pacis: Libre Tres,* Francis W. Kelsy trans. (1925), p. 44.

HUGO GROTIUS

Prolegomena

1. The municipal law of Rome and of other states has been treated by many, who have undertaken to elucidate it by means of commentaries or to reduce it to a convenient digest. That body of law, however, which is concerned with the mutual relations among states or rulers of states, whether derived from nature, or established by divine ordinances, or having its origin in custom and tacit agreement, few have touched upon. Up to the present time no one has treated it in a comprehensive and systematic manner; yet the welfare of mankind demands that this task be accomplished.

2. Cicero justly characterized as of surpassing worth a knowledge of treaties of alliance, conventions, and understandings of peoples, kings and foreign nations; a knowledge, in short, of the whole law of war and peace. And to this knowledge Euripides gives the preference over an understanding of things divine and human; for he represents Theoclymenus as being thus addressed:

> For you, who know the fate of men and gods,
> What is, what shall be, shameful would it be
> To know not what is just.

3. Such a work is all the more necessary because in our day, as in former times, there is no lack of men who view this branch of law with contempt as having no reality outside of an empty name. On the lips of men quite generally is the saying of Euphemus, which Thucydides quotes, that in the case of a king or imperial city nothing is unjust which is expedient. Of like implication is the statement that for those whom fortune favours might makes right, and that the administration of a state cannot be carried on without injustice.

Furthermore, the controversies which arise between peoples or kings generally have Mars as their arbiter. That war is irreconcilable with all law is a view held not alone by the ignorant populace; expressions are often let slip by well-informed and thoughtful men which lend countenance to such a view. Nothing is more common than the assertion of antagonism between law and arms. Thus Ennius says:

> Not on grounds of right is battle joined,
> But rather with the sword do men
> Seek to enforce their claims.

"Prolegomena" of *De Jure Belli Ac Pacis*, in J. B. Scott, ed., *Classics of International Law*, Vol. 2 (1925), pp. 9–30. Reprinted by permission of Carnegie Endowment for International Peace. Some notes have been altered.

Horace, too, described the savage temper of Achilles in this wise:

> Laws, he declares, were not for him ordained;
> By dint of arms he claims all for himself.

Another poet depicts another military leader as commencing war with the words:

> Here peace and violated laws I leave behind.

Antigonus when advanced in years ridiculed a man who brought to him a treatise on justice when he was engaged in besieging cities that did not belong to him. Marius declared that the din of arms made it impossible for him to hear the voice of the laws. Even Pompey, whose expression of countenance was so mild, dared to say: "When I am in arms, am I to think of laws?"

4. Among Christian writers a similar thought finds frequent expression. A single quotation from Tertullian may serve in place of many: "Deception, harshness, and injustice are the regular business of battles." They who so think will no doubt wish to confront us with this passage in Comedy:

> These things uncertain should you, by reason's aid,
> Try to make certain, no more would you gain
> Than if you tried by reason to go mad.

5. Since our discussion concerning law will have been undertaken in vain if there is no law, in order to open the way for a favourable reception of our work and at the same time to fortify it against attacks, this very serious error must be briefly refuted. In order that we may not be obliged to deal with a crowd of opponents, let us assign to them a pleader. And whom should we choose in preference to Carneades? For he had attained to so perfect a mastery of the peculiar tenet of his Academy that he was able to devote the power of his eloquence to the service of falsehood not less readily than to that of truth.

Carneades, then, having undertaken to hold a brief against justice, in particular against that phase of justice with which we are concerned, was able to muster no argument stronger than this, that, for reasons of expediency, men imposed upon themselves laws, which vary according to customs, and among the same peoples often undergo changes as times change; moreover that there is no law of nature, because all creatures, men as well as animals, are impelled by nature toward ends advantageous to themselves; that, consequently, there is no justice, or, if such there be, it is supreme folly, since one does violence to his own interests if he consults the advantage of others.

6. What the philosopher here says, and the poet reaffirms in verse,

> And just from unjust Nature cannot know,

must not for one moment be admitted. Man is, to be sure, an animal, but an animal of a superior kind, much farther removed from all other animals than the different kinds of animals are from one another; evidence on this point may be found in the many traits peculiar to the human species. But among the traits characteristic of man is an impelling desire for society, that is, for the social life—not of any and every sort, but peaceful, and organized according to the measure of his intelligence, with those who are of his own kind; this social trend the Stoics called "sociableness." Stated as a universal truth, therefore, the assertion that every animal is impelled by nature to seek only its own good cannot be conceded.

7. Some of the other animals, in fact, do in a way restrain the appetency for that which is good for themselves alone, to the advantage, now of their offspring, now of other animals of the same species. This aspect of their behaviour has its origin, we believe, in some extrinsic intelligent principle, because with regard to other actions, which involve no more difficulty than those referred to, a like degree of intelligence is not manifest in them. The same thing must be said of children. In children, even before their training has begun, some disposition to do good to others appears, as Plutarch sagely observed; thus sympathy for others comes out spontaneously at that age. The mature man in fact has knowledge which prompts him to similar actions under similar conditions, together with an impelling desire for society, for the gratification of which he alone among animals possesses a special instrument, speech. He has also been endowed with the faculty of knowing and of acting in accordance with general principles. Whatever accords with that faculty is not common to all animals, but peculiar to the nature of man.

8. This maintenance of the social order, which we have roughly sketched, and which is consonant with human intelligence, is the source of law properly so called. To this sphere of law belong the abstaining from that which is another's, the restoration to another of anything of his which we may have, together with any gain which we may have received from it; the obligation to fulfil promises, the making good of a loss incurred through our fault, and the inflicting of penalties upon men according to their deserts.

9. From this signification of the word law there has flowed another and more extended meaning. Since over other animals man has the advantage of possessing not only a strong bent towards social life, of which we have spoken, but also a power of discrimination which enables him to decide what things are agreeable or harmful (as to both things present and things to come), and what can lead to either alternative: in such things it is meet for the nature of man, within the limitations of human intelligence, to follow the direction of a well-tempered judgement, being neither led astray by fear or the allurement of immediate pleasure, nor carried away by rash impulse. Whatever is clearly at variance with such judgement is understood to be contrary also to the law of nature, that is, to the nature of man.

10. To this exercise of judgement belongs moreover the rational allotment to each man, or to each social group, of those things which are

properly theirs, in such a way as to give the preference now to him who is more wise over the less wise, now to a kinsman rather than to a stranger, now to a poor man rather than to a man of means, as the conduct of each or the nature of the thing suggests. Long ago the view came to be held by many, that this discriminating allotment is a part of law, properly and strictly so called; nevertheless law, properly defined, has a far different nature, because its essence lies in leaving to another that which belongs to him, or in fulfilling our obligations to him.

11. What we have been saying would have a degree of validity even if we should concede that which cannot be conceded without the utmost wickedness, that there is no God, or that the affairs of men are of no concern to Him. The very opposite of this view has been implanted in us partly by reason, partly by unbroken tradition, and confirmed by many proofs as well as by miracles attested by all ages. Hence it follows that we must without exception render obedience to God as our Creator, to Whom we owe all that we are and have; especially since, in manifold ways, He has shown Himself supremely good and supremely powerful, so that to those who obey Him He is able to give supremely great rewards, even rewards that are eternal, since He Himself is eternal. We ought, moreover, to believe that He has willed to give rewards, and all the more should we cherish such a belief if He has so promised in plain words; that He has done this, we Christians believe, convinced by the indubitable assurance of testimonies.

12. Herein, then, is another source of law besides the source in nature, that is, the free will of God, to which beyond all cavil our reason tells us we must render obedience. But the law of nature of which we have spoken, comprising alike that which relates to the social life of man and that which is so called in a larger sense, proceeding as it does from the essential traits implanted in man, can nevertheless rightly be attributed to God, because of His having willed that such traits exist in us. In this sense, too, Chrysippus and the Stoics used to say that the origin of law should be sought in no other source than Jupiter himself; and from the name Jupiter the Latin word for Law (*ius*) was probably derived.

13. There is an additional consideration in that, by means of the laws which He has given, God has made those fundamental traits more manifest, even to those who possess feebler reasoning powers; and He has forbidden us to yield to impulses drawing us in opposite directions— affecting now our own interest, now the interest of others—in an effort to control more effectively our more violent impulses and to restrain them within proper limits.

14. But sacred history, besides enjoining rules of conduct, in no slight degree reinforces man's inclination towards sociableness by teaching that all men are sprung from the same first parents. In this sense we can rightly affirm also that which Florentinus asserted from another point of view, that a blood-relationship has been established among us by nature; consequently it is wrong for a man to set a snare for a fellow-man. Among

mankind generally one's parents are as it were divinities, and to them is owed an obedience which, if not unlimited, is nevertheless of an altogether special kind.

15. Again, since it is a rule of the law of nature to abide by pacts (for it was necessary that among men there be some method of obligating themselves one to another, and no other natural method can be imagined), out of this source the bodies of municipal law have arisen. For those who had associated themselves with some group, or had subjected themselves to a man or to men, had either expressly promised, or from the nature of the transaction must be understood impliedly to have promised, that they would conform to that which should have been determined, in the one case by the majority, in the other by those upon whom authority had been conferred.

16. What is said, therefore, in accordance with the view not only of Carneades but also of others, that

> Expediency is, as it were, the mother
> Of what is just and fair,

is not true, if we wish to speak accurately. For the very nature of man, which even if we had no lack of anything would lead us into the mutual relations of society, is the mother of the law of nature. But the mother of municipal law is that obligation which arises from mutual consent; and since this obligation derives its force from the law of nature, nature may be considered, so to say, the great-grandmother of municipal law.

The law of nature nevertheless has the reinforcement of expediency; for the Author of nature willed that as individuals we should be weak, and should lack many things needed in order to live properly, to the end that we might be the more constrained to cultivate the social life. But expediency afforded an opportunity also for municipal law, since that kind of association of which we have spoken, and subjection to authority, have their roots in expediency. From this it follows that those who prescribe laws for others in so doing are accustomed to have, or ought to have, some advantage in view.

17. But just as the laws of each state have in view the advantage of that state, so by mutual consent it has become possible that certain laws should originate as between all states, or a great many states; and it is apparent that the laws thus originating had in view the advantage, not of particular states, but of the great society of states. And this is what is called the law of nations, whenever we distinguish that term from the law of nature.

This division of law Carneades passed over altogether. For he divided all law into the law of nature and the law of particular countries. Nevertheless if undertaking to treat of the body of law which is maintained between states—for he added a statement in regard to war and things acquired by means of war—he would surely have been obliged to make mention of this law.

18. Wrongly, moreover, does Carneades ridicule justice as folly. For since, by his own admission, the national who in his own country obeys its

laws is not foolish, even though, out of regard for that law, he may be obliged to forgo certain things advantageous for himself, so that nation is not foolish which does not press its own advantage to the point of disregarding the laws common to nations. The reason in either case is the same. For just as the national, who violates the law of his country in order to obtain an immediate advantage, breaks down that by which the advantages of himself and his posterity are for all future time assured, so the state which transgresses the laws of nature and of nations cuts away also the bulwarks which safeguard its own future peace. Even if no advantage were to be contemplated from the keeping of the law, it would be a mark of wisdom, not of folly, to allow ourselves to be drawn towards that to which we feel that our nature leads.

19. Wherefore, in general, it is by no means true that

> You must confess that laws were framed
> From fear of the unjust,

a thought which in Plato some one explains thus, that laws were invented from fear of receiving injury, and that men are constrained by a kind of force to cultivate justice. For that relates only to the institutions and laws which have been devised to facilitate the enforcement of right; as when many persons in themselves weak, in order that they might not be overwhelmed by the more powerful, leagued themselves together to establish tribunals and by combined force to maintain these, that as a united whole they might prevail against those with whom as individuals they could not cope.

And in this sense we may readily admit also the truth of the saying that right is that which is acceptable to the stronger; so that we may understand that law fails of its outward effect unless it has a sanction behind it. In this way Solon accomplished very great results, as he himself used to declare,

> By joining force and law together,
> Under a like bond.

20. Nevertheless law, even though without a sanction, is not entirely void of effect. For justice brings peace of conscience, while injustice causes torments and anguish, such as Plato describes, in the breast of tyrants. Justice is approved, and injustice condemned, by the common agreement of good men. But, most important of all, in God injustice finds an enemy, justice a protector. He reserves His judgements for the life after this, yet in such a way that He often causes their effects to become manifest even in this life, as history teaches by numerous examples.

21. Many hold, in fact, that the standard of justice which they insist upon in the case of individuals within the state is inapplicable to a nation or the ruler of a nation. The reason for the error lies in this, first of all, that in respect to law they have in view nothing except the advantage which accrues from it, such advantage being apparent in the case of citizens who, taken singly, are powerless to protect themselves. But great states, since they seem to contain in themselves all things required for the adequate

protection of life, seem not to have need of that virtue which looks toward the outside, and is called justice.

22. But, not to repeat what I have said, that law is not founded on expediency alone, there is no state so powerful that it may not some time need the help of others outside itself, either for purposes of trade, or even to ward off the forces of many foreign nations united against it. In consequence we see that even the most powerful peoples and sovereigns seek alliances, which are quite devoid of significance according to the point of view of those who confine law within the boundaries of states. Most true is the saying, that all things are uncertain the moment men depart from law.

23. If no association of men can be maintained without law, as Aristotle showed by his remarkable illustration drawn from brigands, surely also that association which binds together the human race, or binds many nations together, has need of law; this was perceived by him who said that shameful deeds ought not to be committed even for the sake of one's country. Aristotle takes sharply to task those who, while unwilling to allow any one to exercise authority over themselves except in accordance with law, yet are quite indifferent as to whether foreigners are treated according to law or not.

24. That same Pompey, whom I just now quoted for the opposite view, corrected the statement which a king of Sparta had made, that that state is the most fortunate whose boundaries are fixed by spear and sword; he declared that that state is truly fortunate which has justice for its boundary line. On this point he might have invoked the authority of another king of Sparta, who gave the preference to justice over bravery in war, using this argument, that bravery ought to be directed by a kind of justice, but if all men were just they would have no need for bravery in war.

Bravery itself the Stoics defined as virtue fighting on behalf of equity. Themistius in his address to Valens argues with eloquence that kings who measure up to the rule of wisdom make account not only of the nation which has been committed to them, but of the whole human race, and that they are, as he himself says, not "friends of the Macedonians" alone, or "friends of the Romans," but "friends of mankind." The name of Minos became odious to future ages for no other reason than this, that he limited his fair-dealing to the boundaries of his realm.

25. Least of all should that be admitted which some people imagine, that in war all laws are in abeyance. On the contrary war ought not to be undertaken except for the enforcement of rights; when once undertaken, it should be carried on only within the bounds of law and good faith. Demosthenes well said that war is directed against those who cannot be held in check by judicial processes. For judgements are efficacious against those who feel that they are too weak to resist; against those who are equally strong, or think that they are, wars are undertaken. But in order that wars may be justified, they must be carried on with not less scrupulousness than judicial processes are wont to be.

26. Let the laws be silent, then, in the midst of arms, but only the laws of the State, those that the courts are concerned with, that are adapted

only to a state of peace; not those other laws, which are of perpetual validity and suited to all times. It was exceedingly well said by Dio of Prusa, that between enemies written laws, that is, laws of particular states, are not in force, but that unwritten laws are in force, that is, those which nature prescribes, or the agreement of nations has established. This is set forth by that ancient formula of the Romans, "I think that those things ought to be sought by means of a war that is blameless and righteous."

The ancient Romans, as Varro noted, were slow in undertaking war, and permitted themselves no licence in that matter, because they held the view that a war ought not to be waged except when free from reproach. Camillus said that wars should be carried on justly no less than bravely; Scipio Africanus, that the Roman people commenced and ended wars justly. In another passage you may read: "War has its laws no less than peace." Still another writer admires Fabricius as a great man who maintained his probity in war—a thing most difficult—and believed that even in relation to an enemy there is such a thing as wrongdoing.

27. The historians in many a passage reveal how great in war is the influence of the consciousness that one has justice on his side; they often attribute victory chiefly to this cause. Hence the proverbs, that a soldier's strength is broken or increased by his cause; that he who has taken up arms unjustly rarely comes back in safety; that hope is the comrade of a good cause; and others of the same purport.

No one ought to be disturbed, furthermore, by the successful outcome of unjust enterprises. For it is enough that the fairness of the cause exerts a certain influence, even a strong influence upon actions, although the effect of that influence, as happens in human affairs, is often nullified by the interference of other causes. Even for winning friendships, of which for many reasons nations as well as individuals have need, a reputation for having undertaken war not rashly nor unjustly, and of having waged it in a manner above reproach, is exceedingly efficacious. No one readily allies himself with those in whom he believes that there is only a slight regard for law, for the right, and for good faith.

28. Fully convinced, by the considerations which I have advanced, that there is a common law among nations, which is valid alike for war and in war, I have had many and weighty reasons for undertaking to write upon this subject. Throughout the Christian world I observed a lack of restraint in relation to war, such as even barbarous races should be ashamed of; I observed that men rush to arms for slight causes, or no cause at all, and that when arms have once been taken up there is no longer any respect for law, divine or human; it is as if, in accordance with a general decree, frenzy had openly been let loose for the committing of all crimes.

29. Confronted with such utter ruthlessness many men, who are the very furthest from being bad men, have come to the point of forbidding all use of arms to the Christian, whose rule of conduct above everything else comprises the duty of loving all men. To this opinion sometimes John Ferus and my fellow-countryman Erasmus seem to incline, men who have the ut-

most devotion to peace in both Church and State; but their purpose, as I take it, is, when things have gone in one direction, to force them in the opposite direction, as we are accustomed to do, that they may come back to a true middle ground. But the very effort of pressing too hard in the opposite direction is often so far from being helpful that it does harm, because in such arguments the detection of what is extreme is easy, and results in weakening the influence of other statements which are well within the bounds of truth. For both extremes therefore a remedy must be found, that men may not believe either that nothing is allowable, or that everything is.

30. At the same time through devotion to study in private life I have wished—as the only course now open to me, undeservedly forced out from my native land, which had been graced by so many of my labours—to contribute somewhat to the philosophy of the law, which previously, in public service, I practised with the utmost degree of probity of which I was capable. Many heretofore have purposed to give to this subject a well-ordered presentation; no one has succeeded. And in fact such a result cannot be accomplished unless—a point which until now has not been sufficiently kept in view—those elements which come from positive law are properly separated from those which arise from nature. For the principles of the law of nature, since they are always the same, can easily be brought into a systematic form; but the elements of positive law, since they often undergo change and are different in different places, are outside the domain of systematic treatment, just as other notions of particular things are.

31. If now those who have consecrated themselves to true justice should undertake to treat the parts of the natural and unchangeable philosophy of law, after having removed all that has its origin in the free will of man; if one, for example, should treat legislation, another taxation, another the administration of justice, another the determination of motives, another the proving of facts, then by assembling all these parts a body of jurisprudence could be made up.

32. What procedure we think should be followed we have shown by deed rather than by words in this work, which treats by far the noblest part of jurisprudence.

33. In the first book, having by way of introduction spoken of the origin of law, we have examined the general question, whether there is any such thing as a just war; then, in order to determine the differences between public war and private war, we found it necessary to explain the nature of sovereignty—what nations, what kings possess complete sovereignty; who possess sovereignty only in part, who with right of alienation, who otherwise; then it was necessary to speak also concerning the duty of subjects to their superiors.

34. The second book, having for its object to set forth all the causes from which war can arise, undertakes to explain fully what things are held in common, what may be owned in severalty; what rights persons have over persons, what obligation arises from ownership; what is the rule governing royal successions; what right is established by a pact or a contract; what is the force of treaties of alliance; what of an oath private or

public, and how it is necessary to interpret these; what is due in reparation for damage done; in what the inviolability of ambassadors consists; what law controls the burial of the dead, and what is the nature of punishments.

35. The third book has for its subject, first, what is permissible in war. Having distinguished that which is done with impunity, or even that which among foreign peoples is defended as lawful, from that which actually is free from fault, it proceeds to the different kinds of peace, and all compacts relating to war.

36. The undertaking seemed to me all the more worth while because, as I have said, no one has dealt with the subject-matter as a whole, and those who have treated portions of it have done so in a way to leave much to the labours of others. Of the ancient philosophers nothing in this field remains; either of the Greeks, among whom Aristotle had composed a book with the title *Rights of War,* or—what was especially to be desired— of those who gave their allegiance to the young Christianity. Even the books of the ancient Romans on fetial law have transmitted to us nothing of themselves except the title. Those who have made collections of the cases which are called "cases of conscience" have merely written chapters on war, promises, oaths, and reprisals, just as on other subjects.

37. I have seen also special books on the law of war, some by theologians, as Franciscus de Victoria, Henry of Gorkum, William Matthaei; others by doctors of law, as John Lupus, Franciscus Arias, Giovanni da Legnano, Martinus Laudensis. All of these, however, have said next to nothing upon a most fertile subject; most of them have done their work without system, and in such a way as to intermingle and utterly confuse what belongs to the law of nature, to divine law, to the law of nations, to civil law, and to the body of law which is found in the canons.

38. What all these writers especially lacked, the illumination of history, the very learned Faur undertook to supply in some chapters of his *Semestria,* but in a manner limited by the scope of his own work, and only through the citation of authorities. The same thing was attempted on a larger scale, and by referring a great number of examples to some general statements, by Balthazar Ayala; and still more fully, by Alberico Gentili. Knowing that others can derive profit from Gentili's painstaking, as I acknowledge that I have, I leave it to his readers to pass judgement on the shortcomings of his work as regards method of exposition, arrangement of matter, delimitation of inquiries, and distinctions between the various kinds of law. This only I shall say, that in treating controversial questions it is his frequent practice to base his conclusions on a few examples, which are not in all cases worthy of approval, or even to follow the opinions of modern jurists, formulated in arguments of which not a few were accommodated to the special interests of clients, not to the nature of that which is equitable and upright.

The causes which determine the characterization of a war as lawful or unlawful Ayala did not touch upon. Gentili outlined certain general classes, in the manner which seemed to him best; but he did not so much as refer to many topics which have come up in notable and frequent controversies.

39. We have taken all pains that nothing of this sort escape us; and we have also indicated the sources from which conclusions are drawn, whence it would be an easy matter to verify them, even if any point has been omitted by us. It remains to explain briefly with what helps, and with what care, I have attacked this task.

First of all, I have made it my concern to refer the proofs of things touching the law of nature to certain fundamental conceptions which are beyond question, so that no one can deny them without doing violence to himself. For the principles of that law, if only you pay strict heed to them, are in themselves manifest and clear, almost as evident as are those things which we perceive by the external senses; and the senses do not err if the organs of perception are properly formed and if the other conditions requisite to perception are present. Thus in his *Phoenician Maidens* Euripides represents Polynices, whose cause he makes out to have been manifestly just, as speaking thus:

> Mother, these words, that I have uttered, are not
> Inwrapped with indirection, but, firmly based
> On rules of justice and of good, are plain
> Alike to simple and to wise.

The poet adds immediately a judgement of the chorus, made up of women, and barbarian women at that, approving these words.

40. In order to prove the existence of this law of nature, I have, furthermore, availed myself of the testimony of philosophers, historians, poets, finally also of orators. Not that confidence is to be reposed in them without discrimination; for they were accustomed to serve the interests of their sect, their subject, or their cause. But when many at different times, and in different places, affirm the same thing as certain, that ought to be referred to a universal cause; and this cause, in the lines of inquiry which we are following, must be either a correct conclusion drawn from the principles of nature, or common consent. The former points to the law of nature; the latter, to the law of nations.

The distinction between these kinds of law is not to be drawn from the testimonies themselves (for writers everywhere confuse the terms law of nature and law of nations), but from the character of the matter. For whatever cannot be deduced from certain principles by a sure process of reasoning, and yet is clearly observed everywhere, must have its origin in the free will of man.

41. These two kinds of law, therefore, I have always particularly sought to distinguish from each other and from municipal law. Furthermore, in the law of nations I have distinguished between that which is truly and in all respects law, and that which produces merely a kind of outward effect simulating that primitive law, as, for example, the prohibition to resist by force, or even the duty of defence in any place by public force, in order to secure some advantage, or for the avoidance of serious disadvantages. How necessary it is, in many cases, to observe this distinction, will become apparent in the course of our work.

With not less pains we have separated those things which are strictly and properly legal, out of which the obligation of restitution arises, from those things which are called legal because any other classification of them conflicts with some other stated rule of right reason. In regard to this distinction of law we have already said something above.

42. Among the philosophers Aristotle deservedly holds the foremost place, whether you take into account his order of treatment, or the subtlety of his distinctions, or the weight of his reasons. Would that this preeminence had not, for some centuries back, been turned into a tyranny, so that Truth, to whom Aristotle devoted faithful service, was by no instrumentality more repressed than by Aristotle's name!

For my part, both here and elsewhere I avail myself of the liberty of the early Christians, who had sworn allegiance to the sect of no one of the philosophers, not because they were in agreement with those who said that nothing can be known—than which nothing is more foolish—but because they thought that there was no philosophic sect whose vision had compassed all truth, and none which had not perceived some aspect of truth. Thus they believed that to gather up into a whole the truth which was scattered among the different philosophers and dispersed among the sects, was in reality to establish a body of teaching truly Christian.

43. Among other things—to mention in passing a point not foreign to my subject—it seems to me that not without reason some of the Platonists and early Christians departed from the teachings of Aristotle in this, that he considered the very nature of virtue as a mean in passions and actions. That principle, once adopted, led him to unite distinct virtues, as generosity and frugality, into one; to assign to truth extremes between which, on any fair premiss, there is no possible co-ordination, boastfulness, and dissimulation; and to apply the designation of vice to certain things which either do not exist, or are not in themselves vices, such as contempt for pleasure and for honours, and freedom from anger against men.

44. That this basic principle, when broadly stated, is unsound, becomes clear even from the case of justice. For, being unable to find in passions and acts resulting therefrom the too much and the too little opposed to that virtue, Aristotle sought each extreme in the things themselves with which justice is concerned. Now in the first place this is simply to leap from one class of things over into another class, a fault which he rightly censures in others; then, for a person to accept less than belongs to him may in fact under unusual conditions constitute a fault, in view of that which, according to the circumstances, he owes to himself and to those dependent on him; but in any case the act cannot be at variance with justice, the essence of which lies in abstaining from that which belongs to another.

By equally faulty reasoning Aristotle tries to make out that adultery committed in a burst of passion, or a murder due to anger, is not properly an injustice. Whereas nevertheless injustice has no other essential quality than the unlawful seizure of that which belongs to another; and it does not matter whether injustice arises from avarice, from lust, from anger, or from ill-advised compassion; or from an overmastering desire to achieve eminence, out of which instances of the gravest injustice constantly arise. For to disparage such incitements, with the sole purpose in view that human society may not receive injury, is in truth the concern of justice.

45. To return to the point whence I started, the truth is that some virtues do tend to keep passions under control; but that is not because such control is a proper and essential characteristic of every virtue. Rather it is because right reason, which virtue everywhere follows, in some things prescribes the pursuing of a middle course, in others stimulates to the utmost degree. We cannot, for example, worship God too much; for superstition errs not by worshipping God too much, but by worshipping in a perverse way. Neither can we too much seek after the blessings that shall abide for ever, nor fear too much the everlasting evils, nor have too great hatred for sin.

With truth therefore was it said by Aulus Gellius, that there are some things of which the extent is limited by no boundaries—the greater, the more ample they are, the more excellent. Lactantius, having discussed the passions at great length, says:

> The method of wisdom consists in controlling not the passions, but their causes, since they are stirred from without. And putting a check upon the passions themselves ought not to be the chief concern, because they may be feeble in the greatest crime, and very violent without leading to crime.

Our purpose is to make much account of Aristotle, but reserving in regard to him the same liberty which he, in his devotion to truth, allowed himself with respect to his teachers.

46. History in relation to our subject is useful in two ways: it supplies both illustrations and judgements. The illustrations have greater weight in proportion as they are taken from better times and better peoples; thus we have preferred ancient examples, Greek and Roman, to the rest. And judgements are not to be slighted, especially when they are in agreement with one another; for by such statements the existence of the law of nature, as we have said, is in a measure proved, and by no other means, in fact, is it possible to establish the law of nations.

47. The views of poets and of orators do not have so great weight; and we make frequent use of them not so much for the purpose of gaining acceptance by that means for our argument, as of adding, from their words, some embellishment to that which we wished to say.

48. I frequently appeal to the authority of the books which men inspired by God have either written or approved, nevertheless with a distinction between the Old Testament and the New. There are some who urge that the Old Testament sets forth the law of nature. Without doubt they are in error, for many of its rules come from the free will of God. And yet this is never in conflict with the true law of nature; and up to this point the Old Testament can be used as a source of the law of nature, provided we carefully distinguish between the law of God, which God sometimes executes through men, and the law of men in their relations with one another.

This error we have, so far as possible, avoided, and also another opposed to it, which supposes that after the coming of the New Testament the Old Testament in this respect was no longer of use. We believe the contrary, partly for the reasons which we have already given, partly because the character of the New Testament is such that in its teachings respecting the moral virtues it enjoins the same as the Old Testament or even enjoins greater precepts. In this way we see that the early Christian writers used the witnesses of the Old Testament.

49. The Hebrew writers, moreover, most of all those who have thoroughly understood the speech and customs of their people, are able to contribute not a little to our understanding of the thought of the books which belong to the Old Testament.

50. The New Testament I use in order to explain—and this cannot be learned from any other source—what is permissible to Christians. This, however—contrary to the practice of most men—I have distinguished from the law of nature, considering it as certain that in that most holy law a greater degree of moral perfection is enjoined upon us than the law of nature, alone and by itself, would require. And nevertheless I have not omitted to note the things that are recommended to us rather than enjoined, that we may know that, while the turning aside from what has been enjoined is wrong and involves the risk of punishment, a striving for the highest excellence implies a noble purpose and will not fail of its reward.

51. The authentic synodical canons are collections embodying the general principles of divine law as applied to cases which come up; they either show what the divine law enjoins, or urge us to that which God would fain persuade. And this truly is the mission of the Christian Church, to transmit those things which were transmitted to it by God, and in the way in which they were transmitted.

Furthermore customs which were current, or were considered praiseworthy, among the early Christians and those who rose to the measure of so great a name, deservedly have the force of canons.

Next after these comes the authority of those who, each in his own time, have been distinguished among Christians for their piety and learning, and have not been charged with any serious error; for what these declare with great positiveness, and as if definitely ascertained, ought to have no slight weight for the interpretation of passages in Holy Writ which seem obscure. Their authority is the greater the more there are of them in agreement, and as we approach nearer to the times of pristine purity, when neither desire for domination nor any conspiracy of interests had as yet been able to corrupt the primitive truth.

52. The Schoolmen, who succeeded these writers, often show how strong they are in natural ability. But their lot was cast in an unhappy age, which was ignorant of the liberal arts; wherefore it is less to be wondered at if among many things worthy of praise there are also some things which we should receive with indulgence. Nevertheless when the Schoolmen agree on a point of morals, it rarely happens that they are wrong, since they are especially keen in seeing what may be open to criticism in the

statements of others. And yet in the very ardour of their defence of themselves against opposing views, they furnish a praiseworthy example of moderation; they contend with one another by means of arguments—not, in accordance with the practice which has lately begun to disgrace the calling of letters, with personal abuse, base offspring of a spirit lacking self-mastery.

53. Of those who profess knowledge of the Roman law there are three classes.

The first consists of those whose work appears in the Pandects, the Codes of Theodosius and Justinian, and the Imperial Constitutions called Novellae.

To the second class belong the successors of Irnerius, that is Accursius, Bartolus, and so many other names of those who long ruled the bar.

The third class comprises those who have combined the study of classical literature with that of law.

To the first class I attribute great weight. For they frequently give the very best reasons in order to establish what belongs to the law of nature, and they often furnish evidence in favour of this law and of the law of nations. Nevertheless they, no less than the others, often confuse these terms, frequently calling that the law of nations which is only the law of certain peoples, and that, too, not as established by assent, but perchance taken over through imitation of others or by pure accident. But those provisions which really belong to the law of nations they often treat, without distinction or discrimination, along with those which belong to the Roman law, as may be seen by reference to the title *On Captives and Postliminy*. We have therefore endeavoured to distinguish these two types from each other.

54. The second class, paying no heed to the divine law or to ancient history, sought to adjust all controversies of kings and peoples by application of the laws of the Romans, with occasional use of the canons. But in the case of these men also the unfortunate condition of their times was frequently a handicap which prevented their complete understanding of those laws, though, for the rest, they were skilful enough in tracing out the nature of that which is fair and good. The result is that while they are often very successful in establishing the basis of law, they are at the same time bad interpreters of existing law. But they are to be listened to with the utmost attention when they bear witness to the existence of the usage which constitutes the law of nations in our day.

55. The masters of the third class, who confine themselves within the limits of the Roman law and deal either not at all, or only slightly, with the common law of nations, are of hardly any use in relation to our subject. They combine the subtlety of the Schoolmen with a knowledge of laws and of canons; and in fact two of them, the Spaniards Covarruvias and Vázquez, did not refrain from treating the controversies of peoples and kings, the latter with great freedom, the former with more restraint and not without precision of judgement.

The French have tried rather to introduce history into their study of laws. Among them Bodin and Hotman have gained a great name, the former by an extensive treatise, the latter by separate questions; their statements and lines of reasoning will frequently supply us with material in searching out the truth.

56. In my work as a whole I have, above all else, aimed at three things: to make the reasons for my conclusions as evident as possible; to set forth in a definite order the matters which needed to be treated; and to distinguish clearly between things which seemed to be the same and were not.

57. I have refrained from discussing topics which belong to another subject, such as those that teach what may be advantageous in practice. For such topics have their own special field, that of politics, which Aristotle rightly treats by itself, without introducing extraneous matter into it. Bodin, on the contrary, mixed up politics with the body of law with which we are concerned. In some places nevertheless I have made mention of that which is expedient, but only in passing, and in order to distinguish it more clearly from what is lawful.

58. If any one thinks that I have had in view any controversies of our own times, either those that have arisen or those which can be foreseen as likely to arise, he will do me an injustice. With all truthfulness I aver that, just as mathematicians treat their figures as abstracted from bodies, so in treating law I have withdrawn my mind from every particular fact.

59. As regards manner of expression, I wished not to disgust the reader, whose interests I continually had in mind, by adding prolixity of words to the multiplicity of matters needing to be treated. I have therefore followed, so far as I could, a mode of speaking at the same time concise and suitable for exposition, in order that those who deal with public affairs may have, as it were, in a single view both the kinds of controversies which are wont to arise and the principles by reference to which they may be decided. These points being known, it will be easy to adapt one's argument to the matter at issue, and expand it at one's pleasure.

60. I have now and then quoted the very words of ancient writers, where they seemed to carry weight or to have unusual charm of expression. This I have occasionally done even in the case of Greek writers, but as a rule only when the passage was brief, or such that I dared not hope that I could bring out the beauty of it in a Latin version. Nevertheless in all cases I have added a Latin translation for the convenience of those who have not learned Greek.

61. I beg and adjure all those into whose hands this work shall come, that they assume towards me the same liberty which I have assumed in passing upon the opinions and writings of others. They who shall find me in error will not be more quick to advise me than I to avail myself of their advice.

And now if anything has here been said by me inconsistent with piety, with good morals, with Holy Writ, with the concord of the Christian Church, or with any aspect of truth, let it be as if unsaid.

Selected Bibliography

Classic Works

Aquinas, Thomas. *Summa Theologiae.*
Gentili, Alberico. *De Jure Belli (On the Law of War)* (1598).
———. *De Legationibus (On Embassies)* (1585).
Grotius, Hugo. *De Jure Praedae* (1604).
———. *Mare Liberum* (1609).
———. *De Jure Belli Ac Pacis* (1625).
Pufendorf, Samuel. *Elementorum Jurisprudentiae Universalis* (1660).
———. *De Jure Naturae et Gentium* (1672).
———. *De Officio et Civis Juxta Legem Naturalem* (1673). An abridgement of *De Jure.*
Suarez, Francisco, S.J. *De Legibus, ac Deo Legislatore (On Laws and God the Lawgiver)* (1612).
———. *De Triplici Virtute Theologica: Fide, Spe et Charitate (On the Three Theological Virtues: Faith, Hope, and Charity)* (1621).
De Vitoria, Francisco. *De Indis Noviter Inventis (On the Indians Lately Discovered)* (1539).
———. *De Jure Belli Hispanorum in Barbaros (On the Law of War Made by the Spaniards on the Barbarians)* (1539).
———. *De Jure Gentium et Naturali (On the Jus Gentium and Natural Law)* (1628).
———. *De Poteste Ecclesiae (On the Power of the Church)* (1557).
Wolff, Christian. *Law of Nature Treated According to Scientific Method* (8 vols., 1740–48).
———. *Law of Nations Treated According to Scientific Method* (1749).
———. *Institutes of the Law of Nature and of Nations* (1750).

Specific Aspects of Naturalism

Buckle, Stephen. *Natural Law and the Theory of Property* (1991).
Bull, Hedley, Benedict Kingsbury, and Adam Roberts, eds. *Hugo Grotius and International Relations* (1990).
D'Amato, Anthony. "Is International Law Part of Natural Law?" *Vera Lex* 9 (1989).
———. "Lon Fuller and Substantive International Law," *American Journal of Jurisprudence* 26 (1981): 202–18.
De Aquilar, Jose Manuel, O.P. "The Law of Nations and the Salamanca School of Theology," *Thomist* 9 (1946): 186–221.
D'Èntreves, Alexander Passerin. *An Introduction to Legal Philosophy,* 2nd ed. (1970).
———. *Natural Law: An Historical Survey* (1965).
Doyle, John P. "Francisco Suarez: On Preaching the Gospel to People Like the American Indians," *Fordham International Law Journal* 15 (1991–92).

Finnis, John. *Natural Law and Natural Rights* (1980).

Fuller, Lon. *The Morality of Law* (1964).

George, Robert P. "Recent Criticism of Natural Law Theory," *University of Chicago Law Review* (1988): 1371–1430.

———, ed. *Natural Law Theory: Contemporary Essays* (1992).

Hernandez, Ramon, O.P. "The Internationalization of Francisco De Vitoria and Domingo De Soto," *Fordham International Law Journal* 15 (1991–92): 1031–59.

Kennedy, David. "Primitive Legal Scholarship," *Harvard International Law Journal* 27 (1986): 1–98.

McCoubrey, H. *The Development of Naturalist Legal Theory* (1987).

Midgley, E. *The Natural Law Tradition and the Theory of International Relations* (1975).

Schall, James V., S.J. "Natural Law and the Law of Nations: Some Theoretical Considerations." *Fordham International Law Journal* 15 (1991–92): 997–1030.

Scott, James B. *The Catholic Conception of International Law* (1934).

———. "Francisco Suarez, His Philosophy of Law and of Sanctions," *Georgetown Law Journal* 22 (1934): 405–518.

———. *The Spanish Origin of International Law* (1934).

Verdross, Alfred, and Heribert Franz Koeck. "Natural Law: The Tradition of Universal Reason and Authority," in Ronald St. J. Macdonald and Douglas M. Johnston, eds., *The Structure and Process of International Law: Essays in Legal Philosophy, Doctrine and Theory* (1983), pp. 17–50.

Yasuaki, Onuma, ed. *A Normative Approach to War: Peace, War, Justice in Hugo Grotius* (1993).

3

Legal Positivism

Though its roots may be traced at least to the seventeenth century, Legal Positivism has dominated international jurisprudence in the twentieth century. The essential characteristic of the Positivist approach to international rules is its insistence that such rules are binding only if they are grounded in state consent. Whether that consent is manifested directly by head-of-state treaty signatures, or indirectly by state participation in customary practice, Positivist scholars contend that no other source exists for international law except consent. Prominent early exponents of the Positivist approach include the German professor Johann Jacob Moser (1701–1785), who based his characterizations of international law on state behavior per se; the Swiss diplomat Emerich de Vattel (1714–1767), who emphasized the independence and equality of states as international law's creators; and the English jurist Richard Zouche (1590–1660), whose *Juris et Judicii Fecialis* has been called "the first manual of international law."[1]

Legal Positivists seek fundamentally to ascertain what the law is, rather than what it *ought* to be. They are also united in rejecting the Naturalist premise that law can be rationally derived from some metaphysical source. As evidence of naturalism's alleged inadequacy, Positivists routinely cite the wide variation, and indeed the inconsistency in natural lawyers' conclusions about the law's content. In striving to render international legal analysis more systematic and, many would assert, scientific, modern Positivists have developed a penchant for codification.

Positivism emerged as a general approach to law, focusing at first on domestic legal systems. Ironically, though modern international law is founded largely on Positivist principles, some Positivists deny that international law constitutes a genuine species of "law."

The Command Theory

John Austin (1790–1859) proposes a starkly Positivist conception of law, the "command theory," by which he denies that international law is worthy of the label "law." In *The Province of Jurisprudence Determined* (1832), a published version of his lectures, the British scholar submits that law cannot be "law, properly so called" unless it constitutes a species of *command,* issued by a *sovereign* (superior to the subjects of the law) and backed by a *sanction.*

Austin regards "sovereign power" as "incapable of legal limitation." Law must proceed, he asserts, from a "precisely determined party capable of issuing a command" rather than from some "uncertain aggregate of persons." Because international law does not proceed from a single sovereign, and because states, the intended subjects of international law, are themselves sovereign and thus not susceptible to legal sanction, Austin classifies international law as a form of "positive morality."

John Austin's rejection of the legal status of international rules is of more than semantic importance. As a "law rooted in opinion," international law is no more worthy of study, or of the attention and adherence of governments, than are the "law of honor" or the "law of fashion," other forms of positive morality. In Austin's view:

> laws which regard the conduct of sovereigns or supreme governments in their various relations to one another. . . are imposed upon nations or sovereigns by opinions current among nations. . . . a so called law set by general opinion is not a law in the proper signification of the term. It also follows from the same reasons, that it is not armed with a sanction, and does not impose a duty, in the proper acceptation of the expressions. For a sanction properly so called is an evil annexed to a command. And duty properly so called is an obnoxiousness to evils of the kind.[2]

The Pure Theory of the Law

While rejecting its more dogmatic elements, the Austrian jurist Hans Kelsen (1881–1973) builds upon and refines Austinian Positivism. Professor Kelsen agrees with Austin that a legal rule is analogous to a command, but denies that such a rule rests on any active will. Like Austin, Kelsen acknowledges that coercion represents an essential element of law, but he criticizes Austin's exclusive focus on the negative sanction of fear. In the essay included here, Kelsen probes the role in international law of coercion, especially of war and reprisals, to determine whether international law is truly a legal system analogous to municipal law. Central to Kelsen's conclusion that international law constitutes authentic "law," albeit in "primitive" form, is his view that coercion by one state against another must be deemed illegal ("delictual") unless that forcible action is undertaken as a "sanction" response to a prior illegal act ("delict").

Kelsen's most significant modification of earlier Positivist approaches, however, is his rejection of their dualistic view of the sovereign and legal orders. In Kelsen's monistic conception of the legal order, the state constitutes merely the personification of a system of legal norms. Kelsen not only asserts that the state and law are coincident, but also rejects the conception of international law as a separate system from municipal law. For Kelsen there exists a single, seamless "world of law" based on a *Grundnorm* that must be "presupposed."

To maintain the theoretical purity of this monistic conception of law, Kelsen accords primary status to international law, placing it at the apex of his hierarchy of legal norms and describing municipal law as a "delegation" from international law. This conspicuous departure from Austin demonstrates the great variety of conclusions deducible from core Legal Positivist assumptions.

Analytical Theory

n attempting to chart a mean between the juristic extremes of "law and morality" and "law as an order backed by threats," H.L.A. Hart (1907–1992) produced one of the most influential works of contemporary legal positivism, *The Concept of Law* (1961). Here, Hart embraces the Positivist insistence on a conceptual separation of law and morals, but he acknowledges that this division itself presupposes a moral choice. Hart, who is widely regarded as a leading modern Positivist, nonetheless concedes the existence of a certain minimum core of natural law.

Professor Hart criticizes Austin's insistence on sanction as a necessary element of the legal system, and seeks to elucidate the difference between what an actor *has been obliged* (coerced) to do, and what that actor *has an obligation* (duty) to do. The nature of obligation, and not merely of coercion, is central to Hart's concept of law.

Hart ultimately judges Austin's command theory of Positivism a failure, and ascribes its failure fundamentally to its inability to elucidate the "idea of a rule, without which we cannot hope to elucidate even the most elementary forms of law."[3] Also central to Hart's concept of law, then, is the proposition that a developed legal system must feature two types of rules: "primary rules" stipulating substantive obligations, and "secondary rules" of recognition, change, and adjudication, which serve to define and to unify the legal system. In Hart's words:

> Under rules of the one type, which may well be considered the basic or primary type, human beings are required to do or abstain from certain actions, whether they wish to or not. Rules of the other type are in a sense parasitic upon or secondary to the first; for they provide that human beings may by doing or saying certain things introduce new rules of the primary type, extinguishing or modifying old ones, or in various ways determine their incidence or control their operations. Rules of the first

type impose duties; rules of the second type confer powers, public or private.[4]

Hart defends international law against the Austinian accusation that it is merely a form of positive morality. The British scholar begins by observing that many rules of international law are, in fact, "morally quite indifferent." He contends, however, that international law, like primitive law, lacks secondary rules with which to assess the validity of its substantive provisions. Thus, international law is not really a *legal system* at all, but merely a collection of rules. International law is analogous to municipal law in content, but not in form or function.

Professor Hart concludes that rules are simply accepted standards of conduct, supported by certain forms of social pressure, which can be observed and categorized. The objective mode of inquiry into the behavior of states implied by Hart's Legal Positivist approach, as will be seen in succeeding chapters of this volume, has been shared by a variety of other modern approaches to international rules as well.

Notes

1. "Historical Introduction," in L. Henkin, R. Pugh, O. Schachter, and H. Smit, eds., *International Law: Cases and Materials,* 3rd ed. (St. Paul, Minn.: West, 1993), p. xxv.

2. John Austin, "The Province of Jurisprudence Determined," in Clarence Morris, ed. *The Great Legal Philosophers* (Philadelphia: University of Pennsylvania Press, 1971), p. 352.

3. H.L.A. Hart, *The Concept of Law,* 2nd ed. (Oxford: Oxford University Press, 1994), p. 81.

4. Ibid., pp. 78–79.

HANS KELSEN

The Nature of International Law

1. The Problem of International Peace

In political discussions of today two questions predominate: How can economic life be satisfactorily organized within the national community, the state, without abolishing the personal freedom of the individual? and how can war or any other use of force be prevented within the international community, in the relation between states? In trying to answer the second question we turn at once to the individual state, where in the relations between citizens the goal has been attained in principle. Except under certain extraordinary conditions such as revolution or civil war, the employment of force has been effectively eliminated from the relations between citizens and reserved for a central organ authorized to use force only as a reaction against illegal acts.

It seems natural, therefore, to unite all these individual states, or at least as many as possible, into a world-state, and to concentrate all their means of power and place them at the exclusive disposal of a central government; or in other words, to subject as many states as possible to a legal order which, as far as the degree of its centralization is concerned, would be on a par with the legal order of the states themselves.

At the present time, under present political circumstances, the idea of such a world-state is hardly more than a Utopian scheme, even if this world-state is represented as a relatively decentralized federal state and is referred to by the inoffensive term of a union of states. From a realistic point of view, the solution of the problem of peace can be sought only within the frame of international law, that is to say, by an organization which in the degree of its centralization does not exceed that compatible with the nature of international law. If this degree of centralization is exceeded, the international community is transformed into a national community, a state; for it is essentially in the degree of centralization that an international community constituted by international law differs from a national community constituted by national law, a union of states from a state. The international community is a decentralized community, decentralized in a specific manner, whereas the state is a centralized community. A solution of the peace problem within the frame of international law means, therefore, a solution of the peace problem through an internation-

Lecture 2 from *Law and Peace in International Relations* (Cambridge, Mass.: Harvard University Press, Copyright © 1942, 1970 by the President and Fellows of Harvard College). Reprinted by permission of the publishers.

al organization whose centralization does not go so far that international law will be eliminated in the relations between the states embraced by the organization; a solution of the peace problem by the establishment of a community of states without altering the law governing the relations between these states to such an extent that this law ceases to be international law and becomes national law.

Such a solution of the peace problem is a political task, and, like every political task, has a technical character. It is a question of organizing a community of states through the specific means offered by international law. To achieve this end one must know the nature of international law, its organic structure. Therefore I shall first address myself to the question of the nature of international law. One can hardly formulate this question except by asking whether or not the norms called international law are law in the same sense as the norms of national law. This question is by no means merely a theoretical one. For if international law is law in the same sense as national law, if the international community of states is, in principle, the same social phenomenon as the national community of individuals, it may be presumed that international law is susceptible to the same evolution as national law. If this be true, then a relatively certain way is opened to the successful reform of international legal relations.

2. The Legal Character of International Law

Scientifically formulated, the question whether or not international law is law in the sense of the definition established in the first lecture is the question whether or not the legal material commonly called international law can be described in rules of law, using this term in a purely descriptive sense.[1]

A rule of law, as was stated in the first lecture, is a hypothetical judgment according to which a coercive act, forcible interference in the sphere of a subject's interests, is attached as a consequence to certain conduct of that subject. The coercive measure which the rule of law provides as the consequence is the sanction; the conduct of the subject set forth as the condition is the delict. The sanction is interpreted as a reaction of the legal community against the delict. The delict is undesirable behavior, especially forcible interference in the sphere of interests of another subject, a coercive act. The coercive act is therefore either a delict, a condition of the sanction—and hence forbidden—or a sanction, the consequence of a delict—and hence permitted. This alternative is an essential characteristic of the coercive order called law.

International law is law in this sense if a coercive act on the part of a state, the forcible interference of a state in the sphere of interests of another, is permitted only as a reaction against a delict and the employment of force to any other end is forbidden—only if the coercive act undertaken as a reaction against a delict can be interpreted as a reaction of the international legal community. If it is possible to describe the material which appears in the guise of international law in such a way that the employment of force directed by one state against another can be interpreted only as either delict or sanction, then international law is law in the same sense as national law.

In speaking of international law, reference is made only to general or common international law, not to particular international law. General or common international law is customary law, valid for all the states belonging to the international community. Particular international law is valid for a few states only, and comprises especially norms created by international treaties valid only for the contracting parties. There is as yet no international treaty concluded by all states, no general or common international law created by international treaty. Even treaties concluded by many states, such as the Covenant of the League of Nations or the Kellogg Pact, constitute not general, but particular international law.

The problem must therefore be formulated as follows: first, is there according to general international law such a thing as a delict, conduct of a state usually characterized as illegal? Second, is there according to general international law such a thing as a sanction, a coercive measure provided as the consequence of a delict, and directed against a state which conducts itself illegally—a deprivation of possessions by the employment of force if necessary, a forcible interference in the normally protected sphere of interests of the state responsible for the delict? From what was said in the first lecture, it follows that, juristically, specific conduct of a state can be considered a delict only if international law attaches to this conduct a sanction directed against the state.

3. Delict and Sanction in International Law

It is a commonly accepted fact that there exists in international law such a thing as a delict, that is, conduct of a state which is considered illegal. This follows from the fact that international law is regarded as a system of norms which prescribe certain conduct for states. If a state without a specific reason recognized by international law invades territory which according to international law belongs to another state, or if a state fails to observe a treaty concluded with another state according to international law, its conduct is considered contrary to the order just as the conduct of an individual who lies is considered contrary to the moral order. In this sense there is without doubt a delict in international law.

But is there in international law such a thing as a delict in the specifically juristic sense, that is, is there also a sanction prescribed by international law, a sanction directed against the state responsible for the delict?

By "sanction in international law" many theorists mean the obligation to repair the wrong, especially illegally caused damage. This is, so to speak, a substitute obligation, a duty which arises when a state has failed to fulfill its main or original obligation. The duty to make reparation replaces the obligation violated. It is doubtful, however, whether the obligation to make reparation is provided by general international law as a consequence of the delict or is only the result of a treaty concluded between the state affected by the delict and the state responsible for it. I, personally, incline to the latter view.[2] But even if the obligation to make reparation is provided by general international law as a consequence of the delict, this substitute obligation cannot be considered a sanction. Only the consequence of failure to fulfill this substitute obligation, the last consequence stated by the rule of law, constitutes a true sanction. The specific sanction of a legal order can only be a coercive measure, provided by the legal order in case an obligation is violated, and, if a substitute obligation is established, in case this substitute obligation also is violated. Are there coercive measures provided by general international law as consequences of international delicts? Are there forcible interferences in the normally protected spheres of interests of the states responsible for the delicts? These are the questions.

4. Reprisals

If all the material known under the name of international law be investigated, there appear to be two different kinds of forcible interference in the sphere of interests of a state normally protected by international law. The distinction rests upon the degree of interference: whether this interference is in principle limited or unlimited, whether the action undertaken against a state is aimed solely at the violation of certain interests of this state, or is directed toward its complete submission or total annihilation.

As to the characterization of limited interference in the sphere of interests of one state by another, a generally accepted opinion prevails. Such an interference is considered either as a delict in the sense of international law, or as a reprisal. It is permitted as a reprisal, however, only insofar as it takes place as a reaction against a delict. The idea that a reprisal, a limited interference in the normally protected sphere of interests of another state, is only admissible as a reaction against a wrong committed by this state has been universally accepted and forms an undisputed part of positive international law. It is not essential that interference in the sphere of interests of a state, undertaken as a reprisal, be accompanied by the use of force. But the use of force in a resort to reprisal is permissible, especially if resistance makes it essential. Similarly, the sanctions of national law, punishment and civil execution, are executed by force only in the case of resistance.

There is nothing to prevent calling a reprisal a sanction of international law. Whether this is true also as to unlimited interference in the sphere of interests of another state remains to be seen. Such an interference is usually called war, because it is an action executed by armed force, by the army, the navy, and the air force. This action, too, has a forcible character only if it meets with resistance. The problem therefore becomes: What is the meaning of war according to international law? Is it possible to interpret war, like the limited interference in the sphere of interests of another state, as either a delict or a sanction? In other words, is it possible to say that according to international law war is permitted only as a sanction, and any war which has not the character of a sanction is forbidden by international law, is a delict?

5. The Two Interpretations of War

Two diametrically opposite views exist as to the interpretation of war. According to one opinion, war is neither a delict nor a sanction. Any state that is not expressly bound by special treaty to refrain from warring upon another state, or to resort to war only under certain definite conditions, may proceed to war against any other state on any ground without violating international law. According to this opinion, therefore, war can never constitute a delict, for the behavior of a state which is called war is not forbidden by general international law and hence to this extent is permitted. But, according to this opinion, war cannot constitute a sanction either, for there is in international law no special provision which authorizes the state to resort to war. War is not set up by international law as a specific reaction against illegal conduct on the part of a state.

The opposite opinion, however, holds that according to general international law war is forbidden in principle. It is permitted only as a reaction against an illegal act, a delict, and only when directed against the state responsible for this delict. As with reprisals, war has to be a sanction if it is not to be characterized as a delict. This is the theory of *bellum justum.*

It would be naïve to ask which of these two opinions is the correct one, for each is sponsored by outstanding authorities and defended by weighty arguments. This fact in itself makes any definite choice between the two theories extremely difficult. By what arguments can the thesis be attacked or defended that according to general international law no war is permissible save as a reaction against a wrong suffered, against a delict? The mere statement of the problem in this form suggests that the position of those who represent the theory of *bellum justum* is more difficult to maintain, for the burden of proof is theirs, while the opposite view limits itself to a denial of this thesis, and, as is well known, *negantis major potestas.*

6. The Doctrine of "Bellum Justum"

If it be asked how it is possible to prove the thesis of the *bellum justum* theory—that general international law forbids war in principle—the first difficulty is encountered. According to strict juristic thinking, a certain conduct is prohibited within a certain legal system when a specific sanction is attached to such conduct. The only possible reaction that can be provided by general international law against an unpermitted war is war itself, a kind of "counter-war" against the state which resorted to war in disregard of international law. No other sanction is possible in view of the actual technical condition of general international law. But this implies that war, or to be more exact, counter-war, must be presupposed as a sanction in order that war may be interpreted as a delict. Such a view, however, obviously begs the question, and it is, therefore, logically impracticable to prove the thesis of the *bellum justum* theory. But there is another way to go about it, namely to examine the historical manifestations of the will of the states—diplomatic documents, especially declarations of war and treaties between states. All these show quite clearly that the different states, that is to say, the statesmen representing them, consider war an illegal act, in principle forbidden by general international law, permitted only as a reaction against a wrong suffered. This proves the existence of a legal conviction corresponding to the thesis of the *bellum justum* theory. This conviction manifests itself in the fact that the governments of states resorting to war always try to justify so doing to their own people as well as to the world at large. There is hardly an instance on record in which a state has not tried to proclaim its own cause just and righteous. If such proclamations do not appear in the official declarations of war, they can be found in other documents, or perhaps in the state-controlled press. Never yet has a government declared that it was resorting to war only because it felt at liberty to do so, or because such a step seemed advantageous. An examination of the various justifications for resorting to war reveals that it is usually contended that the other state has done wrong, or is on the verge of doing so, by committing an unwarranted act of aggression, or at least preparing such an act, or by violating certain other legitimate interests, or having the intention of so doing. There can be little doubt that, on the whole, national public opinion, like international public opinion, disapproves of war and permits it only exceptionally as a means to realize a good and just cause. The most radical exponents of war, the most extreme philosophers of imperialism, in their attempts to glorify war and to vilify pacifism, justify war only as a means to a good end.

Even if such justification is of moral rather than strictly legal significance it is of great importance; for, in the last analysis, international morality is the soil which fosters the growth of international law. It is international morality which determines the general direction of the development of international law. Whatever is considered "just" in the sense of international morality has at least a tendency of becoming international "law."

7. The Idea of "Bellum Justum" in Positive International Law

It is easy to prove that the theory of *bellum justum* forms the basis of a number of highly important documents in positive international law, namely, the Treaty of Versailles, the Covenant of the League of Nations, the Kellogg Pact.

Article 231 of the Treaty of Versailles justified the reparations imposed on Germany by maintaining that Germany and its allies were responsible for an act of aggression. This means that Article 231 characterized this aggression as an illegal act, a delict, which would have been impossible if the authors of the Peace Treaty had shared the opinion that every state had a right to resort to war for any reason against any other state. If the aggression which Germany was forced to admit had not been considered "illegal," it could not have been relied on to justify Germany's obligation to make reparation for the loss and damage caused by the aggression. The Treaty of Versailles did not impose upon Germany a "war-indemnity," but a duty to make "reparations" for illegally caused damages. The aggression of Germany and its allies was considered illegal because the war to which they resorted in 1914 was considered to be a war "imposed" upon the Allied and Associated Governments. This can mean only that Germany and its allies resorted to war without sufficient reason, that is, without themselves having been wronged by the Allied and Associated Powers or by any one of them.

Article 15, paragraph 7, of the Covenant of the League of Nations permits members of the League, under certain conditions, to proceed to war against other League members, but only "for the maintenance of right and justice." Only a just war is permitted.

The Kellogg Pact forbids war, but only as an instrument of national policy. This is a very important qualification of the prohibition. A reasonable interpretation of the Kellogg Pact, one not attempting to make of it a practically useless and futile instrument, is that war is not forbidden as a means of *international* policy, especially not as a reaction against violation of international law, as an instrument for the maintenance and realization of international law. This is exactly the idea of the *bellum justum* theory. Since, however, the Covenant of the League of Nations and the Kellogg Pact are only instances of particular international law, these statements dealing with the "illegality" of war must be considered merely indications of the actual existence of a commonly accepted international legal conviction.

8. The Idea of "Bellum Justum" in Primitive Society

The legal conviction just mentioned is by no means an achievement of modern civilization. It is to be found under the most primitive conditions. It is unequivocally expressed even in the relationship of wild tribes. To understand the inter-tribal relationships of primitive society one must realize that primitive man makes a definite distinction between a violation of tribal interests (particularly the killing of a member of his own tribe) by a member of that tribe, and the same deed performed by a member of a foreign tribe. From a sociological point of view, this distinction is of the greatest importance, for primitive man is not yet aware of death due to natural causes. Interpreting the facts of nature solely by social categories, he sees in every death either a punishment imposed by a superhuman authority, or a murder. And murder can be committed either by a visible act of another individual, or by means of magic. Hence death can always be interpreted as murder if for some reason its interpretation as punishment is not possible or desirable. Primitive man considers death and sickness as well not as "natural" but as social phenomena, because to him all nature forms a part of society, that is, of his social group. The dualism of nature and society, a characteristic element of modern thinking, is completely unknown to the primitive mentality.

In the early stages of social development, a violation of the social order attributed to a member of the group will not be vindicated by the group itself through socially organized reaction. There is no punishment of the murderer by the whole group, no duty of the relatives of the murdered person to avenge his death. This does not mean, however, that there is no sanction at all. It only implies that sanctions are not the reaction of the group, that they are not yet socially organized, like the vendetta or the punishment meted out by a tribal chieftain. The first sanction for wrongdoing committed by one of its members within the smallest group—the family, for instance—is a transcendental sanction. A superhuman authority, a god, punishes a crime committed by one in the bosom of his family. The first gods are the souls of deceased ancestors, who jealously watch out for the strict maintenance of social order by their descendants. In the case of murder, it is the spirit of the murdered individual, of the murdered father or the murdered mother, who punishes the murderer by sickness or death. It is extremely significant that the belief in the soul of the dead is socially determined. Direct action of the soul of a murdered man is originally at least confined to his own group; the soul of a murdered man can avenge itself directly only upon the members of his own group, that is to say, his relatives, by spreading sickness or death. It seems that originally at least the soul of the dead was unable to avenge itself directly upon a murderer belonging to another group. In such a case it could only instigate its living relatives to wreak vengeance upon the murderer or upon his group. Only if the relatives of a dead man believe that his death was caused directly or indirectly by a member of another group do they feel themselves obligated to the soul of the dead to avenge the crime. This is the origin as well as the ideological-religious background of the so-called vendetta, which originally was always directed against an outside group.

Normally a war between primitive tribes or groups is essentially a vendetta, an act of revenge; as such it is a reaction against a violation of certain interests, a reaction against what is considered a wrong. The vendetta is probably the original form of socially organized reaction against a wrong, the first socially organized sanction.

Now, if law is the social organization of sanction, the original form of law must have been inter-tribal law, and, as such, a kind of international law. This is the reason why any theory of international law has to consider the origins of law. The original inter-tribal law was, in its very essence, the principle of "just war." Arthur S. Thomson, reporting on the wars of the

Maoris, the primitive aborigines of New Zealand, has this to say: "Every war has an apparent just cause. The motive may have been slight, but there was a lawfulness for it, looking at the question with the ideas of New Zealanders."[3] And the well-known ethnologist A. R. Radcliff-Brown describes the wars between the very primitive Australians as follows: "The waging of war is in some communities, as among the Australian hordes, normally an act of retaliation, carried out by one group against another that is held responsible for an injury suffered, and the procedure is regulated by a recognized body of customs which is equivalent to the international law of modern nations."[4] In general, this is typical of all wars among primitive peoples. If international law is a primitive law—as will be shown later—then it is quite natural that the principle of *bellum justum* has been conserved in this legal order.

9. The Idea of "Bellum Justum" in Antiquity, the Middle Ages, and Modern Times

It is therefore not surprising that one encounters the idea of *bellum justum* in the inter-state law of the ancient Greeks. In his well-known book on the legal customs of the early Greeks and Romans, Coleman Phillippson says: "No war was undertaken without the belligerents alleging a definite cause considered by them as a valid and sufficient justification therefor."[5] Even Roman imperialism believed it could not get along without an ideology by means of which its wars could be justified as legal actions. The law of war was closely connected with the so-called *jus feciale*. Only such wars were considered "just wars" as were undertaken in observance of the rules of the *jus feciale*. These rules had, it is true, essentially only a formal character, but Cicero, who may be regarded as the representative legal philosopher of ancient Rome, and who on this point, too, probably only expressed the generally prevailing public opinion, stated that only such wars could be considered legal actions as were undertaken either for reasons of defense or for reasons of vengeance: *Illa injusta bella sunt quae sunt sine causa suscepta, nam extra ulciscendi aut propulsandorum hostium causam bellum geri justum nullum potest* ("Wars undertaken without reason are unjust wars, for except for the purpose of avenging or repulsing an enemy, no just war can be waged.")[6]

Saint Augustine and Isidoro de Sevilla were influenced in their theory of "just war" by Cicero,[7] and from the writings of these Christian authors the theory of "just war" was taken over by the *Decretum Gratiani*, to be ultimately incorporated into the *Summa Theologiae* of St. Thomas Aquinas. It became the dominating doctrine of the Middle Ages, only to be absorbed by the natural-law theories of the sixteenth, seventeenth, and eighteenth centuries. Grotius in particular expounded the view that according to natural law every war must have a just cause, and that, in the last analysis, this "just cause" can only be a wrong suffered.[8] This idea, which remained predominant until the end of the eighteenth century, disappeared almost entirely from the theories of positive international law during the nineteenth century, although it still formed the basis of public opinion and of the political ideologies of the different governments. Only after the close of the first World War was this doctrine of *bellum justum* again taken up by certain authors.[9]

10. Arguments Against the "Bellum Justum" Theory

The different arguments against the theory that according to general international law war is in principle forbidden, being permissible only as a reaction against a violation of international law, are of varying importance. Certainly the weakest of them, current during the nineteenth century, is that which was most frequently and most successfully relied upon during that period, namely, that it would be inconsistent with the sovereignty of a state to limit its right to resort to war. According to this view, it is especially in war that the sovereignty of a state manifests itself, and sovereignty is the true essence of the state. Undoubtedly, any norm which forbids a state to resort to war against another state, save as a reaction against a wrong suffered by it, is contrary to the idea of the sovereignty of a state. This argument is directed not so much against the theory of *bellum justum*, however, as against international law in general, against every normative legal ordering of the conduct of states. For any legal order obligating states to behave in a certain manner can be conceived only as an authority above the states, and is, therefore, incompatible with the idea of their sovereignty; for to attribute sovereignty to a state means that it is itself the highest authority, above and beyond which there can be no higher authority regulating and determining its conduct. This particular argument does not really constitute a conception of international law opposed to the theory of *bellum justum*. It does not afford a different answer to the question of the content of positive international law. It rather denies international law *in toto* as a legal order obligating and authorizing states. Any discussion of the legal importance of war, however, presupposes the existence of a legal order obligating and authorizing states.

A more serious argument is that everything which can be said in favor of the *bellum justum* theory proves only that war is morally forbidden. It does not prove that positive international law forbids war in principle, permitting it only as a reaction against a wrong suffered. To this it might be replied that should it be possible to prove that states, or the individuals representing them, actually base their reciprocal behavior on the idea that any war which is not a reaction against a wrong itself constitutes a wrong, that only a war waged to right a wrong is a justifiable war, there would seem to be no good reason why this kind of war should not be regarded as a sanction. And if this is so, the judgment regarding the nature of war is definitely a "juristic judgment." Under these circumstances, it is possible to describe the phenomenon "war" in its relation to other phenomena in the form of a legal rule, using the term in a purely descriptive sense. Thus any war that is not merely a sanction can be characterized legally as a "delict."

Particularly serious is the objection that war of one state against another could never be set up as a sanction because for technical reasons no war can function as a sanction. War never guarantees that the wrongdoer alone will always be hit by the evil which a sanction is supposed to mete out. In war not he who is in the "right" is victorious, but he who is the strongest. For this reason, war is out of the question as a reaction against a wrong, when the party which suffered this wrong is the weaker of the two. There can be no question of a sanction unless there exists an organization to apply the measure of coercion with powers so far superior to the power of the wrongdoer that no serious resistance is possible.

The most striking objection to the theory of just war, however, is the one which claims that according to general international law war can be interpreted neither as a sanction nor as a delict. Who is to decide the disputed issue as to whether one state actually has violated a right of another state? General international law knows no tribunal to decide this question. It can be decided, therefore, only through mutual agreement between the parties. But this would be the exception, since a state will hardly admit having violated the rights of another state. If no agreement be reached between the parties to the conflict, the questions of whether or not international law has actually been violated and who is responsible for the violation cannot be uniformly decided, and certainly not—as is now and then believed—decided by the science of law. Not the science of law, not jurists, but only and exclusively the governments of the states in conflict are authorized to decide these questions. If there is no uniform answer to the question of whether in a given case there has been a delict, then there can be no uniform answer to the question of whether the war waged as a reaction against what is claimed to have been a delict is actually a "just war"—whether the character of this war is that of a sanction or of a delict. Thus the distinction between war as sanction and war as delict would become highly problematical. Moreover, there is no apparent difference between the theory which holds that the state has a right to resort to war whenever and against whomever it pleases and the theory which holds that war is permitted only as a reaction against a delict, any other war being itself a delict, but at the same time has to admit that within general international law it is almost impossible satisfactorily to apply these principles in a concrete instance.

11. The Primitive Legal Order

The attempt to meet all these objections is by no means intended to veil the theoretical difficulties of the enterprise. Both the objections raised against the theory of *bellum justum* (and therefore against the legal character of international law in general) are grounded primarily on the technical insufficiency of general international law. This insufficiency is quite apparent, not only as to the points upon which the arguments against the theory of *bellum justum* are based, but also in other highly important issues, as will be shown later.

In its technical aspects, general international law is a primitive law, as is evidenced among other ways by its complete lack of a particular organ charged with the application of legal norms to concrete instances. In primitive law the individual whose legally protected interests have been violated is himself authorized by the legal order to proceed against the wrongdoer with all the coercive measures provided by the legal order. This is called self-help. Every individual takes the law into his own hands. Blood revenge is the most characteristic form of this primitive legal technique. Neither the establishment of the existence of a delict nor the execution of the sanction is conferred upon an authority distinct from the parties involved or interested. In both these aspects the legal order is entirely decentralized. There is neither a court nor a centralized executive power. The relatives of the murdered person, the mourners, must themselves decide whether an avenging action should be undertaken, and if so, against whom they should proceed.

Nevertheless, in a primitive community the man avenging the murder of his father upon one whom he considers to be the murderer is himself regarded not as a murderer but as an organ of the community; for by this very act he executes a norm of the social order constituting the community. It is this norm which empowers him and him only, under certain circumstances and under these circumstances only, to kill the suspected murderer. This same man would not be acting as an organ or instrument of his community, but merely as a murderer himself, should this same action on his part be prompted by circumstances other than those provided by the legal order of his community; should he not be acting merely as an avenger.

The distinction between murder as a delict, and manslaughter as a fulfillment of a duty to avenge, is of the greatest importance for primitive society. It means that killing is only permitted if the killer acts as an organ of his community, if his action is undertaken in execution of the legal order. The coercive measure is reserved to the community, and is, in consequence, a monopoly of the community. The decentralization of the application of the law does not prevent the coercive measures as such from being strictly monopolized. This is the way such events are interpreted in primitive society; and this interpretation is one of the most important ideological foundations of primitive society, although it may well be doubted whether in a concrete instance the killing constitutes merely an avenging act—a sanction—or should itself be regarded as a delict, and despite the fact that blood revenge is hardly a suitable means for protecting the weak against the strong. The latter fact in particular leads to certain phenomena very interesting from a sociological point of view—the institution of sham revenge, certain rituals which take the place of real vendet-

ta, when it would be too risky in the face of the superior forces of the
opponent actually to execute the duty of revenge.

A social order still resting on the principle of self-help may produce a
state of affairs leaving much to be desired. Nevertheless it is possible to
consider this state a legal state, and this decentralized order a legal order;
for this order can be interpreted as an order according to which coercive
measures are a monopoly of the community. And it is permissible to
interpret the primitive social order in this way because the individuals
subjected to this order themselves interpret it in this way.

History teaches that evolution everywhere proceeds from blood revenge toward the institution of courts and the development of a centralized executive power; that is, toward steadily increasing centralization of
the coercive social order. It is entirely justifiable to call the still decentralized coercive social order of primitive society by the name of law, in spite
of its rather crude technique; for this decentralized order constitutes the
first step in an evolution which ultimately leads to the law of the state, a
centralized coercive order. As the embryo in a woman's womb is from the
beginning a human being, so the decentralized coercive order of primitive
self-help is already law—law *in statu nascendi.*

12. International Law as Primitive Law

From what has been said so far it may be inferred that general international law, characterized by the legal technique of self-help, can be interpreted
in the same manner as a primitive legal order, characterized by the institution of blood revenge (vendetta). This primitive law can be understood
only if we distinguish—as does the primitive man—between killing as a
delict and killing as a sanction. In order to understand international law, a
differentiation must be made between war as a delict and war as a sanction,
despite the fact that the practical application of this distinction in a concrete instance might be difficult—in some cases even impossible—and
although war, like vendetta, is technically insufficient as a sanction.

Everything that has been said against interpreting war as a sanction
can also be said against reprisals; yet the opponents of the theory of *bellum
justum,* which acknowledges war only as sanction, do not find it necessary
to use their arguments against interpreting reprisals as sanctions. Should
we, however, contrary to the *bellum justum* theory refuse to regard war as
in principle forbidden (permitted only as a reaction against a delict), we
should no longer be in a position to conceive of general international law
as an order turning the employment of force into a monopoly of the
community. Under these circumstances, general international law could
no longer be considered as a legal order. If the unlimited interference in
the sphere of another's interests called "war" is not in principle forbidden
by general international law, if any state is at liberty to resort to war against
any other state, then international law fails to protect the sphere of interests of the states subjected to its order; the states have no protected sphere

of interests at all; and the condition of affairs created by so-called international law cannot be a legal state. Whether or not international law can be considered as true law depends upon whether it is possible to interpret international law in the sense of the theory of *bellum justum,* whether it is possible to assume that, according to general international law, war is in principle forbidden, being permitted only as a sanction, that is, as a reaction against a delict.

The opponents of the theory of just war, or at least the majority among them, do not intend to question the legal character of international law. On the contrary, they insist upon calling international law true law. For this very reason, they do not deny that reprisals, that is, the limited interference in the sphere of interests of a state, are permitted only as a reaction against a wrong, as a sanction. This is in truth a more than paradoxical result of an interpretation of international law: no state would be entitled to a limited interference in the sphere of interests of another state, but any state would be fully justified in committing an unlimited interference in such a sphere. According to this interpretation, a state violates international law if it causes limited damage to another state, and in this case its enemy is authorized to react against it with reprisals. But the state does not violate international law and does not render itself liable to a sanction if its interference in the sphere of interests of the other state is adequate to afflict the whole population and the whole country of its enemy with death and destruction. This is similar to a social order according to which petty thievery is punished while armed robbery goes free. Such an order is logically not impossible, but it is politically very improbably that a positive social order, especially international law, should have such a content, even if the intention of the order to reserve the employment of force to the community, to establish a monopoly of force in the community, be imperfectly realized.

The technical inadequacies of general international law do indeed to a certain extent justify the interpretation of the opponents of the *bellum justum* theory. But he who accepts this interpretation must be consistent; he must not regard international law as true law. The opposite interpretation, however—that based on the *bellum justum* theory—is also possible, as has been shown in this lecture. The situation is characterized by the possibility of a double interpretation. It is one of the peculiarities of the material which forms the object of the social sciences to be sometimes liable to a double interpretation. Hence, objective science is not able to decide for or against one or the other.

It is not a scientific, but a political decision which gives preference to the *bellum justum* theory. This preference is justified by the fact that only this interpretation conceives of the international order as law, although admittedly primitive law, the first step in an evolution which within the national community, the state, has led to a system of norms which is generally accepted as law. There can be little doubt that the international law of the present contains all the potentialities of such an evolution; it has even shown a definite tendency in this direction. Only if such an evolution could be recognized as inevitable would it be scientifically justified to declare the *bellum justum* theory the only correct interpretation of international law. Such a supposition, however, reflects political wishes rather than scientific thinking. From a strictly scientific point of view a diametrically opposite evolution of international relations is not absolutely excluded. That war is in principle a delict and is permitted only as a sanction is a possible interpretation of international relations, but not the only one. We choose this interpretation, hoping to have recognized the beginning of a development of the future and with the intention of strengthening as far as possible all the elements of present-day international law which tend to justify this interpretation and to promote the evolution we desire.

Notes

1. Cf. my *Théorie générale du droit international public,* Académie du droit international, Recueil des Cours, vol. XLII (1932).

2. Cf. my "Unrecht und Unrechtsfolge im Völkerrecht," *Zeitschrift für öffentliches Recht,* XII (1932), 481 ff.

3. Arthur S. Thomson, *The Story of New Zealand* (1859), pp. 1, 123.

4. A. R. Radcliff-Brown, "Primitive Law," *Encyclopaedia of the Social Sciences,* ed. E.R.A. Seligmann and A. Johnson, IX (1933), p. 203.

5. Coleman Phillippson, *The International Law and Custom of Ancient Greece and Rome* (1911), pp. 11, 179.

6. Cicero, *De republica,* III, 23.

7. Cf. William Ballis, *The Legal Position of War* (1937), pp. 27ff.

8. Hugo Grotius, *De Jure Belli ac Pacis Libri Tres* (Classics of International Law. Oxford: Clarendon Press, 1925), II, 170: "No other just cause for undertaking war can there be excepting injury received."

9. Cf. Leo Strisower, *Der Krieg und die Völkerrechtsordnung* (1919).

H.L.A. HART

International Law

1. Sources of Doubt

The idea of a union of primary and secondary rules to which so important
a place has been assigned in this book may be regarded as a mean between
juristic extremes. For legal theory has sought the key to the understanding
of law sometimes in the simple idea of an order backed by threats and
sometimes in the complex idea of morality. With both of these law has
certainly many affinities and connections; yet, as we have seen, there is a
perennial danger of exaggerating these and of obscuring the special features which distinguish law from other means of social control. It is a
virtue of the idea which we have taken as central that it permits us to see
the multiple relationships between law, coercion, and morality for what
they are, and to consider afresh in what, if any, sense these are necessary.

Though the idea of the union of primary and secondary rules has
these virtues, and though it would accord with usage to treat the existence
of this characteristic union of rules as a sufficient condition for the application of the expression "legal system," we have not claimed that the word
"law" must be defined in its terms. It is because we make no such claim to
identify or regulate in this way the use of words like "law" or "legal," that
this book is offered as an elucidation of the *concept* of law, rather than a
definition of "law" which might naturally be expected to provide a rule or
rules for the use of these expressions. Consistently with this aim, we investigated, in the last chapter, the claim made in the German cases, that the
title of valid law should be withheld from certain rules on account of their
moral iniquity, even though they belonged to an existing system of primary and secondary rules. In the end we rejected this claim; but we did so,
not because it conflicted with the view that rules belonging to such a
system must be called "law," nor because it conflicted with the weight of
usage. Instead we criticized the attempt to narrow the class of valid laws by
the extrusion of what was morally iniquitous, on the ground that to do this
did not advance or clarify either theoretical inquiries or moral deliberation.
For these purposes, the broader concept which is consistent with so much
usage and which would permit us to regard rules however morally iniquitous as law, proved on examination to be adequate.

International law presents us with the converse case. For, though it is
consistent with the usage of the last 150 years to use the expression "law"

Chapter 10 in *The Concept of Law,* 2d ed. (1994), pp. 213–37. © Oxford University Press
1961, 1994. Reprinted by permission of Oxford University Press.

here, the absence of an international legislature, courts with compulsory jurisdiction, and centrally organized sanctions have inspired misgivings, at any rate in the breasts of legal theorists. The absence of these institutions means that the rules for states resemble that simple form of social structure, consisting only of primary rules of obligation, which, when we find it among societies of individuals, we are accustomed to contrast with a developed legal system. It is indeed arguable, as we shall show, that international law not only lacks the secondary rules of change and adjudication which provide for legislature and courts, but also a unifying rule of recognition specifying "sources" of law and providing general criteria for the identification of its rules. These differences are indeed striking and the question "Is international law really law?" can hardly be put aside. But in this case also, we shall neither dismiss the doubts, which many feel, with a simple reminder of the existing usage; nor shall we simply confirm them on the footing that the existence of a union of primary and secondary rules is a necessary as well as a sufficient condition for the proper use of the expression "legal system." Instead we shall inquire into the detailed character of the doubts which have been felt, and, as in the German case, we shall ask whether the common wider usage that speaks of "international law" is likely to obstruct any practical or theoretical aim.

Though we shall devote to it only a single chapter some writers have proposed an even shorter treatment for this question concerning the character of international law. To them it has seemed that the question "Is international law really law?" has only arisen or survived, because a trivial question about the meaning of words has been mistaken for a serious question about the nature of things: since the facts which differentiate international law from municipal law are clear and well known, the only question to be settled is whether we should observe the existing convention or depart from it; and this is a matter for each person to settle for himself. But this short way with the question is surely too short. It is true that among the reasons which have led theorists to hesitate over the extension of the word "law" to international law, a too simple, and indeed absurd view, of what justifies the application of the same word to many different things has played some part. The variety of types of principle which commonly guide the extension of general classifying terms has too often been ignored in jurisprudence. None the less, the sources of doubt about international law are deeper, and more interesting than these mistaken views about the use of words. Moreover, the two alternatives offered by this short way with the question ("Shall we observe the existing convention or shall we depart from it?") are not exhaustive; for, besides them, there is the alternative of making explicit and examining the principles that have in fact guided the existing usage.

The short way suggested would indeed be appropriate if we were dealing with a proper name. If someone were to ask whether the place called "London" is *really* London, all we could do would be to remind him of the convention and leave him to abide by it or choose another name to suit his taste. It would be absurd, in such a case, to ask on what principle London was so called and whether this principle was acceptable. This would be absurd because, whereas the allotment of proper names rests *only* on an *ad hoc* convention, the extension of the general terms of any serious discipline is never without its principle or rationale, though it may not be obvious what that is. When as, in the present case, the extension is queried by those who in effect say, "We know that it is called law, but is it really law?," what is demanded—no doubt obscurely—is that the principle be made explicit and its credentials inspected.

We shall consider two principal sources of doubt concerning the legal character of international law and, with them, the steps which theorists have taken to meet these doubts. Both forms of doubt arise from an adverse comparison of international law with municipal law, which is taken as the clear, standard example of what law is. The first has its roots deep in the conception of law as fundamentally a matter of orders backed by threats and contrasts the character of the *rules* of international law with those of municipal law. The second form of doubt springs from the obscure belief that states are fundamentally incapable of being the subjects of legal obligation, and contrasts the character of the *subjects* of international law with those of municipal law.

2. Obligations and Sanctions

The doubts which we shall consider are often expressed in the opening chapters of books on international law in the form of the question "How can international law be binding?" Yet there is something very confusing in this favourite form of question; and before we can deal with it we must face a prior question to which the answer is by no means clear. This prior question is: what is meant by saying of a whole system of law that it is "binding?" The statement that a particular rule of a system is binding on a particular person is one familiar to lawyers and tolerably clear in meaning. We may paraphrase it by the assertion that the rule in question is a valid rule, and under it the person in question has some obligation or duty. Besides this, there are some situations in which more general statements of this form are made. We may be doubtful in certain circumstances whether one legal system or another applies to a particular person. Such doubts may arise in the conflict of laws or in public international law. We may ask, in the former case, whether French or English Law is binding on a particular person as regards a particular transaction, and in the latter case we may ask whether the inhabitants of, for example, enemy-occupied Belgium, were bound by what the exiled government claimed was Belgian law or by the ordinances of the occupying power. But in both these cases, the questions are questions of law which arise *within* some system of law (municipal or international) and are settled by reference to the rules or principles of that system. They do not call in question the general character of the rules, but only their scope or applicability in given circumstances to particular persons or transactions. Plainly the question, "Is international law binding?" and its cogeners "How can international law be binding?" or "What makes international law binding?" are questions of a different order. They express a doubt not about the applicability, but about the general legal status of international law: this doubt would be more candidly expressed in the form "Can such rules as these be meaningfully and truthfully said ever to give rise to obligations?" As the discussions in the books show, one source of doubt on this point is simply the absence from the system of centrally organized sanctions. This is one point of adverse comparison with municipal law, the rules of which are taken to be unquestionably "binding" and to be paradigms of legal obligation. From this stage the further argument is simple: if for this reason the rules of international law are not "binding," it is surely indefensible to take seriously their classification as law; for however tolerant the modes of common speech may be, this is too great a difference to be overlooked. All speculation about the nature of law begins from the assumption that its existence at least makes certain conduct obligatory.

In considering this argument we shall give it the benefit of every doubt concerning the facts of the international system. We shall take it that neither Article 16 of the Covenant of the League of Nations nor Chapter VII of the United Nations Charter introduced into international law anything which can be equated with the sanctions of municipal law. In spite of the Korean war and of whatever moral may be drawn from the Suez incident, we shall suppose that, whenever their use is of importance, the law enforcement provisions of the Charter are likely to be paralysed by the veto and must be said to exist only on paper.

To argue that international law is not binding because of its lack of organized sanctions is tacitly to accept the analysis of obligation contained in the theory that law is essentially a matter of orders backed by threats. This theory, as we have seen, identifies "having an obligation" or "being bound" with "likely to suffer the sanction or punishment threatened for disobedience." Yet, as we have argued, this identification distorts the role played in all legal thought and discourse of the ideas of obligation and duty. Even in municipal law, where there are effective organized sanctions, we must distinguish, for the variety of reasons given in Chapter III, the meaning of the external predictive statement "I (you) are likely to suffer for disobedience," from the internal normative statement "I (you) have an obligation to act thus" which assesses a particular person's situation from the point of view of rules accepted as guiding standards of behaviour. It is true that not all rules give rise to obligations or duties; and it is also true that the rules which do so generally call for some sacrifice of private interests, and are generally supported by serious demands for conformity and insistent criticism of deviations. Yet once we free ourselves from the predictive analysis and its parent conception of law as essentially an order backed by threats, there seems no good reason for limiting the normative idea of obligation to rules supported by organized sanctions.

We must, however, consider another form of the argument, more plausible because it is not committed to definition of obligation in terms of the likelihood of threatened sanctions. The sceptic may point out that there are in a municipal system, as we have ourselves stressed, certain provisions which are justifiably called necessary; among these are primary rules of obligation, prohibiting the free use of violence, and rules providing for the official use of force as a sanction for these and other rules. If such rules and organized sanctions supporting them are in this sense necessary for municipal law, are they not equally so for international law? That they are may be maintained without insisting that this follows from the very meaning of words like "binding" or "obligation."

The answer to the argument in this form is to be found in those elementary truths about human beings and their environment which constitute the enduring psychological and physical setting of municipal law. In societies of individuals, approximately equal in physical strength and vulnerability, physical sanctions are both necessary and possible. They are required in order that those who would voluntarily submit to the restraints of law shall not be mere victims of malefactors who would, in the absence of such sanctions, reap the advantages of respect for law on the part of others, without respecting it themselves. Among individuals living in close proximity to each other, opportunities for injuring others, by guile, if not by open attack, are so great, and the chances of escape so considerable, that no mere natural deterrents could in any but the simplest forms of society be adequate to restrain those too wicked, too stupid, or too weak to obey the law. Yet, because of the same fact of approximate equality and the patent advantages of submission to a system of restraints, no combination of malefactors is likely to exceed in strength those who would voluntarily co-operate in its maintenance. In these circumstances, which constitute the background of municipal law, sanctions may successfully be used against malefactors with relatively small risks, and the threat of them will add much to whatever natural deterrents there may be. But, just because the simple truisms which hold good for individuals do not hold good for states, and the factual background to international law is so different from that of municipal law, there is neither a similar necessity for sanctions (desirable though it may be that international law should be supported by them) nor a similar prospect of their safe and efficacious use.

This is so because aggression between states is very unlike that between individuals. The use of violence between states must be public, and though there is no international police force, there can be very little certainty that it will remain a matter between aggressor and victim, as a murder or theft, in the absence of a police force, might. To initiate a war is, even for the strongest power, to risk much for an outcome which is rarely predictable with reasonable confidence. On the other hand, because of the inequality of states, there can be no standing assurance that the combined strength of those on the side of international order is likely to preponderate over the powers tempted to aggression. Hence the organization and

use of sanctions may involve fearful risks and the threat of them add little
to the natural deterrents. Against this very different background of fact,
international law has developed in a form different from that of municipal
law. In a population of a modern state, if there were no organized repression and punishment of crime, violence and theft would be hourly expected; but for states, long years of peace have intervened between disastrous wars. These years of peace are only rationally to be expected, given
the risks and stakes of war and the mutual needs of states; but they are
worth regulating by rules which differ from those of municipal law in
(among other things) not providing for their enforcement by any central
organ. Yet what these rules require is thought and spoken of as obligatory;
there is general pressure for conformity to the rules; claims and admissions
are based on them and their breach is held to justify not only insistent
demands for compensation, but reprisals and counter-measures. When the
rules are disregarded, it is not on the footing that they are not binding;
instead efforts are made to conceal the facts. It may of course be said that
such rules are efficacious only so far as they concern issues over which
states are unwilling to fight. This may be so, and may reflect adversely on
the importance of the system and its value to humanity. Yet that even so
much may be secured shows that no simple deduction can be made from
the necessity of organized sanctions to municipal law, in its setting of
physical and psychological facts, to the conclusion that without them
international law, in its very different setting, imposes no obligations, is
not "binding," and so not worth the title of "law."

3. Obligation and the Sovereignty of States

Great Britain, Belgium, Greece, Soviet Russia have rights and obligations
under international law and so are among its subjects. They are random
examples of states which the layman would think of as independent and
the lawyer would recognize as "sovereign." One of the most persistent
sources of perplexity about the obligatory character of international law
has been the difficulty felt in accepting or explaining the fact that a state
which is sovereign may also be "bound" by, or have an obligation under,
international law. This form of scepticism is, in a sense, more extreme than
the objection that international law is not binding because it lacks sanctions. For whereas that would be met if one day international law were
reinforced by a system of sanctions, the present objection is based on a
radical inconsistency, said or felt to exist, in the conception of a state which
is at once sovereign and subject to law.

Examination of this objection involves a scrutiny of the notion of
sovereignty, applied not to a legislature or to some other element or
person *within* a state, but to a state itself. Whenever the word "sovereign"
appears in jurisprudence, there is a tendency to associate with it the idea of
a person above the law whose word is law for his inferiors or subjects. We
have seen in the early chapters of this book how bad a guide this seductive

notion is to the structure of a municipal legal system; but it has been an even more potent source of confusion in the theory of international law. It is, of course, *possible* to think of a state along such lines, as if it were a species of Superman—a Being inherently lawless but the source of law for its subjects. From the sixteenth century onwards, the symbolical identification of state and monarch ("L'état c'est moi") may have encouraged this idea which has been the dubious inspiration of much political as well as legal theory. But it is important for the understanding of international law to shake off these associations. The expression "a state" is not the name of some person or thing inherently or "by nature" outside the law; it is a way of referring to two facts: first, that a population inhabiting a territory lives under that form of ordered government provided by a legal system with its characteristic structure of legislature, courts, and primary rules; and, secondly, that the government enjoys a vaguely defined degree of independence.

The word "state" has certainly its own large area of vagueness but what has been said will suffice to display its central meaning. States such as Great Britain or Brazil, the United States or Italy, again to take random examples, possess a very large measure of independence from both legal and factual control by any authorities or persons outside their borders, and would rank as "sovereign states" in international law. On the other hand, individual states which are members of a federal union, such as the United States, are subject in many different ways to the authority and control of the federal government and constitution. Yet the independence which even these federated states retain is large if we compare it with the position, say, of an English county, of which the word "state" would not be used at all. A county may have a local council discharging, for its area, some of the functions of a legislature, but its meagre powers are subordinate to those of Parliament and, except in certain minor respects, the area of the county is subject to the same laws and government as the rest of the country.

Between these extremes there are many different types and degrees of dependence (and so of independence) between territorial units which possess an ordered government. Colonies, protectorates, suzerainties, trust territories, confederations, present fascinating problems of classification from this point of view. In most cases the dependence of one unit on another is expressed in legal forms, so that what is law in the territory of the dependent unit will, at least on certain issues, ultimately depend on law-making operations in the other.

In some cases, however, the legal system of the dependent territory may not reflect its dependence. This may be so either because it is merely formally independent and the territory is in fact governed, through puppets, from outside; or it may be so because the dependent territory has a real autonomy over its internal but not its external affairs, and its dependence on another country in external affairs does not require expression as part of its domestic law. Dependence of one territorial unit on another in

these various ways is not, however, the only form in which its independence may be limited. The limiting factor may be not the power or authority of another such unit, but an international authority affecting units
which are alike independent of each other. It is possible to imagine many
different forms of international authority and correspondingly many different limitations on the independence of states. The possibilities include,
among many others, a world legislature on the model of the British Parliament, possessing legally unlimited powers to regulate the internal and
external affairs of all; a federal legislature on the model of Congress, with
legal competence only over specified matters or one limited by guarantees
of specific rights of the constituent units; a regime in which the only form
of legal control consists of rules generally accepted as applicable to all; and
finally a regime in which the only form of obligation recognized is contrac-
tual or self-imposed, so that a state's independence is legally limited only
by its own act.

It is salutary to consider this range of possibilities because merely to
realize that there are many possible forms and degrees of dependence and
independence, is a step towards answering the claim that because states are
sovereign they "*cannot*" be subject to or bound by international law or
"*can*" only be bound by some specific form of international law. For the
word "sovereign" means here no more than "independent"; and, like the
latter, is negative in force: a sovereign state is one *not* subject to certain
types of control, and its sovereignty is that area of conduct in which it is
autonomous. Some measure of autonomy is imported, as we have seen, by
the very meaning of the word state but the contention that this "*must*" be
unlimited or "*can*" only be limited by certain types of obligation is at best
the assertion of a claim that states ought to be free of all other restraints,
and at worst is an unreasoned dogma. For if in fact we find that there exists
among states a given form of international authority, the sovereignty of
states is to that extent limited, and it has just that extent which the rules
allow. Hence we can only know which states are sovereign, and what the
extent of their sovereignty is, when we know what the rules are; just as we
can only know whether an Englishman or an American is free and the
extent of his freedom when we know what English or American law is. The
rules of international law are indeed vague and conflicting on many points,
so that doubt about the area of independence left to states is far greater
than that concerning the extent of a citizen's freedom under municipal
law. None the less, these difficulties do not validate the *a priori* argument
which attempts to deduce the general character of international law from
an absolute sovereignty, which is assumed, without reference to international law, to belong to states.

It is worth observing that an uncritical use of the idea of sovereignty
has spread similar confusion in the theory both of municipal and international law, and demands in both a similar corrective. Under its influence,
we are led to believe that there *must* in every municipal legal system be a
sovereign legislator subject to no legal limitations; just as we are led to

believe that international law *must* be of a certain character because states are sovereign and incapable of legal limitation save by themselves. In both cases, belief in the necessary existence of the legally unlimited sovereign prejudges a question which we can only answer when we examine the actual rules. The question for municipal law is: what is the extent of the supreme legislative authority recognized in this system? For international law it is: what is the maximum area of autonomy which the rules allow to states?

Thus the simplest answer to the present objection is that it inverts the order in which questions must be considered. There is no way of knowing what sovereignty states have, till we know what the forms of international law are and whether or not they are mere empty forms. Much juristic debate has been confused because this principle has been ignored, and it is profitable to consider in its light those theories of international law which are known as "voluntarist" or theories of "auto-limitation." These attempted to reconcile the (absolute) sovereignty of states with the existence of binding rules of international law, by treating all international obligations as self-imposed like the obligation which arises from a promise. Such theories are in fact the counterpart in international law of the social contract theories of political science. The latter sought to explain the facts that individuals, "naturally" free and independent, were yet bound by municipal law, by treating the obligation to obey the law as one arising from a contract which those bound had made with each other, and in some cases with their rulers. We shall not consider here the well-known objections to this theory when taken literally, nor its value when taken merely as an illuminating analogy. Instead we shall draw from its history a threefold argument against the voluntarist theories of international law.

First, these theories fail completely to explain how it is known that states "*can*" only be bound by self-imposed obligations, or why this view of their sovereignty should be accepted, in advance of any examination of the actual character of international law. Is there anything more to support it besides the fact that it has often been repeated? Secondly, there is something incoherent in the argument designed to show that states, because of their sovereignty, *can* only be subject to or bound by rules which they have imposed upon themselves. In some very extreme forms of "auto-limitation" theory, a state's agreement or treaty engagements are treated as mere declarations of its proposed future conduct, and failure to perform is not considered to be a breach of any obligation. This, though very much at variance with the facts, has at least the merit of consistency: it is the simple theory that the absolute sovereignty of states is inconsistent with obligation of any kind, so that, like Parliament, a state cannot bind itself. The less extreme view that a state may impose obligations on itself by promise, agreement, or treaty is not, however, consistent with the theory that states are subject only to rules which they have thus imposed on themselves. For, in order that words, spoken or written, should in certain circumstances function as a promise, agreement, or treaty, and so give rise to obligations and confer rights which others may claim, *rules* must already exist providing that a state is bound to do whatever it undertakes by appropriate words to do. Such rules presupposed in the very notion of a self-imposed obligation obviously cannot derive *their* obligatory status from a self-imposed obligation to obey them.

It is true that every specific *action* which a given state was bound to do might in theory derive its obligatory character from a promise; none the less this could only be the case if the *rule* that promises, &c., create obligations is applicable to the state independently of any promise. In any society, whether composed of individuals or states, what is necessary and sufficient, in order that the words of a promise, agreement, or treaty should give rise to obligations, is that rules providing for this and specifying a procedure for these self-binding operations should be generally, though they need not be universally, acknowledged. Where they are acknowledged the individual or state who wittingly uses these procedures is bound thereby, whether he or it chooses to be bound or not. Hence, even this most voluntary form of social obligation involves some rules which are binding independently of the choice of the party bound by them, and this, in the case of states, is inconsistent with the supposition that their sovereignty demands freedom from all such rules.

Thirdly there are the facts. We must distinguish the *a priori* claim just criticized, that states *can* only be bound by self-imposed obligations, from the claim that though they could be bound in other ways under a different system, in fact no other form of obligation for states exists under the present rules of international law. It is, of course, possible that the system might be one of this wholly consensual form, and both assertions and repudiations of this view of its character are to be found in the writings of jurists, in the opinions of judges, even of international courts, and in the declarations of states. Only a dispassionate survey of the actual practice of states can show whether this view is correct or not. It is true that modern international law is very largely treaty law, and elaborate attempts have been made to show that rules which appear to be binding on states without their prior consent do in fact rest on consent, though this may have been given only "tacitly" or has to be "inferred." Though not all are fictions, some at least of these attempts to reduce to one the forms of international obligation excite the same suspicion as the notion of a "tacit command" which, as we have seen, was designed to perform a similar, though more obviously spurious, simplification of municipal law.

A detailed scrutiny of the claim that all international obligation arises from the consent of the party bound, cannot be undertaken here, but two clear and important exceptions to this doctrine must be noticed. The first is the case of a new state. It has never been doubted that when a new, independent state emerges into existence, as did Iraq in 1932, and Israel in 1948, it is bound by the general obligations of international law including, among others, the rules that give binding force to treaties. Here the attempt to rest the new state's international obligations on a "tacit" or "inferred" consent seems wholly threadbare. The second case is that of a state acquiring territory or undergoing some other change, which brings with it, for the first time, the incidence of obligations under rules which previously it had no opportunity either to observe or break, and to which it had no occasion to give or withhold consent. If a state, previously without access to the sea, acquires maritime territory, it is clear that this is enough to make it subject to all the rules of international law relating to the territorial waters and the high seas. Besides these, there are more debatable cases, mainly relating to the effect on non-parties of general or multilateral treaties; but these two important exceptions are enough to justify the suspicion that the general theory that all international obligation is self-imposed has been inspired by too much abstract dogma and too little respect for the facts.

4. International Law and Morality

[Previously] we considered the simple form of social structure which consists of primary rules of obligation alone, and we saw that, for all but the smallest most tightly knit and isolated societies, it suffered from grave defects. Such a regime must be static, its rules altering only by the slow processes of growth and decay; the identification of the rules must be uncertain; and the ascertainment of the fact of their violation in particular cases, and the application of social pressure to offenders must be haphazard, time-wasting, and weak. We found it illuminating to conceive the secondary rules of recognition, change, and adjudication characteristic of municipal law as different though related remedies for these different defects.

In form, international law resembles such a regime of primary rules, even though the content of its often elaborate rules are very unlike those of a primitive society, and many of its concepts, methods, and techniques are the same as those of modern municipal law. Very often jurists have thought that these formal differences between international and municipal law can best be expressed by classifying the former as "morality." Yet it seems clear that to mark the difference in this way is to invite confusion.

Sometimes insistence that the rules governing the relations between states are only moral rules, is inspired by the old dogmatism, that any form of social structure that is not reducible to orders backed by threats can only be a form of "morality." It is, of course, possible to use the word "morality" in this very comprehensive way; so used, it provides a conceptual wastepaper basket into which will go the rules of games, clubs, etiquette, the fundamental provisions of constitutional law and international law, together with rules and principles which we ordinarily think of as moral ones, such as the common prohibitions of cruelty, dishonesty, or lying. The objection to this procedure is that between what is thus classed together as "morality" there are such important differences of both form and social function, that no conceivable purpose, practical or theoretical, could be served by so crude a classification. Within the category of morality thus artificially widened, we should have to mark out afresh the old distinctions which it blurs.

In the particular case of international law there are a number of different reasons for resisting the classification of its rules as "morality." The first is that states often reproach each other for immoral conduct or praise themselves or others for living up to the standard of international morality. No doubt *one* of the virtues which states may show or fail to show is that of abiding by international law, but that does not mean that that law is morality. In fact the appraisal of states' conduct in terms of morality is recognizably different from the formulation of claims, demands, and the acknowledgements of rights and obligations under the rules of international law. [Previously] we listed certain features which might be taken as defining characteristics of social morality: among them was the distinctive form of moral pressure by which moral rules are primarily supported. This consists not of appeals to fear or threats of retaliation or demands for compensation, but of appeals to conscience, made in the expectation that once the person addressed is reminded of the moral principle at stake, he may be led by guilt or shame to respect it and make amends.

Claims under international law are not couched in such terms though of course, as in municipal law, they may be joined with a moral appeal. What predominate in the arguments, often technical, which states address to each other over disputed matters of international law, are references to precedents, treaties, and juristic writings; often no mention is made of moral right or wrong, good or bad. Hence the claim that the Peking Government has or has not a right under international law to expel the Nationalist forces from Formosa is very different from the question whether this is fair, just, or a morally good or bad thing to do, and is backed by characteristically different arguments. No doubt in the relations between states there are half-way houses between what is clearly law and what is clearly morality, analogous to the standards of politeness and courtesy recognized in private life. Such is the sphere of international "comity" exemplified in the privilege extended to diplomatic envoys of receiving goods intended for personal use free of duty.

A more important ground of distinction is the following. The rules of international law, like those of municipal law, are often morally quite indifferent. A rule may exist because it is convenient or necessary to have some clear fixed rule about the subjects with which it is concerned, but not because any moral importance is attached to the particular rule. It may well be but one of a large number of possible rules, any one of which would have done equally well. Hence legal rules, municipal and international, commonly contain much specific detail, and draw arbitrary distinctions, which would be unintelligible as elements in moral rules or principles. It is true that we must not be dogmatic about the possible content of social morality: as we saw [previously] the morality of a social group may contain much by way of injunction which may appear absurd or superstitious when viewed in the light of modern knowledge. So it is possible, though difficult, to imagine that men with general beliefs very different from ours, might come to attach *moral* importance to driving on the left instead of the right of the road or could come to feel moral guilt if they broke a promise witnessed by two witnesses, but no such guilt if it was witnessed by one. Though such strange moralities are possible, it yet remains true that a morality cannot (logically) contain rules which are generally held by those who subscribe to them to be in no way preferable to alternatives and of no intrinsic importance. Law, however, though it also contains much that is of moral importance, can and does contain just such rules, and the arbitrary distinctions, formalities, and highly specific detail which would be most difficult to understand as part of morality, are consequently natural and easily comprehensible features of law. For one of the typical functions of law, unlike morality, is to introduce just these elements in order to maximize certainty and predictability and to facilitate the proof or assessments of claims. Regard for forms and detail carried to excess, has earned for law the reproaches of "formalism" and "legalism"; yet it is important to remember that these vices are exaggerations of some of the law's distinctive qualities.

It is for this reason that just as we expect a municipal legal system, but not morality, to tell us how many witnesses a validly executed will must have, so we expect international law, but not morality, to tell us such things as the number of days a belligerent vessel may stay for refueling or repairs in a neutral port; the width of territorial waters; the methods to be used in their measurement. All these things are necessary and desirable provisions for *legal rules* to make, but so long as the sense is retained that such rules may equally well take any of several forms, or are important only as one among many possible means to specific ends, they remain distinct from rules which have the status in individual or social life characteristic of morality. Of course not all the rules of international law are of this formal, or arbitrary, or morally neutral kind. The point is only that legal rules *can* and moral rules *cannot* be of this kind.

The difference in character between international law and anything which we naturally think of as morality has another aspect. Though the effect of a law requiring or proscribing certain practices might ultimately be to bring about changes in the morality of a group, the notion of a legislature making or repealing moral rules is, as we saw [previously], an absurd one. A legislature cannot introduce a new rule and give it the status of a moral rule by its *fiat*, just as it cannot, by the same means, give a rule the status of a tradition, though the reasons why this is so may not be the same in the two cases. Accordingly morality does not merely lack or happen not to have a legislature; the very idea of change by human legislative *fiat* is repugnant to the idea of morality. This is so because we conceive of morality as the ultimate standard by which human actions (legislative or otherwise) are evaluated. The contrast with international law is clear. There is nothing in the nature or function of international law which is similarly inconsistent with the idea that the rules might be subject to legislative change; the lack of a legislature is just a lack which many think of as a defect one day to be repaired.

Finally we must notice a parallel in the theory of international law between the argument, criticized [previously], that even if particular rules of municipal law may conflict with morality, none the less the system as a whole must rest on a generally diffused conviction that there is a moral obligation to obey its rules, though this may be overridden in special exceptional cases. It has often been said in the discussion of the "foundations" of international law, that in the last resort, the rules of international law *must* rest on the conviction of states that there is a moral obligation to obey them; yet, if this means more than that the obligations which they recognize are not enforceable by officially organized sanctions, there seems no reason to accept it. Of course it is possible to think of circumstances which would certainly justify our saying that a state considered some course of conduct required by international law morally obligatory, and acted for that reason. It might, for example, continue to perform the obligations of an onerous treaty because of the manifest harm to humanity that would follow if confidence in treaties was severely shaken, or because of the sense that it was only fair to shoulder the irksome burdens of a code from which it, in its turn, had profited in the past when the burden fell on others. Precisely whose motives, thoughts and feelings on such matters of moral conviction are to be attributed to the state is a question which need not detain us here.

But though there *may* be such a sense of moral obligation it is difficult to see why or in what sense it *must* exist as a condition of the existence of international law. It is clear that in the practice of states certain rules are regularly respected even at the cost of certain sacrifices; claims are formulated by reference to them; breaches of the rules expose the offender to serious criticism and are held to justify claims for compensation or retaliation. These, surely, are all the elements required to support the statement that there exist among states rules imposing obligations upon them. The proof that "binding" rules in any society exist, is simply that they are thought of, spoken of, and function as such. What more is required by way of "foundations" and why, if more is required, must it be a foundation of moral obligation? It is, of course, true that rules could not exist or function in the relations between states unless a preponderant majority accepted the rules and voluntarily co-operated in maintaining them. It is true also that the pressure exercised on those who break or threaten to break the rules is often relatively weak, and has usually been decentralized or unorganized. But as in the case of individuals, who voluntarily accept the far more strongly coercive system of municipal law, the motives for voluntarily supporting such a system may be extremely diverse. It may well be that any form of legal order is at its healthiest when there is a generally diffused sense that it is morally obligatory to conform to it. None the less, adherence to law may not be motivated by it, but by calculations of long-term interest, or by the wish to continue a tradition or by disinterested concern for others. There seems no good reason for identifying any of these as a necessary condition of the existence of law either among individuals or states.

5. Analogies of Form and Content

To the innocent eye, the formal structure of international law lacking a legislature, courts with compulsory jurisdiction and officially organized sanctions, appears very different from that of municipal law. It resembles, as we have said, in form though not at all in content, a simple regime of primary or customary law. Yet some theorists, in their anxiety to defend against the sceptic the title of international law to be called "law," have succumbed to the temptation to minimize these formal differences, and to exaggerate the analogies which can be found in international law to legislation or other desirable formal features of municipal law. Thus, it has been claimed that war, ending with a treaty whereby the defeated power cedes territory, or assumes obligations, or accepts some diminished form of independence, is essentially a legislative act; for, like legislation, it is an imposed legal change. Few would now be impressed by this analogy, or think that it helped to show that international law had an equal title with municipal law to be called "law"; for one of the salient differences between municipal and international law is that the former usually does not, and the latter does, recognize the validity of agreements extorted by violence.

A variety of other, more respectable analogies have been stressed by those who consider the title of "law" to depend on them. The fact that in almost all cases the judgment of the International Court and its predecessor, the Permanent Court of International Justice, have been duly carried out by the parties, has often been emphasized as if this somehow offset the fact that, in contrast with municipal courts, no state can be brought before these international tribunals without its prior consent. Analogies have also been found between the use of force, legally regulated and officially administered, as a sanction in municipal law and "decentralized sanctions," i.e., the resort to war or forceful retaliation by a state which claims that its rights under international law have been violated by another. That there is some analogy is plain; but its significance must be assessed in the light of the equally plain fact that, whereas a municipal court has a compulsory jurisdiction to investigate the rights and wrongs of "self help," and to punish a wrongful resort to it, no international court has a similar jurisdiction.

Some of these dubious analogies may be considered to have been much strengthened by the obligations which states have assumed under the United Nations Charter. But, again, any assessment of their strength is worth little if it ignores the extent to which the law enforcement provisions of the Charter, admirable on paper, have been paralysed by the veto and the ideological divisions and alliances of the great powers. The reply, sometimes made, that the law-enforcement provisions of municipal law *might* also be paralysed by a general strike is scarcely convincing; for in our comparison between municipal law and international law we are concerned with what exists in fact, and here the facts are undeniably different.

There is, however, one suggested formal analogy between international and municipal law which deserves some scrutiny here. Kelsen and many modern theorists insist that, like municipal law, international law possesses and indeed must possess a "basic norm," or what we have termed a rule of recognition, by reference to which the validity of the other rules of the system is assessed, and in virtue of which the rules constitute a single system. The opposed view is that this analogy of structure is false: international law simply consists of a *set* of separate primary rules of obligation which are not united in this manner. It is, in the usual terminology of international lawyers, a set of customary rules of which the rule giving binding force to treaties is one. It is notorious that those who have embarked on the task have found very great difficulties in formulating the "basic norm" of international law. Candidates for this position include the principle *pacta sunt servanda*. This has, however, been abandoned by most theorists, since it seems incompatible with the fact that not all obligations under international law arise from "*pacta*," however widely that term is construed. So it has been replaced by something less familiar: the so-called rule that "States should behave as they customarily behave."

We shall not discuss the merits of these and other rival formulations of the basic norm of international law; instead we shall question the assumption that it must contain such an element. Here the first and perhaps the last question to ask is: why should we make this *a priori* assumption (for that is what it is) and so prejudge the actual character of the rules of international law? For it is surely conceivable (and perhaps has often been the case) that a society may live by rules imposing obligations on its members as "binding," even though they are regarded simply as a set of separate rules, not unified by or deriving their validity from any more basic rule. It is plain that the mere existence of rules does not involve the existence of such a basic rule. In most modern societies there are rules of etiquette, and, though we do not think of them as imposing obligations, we may well talk of such rules as existing; yet we would not look for, nor could we find, a basic rule of etiquette from which the validity of the separate rules was derivable. Such rules do not form a system but a mere set, and, of course, the inconveniences of this form of social control, where matters more important than those of etiquette are at stake, are considerable. They have already been described [previously]. Yet if rules are in fact accepted as standards of conduct, and supported with appropriate forms of social pressure distinctive of obligatory rules, nothing more is required to show that they are binding rules, even though, in this simple form of social structure, we have not something which we do have in municipal law: namely a way of demonstrating the validity of individual rules by reference to some ultimate rule of the system.

There are of course a number of questions which we can ask about rules which constitute not a system but a simple set. We can, for example, ask questions about their historical origin, or questions concerning the causal influences that have fostered the growth of the rules. We can also ask questions about the value of the rules to those who live by them, and whether they regard themselves as morally bound to obey them or obey from some other motive. But we cannot ask in the simpler case one kind of question which we can ask concerning the rules of a system enriched, as municipal law is, by a basic norm or secondary rule of recognition. In the simpler case we cannot ask: "From what ultimate provision of the system do the separate rules derive their validity or 'binding force'?" For there is no such provision and need be none. It is, therefore, a mistake to suppose that a basic rule or rule of recognition is a generally necessary condition of the existence of rules of obligation or "binding" rules. This is not a necessity, but a luxury, found in advanced social systems whose members not merely come to accept separate rules piecemeal, but are committed to the acceptance in advance of general classes of rule, marked out by general criteria of validity. In the simpler form of society we must wait and see whether a rule gets accepted as a rule or not; in a system with a basic rule of recognition we can say before a rule is actually made, that it *will* be valid *if* it conforms to the requirements of the rule of recognition.

The same point may be presented in a different form. When such a rule of recognition is added to the simple set of separate rules, it not only brings with it the advantages of system and ease of identification, but it makes possible for the first time a new form of statement. These are internal statements about the validity of the rules; for we can now ask in a new sense, "What provision of the system makes this rule binding?" or, in Kelsen's language, "What, within the system, is the reason of its validity?" The answers to these new questions are provided by the basic rule of recognition. But though, in the simpler structure, the validity of the rules cannot thus be demonstrated by reference to any more basic rule, this does not mean that there is some question about the rules or their binding force or validity which is left unexplained. It is not the case that there is some mystery as to why the rules in such a simple social structure are binding, which a basic rule, if only we could find it, would resolve. The rules of the simple structure are, like the basic rule of the more advanced systems, binding if they are accepted and function as such. These simple truths about different forms of social structure can, however, easily be obscured by the obstinate search for unity and system where these desirable elements are not in fact to be found.

There is indeed something comic in the efforts made to fashion a basic rule for the most simple forms of social structure which exist without one. It is as if we were to insist that a naked savage *must* really be dressed in some invisible variety of modern dress. Unfortunately, there is also here a standing possibility of confusion. We may be persuaded to treat as a basic rule, something which is an empty repetition of the mere fact that the society concerned (whether of individuals or states) observes certain standards of conduct as obligatory rules. This is surely the status of the strange basic norm which has been suggested for international law: "States should behave as they have customarily behaved." For it says nothing more than that those who accept certain rules must also observe a rule that the rules ought to be observed. This is a mere useless reduplication of the fact that a set of rules are accepted by states as binding rules.

Again once we emancipate ourselves from the assumption that international law *must* contain a basic rule, the question to be faced is one of fact. What is the actual character of the rules as they function in the relations between states? Different interpretations of the phenomena to be observed are of course possible; but it is submitted that there is no basic rule providing general criteria of validity for the rules of international law, and that the rules which are in fact operative constitute not a system but a set of rules, among which are the rules providing for the binding force of treaties. It is true that, on many important matters, the relations between states are regulated by multilateral treaties, and it is sometimes argued that these may bind states that are not parties. If this were generally recognized, such treaties would in fact be legislative enactments and international law would have distinct criteria of validity for its rules. A basic rule of recognition could then be formulated which would represent an actual feature of the system and would be more than an empty restatement of the fact that a set of rules are in fact observed by states. Perhaps international law is at present in a stage of transition towards acceptance of this and other forms which would bring it nearer in structure to a municipal system. If, and when, this transition is completed the formal analogies, which at present seem thin and even delusive, would acquire substance, and the sceptic's last doubts about the legal "quality" of international law may then be laid to rest. Till this stage is reached the analogies are surely those of function and content, not of form. Those of function emerge most clearly when we reflect on the ways in which international law differs from morality, some of which we examined in the last section. The analogies of content consist in the range of principles, concepts, and methods which are common to both municipal and international law, and make the lawyers' technique freely transferable from the one to the other. Bentham, the inventor of the expression "international law," defended it simply by saying that it was "sufficiently analogous"[1] to municipal law. To this, two comments are perhaps worth adding. First, that the analogy is one of content not of form: secondly, that, in this analogy of content, no other social rules are so close to municipal law as those of international law.

Note

1. Jeremy Bentham, *Principles of Morals and Legislation* (1789), XVII. 25, n. I.

Selected Bibliography

Classic Works on Legal Positivism

Austin, John. *The Province of Jurisprudence Determined* (1832).
Bentham, Jeremy. *Introduction to the Principles of Morals and Legislation* (1789).
van Bynkershoek, Cornelius. *Quaestiones Juris Publici* (1737).
———. *De Foro Legatorum* (1721).
Hart, H.L.A. *The Concept of Law* (1961).
———. *Law, Liberty, and Morality* (1962).
Kelsen, Hans. *General Theory of Law and the State* (1945).
———. *General Theory of Norms (Allgemeine Theorie der Normen)*, Michael Hartney, trans. (1991).
———. *Principles of International Law* (1952).
———. *Pure Theory of Law* (1967).
———. *What Is Justice? Justice, Law, and Politics in the Mirror of Science* (1957).
Moser, Johann Jakob. *Neues deutsches Staatsrecht*, 12 vols. (1777–80).
Oppenheim, Lassa. "The Science of International Law: Its Task and Method," *American Journal of International Law* (1908): 313–56.
de Vattel, Emerich. *Le Droit des Gens* (1758).
Zouche, Richard. *Jus et Judicium Feciale, sive Jus Inter Gentes et Quaestionum de Eodem Explication* (1650).

Recent Reviews and Critiques

Ago, Roberto. "Positive Law and International Law," *American Journal of International Law* 51 (1957): 691–733.
Bos, Maarten. "Will and Order in the Nation-State System: Observations on Positivism and Positive International Law," in Ronald St. J. Macdonald and Douglas M. Johnston, eds., *The Structure and Process of International Law: Essays in Legal Philosophy, Doctrine and Theory* (1983), pp. 51–78.
Boyle, Francis A. *World Politics and International Law* (1985).
D'Amato, Anthony. "The Moral Dilemma of Positivism," *Valparaiso University Law Review* 20 (1985): 43–54.

4

Classical Realism

The philosophical roots of Political Realism may be traced as far back as Thucydides and Machiavelli. Nevertheless, the "Classical Realist" approach associated with E. H. Carr, Hans Morgenthau, George Kennan, and other scholars developed primarily during World War II and the succeeding three decades. Classical Realism, which is so labeled to distinguish it from the later "Neorealism," represented largely a reaction to the perceived failures of late nineteenth- and early twentieth-century statecraft. Diplomats and state leaders then, charged the Classical Realists, had wrongly sought to establish an international order based on law, one in which conflicts would be resolved by neutral adjudication rather than by armed force. Their "utopian" efforts—embodied in the arbitration treaties, the Hague Conferences, the League of Nations, and the Permanent Court of International Justice—had relied heavily on Legal Positivism, and had reflected its misplaced emphasis on the elaboration of international rules and the development of international institutions.

Morgenthau and his Classical Realist colleagues were determined to supplant "idealism" with a *Realpolitik* approach. They argued that national interest, rather than legal rules, should guide foreign policy, and that power relationships, rather than legal institutions, proved the ultimate determinants of international affairs. International law might be regularly observed, they conceded, but it did not fundamentally "matter."

E. H. Carr

Edward Hallett Carr's *The Twenty Years' Crisis 1919–1939*[1] has been dubbed "the first 'scientific' treatment of modern world politics."[2] Published in 1939 as the shadow of a second world war loomed, Carr's treatise

94

is commonly credited with launching the "idealist-realist" debate.[3] Professor Carr's celebrated critique of "utopianism" constituted, moreover, a fundamental challenge to international law's efficacy.[4]

Carr declares that international law cannot "be understood independently of the political foundation on which it rests and of the political interests which it serves." "Behind all law," he maintains, lies a "necessary political background. The ultimate authority derives from politics." Hence, "international legal" approaches to "political" problems are misguided. Reflecting on the troubled political circumstances of his time, the Briton observes: "[T]o bring about revision in the international society by means other than war is the most vital problem of contemporary international politics. The first step is to extricate ourselves from the *blind alley of arbitration and judicial settlement,* where no solution of this problem is to be found." Given international law's inherent limitations, Carr counsels "the wise politician" and "the wise student of politics" to "devote a great deal of attention to *political* disputes."

Hans Morgenthau

"Deeply influenced" by Carr[5] was Hans J. Morgenthau, author of the 1948 classic, *Politics Among Nations: The Struggle for Power and Peace.*[6] Francis Boyle has written of Morgenthau's seminal text:

> The definitive exposition of a modern theory of political realism. . . , the work set the discipline of [International Relations] on its feet and remained its greatest classic. The book was written with the power, brilliance, and analytical insight of an international lawyer who had been profoundly disillusioned by the experience of World War II. Little sympathy remained for international law and organizations precisely because they had been tragically repudiated by history itself.[7]

At the time of its publication, *Politics Among Nations* read like a "declaration of war"[8] against the "legalist-moralist" approach to International Relations. That declaration was heard by a vast audience, for of "the textbooks in international relations published during the first two decades after World War II," Morgenthau's "had the greatest impact on. . . university teaching."[9]

Professor Morgenthau begins his work with the fundamental premise that "international politics is of necessity power politics," and introduces his discussion of international law with a chapter tellingly entitled, "The Main Problems of International Law." As a former law professor, Morgenthau is quick to acknowledge that international law exists and that "in most instances" it has been "scrupulously observed." Nevertheless, "to recognize" the existence of international law, he notes, is "not tantamount to asserting that [international law] is as effective a legal system as the national legal systems are and that, more particularly, it is *effective* in regulating or restraining the struggle for power on the international scene." The reason for international law's ineffectiveness is rooted in its very nature. "It is," writes Morgenthau, "a primitive type of law primarily because it is almost completely decentralized law."

In a detailed thirty-page treatment, Morgenthau underscores the decentralization of international law in each of its three basic functions: legislation, adjudication, and enforcement. His specific analysis of international law's "legislature decentralization," and hence of its "imprecision," typifies Morgenthau's overall approach:

> Governments. . . are always anxious to shake off the restraining influence which international law might have upon their international policies, to use international law instead for the promotion of their national interests, and to evade legal obligations which might be harmful to them. They have used the imprecision of international law as a ready-made tool for furthering their ends. They have done so by advancing unsupported claims to legal rights and by distorting the meaning of generally recognized rules of international law.

He concludes: "Thus the lack of precision, inherent in the decentralized nature of international law, is breeding ever more lack of precision, and the debilitating vice, which was present at its birth, continues to sap its strength." Such devastating rhetoric illustrates well "the methodically ruthless vitality of Morgenthau's attack upon the legalist-moralist approach" to International Relations.[10]

George F. Kennan

One of the most prominent American-born Classical Realists was George F. Kennan, the intellectual architect of U.S. "containment" policy. In his lecture reprinted here, Kennan faults the legalistic approach for the twentieth-century rise of the "total victory" concept, one which has brought with it the notion of "total war." Because international legalism imbues war, as the primary means of international law enforcement, with moral legitimacy, Kennan argues that legalism renders "violence more enduring, more terrible, and more destructive to political stability."

Stanley Hoffmann

In 1971, *The Relevance of International Law*[11] was published to mark the sixty-fifth birthday of Leo Gross, an esteemed professor of international law at the Fletcher School of Law and Diplomacy. The ostensible purpose of the *festschrift* was to assess international law's relevance "to the problems of war and peace, to the challenge Third World Countries present[ed] to the stability of the international system, to the growth of international organizations, and to the subsequent evolution of 'world order.'"[12] Ironically, however, a prominent essay by co-editor Stanley Hoffmann "strove mightily to refute what was supposed to be the book's main proposition, namely, that international law and organizations were indeed relevant to international politics," and hence to the discipline of International Relations.[13]

In "International Law and the Control of Force," Hoffmann advances what might be described as a quintessentially Classical Realist argument. He maintains that international law represents "the law of a milieu that has no central power," and that "resort to violence" is "the essence of the group" of "rival societies" that comprise the modern state system. Because the world's "fundamental structure," a "state of nature," has not changed, Hoffmann explains, "legal attempts at constraint have so far been in vain." Referring sardonically to international law as the most powerful training ground for imagination, he charges:

[I]n a clash between inadequate law and supreme political interests, law bows—and lawyers are reduced to serve either as a chorus of lamenters with fists raised at the sky and state or as a clique of national justifiers in the most sophisticatedly subservient or sinuous fashion.

In a reference to Dean Acheson's remarks reprinted here, Professor Hoffmann concludes, rather pessimistically:

Law bows because, as Acheson—a lawyer—put it in unforgettably blunt terms, it raises a "moral" rather than a "real" issue—i.e., law is so inadequate, tries to reform behavior in so unrealistic a way that it ceases being "part of political reality"; if "the survival of states is not a matter of law," if furthermore the international system is one which raises problems of survival incessantly, then we are left with the sad conclusion that in the last analysis, in this crucial area, the states are still above the law.

Hoffmann's suggestions—that states were not constrained by international law in circumstances of paramount national interest, and that international law then might no longer be part of political reality—offered scant incentive for IR scholars to study international law per se. Indeed, very few would undertake such studies in the 1970s or thereafter.

Notes

1. E. H. Carr, *The Twenty Years' Crisis, 1919–1939* (London: Macmillan, 1939). All subsequent references to Carr will be drawn from the Harper Torchbooks reprint of the 1946 second edition of Carr (New York: Harper & Row, 1964), pp. 170–207.
2. Stanley Hoffmann, "An American Social Science: International Relations," *Daedalus* 106 (1977): 43. For a brief discussion of Carr, see James E. Dougherty and Robert L. Pfaltzgraff, Jr., *Contending Theories of International Relations,* 3rd ed. (New York: Harper & Row, 1990), pp. 4–7.
3. J. Martin Rochester, "The Rise and Fall of International Organization as a Field of Study," *International Organization* 40 (1986): 781.
4. For an overview of Carr's argument and its influence on Morgenthau, see Francis A. Boyle, *World Politics and International Law* (Durham, N.C.: Duke University Press, 1985), pp. 12–13.

5. Discussion with Professor Morgenthau, April 1973, cited by Boyle, ibid., p. 12. For a review of Morgenthau's views on international law, see Greg Russell, *Hans Morgenthau and the Ethics of American Statecraft* (Baton Rouge: Louisiana State University Press, 1990), pp. 172–75.

6. Hans J. Morgenthau, *Politics Among Nations: The Struggle for Power and Peace* (New York: Knopf, 1948). All subsequent references to Morgenthau will be drawn from this edition.

7. Boyle, *World Politics and International Law*, p. 11.

8. Discussion with Stanley Hoffmann, September 1973, cited by Boyle, ibid., pp. 12, 298n.

9. Dougherty and Pfaltzgraff, *Contending Theories of International Relations*, pp. 8–9.

10. Boyle, *World Politics and International Law*, p. 13.

11. Karl Deutsch and Stanley Hoffmann, eds., *The Relevance of International Law* (Garden City, N.Y.: Anchor Books, 1971).

12. Boyle, *World Politics and International Law*, p. 3.

13. Ibid., pp. 3–4. Hoffman himself noted, "It may be strange for the co-editor of a volume on the relevance of international law to contribute an essay that could, with only a little flippancy, be taken as an attempt to show the irrelevance of international law." Stanley Hoffmann, "International Law and the Control of Force," in Deutsch and Hoffmann, eds., *The Relevance of International Law*, p. 34. All excerpts will be drawn from pages 36 to 47 of this essay.

GEORGE F. KENNAN

Diplomacy in the Modern World

These lectures were designed as historical exercises, as contributions to the analysis of past events in the field of American diplomacy; and normally they might have been permitted to stand as such. But the background of current events against which they have been given has been so absorbing, and your own preoccupation with these events so obvious and understandable, that I know you will feel that what I have said has not been given its maximum usefulness if I do not add a word about its relevance to our problems of today.

Before I do this, there is one more thing I would like to say about the past. I fear that the impression I have given you of our past performance in the diplomatic field may have been a darker and gloomier one than is really in my mind. I ought to record, I think, my own recognition that the annals of American diplomacy in this half-century contain many positive aspects as well as negative ones. Let us remember that for us this has been a period of tremendous and most trying transition. We entered upon it with the concepts and methods of a small neutral nation. I know this approach well. I have seen it in some of the foreign offices of other countries where I have been privileged to do business on behalf of our government. It is an approach which I like and respect, and for which I must confess a certain nostalgia. It can have in it, and usually does, great quality and dignity. The Department of State as it existed at the turn of the century, and as it still was in large measure in the 1920's when I entered it, was a quaint old place, with its law-office atmosphere, its cool dark corridors, its swinging doors, its brass cuspidors, its black leather rocking chairs, and the grand-father's clock in the Secretary of State's office. There was a real old-fashioned dignity and simplicity about it. It was staffed in those earlier days by professional personnel some of whom were men of great experience and competence. And it was headed more often than otherwise by Americans of genuine stature and quality.

I should be most unhappy if anything said in these lectures should seem a mark of disrespect for such men as John Hay, Elihu Root, Charles Evans Hughes, or Henry Stimson. These men embodied that pattern of integrity of mind and spirit, moderation and delicacy of character, irreproachable loyalty in personal relations, modesty of person combined with dignity of office, and kindliness and generosity in the approach to all who were weaker and more dependent, which constitutes, it seems to me, our

Chapter 6 in *American Diplomacy,* expanded ed. (University of Chicago Press, 1984), pp. 91–103. Reprinted with permission.

finest contribution to the variety of the human species in this world and comes closest to embodying our national ideal and genius. They were men so measured and prudent in their judgment of others, so careful to reserve that judgment until they felt they had the facts, so well aware of the danger of inadequate evidence and hasty conclusion, that we would be making ourselves ridiculous if we were to attend their memories and the evidences of their handiwork in any other spirit.

We are another generation, and we cannot be fully the judges either of the demands which faced our elders or of the adequacy of their responses. For the performance of these men in public office I can feel only the sort of sympathy and admiration which one felt for the struggles and works of one's own father, coupled with the invariable conviction of children everywhere that there were features of the modern world which Father understood very poorly and we children understood much better. And if, today, we think we see blind spots or weak spots in their approaches to foreign policy, we would do well to remember what Gibbon said of the great Byzantine general, Belisarius: "His imperfections flowed from the contagion of the times: his virtues were his own."

But, notwithstanding all this, it is clear that there has been in the past a very significant gap between challenge and response in our conduct of foreign policy; that this gap still exists; and that, whereas fifty years ago it was not very dangerous to us, today it puts us in grave peril. We can afford no complacency about these things in the year 1951, and we have no choice but to face up unsparingly to our weaknesses.

I think you have seen quite clearly from the earlier lectures what I hold these weaknesses to be. I do not need to recapitulate them in any great detail. They are ones which relate both to machinery and to concept—both to means and to objectives.

On the question of the machinery of government, we have seen that a good deal of our trouble seems to have stemmed from the extent to which the executive has felt itself beholden to short-term trends of public opinion in the country and from what we might call the erratic and subjective nature of public reaction to foreign-policy questions. I would like to emphasize that I do not consider public reaction to foreign-policy questions to be erratic and undependable over the long term; but I think the record indicates that in the short term our public opinion, or what passes for our public opinion in the thinking of official Washington, can be easily led astray into areas of emotionalism and subjectivity which make it a poor and inadequate guide for national action.

What can we do about this?

As one who has occupied himself professionally with foreign affairs for a quarter of a century, I cannot refrain from saying that I firmly believe that we could make much more effective use of the principle of professionalism in the conduct of foreign policy; that we could, if we wished, develop a corps of professional officers superior to anything that exists or ever has existed in this field; and that, by treating these men with respect and drawing on their insight and experience, we could help ourselves considerably. However, I am quite prepared to recognize that this runs counter to strong prejudices and preconceptions in sections of our public mind, particularly in Congress and the press, and that for this reason we are probably condemned to continue relying almost exclusively on what we might call "diplomacy by dilettantism."

That being the case, we still have with us, in what is obviously a very acute form, the problem of the machinery for decision-making and for the implementation of policy in our government. Whatever else may be said about these facilities to date, it can hardly be said that they are distinguished by such things as privacy, deliberateness, or the long-term approach. The difficulties we encounter here are so plain to all of you at this moment that I shall not attempt to adumbrate them. The subject of their correction is an extremely complex one, involving many facets of governmental organization and method. There are those who feel that these difficulties can be satisfactorily disposed of within our present constitutional framework and that they are simply a question of proper personal leadership in government. There are others who doubt that the problem is soluble without constitutional reform—reform which would give us a parliamentary system more nearly like that which exists in England and most other parliamentary countries, a system in which a government falls if it loses the confidence of its parliament, and in which there is opportunity to consult the people on the great issues and at the crucial moments and to adjust governmental responsibilities in accordance with the peoples' decision.

I must say that if I had any doubts before as to whether it is this that our country requires, those doubts have been pretty well resolved in my mind by the events of the past weeks and months. I find it hard to see how we can live up to our responsibilities as a great power unless we are able to resolve, in a manner better than we have done recently, the great challenges to the soundness of government policy and to the claim of an administration to speak for the mass of the people in foreign affairs.

Here again, I am afraid, the chances of change in the direction I have indicated are so slight that we must dismiss the possibility as one that might have any particular relevance to our present problems.

This leaves us substantially with the question of concept. This is the field in which the scholar's voice can be most useful, and for which it seems to me that this examination of the past yields the most instructive results.

As you have no doubt surmised, I see the most serious fault of our past policy formulation to lie in something that I might call the legalistic-moralistic approach to international problems. This approach runs like a red skein through our foreign policy of the last fifty years. It has in it something of the old emphasis on arbitration treaties, something of the Hague Conferences and schemes for universal disarmament, something of the more ambitious American concepts of the role of international law, something of the League of Nations and the United Nations, something of the Kellogg Pact, something of the idea of a universal "Article 51" pact, something of the belief in World Law and World Government. But it is none of these, entirely. Let me try to describe it.

It is the belief that it should be possible to suppress the chaotic and dangerous aspirations of governments in the international field by the acceptance of some system of legal rules and restraints. This belief undoubtedly represents in part an attempt to transpose the Anglo-Saxon concept of individual law into the international field and to make it applicable to governments as it is applicable here at home to individuals. It must also stem in part from the memory of the origin of our own political system—from the recollection that we were able, through acceptance of a common institutional and juridical framework, to reduce to harmless dimensions the conflicts of interest and aspiration among the original thirteen colonies and to bring them all into an ordered and peaceful relationship with one another. Remembering this, people are unable to understand that what might have been possible for the thirteen colonies in a given set of circumstances might not be possible in the wider international field.

It is the essence of this belief that, instead of taking the awkward conflicts of national interest and dealing with them on their merits with a view to finding the solutions least unsettling to the stability of international life, it would be better to find some formal criteria of a juridical nature by which the permissible behavior of states could be defined. There would then be judicial entities competent to measure the actions of governments against these criteria and to decide when their behavior was acceptable and when unacceptable. Behind all this, of course, lies the American assumption that the things for which other peoples in this world are apt to contend are for the most part neither creditable nor important and might justly be expected to take second place behind the desirability of an orderly world, untroubled by international violence. To the American mind, it is implausible that people should have positive aspirations, and ones that they regard as legitimate, more important to them than the peacefulness and orderliness of international life. From this standpoint, it is not apparent why other peoples should not join us in accepting the rules of the game in international politics, just as we accept such rules in the competition of sport in order that the game may not become too cruel and too destructive and may not assume an importance we did not mean it to have.

If they were to do this, the reasoning runs, then the troublesome and chaotic manifestations of the national ego could be contained and rendered either unsubstantial or subject to easy disposal by some method familiar and comprehensible to our American usage. Departing from this background, the mind of American statesmanship, stemming as it does in so large a part from the legal profession in our country, gropes with unfailing persistence for some institutional framework which would be capable of fulfilling this function.

I cannot undertake in this short lecture to deal exhaustively with this thesis or to point out all the elements of unsoundness which I feel it contains. But some of its more outstanding weaknesses are worthy of mention.

In the first place, the idea of the subordination of a large number of states to an international juridical regime, limiting their possibilities for aggression and injury to other states, implies that these are all states like our own, reasonably content with their international borders and status, at least to the extent that they would be willing to refrain from pressing for change without international agreement. Actually, this has generally been true only of a portion of international society. We tend to underestimate the violence of national maladjustments and discontents elsewhere in the world if we think that they would always appear to other people as less important than the preservation of the juridical tidiness of international life.

Second, while this concept is often associated with a revolt against nationalism, it is a curious thing that it actually tends to confer upon the concept of nationality and national sovereignty an absolute value it did not have before. The very principle of "one government, one vote," regardless of physical or political differences between states, glorifies the concept of national sovereignty and makes it the exclusive form of participation in international life. It envisages a world composed exclusively of sovereign national states with a full equality of status. In doing this, it ignores the tremendous variations in the firmness and soundness of national divisions: the fact that the origins of state borders and national personalities were in many instances fortuitous or at least poorly related to realities. It also ignores the law of change. The national state pattern is not, should not be, and cannot be a fixed and static thing. By nature, it is an unstable phenomenon in a constant state of change and flux. History has shown that the will and the capacity of individual peoples to contribute to their world environment is constantly changing. It is only logical that the organizational forms (and what else are such things as borders and governments?) should change with them. The function of a system of international relationships is not to inhibit this process of change by imposing a legal strait jacket upon it but rather to facilitate it: to ease its transitions, to temper the asperities to which it often leads, to isolate and moderate the conflicts to which it gives rise, and to see that these conflicts do not assume forms too unsettling for international life in general. But this is a task for diplomacy, in the most old-fashioned sense of the term. For this, law is too abstract, too inflexible, too hard to adjust to the demands of the unpredictable and the unexpected.

By the same token, the American concept of world law ignores those means of international offense—those means of the projection of power and coercion over other peoples—which by-pass institutional forms entirely or even exploit them against themselves: such things as ideological attack, intimidation, penetration, and disguised seizure of the institutional paraphernalia of national sovereignty. It ignores, in other words, the device of the puppet state and the set of techniques by which states can be converted into puppets with no formal violation of, or challenge to, the outward attributes of their sovereignty and their independence.

This is one of the things that have caused the peoples of the satellite countries of eastern Europe to look with a certain tinge of bitterness on the United Nations. The organization failed so completely to save them from domination by a great neighboring country, a domination no less invidious by virtue of the fact that it came into being by processes we could not call "aggression." And there is indeed some justification for their feeling, because the legalistic approach to international affairs ignores in general the international significance of political problems and the deeper sources of international instability. It assumes that civil wars will remain civil and not grow into international wars. It assumes the ability of each people to solve its own internal political problems in a manner not provocative of its international environment. It assumes that each nation will always be able to construct a government qualified to speak for it and cast its vote in the international arena and that this government will be acceptable to the rest of the international community in this capacity. It assumes, in other words, that domestic issues will not become international issues and that the world community will not be put in the position of having to make choices between rival claimants for power within the confines of the individual state.

Finally, this legalistic approach to international relations is faulty in its assumptions concerning the possibility of sanctions against offenses and violations. In general, it looks to collective action to provide such sanction against the bad behavior of states. In doing so, it forgets the limitations on the effectiveness of military coalition. It forgets that, as a circle of military associates widens in any conceivable political-military venture, the theoretical total of available military strength may increase, but only at the cost of compactness and ease of control. And the wider a coalition becomes, the more difficult it becomes to retain political unity and general agreement on the purposes and effects of what is being done. As we are seeing in the case of Korea, joint military operations against an aggressor have a different meaning for each participant and raise specific political issues for each one which are extraneous to the action in question and affect many other facets of international life. The wider the circle of military associates, the more cumbersome the problem of political control over their actions, and the more circumscribed the least common denominator of agreement. This law of diminishing returns lies so heavily on the possibilities for multilateral military action that it makes it doubtful whether the participation of smaller states can really add very much to the ability of the great powers to assure stability of international life. And this is tremendously important, for it brings us back to the realization that even under a system of world law the sanction against destructive international behavior might continue to rest basically, as it has in the past, on the alliances and relationships among the great powers themselves. There might be a state, or perhaps more than one state, which all the rest of the world community together could not successfully coerce into following a line of action to which it was violently averse. And if this is true, where are we? It seems to me that we are right back in the realm of the forgotten art of diplomacy from which we have spent fifty years trying to escape.

These, then, are some of the theoretical deficiencies that appear to me to be inherent in the legalistic approach to international affairs. But there is a greater deficiency still that I should like to mention before I close. That is the inevitable association of legalistic ideas with moralistic ones: the carrying over into the affairs of states of the concepts of right and wrong, the assumption that state behavior is a fit subject for moral judgment. Whoever says there is a law must of course be indignant against the law-breaker and feel a moral superiority to him. And when such indignation spills over into military contest, it knows no bounds short of the reduction of the lawbreaker to the point of complete submissiveness—namely, unconditional surrender. It is a curious thing, but it is true, that the legalistic approach to world affairs, rooted as it unquestionably is in a desire to do away with war and violence, makes violence more enduring, more terrible, and more destructive to political stability than did the older motives of national interest. A war fought in the name of high moral principle finds no early end short of some form of total domination.

In this way, we see that the legalistic approach to international problems is closely identified with the concept of total war and total victory, and the manifestations of the one spill over only too easily into the manifestations of the other. And the concept of total war is something we would all do well to think about a little in these troubled times. This is a relatively new concept, in Western civilization at any rate. It did not really appear on the scene until World War I. It characterized both of these great world wars, and both of them—as I have pointed out—were followed by great instability and disillusionment. But it is not only a question now of the desirability of this concept; it is a question of its feasibility. Actually, I wonder whether even in the past total victory was not really an illusion from the standpoint of the victors. In a sense, there is not total victory short of genocide, unless it be a victory over the minds of men. But the total military victories are rarely victories over the minds of men. And we now face the fact that it is very questionable whether in a new global conflict there could ever be any such thing as total *military* victory. I personally do not believe that there could. There might be a great weakening of the armed forces of one side or another, but I think it out of the question that there should be such a thing as a general and formal submission of the national will on either side. The attempt to achieve this unattainable goal, however, could wreak upon civilization another set of injuries fully as serious as those caused by World War I or World War II, and I leave it to you to answer the question as to how civilization could survive them.

It was asserted not long ago by a prominent American that "war's very object is victory" and that "in war there can be no substitute for victory." Perhaps the confusion here lies in what is meant by the term "victory." Perhaps the term is actually misplaced. Perhaps there can be such a thing as "victory" in a battle, whereas in war there can be only the achievement or nonachievement of your objectives. In the old days, wartime objectives were generally limited and practical ones, and it was common to measure the success of your military operations by the extent to which they brought you closer to your objectives. But where your objectives are moral and ideological ones and run to changing the attitudes and traditions of an entire people or the personality of a regime, then victory is probably something not to be achieved entirely by military means or indeed in any short space of time at all; and perhaps that is the source of our confusion.

In any case, I am frank to say that I think there is no more dangerous delusion, none that has done us a greater disservice in the past or that threatens to do us a greater disservice in the future, than the concept of total victory. And I fear that it springs in large measure from the basic faults in the approach to international affairs which I have been discussing here. If we are to get away from it, this will not mean that we shall have to abandon our respect for international law, or our hopes for its future usefulness as the gentle civilizer of events which I mentioned in one of the earlier lectures. Nor will it mean that we have to go in for anything that can properly be termed "appeasement"—if one may use a word so cheapened and deflated by the abuse to which it has been recently subjected. But it will mean the emergence of a new attitude among us toward many things outside our borders that are irritating and unpleasant today—an attitude more like that of the doctor toward those physical phenomena in the human body that are neither pleasing nor fortunate—an attitude of detachment and soberness and readiness to reserve judgment. It will mean that we will have the modesty to admit that our own national interest is all that we are really capable of knowing and understanding—and the courage to recognize that if our own purposes and undertakings here at home are decent ones, unsullied by arrogance or hostility toward other people or delusions of superiority, then the pursuit of our national interest can never fail to be conducive to a better world. This concept is less ambitious and less inviting in its immediate prospects than those to which we have so often inclined, and less pleasing to our image of ourselves. To many it may seem to smack of cynicism and reaction. I cannot share these doubts. Whatever is realistic in concept, and founded in an endeavor to see both ourselves and others as we really are, cannot be illiberal.

DEAN ACHESON

Remarks

To talk of the legal aspects of the Cuban incident reminds me of the story of the women discussing the Quiz Program scandals. One said that she felt the scandals presented serious moral issues. The other answered, "And I always say that moral issues are more important than real issues." Mr. Chayes has cited legal principles to justify the actions taken by our Government in October of 1962, observing in passing that "law was not wholly irrelevant."

Today, in the analyses presented, several legal theories to justify the Cuban quarantine have appeared. Professor Hart has been quoted to the effect that a legal system is all-pervasive, and that an all-pervasive system will necessarily provide an answer for all problems which arise within it. Others found justification within treaties or agreements; still others within the realm of "generally accepted" ideas. What can one expect to find? Clearly, a simple answer that the action was lawful or unlawful will not be found.

In my estimation, however, the quarantine is not a legal issue or an issue of international law as these terms should be understood. Much of what is called international law is a body of ethical distillation, and one must take care not to confuse this distillation with law. We should not rationalize general legal policy restricting sovereignty from international documents composed for specific purposes.

Further, the law through its long history has been respectful of power, especially that power which is close to the sanctions of law. This point is exemplified in the history of English law during the era of Richard II. The Court of the King's Bench was asked to pass on the validity of the Duke of York's claim to the English Crown. The Court refused to consider the question, since it "concerned the king's own estate & regalie." The Court indeed assumed a respectful attitude toward power.

There are indications in our country today which suggest that some segments of our sovereign people resist judicial entry into the inner sanctuary of power. In the field of labor-management relations, where law had once entered boldly, it has withdrawn before power. The same court that was willing to apply a yet-to-be announced doctrine of law to apportionment of legislative representatives has left the issue of featherbedding, where no rules were applicable, to power. Again in the steel price controversy, law has left the arbitrament to other principles.

From Proceedings of the American Society of International Law, 57th Annual Meeting (1963), pp. 13–15. © The American Society of International Law. Reprinted by permission.

I must conclude that the propriety of the Cuban quarantine is not a legal issue. The power, position and prestige of the United States had been challenged by another state; and law simply does not deal with such questions of ultimate power—power that comes close to the sources of sovereignty. I cannot believe that there are principles of law that say we must accept destruction of our way of life. One would be surprised if practical men, trained in legal history and thought, had devised and brought to a state of general acceptance a principle condemnatory of an action so essential to the continuation of pre-eminent power as that taken by the United States last October. Such a principle would be as harmful to the development of restraining procedures as it would be futile. No law can destroy the state creating the law. The survival of states is not a matter of law.

However, in the action taken in the Cuban quarantine, one can see the influence of accepted legal principles. These principles are procedural devices designed to reduce the severity of a possible clash. Those devices cause wise delay before drastic action, create a "cooling off" period, permit the consideration of others' views. The importance of the Organization of American States was also procedural, and emphasized the desirability of collective action, thus creating a common denominator of action. Some of these desirable consequences are familiar to us in the domestic industrial area.

In October the United States was faced with grave problems of policy and procedure in relation to its own and outside interests. The action taken was the right action. "Right" means more than legally justifiable, or even successful. The United States resolved very grave issues of policy in a way consonant with ethical restraint.

The most perplexing aspect of the decision was the difficulty of comparing, of weighing, competing considerations. How could one weigh the desirability of less drastic action at the outset against the undesirability of losing sight of the missiles, or having them used against us, which might be avoided by more drastic action from the onset, such as destroying the weapons. The President had no scales in which to test these weights, no policy litmus paper. Wisdom for the decision was not to be found in law, but in judgment. Principles, certainly legal principles, do not decide concrete cases.

Selected Bibliography

Works on Classical Realism

Acheson, Dean. *Fragments of My Fleece* (1971), p. 156.
Carr, E. H. *The Twenty Years Crisis, 1919–1939*.
Hoffmann, Stanley. "International Law and the Control of Force," in Karl W. Deutsch and Staley Hoffmann, eds., *The Relevance of International Law* (1968).
Kennan, George F. *American Diplomacy, 1900–1950* (1951).
Kissinger, Henry A. "The Nature of Leadership," in *American Foreign Policy* (1969), pp. 27–43.
Morgenthau, Hans J. *In Defense of the National Interest* (1951), esp. p. 144.
———. *Politics Among Nations: The Struggle for Power and Peace* (1948).
———. "Positivism, Functionalism, and International Law," *American Journal of International Law* 34 (1940): 260–84.
———. *Scientific Man vs. Power Politics* (1946).
Niebuhr, Reinhold. *Moral Man and Immoral Society* (1960).
———. *The Nature and Destiny of Man: Human Nature* (1943).
Spykman, Nicholas John. *America's Strategy in World Politics* (1942).
Wolfers, Arnold. "Introduction: Political Theory and International Relations," in Arnold Wolfers and Lawrence W. Martins, eds., *The Anglo-American Tradition in Foreign Affairs* (1956).
———. "National Security as an Ambiguous Symbol," in *Discord and Collaboration* (1962), pp. 147–65.

The Evolution of Realist Thought

Ashley, Richard, "Political Realism and Human Interests," *International Studies Quarterly* 25 (1981): 204–37.
Smith, Michael Joseph. *Realist Thought from Weber to Kissinger* (1986).

5

The New Haven School

Borrowing and adapting the tools of a variety of social science disciplines—
from economics and political science to psychology and sociology—the
originators of the New Haven approach developed what they have called a
"policy-oriented jurisprudence." Myres S. McDougal, a Yale law professor
and one-time president of the American Society of International Law, and
Harold D. Lasswell, a Yale professor of law and political science and one-
time president of the American Political Science Association, have developed a truly interdisciplinary approach to the study of international rules.

Like the Positivist approach, the New Haven approach purports to
discover the content of international law through empirical observation.
However, the New Haven approach focuses on a much wider slice of social
reality than the rule-governed behavior of states, which delimits the inquiry of most Positivists. Like the Classical Realists, the adherents to this
approach recognize the severe limitations of the Positivist conception of
law as a body of rules.

Believing that a rule-based conception of international law was incapable of accurately describing or governing international affairs, the Classical Realists concluded that law is largely irrelevant to the relations of
sovereign states, which should instead be governed by the prudent pursuit
of national interests. Adherents of the New Haven School, rather than
rejecting international law in favor of political prudence, seek to *include*
within the ambit of the legal analysis factors and contextual elements
previously considered extraneous to the law. In so doing, they incorporate
the prudential analysis so central to the Classical Realist project within the
framework of the legal process. The New Haven approach has thus radically expanded the scope of international legal inquiry to include explicit
discussion of the values, interests, goals, and conditioning factors affecting
the process of authoritative decision-making. By focusing on the *process* by

which authoritative decisions are reached, rather than on a static body of rules, these scholars seek to extricate the study of international rules from the increasing formalism and ultimate irrelevancy into which Classical Realists suggest the dominant Positivist approach is slipping.

The methodology adopted by the New Haven approach attempts to provide a "map" of social reality by viewing legal principles in their wider social context. To do this, the New Haven approach utilizes an elaborate analytical structure, based on a "meta-language" in which the terms are given highly specialized meanings. The analytical tools of the New Haven approach, such as phase analysis, value analysis, and the analysis of decision functions, essentially provide checklists of factors to be considered in examining the context of decision-making. These tools are intended to clarify the goals to be pursued, describe past trends in decision-making, and provide insight into conditioning factors.

The explicit purpose of this methodology is to develop "a prescriptive framework for the performance of optimally rational decisionmaking." While practitioners of the New Haven approach reject the Naturalist notion that international law can simply be *discovered* by the application of reason or the study of some higher law, they do argue that law necessarily serves social purposes, and that law must be *constructed* so as to give effect to the fundamental goals of the community it serves. International law does, therefore, serve a "higher purpose" than the ends of the individual states whose patterned behavior composes it. The New Haven scholars have freely acknowledged the necessity of making value choices in the application of their methodology, arguing that such choices are inevitable in all approaches, and that they should be made explicit by policymakers and scholars. New Haven scholars have adopted "human dignity" as their core value for formulating international legal principles.

Critics have argued that, by linking legal decision-making explicitly to the values underlying the world public order (which are difficult to demonstrate empirically), the New Haven approach has made law too indeterminate and discretionary to be useful. If judgments about the values of the international community replace reliance on formal rules, critics argue, law becomes conflated with politics or social science and ceases to perform any independently useful function. In response to this, defenders of the New Haven approach argue that the explicit consideration of values in making legal decisions is preferable to the covert approach to values represented by the Positivist fiction that "rules automatically decide cases."

The New Haven approach attempts to transcend the long-standing debate about the legal quality of international law by defining "law" as a product of both authority (legitimacy) and control (effect on behavior). Rules that are both authoritative and controlling may appropriately be called legal rules. Therefore, the New Haven approach is concerned with both subjective perspectives and the objective behavior of states in assessing international rules.

The essential insights of the New Haven approach—its focus on process and its policy orientation—have been influential in the development of later theories about international rules and norms. The New Stream of international jurisprudence, for instance, takes as its starting point the rejection of the possibility of a purely scientific, neutral approach to international rules, an insight of the American Legal Realists that has been incorporated into international jurisprudence by the New Haven approach. The Institutionalists also owe a great deal to the New Haven approach's contextualism in studying international legal decision-making. Under the rubric of studying the "arena" in which decisions affecting a particular international issue area are made, New Haven scholars have long performed an analysis very similar to that which Institutionalists now utilize in the study of international "regimes."

In addition to its contributions to other approaches, work within the New Haven approach continues to be carried on by a diverse group of scholars who have used the New Haven "toolbox" to reach a variety of different policy conclusions. Richard Falk, a professor of political science at Princeton University, and other participants in the World Order Models Project have drawn upon the jurisprudence of the New Haven School. W. Michael Reisman, who teaches at the Yale Law School and has been a frequent collaborator with Myres McDougal, is among the most prolific and the most "orthodox," in the sense of agreement with the policy conclusions of McDougal and Lasswell, of those currently doing work from this approach. Finally, the influence of the New Haven approach has been felt outside the United States, where it is considered one of the significant American contributions to international legal theory.

MYRES S. MCDOUGAL AND HAROLD D. LASSWELL

The Identification and Appraisal of Diverse Systems of Public Order

It is a commonplace observation that the world arena today exhibits a number of systems of public order, each demanding and embodying the values of human dignity in very different degree. Yet the problems connected with the identification of public order systems, and their appraisal in terms of impact upon the values of human dignity, have received so little systematic attention that scholars of many nations, in no sense exclusive of the United States, continue inadvertently to contribute to the confusions of everyday life manifest in the whole world community and all its component regions.[1]

The consequences of continued confusion are to impede the continuing efforts that are indispensable to the building of the new institutions of which there is such desperate need. Among traditional legal scholars it has long been customary to give unquestioning verbal deference to the proposition that if there is any international law at all, it is a universal law, embracing the organized governments of the world community as a whole, or at least all those bodies politic admitted to the ever-enlarging European "family of nations."[2] The existence of regional diversities in the interpretation of allegedly universal prescriptions, and in the fundamental policies about the allocation of power and other values sought by such interpretation, has been cloaked in the shadows of "decent mystery" by hopeful insistence that such divergent interpretations are but occasional aberrations which will disappear when the real universality of the relevant concepts is appropriately understood.

This make-believe universalism has had the effect of undercutting the authority of every doctrine put forward in the name of the whole body of nations. Even prescriptions rationally designed to serve community interest, when properly invoked and generally applied, have suffered the onus of bearing a classificatory label identical with the symbol which is also employed to identify propositions whose authority is dubious in the extreme, or wholly nonexistent. Professional lawyers and men of affairs the world over exhibit the most extreme oscillation between overaffirmation of the authoritativeness of what they term "international law" and overdenial of the validity of any significant claims put forward in the name of such a system.

Among Anglo-American jurists it is thus habitual to wage a silent war

From *American Journal of International Law* 53 (1959): 1. ©The American Society of International Law. Reprinted by permission. Some notes have been altered.

of attrition against the conception of a comprehensive international law on behalf of terms like "conflict of laws" or "comity," which they treat as an arcanum, to be opened only by the exercise of transcendent subtleties legitimized under the recognized legerdemain of principles of jurisdiction, derived from territorial sovereignty, nationality, and other technical concepts.[3]

Not the least obstructive result of this confusion is the failure to keep at the focus of responsible world attention both the *future-oriented* nature of the challenge contained in the idea of universal legal order and the crucial fact that a legal order of inclusive scope can come into existence only in a process of interaction in which every particular legal advance both strengthens a world public order and is in turn itself supported and strengthened by that order. The processes of law have as their proper office the synthesizing and stabilizing of creative efforts toward a new order by the procedures and structures of authority, thereby consolidating gains and providing guidance for the next steps along the path toward a universal system. By pretending in one mood that international law is a contemporary and presumably well-constructed edifice while insinuating in another that it is a pretentious and dubious fantasy, the true dimensions of the task are concealed. Effective, comprehensive universality, despite the faint shadows of worldwide organization, does not now exist. It is for the future, and can be expected only as a reward of clarification and of relevant effort.

A pervasive present illusion is that lip service to the claim of universality for contemporary international law serves the cause of universality. On the contrary, the invocation of spurious universalism on all questions diverts creative concern from the vital issues on which the diverse systems of public order that now dominate the world scene are *not* united, and which, if they are to be resolved by peaceable persuasion rather than bellicose coercion, must be brought into the open and kept there as unremitting challenges to take appropriate action. Obscurity helps to perpetuate the divisions of the world and in the deepest sense serves the interest of no one, for all mortals are in deadly peril of inadvertent as well as planned destruction in the wake of nuclear conflict.

Having full regard to the common interest in removing the cloud that overcasts the future, it must not, however, be supposed that all interests are identical, or that the existing decision-makers of all nation states are without what they regard as important stakes in continuing, rather than terminating, the present state of danger.

In view of the universal testimony in public and private about the suicidal peril of continuing the arms race, one may well exclaim, "How can such things be?" Are the top officials of the world so depraved in mind and character, so insistent upon egocentric power, that they would rather risk the end of man than agree to a genuinely universal system of public order?

With the demoniac case of Adolf Hitler fresh in mind, we cannot deny the possibility that totalitarian systems of public order are capable of bringing into power and keeping in power a personality whose self-image is so inflated by unconscious processes that he is ready to ruin the world if he cannot rule it. The bitter and shocking revelations by Khrushchev of the last mad years of Stalin provide us with another example of the pathologic horrors of systems that feed on dreams of world dominion imposed by blends of fascination and terror.

Despite these ominous precedents we do not assert that the primary danger from the present anarchic state of the world, so far as issues of elementary safety are concerned, is the spawning of another paranoidal Caesar in Moscow. The continuing threat is more humdrum than that. We do not even need to make the assumption of malevolence, of individual depravity that prefers office to the sacrifices necessary to abate the nuclear danger. A much simpler explanation may very well account for the failure of leaders, notably of totalitarian leaders, to make whatever short-range sacrifices may appear necessary in order to install the operations essential to a truly universal system of international law.

We refer to the conditions that surround the political leader of totalitarian systems. Such a leader has come to the top by surviving the chronic uncertainties and risks of a police state. His every move is reacted to instantly, not by peaceably disposed competitors in free debate and election, who are campaigning for votes, but by ambitious assistants and nominal colleagues, whose only route to greater power is ruthless conspiracy and coercion, and who thus are necessarily out to ruin his career, if not to end his life. It cannot be assumed that under these menacing conditions the apparent leader of a totalitarian junta can lightly allow himself to appear to acquiesce, for example, in measures that authorize the bringing of foreign personnel into the arsenals of the totalitarian garrison. The overwhelming probability would appear to be that the first leaders who move in this direction will forfeit their political influence, and possibly their lives. These top figures, despite all their braggadocio and bombast, have been effectively paralyzed as leaders of cooperative achievement by a polity of mutual and deadly intimidation; they gyrate in endless convolution while the arms race gains breadth and malignance.

Yet the spokesmen of totalitarian powers are the ones who, professing to be more orthodox keepers of the faith than their bourgeois opponents, pay most punctilious deference to the supposed universality of international law. And why? Strange as it may seem at first glance, the most convincing interpretation is that the existing imperfections of the system can be used by them to help prevent further advances toward a world order with genuine measures of security. For it is in the name of such allegedly universal doctrines of international law as sovereignty, domestic jurisdiction, nonintervention, independence, and equality—all of which appear to fortify claims to freedom from external obligation—that the case is made to resist the institutional reconstructions which are indispensable to security.

In this grave posture of world affairs it can only make sense to put aside the veil that is provided by false conceptions of the universality of international law. An indispensable step toward a truly comprehensive system of world order is to disabuse all minds of the false myth that universal words imply universal deeds. The effective authority of any legal system depends in the long run upon the underlying common interests of the participants in the system and their recognition of such common interests, reflected in continuing predispositions to support the prescriptions and the procedures that comprise the system. The discrediting of claims to universality which are in fact false is thus a first necessary step toward clarifying the common goals, interpretations, and procedures essential to achieving an effective international order capable of drawing upon the continuous support essential to global security by consent. By piercing the veil of pseudo-universality we may, further, diminish the degree of unwitting support that totalitarian powers obtain from the persisting failure of many scholars and leaders of the non-Soviet world to disclose the true state of affairs. Too many people, professional and lay, have failed to see that insistence upon universality as now "existing" serves as a tactical screen to disguise the strategic goal of advancing toward an imposed universalization of the totalitarian form of public order. Soviet leaders hope to benefit the totalitarian objective by keeping the bodies politic of the non-Soviet world sufficiently divided to forestall joint exposure of the Soviet position and to prevent continuing conjoint pressure for progress by cooperation toward a world order of human dignity.

For the visible future at least the lead must of course be taken by scholars and public figures physically located in the non-Soviet world. It is obvious that scholars who reside in the non-Soviet world have much more freedom in the expression of unconventional ideas than their opposite numbers. In part this comes from the diverse social environments where they live and from which they draw support. In part the critical factor is ideological, reflecting freedom from, rather than subjection to, a deterministic materialistic metaphysics. The non-Soviet world has several well-established modern and industrial societies which make no demands to go beyond their national frontiers for the purpose of subordinating other peoples to a centrally administered socio-economic and political structure.

Scholars and public figures in the nontotalitarian world can use this relatively favorable environment to make critical appraisals—of the national self as well as the self of other nations. It is therefore feasible for them to dissolve the curtains of confusion created by the common practice of glorifying specific institutional practices instead of glorifying the goal values of human dignity and engaging in a *continuous reappraisal of the circumstances in which specific institutional combinations can make the greatest net contribution to the overarching goal.*

Fortunately, advantage may be taken of the fact that the major systems of public order are in many fundamental respects rhetorically unified. All systems proclaim the dignity of the human individual and the ideal of a worldwide public order in which this ideal is authoritatively pursued and effectively approximated. They differ in many details of the institutionalized patterns of practice by which they seek to achieve such goals in specific areas and in the world as a whole.

The important point is that varying detailed practices by which over-riding goals are sought need not necessarily be fatal to the future of mankind but can be made creative in promoting and expanding freedom, security, and abundance. The modern world is a caldron of aspiration for a better life on the part of millions of human beings hitherto devoid of any expectation of receiving serious consideration. Unless the institutional details of all systems of public order are open to reconsideration in the light of the contribution that they make to the realization of human dignity in theory and fact, the plight of the world community will remain as precarious as we know it to be today.

Not the least of the institutionalized devices that call for reappraisal are the doctrines and operations having the name of international law. We suggest that major contributions to world order would be the divorce of many of these putative principles from the contexts that give them spurious significance and the vindication of authoritative prescriptions that have genuine relevance to the goal values of human dignity.

The task is a prime responsibility of the scholarly world, and especially of jurisprudence and the social sciences generally. Some of the work has been done by traditional scholars, though too often in scattered and incomplete form. We shall outline a map of the undertaking that we have in mind and in whose execution we invite all like-minded scholars to participate. It will be made evident that we are calling, not for a single research project to be done once and for all, but for a continuing process designed to become part of the intelligence and appraisal functions of the world community. In common with all institutional details this inquiry will be open to perpetual reappraisal.

The map we recommend begins with (a) orienting ourselves in the world social process, (b) identifying within this a process distinctively specialized to power, (c) characterizing as the legal process those decisions that are at once authoritative and controlling, and (d) defining as the public order those features of the whole social process which receive protection by the legal process. From this map we proceed to (e) outline our commitment to the realization of a universal system of public order consistent and compatible with human dignity, (f) analyze the intellectual tasks that confront the scholar who accepts this overriding goal, (g) indicate some of the specific questions that arise in the consideration of any system of public order, and (h) refer to the scholarly procedures by which the task of inquiry can be executed on a satisfactory scale of depth and coverage.[4]

World Social Process

Systems of public order are embedded in a larger context of world events which is the entire social process of the globe. We speak of "process" because there is interaction, of "social" because living beings are the active participants, of "world" because the expanding circles of interaction among men ultimately reach the remotest inhabitants of the globe. Interaction is a matter of going and coming, of buying and selling, of looking and listening, and more. The most far-reaching dimension is the taking of one another into account in the making of choices, whether these choices have to do with comprehensive affairs of state or private concerns of family safety. Such subjective events of mutual assessment tie people into the same process even when they retire behind the ramparts of castles and garrisons to prepare against an eventual day of reckoning.

The participants in the world social process are acting individually in their own behalf and in concert with others with whom they share symbols of common identity and ways of life of varying degrees of elaboration. Whether acting through one channel or the other, the fundamental goal stays ever the same, the maximization of values within the limits of capability. A value is a preferred event; and if we were to begin to list all the specific items of food and drink, of dress, of housing, and of other enjoyments, we should quickly recognize the unwieldiness of the task. Hence for the purpose of comparing individuals and peoples with one another we find it expedient to employ a brief list of categories where there is place for health, safety, and comfort (well-being), for affection, respect, skill, enlightenment, rectitude, wealth, and power. Human beings the world over devote their lives to the incessant shaping and sharing of values, activities which they accomplish by making use of patterns of varying degrees of distinctiveness.

Each identifiable "practice" is a pattern of subjectivities (perspectives) and of operations. The practices which are relatively specialized to the shaping and sharing of value we identify as an "institution." Hence we recognize institutions of government, specialized to the shaping and sharing of power; economic institutions, which focus upon the production, distribution, and consumption of wealth; religious and ethical institutions, specialized to the grounding and specification of responsible conduct; mass media and other institutions of enlightenment; schools of arts, trades, and professions, and associated institutions of skill; pervasive patterns of social class, which are basic institutions of respect; the institutions of family and friendship (affection); and of health, comfort, and safety (well-being). These institutions, organized and unorganized, utilize the resources of nature in greater or less degree in the shaping and sharing of preferred outcomes of the social process.

When we consider the globe as a whole, we perceive that it is composed of communities of diverse size and degrees of institutional distinctiveness (culture). A short time ago Western Europe and North America were the sole possessors of modern science and technology, and of related patterns of culture. Today the culture of science is spreading toward universality as ancient civilizations are revived and the relatively isolated folk societies of Asia, Africa, South America, and the Pacific come within the orbit of modernization and industrialization.

World Power Process

Within the vast social process of man pursuing values through institutions utilizing resources, we are especially concerned with the characteristic features of the power process. A social situation relatively specialized to the shaping and sharing of power outcomes is an "arena"; and it is evident that the world at any given cross section in time is a series of arenas ranging in comprehensiveness from the globe as a whole through great continental, hemispheric, and oceanic clusters to nation states, provinces, and cities and on down to the humblest village and township. The identifying characteristic of an arena is a structure of expectations shared among the members of a community. The assumption is that a decision process occurs in the community; that is, choices affecting the community are made which, if opposed, will in all probability be enforced against opposition. Enforcement implies severe sanction.

When we scrutinize an arena in more detail, going beyond the minimum necessary for bare definitional purposes, it is possible to identify several categories of participants. Some are official organizations or governments —national and international. Others are specialized to bring influence to bear upon those who make the important decisions (political parties, political orders, pressure groups, gangs). Some are associations which, though active in the social process, do not concentrate upon power but primarily seek other values. The ultimate actor is always the individual human being who may act alone or through any organization.

Whatever the type of participants—group or individual—the actual conduct of participants in the power process depends in part upon their perspectives, which are value demands, group identifications and expectations. They may demand, for example, a rising standard of living; and the rising standard may be sought on behalf of the family with which one is identified, or on the basis of identification with depressed classes in a community. Demands may be accompanied by structures of expectation that place great reliance upon strategies of persuasion (or coercion) as the most likely means of influencing results.

Each participant has at his disposal values that he employs as bases for the influencing of outcomes. An inventory discloses that all values— power, wealth, respect, and so on—may be used to affect a decision outcome.

Base values are made effective by the strategies used to affect outcomes. Strategies are often classified according to the degree to which they rely upon symbols or material resources. Diplomacy depends primarily upon symbols in the form of offers, counteroffers, and agreements among elite figures. Ideological strategy also uses symbols as the principal means of action, the distinctive mode being communications which are directed to large audiences. Economic instruments are goods and services; military strategy employs weapons. Every strategy uses indulgences (such as economic aid to allies) or deprivations (such as boycott of unfriendly powers), and proceeds in isolation or coalition. The coalitions within an arena at a given time reflect the number and strength of the participants interacting in the arena. During the nineteenth century the world arena was dominated by a few great powers; in recent times the structure has to an increasing degree been bipolar.

The strategies of participants succeed or fail in the degree to which they culminate in military victory or defeat, or in the winning or losing of votes in intergovernmental organizations or direct negotiation among nation states.

The outcomes affect the value position of every participant in the world context in terms of every value and institutional practice. In addition, postoutcome effects may change the basic composition and modes of operation of the entire world community.

The Legal Process

Within the decision-making process our chief interest is in the legal process, by which we mean the making of authoritative and controlling decisions. Authority is the structure of expectation concerning who, with what qualifications and mode of selection, is competent to make which decisions by what criteria and what procedures. By control we refer to an effective voice in decision, whether authorized or not. The conjunction of common expectations concerning authority with a high degree of corroboration in actual operation is what we understand by law.

In order to identify and compare the role of law in the processes of power it is serviceable to distinguish seven functional phases of decision-making and execution. (1) *Prescription* is the articulation of general requirements of conduct. Among the organs specialized to this function are constitutional conventions and legislatures. International law is articulated principally in the daily activities of foreign offices as they justify or attack, accept or reject, the claims put forward by themselves or others. Prior in time to prescription in a given sequence is (2) *recommendation,* or the promoting of prescriptions. This function is actively performed by such official and semi-official bodies as international governmental organizations, national and transnational political parties, and pressure groups. Also the (3) *intelligence* function is typically prior in time to prescription or recommendation; it includes the gathering and processing of information about past events and the making of estimates of the future, especially of the costs and gains of alternative policies. Official organs of intelligence are partly specialized to secret intelligence; but a very large part is open, and in free countries is very largely supplied by the press and by research and scholarly agencies. Since its founding, the United Nations has performed a vast intelligence operation for all. (4) *Invocation* consists in making a preliminary appeal to a prescription in the hope of influencing results. Hence invoking activities are conspicuous in negotiation; they also include the justifying of claims defended or attacked by counsel before tribunals of the world community. Invocation is the function of public officers or the community agents who are confronted by the responsibility for labeling specific patterns of conduct in reference to legal norms. (5) *Application* is the final characterization of a situation in reference to relevant prescriptions. When a court speaks at the end of litigation, or an administrative organ decides a concrete case, each operation is an applying activity. (6) The *appraisal* function formulates the relationship between official aims and subsequent levels of performance. Among special agencies of appraisal are auditors, inspectors, and censors. Although the appraising function might be included with intelligence, its prominence in political controversy justifies independent recognition. The function of (7) *termination* is the putting to an end of authoritative prescriptions and of arrangements arising within them.

A Public Order System

Within the distinctions thus developed, we are able to clarify what is meant by a system of public order. The reference is to the basic features of the social process in a community—including both the identity and pre-ferred distribution pattern of basic goal values, and the implementing institutions—that are accorded protection by the legal process. Since the legal process is among the basic patterns of a community, the public order includes the protection of the legal order itself, with authority being used as a base of power to protect authority.

In this perspective it is evident that our world is composed of a series of community contexts beginning with the globe as a whole and diminish-ing in territorial range and scope. To the extent that it can be demon-strated that the globe as a whole is a public order system, and only to that extent, do we speak of universal international law. To the degree that territories larger than national states comprise a public order system, we refer to regional international law. Great Britain, for example, has figured simultaneously in more than one large region, and if we add the bilateral contexts which in some cases can be regarded as public order systems, Great Britain plays a role in many such configurations. Obviously today it is more accurate to speak of international *laws* or multinational law than of international *law*.

Clearly, systems of public order differ not only in territorial compre-hensiveness but also in the completeness of arrangements in terms of the different value processes regulated, and in the internal balance of compe-tence for decision *inclusive* of the entire area in question and that for de-cision relating *exclusively* to component areas within it. To the extent that there is universal international law some prescriptions are inclusive of the globe; other prescriptions recognize self-direction by smaller units. Re-gional international law has a corresponding separation between region-wide prescriptions and subregional units. Similarly, nation states like the United States distinguish between the inclusiveness of federal authority and the proper domain of the internal states.

Among major distinctions between public order systems are the de-gree to which *specialized organs* have been developed to conduct the decision process in the inclusive territory, and the degree to which the organs employed by each component unit also carry on the decision process for the whole. It requires no demonstration that international law is largely the creation of organs of the latter type, since the bulk of the world legal system has grown up in the "custom" of communicating foreign offices, supplemented by special conferences, and more recently by intergovernmental bodies whose tasks, speaking formalistically, are not "legislative" (that is, are not regarded as performing "prescriptive" functions).

It is not possible at present to describe the public order structure of the world community, since for the most part existing knowledge is fragmentary and noncomparable. Nor can we proceed with confidence to set detailed limits upon the relative completeness of legal systems and hence of systems and near-systems of public order. It is sufficient to say that, whatever lines are drawn between a system that the scientific observer calls "complete" and systems that are "incomplete," the present absence of authoritative and controlling arrangements for minimum security will preclude the acceptance of the entire world community, as at present constituted, from being classified among complete legal systems and hence among complete public orders.

Toward a Universal Order of Human Dignity

Our overriding aim is to clarify and aid in the implementation of a universal order of human dignity. We postulate this goal, deliberately leaving everyone free to justify it in terms of his preferred theological or philosophical tradition.

The essential meaning of human dignity as we understand it can be succinctly stated: it refers to a social process in which values are widely and not narrowly shared, and in which private choice, rather than coercion, is emphasized as the predominant modality of power.

Given this overarching goal and the present posture of world affairs, what can scholars do individually and through the organizations available to them to further the objective? Manifestly, five intellectual tasks are pertinent to the solution of this as of any legal problem.

First, clarification of goal. Clarification can proceed in two directions, in justification of the commitment to the goal or in detailed specification of what is meant in terms of social and power processes, and legal and public order systems. If we were to specify in detail the meaning of "widely shared participation" in social values, we would consider each of the value-institution processes of society in turn.

Second, description of trend. Having clarified the goal of human dignity, the next intellectual task is the discovery of the degree to which historical and contemporary events conform to or deviate from the goal.

Third, analysis of conditioning factors. Simple historical sequences are not enough to provide understanding of the factors which affect decision. We need to ascertain the factors that condition the degree to which goals have been achieved or failed of achievement.

Fourth, projection of future developments. Assuming that our individual or group efforts will not significantly influence the future, what are the probable limits within which goal values will be achieved?

Fifth, invention and consideration of policy alternatives. Assuming that our efforts may have some impact upon the future, what policy alternatives will maximize our goals (at minimum cost in terms of all values)?

Each of these five intellectual tasks may be illustrated in further detail. We begin with the clarification of goals and indicate with a series of questions about each value what we mean by the sharing of values.

Power. To what extent is power widely or narrowly held? E.g. how many members of the community are involved in amending the constitution or enacting other prescriptions; or in the function of intelligence, recommendation, invocation, application, appraisal, termination? (The involvement may be direct, as in referenda, or indirect, as in representation.) To what extent are the processes of adjustment coercive or persuasive? E.g. how intense is the expectation of violence? Of peaceful agreement?

Wealth. To what extent is the economy focused upon savings and investments? Upon rising levels of consumption? Upon shorter hours of work? E.g. what tax and other fiscal measures make for forced saving or discourage saving and investment? Is there compulsory labor? Are there minimum income guarantees?

Respect. What is the commitment to caste or to mobile class forms of society? E.g. does status depend upon position of family at birth? Or upon any other characteristic besides individual merit? To what extent is minimum respect accorded to everyone on the basis of mere membership in the human race, e.g. prohibition of humiliating penalties, protection of privacy, protection of freedom of agreement against official and private limitation? To what extent are individual differences protected when they depend upon government, e.g. protection of reputation?

Well-Being. To what extent is continued increase of numbers encouraged even at the expense of immediate improvement of the values available to individuals? E.g. are birth restrictions promoted or opposed? What are the policies regarding care of the old? To what degree is the living population sought to be protected from mental and physical deprivation, e.g. accident, disease, and defect prevention; prevention of private and public violence? To what degree is the health, comfort, or safety of the population restored after deprivations have occurred, e.g. arrangements for care and cure?

Skill. To what degree is the body politic committed to optimum opportunity for the discovery and cultivation of socially acceptable skills on the part of everyone? E.g. is there universal and equal access to educational facilities? Does the access continue to whatever level the individual is capable (and motivated) to make use of? In what measure does the body politic provide optimum opportunity for the exercise of accepted skills? E.g. are there employment guarantees or suitable levels? Are new skills recognized and assisted readily, e.g. prohibitions upon skill monopolies?

Enlightenment. To what extent does the community protect the gathering, transmission, and dissemination of information, e.g. guarantee freedom of press, of research, of research reporting? To what degree does the community provide positive aid, e.g. encourage the use of competent sources (though not permitting monopoly)?

Rectitude. To what degree does the body politic protect freedom of worship and of religious propaganda? To what extent is positive assistance given to foster freedom of worship and religious propaganda, e.g. aid to doctrinal schools?

Affection. What is the protection given the family and other institutions of congeniality? E.g. what are the barriers against disruption? What affirmative aid is given, e.g. freedom in the choice of partner, in group formation, in financial and other modes of help?

Next we turn to the description of trends. Our concern is for trends throughout the world community with special reference to all the bodies politic, however incomplete their level of political organization. The term "trend" is used to designate the present distribution of goals sought, the degree of their contemporary realization, and the extent to which this realization has become greater or less through time.

It is perhaps obvious that we are not to be satisfied with taking note of the fact that the ideal of human dignity is verbally accepted. We therefore propose to go beyond the dominant beliefs, assumptions, and loyalties (the myth) of any given society and look into its operational technique. It is therefore ultimately necessary to conduct the studies that reveal the true state of affairs throughout the entire social process. Then we can sum up the state of public order according to the degree of effective sharing and the basic institutions that receive protection.

Each value-institution pattern has a specialized system of myth and of operational technique. The myth falls into three parts: doctrine, formula, folklore. Political doctrines, for instance, include the prevailing philosophies of politics and law. Economic doctrines include theoretical justifications of capitalism or socialism. Respect doctrines either justify social class discrimination or the opposite. And every other value has its doctrinal myth.

The political formula takes in all the constitutional, statutory, and other authoritative prescriptions of the legal order that relate to the decision process. It is possible to find corresponding rules for the other values, such as wealth. Some of these rules receive legal backing; others are not supported by the community as a whole but depend solely upon the support of a component group.

The political myth also includes popular lore about the heroes and villains of yesterday and today, and the notable events of history (and the future); similarly, for wealth, enlightenment, and the other values.

The operational technique exhibits the extent to which the perspectives constituting a myth are adhered to or deviated from.

The foregoing categories provide a broad reference frame within which more detailed consideration can be given to the patterns of authority and control, and particularly the patterns of international law, characteristic of each legal system. We shall devote a separate section to the outlining of such questions.

Turning to the third intellectual task, the analysis of conditioning factors, it is necessary to make an inventory of the categories of factors to be investigated by the scholarly community. Scholarship which would be creative must look behind technical formulas and authoritative procedures to the conditions that importantly determine which formulas and procedures are in fact employed. Relevant comparisons must take into account entire contexts rather than rely upon a few isolated variables divorced from the setting in which they occur. We shall go no further than to indicate the five sets of conditioning (interacting) factors that must eventually receive attention. First, we mention *culture,* which is the term that characterizes the most distinctive patterns of value distribution and institutional practice to be found in the world community. Second, *class;* this word covers the position of individuals or groups in terms of the control of values. One may be upper, middle, or lower (elite, mid-elite, or rank and file) in control over each value. Third, *interest;* the word is used to refer to groups less inclusive than a class or unbound by class. Specific occupational skills, for example, may cut across lines of class. Fourth, *personality;* the term designates the basic value orientations, practices, and mechanisms characteristic of an individual. Fifth, *crisis* level; this expression, referring to conflict situations of extreme intensity, applies to each of the foregoing categories, but can be separated for convenience. In addition to those factors which pertain directly to values and institutions, place must be found for the impact of the entire resource environment, and of basic genetic capabilities, upon mankind.

The fourth task, that of projection of future developments that are likely to affect international law, requires a disciplined consideration of past trends conjointly with the available stock of scientific knowledge. One alternative—that of the total extinction of man—we can rule out of consideration for obvious reasons. But there are drastic new developments that we can wisely anticipate, notably in the field of science and technology. We are already in the early phases of penetrating outer space; and it is not too early to consider a range of contingencies which will arise as we come close to planetary exploration. The explosive growth of machine simulators of the brain, of experimental embryology, and of simple devices of contraception have given some intimation of how our fundamental ideas are likely to undergo drastic revision. If one projects present prospects in the physics of particles and energies, one perceives all sorts of major developments affecting man and his resource environment. We shall keep the present discussion within manageable limits by postponing further consideration of these potentialities.

The ever-present question in everyone's mind is whether we can invent or recognize policy alternatives that are likely to move us most rapidly and at least social cost toward a more perfect realization of a universal international law of human dignity. We shall have space to refer to one fundamental alternative to which the present analysis is intended to contribute. If we are to move knowingly and skillfully toward the goal, it will be necessary for the scholarly community to perfect the intelligence and appraisal functions of those who are striving toward the realization of human dignity.

We turn to a more specific consideration of the existing state of affairs.

Comparing International Systems of Public Order

The questions with which we are concerned are those pertinent to the ultimate appraisal of the success or failure of any system of public order as instruments of the overarching goal of human dignity. We are chiefly interested in international systems, and particularly in the external impact of each system. Specific interpretations of many universalistic terms and propositions differ greatly on particular problems. Hence it is especially important to examine the diverse systems of public order whose several commitments affect the flow of events in the world arena.

The following questions about any particular system of public order, to be asked here of any grouping of states, are directed to the identification of its fundamental categories and techniques and to the appraisal of both its inner operations and its external interactions in terms of impact upon the values of human dignity. With respect to each specific inquiry, we ask a double question: What is the proclaimed, explicit myth or implied assumption about myth? How in fact is the proclaimed or assumed myth interpreted and applied in particular instances of social interaction? We are concerned both for what values are expressed in the basic conceptual structure of the system about important problems and for how these concepts are applied in practice to affect the sharing of values and the degree of achievement of the basic goal values.

Relevant questions might be directed toward every aspect of social interaction, including any or all of the traditional problems of international law. For convenience we group questions about the conceptions and applications of any particular system of public order under the following three main headings: (1) Conceptions of Law (including perspectives of authority and techniques of effective control, as well as myth and practice about the interrelations of authority and control); (2) Features of Power Processes Protected by Law; and (3) Features of Basic Value Processes Protected by Law. It may be emphasized again that the questions we ask are intended to be suggestive only and not exhaustive.

1. Conceptions of Law

The important questions here relate to both perspectives of authority and techniques in effective control. Most generally the questions are: What processes, structures, and functions of authority are established or recommended? What processes, structures, and functions of effective control are established or recommended? And what interrelations between authority and effective control are established, assumed, or demanded?[5]

Concerning authority, more specifically, important questions relate to perspectives about both decision-makers and criteria for decision-making.

First, in regard to decision-makers: Who are regarded as authoritative decision-makers and by what processes are they established and identified as authoritative? What is the degree of community participation in such processes of establishment and identification? Are decision-makers in the various authority functions distinguished from parties to the interactions regulated? Do they include both national and international officials? Do they include representatives of nongovernmental groups or parties? Who, with what qualifications, are selected by whom and how? What constitutive, legislative, executive, judicial, and administrative structures of authority are established or recommended? How, in sum, must such structures be appraised in terms of such fundamental *continua* as democracy-despotism, centralization-decentralization, concentration-deconcentration, pluralization-monopolization, and regimentation-individuation?

Second, in reference to criteria for decision: By what distinctive criteria—in terms both of the scope, range, and domain of values affected and of procedures by which decision outcomes are to be brought about—does the system of public order under inquiry recommend that decisions be taken? How are perspectives of authority grounded in terms of fundamental justifications of decision? Are ultimate references to transempirical or empirical events? If transempirical, are the references religious or metaphysical? If metaphysical, idealistic or materialistic? If ultimate reference is empirical, is it to events within or without the social process? If transcendent of the social process, how characterized? If within the social process, is it by unclarified demand for "precedent," "logic," "validity" or other alleged rectitude norms or by systematic reference to expectations about social process values? If reference is to social process values, is demand made for caste or human dignity values? If the system declares an overriding goal of human dignity, what particular values and institutional practices are included in the conception of such a goal? What degrees in the sharing of particular values are specified as required by human dignity? With what degree of universalism or inclusiveness are criteria of authority, whatever their ultimate reference, asserted and demanded? For what "community" is "common interest" proclaimed?

Important questions about criteria for procedures relate both to the structures of authority established or recommended for each policy function indicated above—prescription, intelligence, recommending, invoking, applying, appraising, terminating—and to the impact of the modalities by which each function is performed upon human dignity values. For each function the two most general questions are: What structures of authority (constitutive, legislative, executive, judicial, administrative) are specialized to the performance of this function? How does the performance, which is in fact established or recommended, make impact upon all demanded values? Impressionistic indication of the type of more specific, relevant questions with respect to each function may be indicated *seriatim:*

Prescription. What is the relative reliance, in the performance of this function, upon specialized organizations or tribunals, upon explicit agreement by participants in an arena, and upon unilateral decision by contending participants in the name of "customary law"? What principles and procedures are afforded for expediting the achievement of consensus and the making of agreements? To what "sources" of policy (prior uniformities in behavior and subjectivities of "rightness," general principles of mature systems, considerations of equity and fairness, opinions of the learned, and so on) are unilateral decision-makers authorized to turn in shaping and justifying decision? Does the system purport to accept the notion of "customary law" but reject the inherited general principles of mature societies? To what degree is there community participation in, and acceptance of, all procedures?

Intelligence. How effective and economic are specialized structures in bringing to the attention of decision-makers the information required for rational decision? How widely is available information shared in the community?

Recommending. How many different types of participants are permitted to engage in this function? How open is participation in advocacy of policies or decisions? Are opposition groups permitted or encouraged? Are the mass media of communication accessible to all?

Invoking. What is the degree in equality of access by all types of participants to the invoking machinery of the community? What participants are admitted to what arenas for invoking what prescriptions?

Applying. Is arrangement made or recommended for the impartial, third-party application of community prescriptions? Are appropriate procedures, and dispositions of effective power, afforded for prompt enforcement? Are procedures for enforcement compatible with human dignity?

Appraising. How effective are the structures afforded for appraising the economy and legality of decision? How open is the sharing of results of appraisals? May private groups make appraisals of the legality of government?

Terminating. How efficient is provision for the termination of obsolete prescription? Do the procedures afforded give effective expression to the demands of the people affected? What is the relative reliance upon termination by consensus of the parties affected and upon unilateral decision by one party? Is an appropriate balance sought and achieved between stability in expectations and necessary change, with minimum costs in terms of all values?

Concerning effective control, more specifically, the important general questions are two: What processes, structures, and functions of effective control are brought to bear in support of, and in turn receive reciprocal protection from, authority? And, in contrast, what processes of effective power escape the control of authority? The first of these questions will be developed in some detail below. The second requires only brief illustration. The thrust of the inquiry is whether all participants in power processes and all instruments of policy are effectively made subject to processes of authority.[6] In what degree do political parties, pressure groups, and other private associations achieve a privileged position above the law or become subordinated to the legal process? In what degree are the varying instruments of policy—diplomatic, ideological, economic, military—subjected to or freed from the regime of law? More comprehensive illustration might of course outline detailed inquiry about democracy of access to—and dispersal of information about—effective power processes. The most complete inquiry would parallel that with respect to the process of authority.

2. Features of Power Processes Protected by Law

The first questions here relate to the allocation of competence, protected by processes of authority, between particular states and larger groupings, or the general community of states.[7] What inclusive competence is protected in the general community or larger groupings of states? What exclusive competence is protected in particular states? How economic is the balance achieved for the production and sharing of the values of human dignity for all mankind? Is it the balance which is best calculated to maintain minimum security, in the sense of freedom from intense coercion or threats of such coercion and freedom to promote the greatest production and widest sharing of other values? To what degree does the inclusive competence protected both secure democratic access by peoples to participation in decision-making which affects them and achieve an assumption of responsibility adequate to maintain application of inclusive policies in arenas both internal and external to particular states? To what degree does the exclusive competence protected secure states from arbitrary external intervention and promote freedom for initiative, experiment, and diversity in effective adaptation of policies to all the peculiarities of the most local contexts? Are technical concepts proffered by the particular system under inquiry—such as "international concern," and equivalents, for protecting inclusive competence, and "sovereignty" and equivalents (including "domestic jurisdiction," "independence," "equality," and "nonintervention") for the protection of exclusive competence— designed and interpreted in fact to promote a rational, productive balance between competences? Is "sovereignty," for example, subordinated to or regarded as a part of international law, or is it conceived as a "discretionary power which overrides the law"?[8] Is "international concern" interpreted in practice to protect inclusive decision which is genuinely inclusive, or used as a cloak to conceal arbitrary exclusive decision?

For the more detailed posing of these and other relevant questions, brief reference may be made *seriatim* to each of the important elements or phases in a power process: participants, arenas, bases of power, strategies, outcomes, and effects.

Participants
Which of the effective participants in the world power process are accepted as full participants in processes of authority—that is, given access to authority structures and functions for the protection of their interests and subordinated to authority for ensuring their responsibility to community

policies? Which effective participants are admitted, or subjected, in lesser degree to what authority structures and functions? By what criteria are different types of participants accepted or rejected in varying degree? What territorially organized communities are accepted as authorized participants in what degree? What provision is made for regional groupings of territorial communities? Is the ultimate goal a monolithic "single state" or a pluralism of balanced regions? What role is accorded international governmental organizations? Are they conceded an independent role or regarded as mere diplomatic appendages of states? What role is accorded nongovernmental groups? Are differences made between political parties and other private associations? Are individual human beings a recognized category of participants in processes of authority or are they regarded as mere objects of authority?

Arenas

Are the various particular arenas provided for the performance of authority functions adequate to promote the resolution of controversies by persuasive rather than coercive means and to reduce to a minimum the number of decisions not taken in accordance with authority?

Are special criteria, other than those stipulated for the identification of generally authorized participants, imposed to regulate admission to particular arenas? When a new territorially organized community emerges, by changes in effective control and authoritative arrangements, from an older community, do authoritative prescriptions make a distinction between emergence by consent and by violence? Between indigenous internal change and change stimulated by external intervention by peoples from other communities? Between change in the name of a totalitarian world order and in genuine demand for indigenous freedom? Do relevant prescriptions achieve an economic balance between maintaining security in the larger community and promoting genuine self-direction in the lesser communities?

Are principles and procedures about membership, representation, and credentials stipulated for international government organizations compatible with easy access by all interested participants, or do they create controversy and continuous world tension?

Is provision made for the reciprocal recognition and protection by governmental participants of the private associations they variously charter and foster for the greater production of specific values, such as wealth and enlightenment? How open is the access of individual human beings to governmental arenas, political parties, pressure groups, and private associations?

Are decisions about recognition, membership, representation, and credentials established as inclusive or exclusive?

Bases of Power

A. Resources. By what criteria may exclusive claims to resources such as land masses, internal waters, and air space be established? Is peaceful use and succession protected against violent seizure?

By what criteria is a balance achieved between exclusive and inclusive claims to sharable and strategic resources, such as the oceans, international rivers, international waterways, polar regions, and outer space?[9] Does the balance achieved promote the most productive and conserving use for the benefit of all?

B. *People.* By what criteria are varying degrees of control over people as bases of power honored and protected? What discriminations are permitted between "nationals" and "aliens"? By what criteria may a territorial community impose its nationality upon or withdraw its nationality from an individual for varying purposes? What are the limits upon naturalization and denaturalization? What selective admissions, exclusions, and corrective measures, with respect to both physical access to territory and all value processes, is a territorial community permitted to impose for power purposes upon its nationals and upon aliens? Do relevant prescriptions protect the utmost individual voluntarism in affiliation and activity that is compatible with a reasonable community security?

C. *Institutions.* How adequately are participants protected in their freedom of decision, as to both internal and external arrangements, from external dictation? Are principles of nonintervention fashioned to catch the more subtle modalities of coercion or only the cruder, physical forms? Are protected freedoms appropriately balanced by imposition of responsibility for the maintenance of internal institutions adequate to the performance of community responsibility? Is "self-determination" invoked to secure and protect a genuine self-direction of people or merely as a slogan to promote destruction of existing communities?

Is the equality between states which is protected a real equality in sharing of power and responsibility or is it a pseudo-equality which defers by verbal legerdemain to the security considerations of the greater powers? Is it tacitly expected that discriminations will be made which are not explicitly provided?

Strategies

With respect to each instrument of policy—diplomatic, ideological, economic, and military—what are the prescriptions about who can employ the instrument, with respect to whom, for what objectives, under what conditions, by what methods, and with what intensities in effects?

How adequate are prescriptions for promoting the persuasive, noncoercive use of instruments of policy?[10] Are adequate immunities and facilities afforded to diplomats and others to facilitate negotiation? Does the "peaceful settlement" demanded by a system express a real willingness to compromise and to seek an integrated solution in community of interest or is it a mere tactic in the poising of an opponent for ultimate destruction? Are provisions about the formation, application, interpretation, and termination of agreements rationally designed to protect the reasonable, mutual expectations of parties? When the "validity" of agreements is found not in the mutual expectations of parties but in alleged *objective* conditions, by what criteria is it decided which conditions create validity and which do not?

Do prescriptions contain a clear prohibition of the use of instruments of policy in modalities so coercive that they threaten a target participant's continuing bases of power and independence in decision? Does the prohibition upon too intense coercion extend to all instruments of policy, singly or in combination, or only to the military instruments? Is the use of force limited to the conservation, rather than to the expansion, of values? Do prescriptions in the law of war about permissible combatants, areas of operations, objectives of attack, instruments and means of attack, and degrees of destruction achieve a reasonable balance between humanitarianism and military necessity? Do the prohibitions of coercion and violence impose a community-wide responsibility or are "neutrals" tolerated?[11]

Outcome and Effects
By what criteria—territoriality, nationality, passive personality, protection of special interests, universality, et cetera—are states accorded exclusive competence to prescribe and apply law for particular events or value changes? By what criteria—"acts of state," "immunities," et cetera—is it expected that a state which has acquired effective control over persons or resources will defer in decision to the law prescribed by another state? What varying degrees of competence are accorded states with respect to events within their own territory, in the territory of other states, and in areas open to many or all? Do relevant prescriptions both permit states substantially affected in their community value processes by particular events to assert competence over such events and, when two or more states are so affected, promote compromise by requiring claimants to take into account the degree of involvement of the values of others in the same or comparable events? Do the prescriptions as a whole establish an appropriate stability in the expectations of participants that controversies will be handled in agreed ways without the disruptions of arbitrary assertion of power? Do they achieve an appropriate balance between subordinating nongovernmental participants—individuals and private associations—to inclusive community authority and freeing such participants from parochial and arbitrary restraint for creative initiative in ordered exploitation of the world's resources, sharable and nonsharable?

Do prescriptions about aggregate changes—state and governmental succession—achieve a necessary balance between continuity in the application of general community policy and freedom for local communities to direct internal changes as they deem their unique conditions to require?

3. Features of Basic Value Processes Protected by Law

Ideally our inquiry here should extend to detailed examination of all the remaining community value processes—such as with respect to wealth, enlightenment, respect, well-being, skill, rectitude, and affection or congenial personal relations—in a manner comparable to that employed above with respect to power processes. Such inquiry would survey the degree to which authority has been brought to the protection of claims made with respect to general participation in interactions in which a particular value is shaped and shared, to access to certain particular situations of shaping and sharing, to continuing control of certain values as base values to affect the shaping and sharing of the value demanded, to the employment of strategies of varying degrees of persuasion and coercion in interactions, and to certain outcomes in enjoyment or consumption of the value demanded. An omnipresent question would, of course, be with respect to each detail of every process whether participation is kept open and free to access by all interested parties or reserved as monopoly for a few.

For brief indication of the general method of inquiry we make reference only to a few important questions with respect to certain important values. We begin with "security," in its *maximum* sense of the sum of position, potential, and expectancy with respect to all values, and then proceed to other values.

Security
By "security" we here refer to demands for the maintenance of a public order which affords full opportunity to preserve and increase all values by peaceful procedures, free from more than a minimum level of coercion or threats of such coercion. In terms of the general analysis of power the questions grouped under the rubric of security emphasize not so much the sharing as the mode by which the social process is carried on. Obviously the fundamental goal of human dignity commits us to the minimum use of coercion compatible with the most advantageous net position for all value outcomes.

For inquiry into any particular system, some of the more general questions may be indicated as follows: What policies are recommended as appropriate for the international community in regard to coercion? What objectives are asserted as permissible, and what impermissible, for employment of coercion? What operational meaning is given to proclaimed policies in terms of policies sought in fact? How are proclaimed and actual policies translated into specific conceptions of permissible and impermissible coercion? What, on the one hand, are the recommended conceptions of "aggression," "breaches of the peace," "threats to the peace," and "intervention," and, on the other, of "self-defense," "collective self-defense," and "police action"? Are these concepts given an operational meaning which in fact authorizes, and promotes, the defense of independence and territorial integrity? Are all instruments of coercion, including the techniques of externally instigated *coups d'état,* brought within their compass? What factors in the context of the world arena are recommended to decision-makers for consideration in the making of specific interpretations in concrete instances? What structures of community authority are approved and recommended for application and enforcement of community policies? What recommendations are made about the procedures by which decisions are to be taken? What specific sanctions are approved and recommended for securing conformity to community policies? Is there willingness to place adequate effective power at the disposal of community organization or agency? Is there willingness to take the measures in reference to other values, such as in regard to standards of living, freedom of communication and inquiry, respect for human dignity, which are necessary to predispose peoples to the maintenance of a secure public order?

Wealth—Economic Growth and Trade
The demand of the lower-income groups and nations around the globe to live a better life in the material sense has confronted the world community with most acute problems. Important questions about any projected system of world public order are: Does this order protect an economy which seeks an appropriate division of labor and the development and exploitation of resources on a world (or universal) scale or some lesser scale? By what policies, persuasive and coercive, are resources allocated? Do these policies embrace the most productive sharing of sharable resources? Are appropriate institutions provided for planning and development functions? What balance is achieved between the public and the private control of resources, or between central and decentralized control? Does this balance promote or retard the democratic functioning of other value processes? Are wealth considerations subordinated to the power considerations? How adequate is the protection and regulation of private claims to resources, and of the wealth activities of private associations across state lines? Are appropriate institutions provided for the most productive international exchange? What accommodation is afforded between free markets and state trading?

Respect—The Articulation and Implementation of Human Rights
The criterion of human dignity is most obviously applicable in relations including the degree of effective freedom of choice given to individuals in society. To respect anyone is to protect his choosing function so long as its exercise does not seriously imperil the corresponding freedom of others. For inquiry into how diverse systems of public order have distinctive approaches to all that affects human rights, we suggest questions like: Does this system begin with a presumption in favor of private choice? In favor of privacy? Does it provide equality of access to value processes upon grounds of merit or foster discriminations based upon caste, race, alienage, color, sex, and so on? Does it prohibit or permit value deprivations incompatible with common humanity? Does it provide positive assistance to individuals on the basis of common humanity in overcoming handicaps? For what territorial community does the system demand human right? What specific content does it recommend, or reject, for international prescription, by agreement or by customary derivation? Does this content embrace all or only a few values? How closely does it approximate, exceed, or fall short of such demands as are asserted in the Universal Declaration of Human Rights? What particular modalities, by inclusive decision, for

the implementation of particular human rights does it accept or reject? Is there acceptance of disinterested, third-party decisions?

Enlightenment and Top Skills

It is generally recognized by observers of the world scene that barriers to the gathering, transmission, and dissemination of current information of events around the globe help to sustain the local monopolies of intelligence that stand in the path of peace and order. Further, the enormous significance of scientific and technological know-how has emphasized the importance of prompt enlightenment as to fundamental discoveries about nature or society.

The relevant questions for spotlighting divergence in approach are as above: What positive facilities, governmental and private, are afforded for promoting inquiry, communication, education, and training? How open is access to all processes? Are discriminations made on grounds other than merit? Is freedom of expression, assembly, and association encouraged? Does the system promote the sharing of information, scientific knowledge, and cultural exchange, across state lines? What content and modes of implementation are proposed for international prescription? What limits are imposed upon the use of the ideological instrument for purposes of coercion?

Well-Being

The importance of maintaining optimum standards of safety, health, and comfort is as axiomatic as the interdependence of all peoples with respect to such standards. Relevant questions relate both to the facilities provided— including all degrees of governmental involvement—for medical care, prevention of disease, healthful housing, appropriate food and clothing, sanitation, working conditions, leisure and recreation, et cetera, and for the area of community concern and effective prescription and application of policy.

Rectitude

The reference here is to the consensus in conceptions of right and wrong sufficient to support all other institutional patterns of the world community toward which we aim. A society of human dignity implies a high degree of unity as to goal values and to the noncoercive practices by which goals are clarified and put into effect. More specifically, what is involved is a high degree of effective application in public and private of the formal standards of responsibility which are essential to attain and maintain the desired society.

Immediate questions relate to varying conceptions of individual and collective responsibility in national and international systems of criminal law and to accommodations between diverse systems, by extradition, protection of political offenders, rights of asylum, and so on. Longer-term questions relate to potentialities for adjusting national criminal laws and procedures to more comprehensive unities, for adapting local systems of ethics (with or without religious and metaphysical derivation) to more comprehensive unities, and for adapting prevailing moral sentiments for larger unities. Recurrent inquiry seeks the degree of freedom of choice in beliefs about right and wrong and the adequacy of facilities for the enjoyment of rectitude beliefs.

Affection (Including Loyalties)

Goals here include the development of a sense of belonging to the whole community of mankind and concern for the common good (positive identification), the spread of congenial personal relationships in all groups regardless of cultural or class characteristics, and the development of nondestructive human personalities capable of entering into friendly contact with others. Relevant questions relate to authoritative formulae and procedures affecting the comprehensiveness of loyalties and memberships and the congeniality of personal relations. Of special concern are any potentialities for adapting local doctrinal systems and sentiments to larger loyalties and for adjusting national and international prescriptions for facilitating more comprehensive memberships. The humanitarianism in family law and the degree to which this humanitarianism is projected across state lines are of obvious pertinence.

What the Scholar Does in Gathering and Processing Data

There remain for brief consideration some of the technical problems that relate to the operations by which scholars gather and process the data required to identify and appraise systems of public order. We shall briefly characterize the strategy by which the facts of any given community context can be obtained. Broadly conceived, the most promising strategy of inquiry moves from the well known to the less known, in this case implying that a beginning is made by employing the operations familiar to all legal scholars, then proceeding to the phases of the situation for which the social and behavioral sciences provide the sharpest instruments. Legal scholars in international law must take direct responsibility for the plan as a whole, and for the execution of those parts that require the traditional training of lawyers. It is also essential that the legal scholar work in close association with specialists from related fields whose contributions are called for. Briefly:

Operation 1. Establish the provisional identity of a public order system within a community context by means of an inventory of explicit legal formulae.

The inventory can be made by examining constitutional charters, statutes, and doctrines purportedly applied by decision-makers in specific controversies. What value patterns and basic institutional practices are given *explicit* protection or aid in fulfillment? What value-institution patterns receive *implicit* support (that is, what does the scholar infer from the formal material, even though the language is somewhat ambiguous)?

By extending research through past time, changes of trend in the public order system, as tentatively understood, can be described.

Operation 2. Add accuracy and detail to the inventory obtained by means of *Operation 1* by describing the frequency with which each prescription found in the legal formulae is invoked or purportedly applied in controversies.

In the formal decision process authoritative prescriptions are mentioned with varying degrees of frequency by the parties who seek to justify their claims, and by decision-makers who are performing functions of invocation or application. It is also true that authoritative prescriptions may be ignored in circumstances to which they refer (as viewed by the scholar-observer). It is pertinent also to note that authoritative language is often referred to *outside* the formal decision process (for instance, between private negotiators). Moreover, prescriptions *might* have been used in factual situations outside the legal process, though actually no one invoked them in controversies difficult if not impossible to distinguish from those which were eventually brought to the formal attention of decision-makers.

The data gathered by *Operation 2* makes it possible to relate the language of authority more directly to the facts of control. As a matter of definition it will often be clarifying for the scholar to specify the minimum level of frequency of invocation and purported application that he requires before accepting a particular pattern of authority and control as "law." The information assembled by *Operation 2* makes it feasible to classify specific authoritative statements, not only as law but as obsolete or obsolescent or emergent law. By extending research historically the trends in the role of each statement can be revealed.

Operation 3. Analyze all other sources for the purpose of making a fuller identification of the systems of public order provisionally revealed by the preceding operations. Describe the legal process in the context of the decision process as a whole, and of the social process within the entire community context.

Most of the scholarly effort at this phase is devoted to obtaining data by methods that are not conventional to traditionally trained legal scholars. Hence reliance is put upon the finding of specialists upon the value-institution processes of wealth, respect, well-being, and so on. Likewise specialists upon the inherited nature of man and the physical resources by which he is surrounded, and with which he interacts, are to be made use of. The data obtained in *Operations 1 and 2*, which deal with aspects of the legal process, must be put in the context of all categories of significant factors (culture, class, interest, personality, crisis).[12]

To some extent the procedures of data-gathering in *Operation 3* will be the interview or participant observation. Insofar as materials must be gathered which are residues of the historical process, the basic methods are those familiar to historians. The growing application of experimental method has resulted in the use of "pre-tests" whose purpose is to reveal the direction and intensity of the predispositions current in a given group. These devices open up the future possibility of proceeding in more informed fashion to devise facilitating strategies for the realization of public order objectives.

All the facts assembled in each operation above will of course be contributory to the five intellectual tasks to be performed by scholars in the fields of international law. The data will interact with the clarification of values, the characterization of trend, the analysis of conditioning factors, the projection of future developments, and the invention and appraisal of alternative policies for the optimum realization of the clarified values of human dignity.

The Contemporary Challenge to Scholars

For some decades scholars of international law have been preoccupied with the task of establishing that the subject of their professional concern was in fact law and could not be dismissed as a miscellany of maxims principally useful for the admonishing of decision-makers to act ethically. The implicit assumption appears to have been that unless the universality of international law is established, there is no international law whatsoever; and further, that the most effective means of moving the world toward a universal body of law is to assert its contemporary reality in fact.

It is high time that the community of scholars abandon a conception of their role in history whose principal effect is to condemn them to inaccuracy and futility. The inaccuracy consists in the assertion of universality in fact, and relative futility is demonstrated by the contemporary division of the globe into diverse systems of public order whose leaders use the appeal to universality as a pawn and a screen in the tactics of world power.

The challenge to scholars is to resume their proper function, which is to assist all who will listen to distinguish clearly between the current facts of the global context and estimates of future developments—and between estimates of policy alternatives that will merely move the world closer to some universal system of law and public order, however unfree, and alternatives that will in fact foster the common objective so frequently proclaimed by the authorized spokesmen of existing nation states—namely, the goal of realizing human dignity in theory and fact.

More specifically the challenge to scholars of international law is twofold: (1) to develop a jurisprudence—a comprehensive theory and appropriate methods of inquiry—which will assist the peoples of the world to distinguish public orders based on human dignity and public orders based either on a law which denies human dignity or a denial of law itself for the simple supremacy of naked force; and (2) to invent and recommend the authority structures and functions (principles and procedures) necessary to a world public order that harmonizes with the growing aspirations of the overwhelming numbers of the peoples of the globe and is in accord with the proclaimed values of human dignity enunciated by the moral leaders of mankind.

In this perilous epoch of threatened catastrophe legal scholars have an opportunity of unparalleled urgency to assist in performing at least two indispensable functions: the functions of providing intelligence and of making recommendations to all who have the will and capability of decision.

As old orders crumble and dissolve under the ever-accelerating impact of scientific, technological, and other changes, the future becomes increasingly plastic in our hands, holding out the possibility of molding a world order nearer to the aspirations of human dignity, or of losing out to the most ruthless and comprehensive tyranny that man has ever known.

The impact of scholarly research and analysis can be to disclose to as many as possible of the effective leaders, and constituencies of leaders, throughout the globe the compatibility between their aspirations and the policies that expedite peaceful cooperation on behalf of a public order of human dignity. In a sense the present incompatibility is already obvious to every individual who possesses even a modicum of authentic information about the chronic threat of accidental as well as deliberate disaster. Besides the aspiration to remain alive, and to keep family and nation alive, there are legitimate aspirations to remain in a potent power position for all values. Research and analysis can indicate to the leader even of non-democratic regimes which policies, if adopted, are likely to maintain them in an advantageous position, as they guide their peoples through peaceful transitions toward a more perfect realization of public orders of freedom and responsibility on a local and global scale.

Scholars are in a position to make, to apply, and to disseminate awareness of the basic distinction between preferred goals and specific institutions. The goal of widespread participation in all values throughout the social process is the fundamental criterion of policy. This must receive specific form, for example, in institutional practices of popular government, of graduated income distribution, and of an open class system. It is of the utmost importance that particular institutional devices shall be open to continuous and competent investigation to assess the actual contribution that they are making to the overriding goal. Productive controversy can rage over the definition of human dignity in specific institutional terms, and also over the technical measurements applied by scholars to the appraisal of their operations. Instead of institutional symbols such as "capitalism" versus "socialism," "territorial" versus "functional" representation, "centralized" versus "decentralized" planning, considered abstractly and affirmed dogmatically, the focus of attention and debate can usefully shift to the appraisal of contemporary structures according to their positive or negative impact upon present and prospective value-shaping and sharing.

The task of appraisal, as we have continually emphasized, is more than the examination of statues, treaties, regulations, and proclaimed judicial doctrines. The relevant context that requires investigation is the constellation of factors affecting the creation and interpretation of authoritative language throughout the entire decision process. Under ascertainable circumstances appropriately authoritative language can foster the realization of effective systems of public order at every level of inclusiveness up to and including the community of mankind, systems consistent and compatible with the overriding goal of human dignity. As a contemporary step in the direction of such universality it is imperative that spokesmen for the field of international law cease proclaiming the present universality of international law and drop the assumption that it is a matter of indifference what system of public order achieves universality. This is the challenging opportunity that "our time of trouble" and "age of anxiety" offers to all scholars everywhere.

Notes

1. Criteria have not been elaborated for even preliminary identification of existing international systems, which vary in territorial spread from two-power arrangements upward toward demanded or asserted universality. Suggestions are variously made in the literature of possibly useful classifications of systems in such terms as Western European (and North Atlantic), American (North, South), Soviet (European, Asian), British Commonwealth, Islamic, Hindu, Burmese, Southeastern Asian, and so on.

2. The common assumption is thus stated in Sauer, "Universal Principles in International Law," 42 Tr. Grotius Soc. 181 (1957): "It goes without saying that the notion of present-day international law implies universality because this law means a law for all nations of the world." Dr. Sauer notes a certain shrinkage, however, and observes "that the present condition of universal international law is a sad one." Id. 184.

The "universality" asserted or demanded, too often in attempted self-fulfilling description, by different writers and spokesmen exhibits of course many varying nuances in reference. Sometimes reference is made to the range of participants alleged to be subject to authoritative prescription and it is insisted that a single international law governs Western and non-Western, Christian and non-Christian, or Communist and non-Communist, states alike. On other occasions the emphasis in reference is upon alleged uniformity in application of prescriptions—that is, that the same results are achieved in the same or comparable contexts when the only difference lies in the identity of the parties to the controversy. Still again "universality" may merely express a demand that all states accept and implement the same set of policies relating to their external interactions. On rare occasions, the reference is explicitly and candidly to mere words, accompanied by demands that future interpretations of the words be made to conform to the requirements of a projected world order. Cf. Dickinson, Law and Peace 122 (1951).

3. For depiction and analysis see Katzenbach, "Conflicts on an Unruly Horse: Reciprocal Claims and Tolerances in Interstate and International Law," 65 Yale L.J. 1087 (1956): Yntema, "The Objectives of Private International Law," 31 Canadian Bar Rev. 721 (1957).

4. For background and development of social process analysis with special reference to law and politics see, among other studies, Lasswell and McDougal,

"Legal Education and Public Policy: Professional Training in the Public Interest," in McDougal & Associates, Studies in World Public Order 42 (1960): Lasswell and Kaplan, Power and Society (1950).

5. We recognize of course that authority and control may overlap and it is indeed precisely this overlap that we recommend as the most useful reference of the word "law." The asking of separate questions about authority and control may, we hope, promote realism in inquiry about their interrelations.

6. Cf. Lipson, "The New Face of Socialist Legality," 7 Problems of Communism (No. 4, July-August 1958) 22, 29:

> What the reformers have not touched and will not touch is the political basis that necessarily prevents "socialist legality," Soviet-style, from meeting the standards of legality upheld by other countries. There will be no sure legal guarantees that the *troikas* and purges will not recur, that the cult of (some other) personality will not again become the religion of the state, and that terror will not lay waste another generation of Soviet citizens; indeed, there can be none as long as the party, and the elements of Soviet society striving for supremacy through or against the party, remain unwilling to grant effective autonomy to the legal system, keeping it above the political struggle as a safeguard of general order and liberty.

7. It is convenient to use the traditional words, "general community of states," without imputation of universality, to refer to the largest grouping seeking common values.

8. Jenks, The Common Law of Mankind 120 (1958).

9. These questions are developed in more detail in McDougal & Burke, "Crisis in the Law of the Sea: Community Perspectives Versus National Egoism," in M. McDougal & Associates, Studies in World Public Order 844 (1960): McDougal & Lipson, "Perspectives for a Law of Outer Space," id. 912.

10. The distinction between persuasion and coercion may be clarified in terms of the number and cost of alternatives open to a participant. By persuasion we refer to interactions which leave open a number of alternatives with expectations of high gain and low cost. By coercion we refer to interactions which leave open few alternatives, with expectations of little or no gain and high costs.

We assume that the participants consciously pursue a range of realizable alternatives in representative situations in the social process. This assumption is necessary to indicate that people who have been trained to demand and expect few alternatives are not free.

11. More detailed inquiry is outlined in McDougal & Feliciano, "International Coercion and World Public Order: The General Principles of the Law of War," in McDougal & Associates, Studies in World Public Order 237 (1960).

12. Compact summaries of the methods and findings of contemporary social science can be found in UNESCO's International Science Bulletin. See further Lasswell, "The Scientific Study of International Relations," 12 Y.B. of World Affairs 1 (1958).

Selected Bibliography

Prominent Works on the New Haven School

Lasswell, Harold D., and Myres McDougal. "Legal Education and Public Policy: Professional Training in the Public Interest," *Yale Law Journal* 52 (1943): 203–95. (articulation of original plan)

McDougal, Myres S. "International Law, Power and Policy: A Contemporary Conception," *Recueil des Cours* 82 (1953). (McDougal's Hague lecture)

———. "International Law and Social Science: A Mild Plea in Avoidance," *American Journal of International Law* 66 (1972): 77–81.

———. "Law as a Process of Decision: A Policy-Oriented Approach to Legal Study," *Natural Law Forum* 1 (1956): 53ff.

———. "The Policy-Science Approach to International Legal Studies," in *Lectures on International Law and the United Nations* (1957).

———. "The Role of Law in World Politics," *Mississippi Law Journal* 20 (1949): 253–83.

———. "Some Basic Theoretical Concepts About International Law: A Policy-Oriented Framework for Inquiry," *Journal of Conflict Resolution* 4 (1960): 337–54.

———, and Harold D. Lasswell. "The Identification and Appraisal of Diverse Systems of Public Order," *American Journal of International Law* 53 (1959): 1–29.

———, Harold D. Lasswell, and W. Michael Reisman. "Theories About International Law: Prologue to a Configurative Jurisprudence," *Virginia Journal of International Law* 8 (1968): 188–299.

———, and W. Michael Reisman. "International Law in Policy-Oriented Perspective," in Ronald St. J. Macdonald and Douglas M. Johnston, eds., *The Structure and Process of International Law* (1983): 103–30.

———, and W. Michael Reisman. "The World Constitutive Process of Authoritative Decision," *Journal of Legal Education* 19 (1967): 253–300, 403–37.

———, and W. Michael Reisman, eds. *International Law Essays: A Supplement to International Law in Contemporary Perspective* (1981).

———, et al. *Studies in World Public Order* (1960). (collection of most of McDougal's important early work)

Reisman, W. Michael, and Burns H. Weston, eds. *Toward World Order and Human Dignity* (1976). (includes a complete bibliography of McDougal's work through 1976)

Recent Applications of the New Haven Approach

Chen, Lung-Chu. *An Introduction to Contemporary International Law: A Policy-Oriented Perspective* (1989).

Falk, Richard A. *Explorations at the Edge of Time* (1992).

———. "Introduction," in Richard A. Falk and Hanreider, eds., *International Law and International Organization* (1968).

———. *The Status of Law in International Society* (1970).

Kothari, Rajni. *Footsteps into the Future: Diagnosis of the Present World and a Design for an Alternative* (1974).

Mendlovitz, Saul H. *On the Creation of a Just World Order: Preferred Worlds for the 1990s* (1975).

Moore, John Norton. "The Secret War in Central America and the Future of World Order," *American Journal of International Law* 80 (1986): 43–127.

Reviews of the New Haven Approach

Anderson, Stanley V. "A Critique of Professor Myres S. McDougal's Doctrine of Interpretation by Major Purposes," *American Journal of International Law* 57 (1963): 378–83.

Dorsey, Gray L. "The McDougal-Lasswell Proposal to Build a World Public Order," *American Journal of International Law* 82 (1988): 41–51.

Falk, Richard A. "McDougal and Feliciano's Law and Minimum World Public Order," *Natural Law Forum* 8 (1963): 171–84.

Gottlieb, Gidon. "The Conceptual World of the Yale School of International Law," *World Politics* 21 (1968): 120–29.

Reisman, W. Michael, Oscar Schachter, and Burns H. Weston. "McDougal's Jurisprudence: Utility, Influence, Controversy," *Proceedings of the American Society of International Law* 79 (1985): 266–80.

Schechter, Michael G. "The New Haven School of International Law, Regime Theorists, Their Critics and Beyond." Paper presented at the Annual Meeting of the ISA, March 1993.

Stone, Julius. "Policy-Oriented World Power Process," *Hastings International and Comparative Law Review* 7 (1984): 273–92.

Tipson, Frederick S. "The Lasswell-McDougal Enterprise: Toward a World Order of Human Dignity," *Virginia Journal of International Law* 14 (1974): 535–85.

Trimble, Phillip R. "International Law, World Order, and Critical Legal Studies," *Stanford Law Review* 42 (1990): 811–45.

Young, Oran R. "International Law and Social Science: The Contributions of Myres S. McDougal," *American Journal of International Law* 60 (1972): 60–76.

6

Structural Realism

According to Kenneth N. Waltz, a founder of the approach, Structural Realism "presents a systematic portrait of international politics depicting component units according to the manner of their arrangement."[1] States, which are deemed the major actors in world affairs, are conceived as unitary actors motivated primarily by the will to survive. Anarchy—the absence of a central monopoly of legitimate force—is the essential structural quality of the system. This structural quality provides an adequate explanation both for competition of states and for the observable though severely limited instances of state cooperation. International regimes, institutions, rules, and norms are not independent causal factors, according to the Structural Realists (or "Neorealists"), and affect the prospects for international cooperation only at the margins.

Waltz has noted several ways in which Structural Realism differs from the Classical Realist approach.[2] First, it is considerably more theoretically ambitious. The essential insight of E. H. Carr, Hans Morgenthau, and other Classical Realists was that international politics was necessarily power politics, conducted in an anarchical setting. Because of their healthy respect for the contingent aspects of international life, they believed little systematic theory concerning international relations was possible. Without abandoning the essential insights of Classical Realists, the Structuralists have sought to elaborate a theory of international politics that takes account of its anarchical and contingent nature, rather than rejecting the theoretical enterprise altogether.

Second, while Classical Realism posits power as the primary utility function of states and suggests that a rational state will always seek to maximize its power, Structural Realists contend that survival and security are the ends of states, and power merely useful as a means to those ends.

This requires a more complex conception of the levers of international behavior, one that takes account of the structure and historical position in which a state finds itself. For power maximization will not benefit a state in every instance (e.g., when it provokes an arms race), and states employ a variety of means in seeking to ensure their survival.

Ultimately, Structural Realists are distinguished from Classical Realists by their focus on systemic or structural causes of conflict and cooperation in international relations. Classical Realists are not unconcerned with the extent to which systemic characteristics, such as the scarcity of resources in an anarchical world, can contribute to international conflict. However, Classical Realists tend to focus more attention on the characteristics of states that lead to conflict than on the characteristics of the system. Morgenthau, for instance, speaks eloquently of "the *animus dominandi*, the desire for power," which is deeply rooted in human nature and manifests itself in the affairs of states. Structural Realists, on the other hand, look to systemic factors for the cause of international conflict, and reject the assumption that lust for power inherent in human nature is a sufficient explanation for such conflict. According to Waltz: "In an anarchic domain, a state of war exists if all parties lust for power. But so too will a state of war exist if all states seek only to ensure their own safety."[3]

These distinctions between Structural Realism and Classical Realism, however, receive scant attention from Structuralists in comparison with the attention devoted to distinguishing Realism from the newer Institutionalist approaches. Some of these Institutionalists seek to appropriate, even to co-opt, the essential insights of the Classical Realists and to harness them in support of Institutionalist ends. The article by Joseph M. Grieco reprinted in this chapter is an outstanding example of the effort by Neorealists to reestablish the essential linkage between the Classical Realist insights and uniquely Realist conclusions.

By beginning with an insufficiently robust notion of the implications of international anarchy and an excessively atomistic conception of states as actors on the international stage, the Institutionalists, Grieco argues, have failed to engage the full ramifications of Realist insights they claim to accept. Structural Realists consider states to be *positional* actors, motivated not so much by the prospect of absolute gains as the need to maintain or enhance their position vis-à-vis other states in order to ensure survival. This is the element of Realist thought that is lost on Institutionalists, Grieco argues.

The debate between Structural Realists and Institutionalists, then, is primarily concerned with the relative explanatory power of the approaches. The primary project for Structural Realists is less one of prescription than of explanation and prediction. The debate does, however, have significant implications for the possibility of international prescription and normative constraint. By its stark emphasis on the causal effect of the structure of international relations in determining real-world outcomes, the Structural approach implicitly diminishes the potential domain of prescriptive and normative causation—the primary domain of international rules. Hence, Waltz's systemic Realism leaves little or no room for international rules as independent causal agents; such rules are merely epiphenomenal.

Notes

1. Kenneth N. Waltz, "The Origins of War in Neorealist Theory," *Journal of Interdisciplinary History* 18 (1988): 618.

2. Ibid., pp. 615–17.

3. Ibid., p. 620.

JOSEPH M. GRIECO

Anarchy and the Limits of Cooperation: A Realist Critique of the Newest Liberal Institutionalism

Realism has dominated international relations theory at least since World War II.[1] For realists, international anarchy fosters competition and conflict among states and inhibits their willingness to cooperate even when they share common interests. Realist theory also argues that international institutions are unable to mitigate anarchy's constraining effects on inter-state cooperation. Realism, then, presents a pessimistic analysis of the prospects for international cooperation and of the capabilities of international institutions.

The major challenger to realism has been what I shall call liberal institutionalism. Prior to the current decade, it appeared in three successive presentations—functionalist integration theory in the 1940s and early 1950s, neofunctionalist regional integration theory in the 1950s and 1960s, and interdependence theory in the 1970s.[2] All three versions rejected realism's propositions about states and its gloomy understanding of world politics. Most significantly, they argued that international institutions can help states cooperate. Thus, compared to realism, these earlier versions of liberal institutionalism offered a more hopeful prognosis for international cooperation and a more optimistic assessment of the capacity of institutions to help states achieve it.

International tensions and conflicts during the 1970s undermined liberal institutionalism and reconfirmed realism in large measure. Yet, that difficult decade did not witness a collapse of the international system, and, in the light of continuing modest levels of inter-state cooperation, a new liberal institutionalist challenge to realism came forward during the early 1980s.[3] What is distinctive about this newest liberal institutionalism is its claim that it accepts a number of core realist propositions, including, apparently, the realist argument that anarchy impedes the achievement of international cooperation. However, the core liberal arguments—that realism overemphasizes conflict and underestimates the capacities of international institutions to promote cooperation—remain firmly intact. The new liberal institutionalists basically argue that even if the realists are correct in believing that anarchy constrains the willingness of states to cooperate, states nevertheless can work together and can do so especially with the assistance of international institutions.

From *International Organization* 42 (1988). Reprinted by permission of the MIT Press, Cambridge, Mass. Some notes have been altered.

This point is crucial for students of international relations. If neo-liberal institutionalists are correct, then they have dealt realism a major blow while providing the intellectual justification for treating their own approach, and the tradition from which it emerges, as the most effective for understanding world politics.

This essay's principal argument is that, in fact, neoliberal institutionalism misconstrues the realist analysis of international anarchy and therefore it misunderstands the realist analysis of the impact of anarchy on the preferences and actions of states. Indeed, the new liberal institutionalism fails to address a major constraint on the willingness of states to cooperate which is generated by international anarchy and which is identified by realism. As a result, the new theory's optimism about international cooperation is likely to be proven wrong.

Neoliberalism's claims about cooperation are based on its belief that states are atomistic actors. It argues that states seek to maximize their individual *absolute* gains and are indifferent to the gains achieved by others. Cheating, the new theory suggests, is the greatest impediment to cooperation among rationally egoistic states, but international institutions, the new theory also suggests, can help states overcome this barrier to joint action. Realists understand that states seek absolute gains and worry about compliance. However, realists find that states are *positional*, not atomistic, in character, and therefore realists argue that, in addition to concerns about cheating, states in cooperative arrangements also worry that their partners might gain more from cooperation than they do. For realists, a state will focus both on its absolute and relative gains from cooperation, and a state that is satisfied with a partner's compliance in a joint arrangement might nevertheless exit from it because the partner is achieving relatively greater gains. Realism, then, finds that there are at least two major barriers to international cooperation: state concerns about cheating and state concerns about relative achievements of gains. Neoliberal institutionalism pays attention exclusively to the former, and is unable to identify, analyze, or account for the latter.

Realism's identification of the relative gains problem for cooperation is based on its insight that states in anarchy fear for their survival as independent actors. According to realists, states worry that today's friend may be tomorrow's enemy in war, and fear that achievements of joint gains that advantage a friend in the present might produce a more dangerous *potential* foe in the future. As a result, states must give serious attention to the gains of partners. Neoliberals fail to consider the threat of war arising from international anarchy, and this allows them to ignore the matter of relative gains and to assume that states only desire absolute gains. Yet, in doing so, they fail to identify a major source of state inhibitions about international cooperation.

In sum, I suggest that realism, its emphasis on conflict and competition notwithstanding, offers a more complete understanding of the problem of international cooperation than does its latest liberal challenger. If that is true, then realism is still the most powerful theory of international politics.

1. Realism and Liberal Institutionalism

Realism encompasses five propositions. First, states are the major actors in world affairs. Second, the international environment severely penalizes states if they fail to protect their vital interests or if they pursue objectives beyond their means; hence, states are "sensitive to costs" and behave as unitary-rational agents. Third, international anarchy is the principal force shaping the motives and actions of states. Fourth, states in anarchy are preoccupied with power and security, are predisposed towards conflict and competition, and often fail to cooperate even in the face of common interests. Finally, international institutions affect the prospects for cooperation only marginally.

Liberal institutionalists sought to refute this realist understanding of world politics. First, they rejected realism's proposition about the centrality of states. For functionalists, the key new actors in world politics appeared to be specialized international agencies and their technical experts; for neofunctionalists, they were labor unions, political parties, trade associations, and supranational bureaucracies; and for the interdependence school, they were multinational corporations and transnational and transgovernmental coalitions. Second, liberal institutionalists attacked the realist view that states are unitary or rational agents. Authority was already decentralized within modern states, functionalists argued, and it was undergoing a similar process internationally. Modern states, according to interdependence theorists, were increasingly characterized by "multiple channels of access," which, in turn, progressively enfeebled the grip on foreign policy previously held by central decision makers.

Third, liberals argued that states were becoming less concerned about power and security. Internationally, nuclear weapons and mobilized national populations were rendering war prohibitively costly. Moreover, increases in inter-nation economic contacts left states increasingly dependent upon one another for the attainment of such national goals as growth, full employment, and price stability. Domestically, industrialization had created the present "social century": the advanced democracies (and, more slowly, socialist and developing countries) were becoming welfare states less oriented towards power and prestige and more towards economic growth and social security. Thus, liberals rejected realism's fourth proposition that states are fundamentally disinclined to cooperate, finding instead that states increasingly viewed one another not as enemies, but instead as partners needed to secure greater comfort and well-being for their home publics.

Finally, liberal institutionalists rejected realism's pessimism about international institutions. For functionalist theory, specialized agencies like the International Labor Organization could promote cooperation because they performed valuable tasks without frontally challenging state sovereignty. For neofunctionalist theory, supranational bodies like the European Economic Community were "the appropriate regional counterpart to the national state which no longer feels capable of realizing welfare goals within its own narrow borders."[4] Finally, interdependence theory suggested that "in a world of multiple issues imperfectly linked, in which coalitions are formed transnationally and transgovernmentally, the potential role of international institutions in political bargaining is greatly increased."[5]

Postwar events, and especially those of the 1970s, appeared to support realist theory and to invalidate liberal institutionalism. States remained autonomous in setting foreign policy goals; they retained the loyalty of government officials active in "transgovernmental networks"; and they recast the terms of their relationships with such seemingly powerful transnational actors as high-technology multinational corporations. Industrialized states varied in their economic performance during the 1970s in the face of similar challenges (oil shortages, recession, and inflation). Scholars linked these differences in performance to divergences, and not convergence, in their domestic political–economic structures. A number of events during the 1970s and early 1980s also demonstrated that the use of force continued to be a pervasive feature of world politics: increases in East–West tensions and the continuation of the Soviet–American arms competition; direct and indirect military intervention and counter-intervention by the superpowers in Africa, Central America, and Southwest Asia; and the Yom Kippur and Iran–Iraq wars. International institutions appeared to be unable to reshape state interest; instead, they were often embroiled in and paralyzed by East–West and North–South disputes. Finally, supranationalism in West Europe was replaced by old-fashioned intergovernmental bargaining, and the advanced democracies frequently experienced serious trade and monetary conflicts and sharp discord over economic relations with the Soviet Union.

And yet, international cooperation did not collapse during the 1970s as it had during the 1930s. In finance, private banks and governments in developed countries worked with the International Monetary Fund to contain the international debt crisis. In trade, the advanced states completed the Tokyo Round negotiations under the General Agreement on Tariffs and Trade. In energy, the advanced states failed to coordinate responses to the oil crises of 1973–1974 and 1979, but cooperated effectively—through the International Energy Agency—following the outbreak of the Iran–Iraq war in 1980. Finally, in high technology, the European states initiated and pursued during the 1970s a host of joint projects in high technology such as Airbus Industrie, the ARIANE rocket program, and the ESPRIT information technology effort. Governments had not transformed their foreign policies, and world politics were not in transition, but *states* achieved cooperation through *international institutions* even in the harsh 1970s. This set the stage for a renewed, albeit truncated, liberal challenge to realism in the 1980s.

2. The New Liberal Institutionalism

In contrast to earlier presentations of liberal institutionalism, the newest liberalism accepts realist arguments that states are the major actors in world affairs and are unitary–rational agents. It also claims to accept realism's emphasis on anarchy to explain state motives and actions. Robert Axelrod, for example, seeks to address this question: "Under what conditions will cooperation emerge in a world of egoists without central authority?"[6] Similarly, Axelrod and Robert Keohane observe of world politics that "there is no common government to enforce rules, and by the standards of domestic society, international institutions are weak."[7]

Yet neoliberals argue that realism is wrong to discount the possibilities for international cooperation and the capacities of international institutions. Neoliberals claim that, contrary to realism and in accordance with traditional liberal views, institutions can help states work together. Thus, neoliberals argue, the prospects for international cooperation are better than realism allows. These points of convergence and divergence among the three perspectives are summarized in Table 1.

Neoliberals begin with assertions of acceptance of several key realist propositions; however, they end with a rejection of realism and with claims of affirmation of the central tenets of the liberal institutionalist tradition. To develop this argument, neoliberals first observe that states in anarchy often face mixed interests and, in particular, situations which can be depicted by Prisoner's Dilemma. In the game, each state prefers mutual cooperation to mutual noncooperation (CC>DD), but also successful cheating to mutual cooperation (DC>CC) and mutual defection to victimization by another's cheating (DD>CD); overall, then, DC>CC>DD>CD. In these circumstances, and in the absence of a centralized authority or some other countervailing force to bind states to their promises, each defects regardless of what it expects the other to do.

However, neoliberals stress that countervailing forces often do exist—forces that cause states to keep their promises and thus to resolve the Prisoner's Dilemma. They argue that states may pursue a strategy of tit-for-tat and cooperate on a conditional basis—that is, each adheres to its promises so long as partners do so. They also suggest that conditional cooperation is more likely to occur in Prisoner's Dilemma if the game is highly iterated, since states that interact repeatedly in either a mutually beneficial or harmful manner are likely to find that mutual cooperation is their best long-term strategy. Finally, conditional cooperation is more attractive to states if the costs of verifying one another's compliance, and of sanctioning cheaters, are low compared to the benefits of joint action. Thus, conditional cooperation among states may evolve in the face of international anarchy and mixed interests through strategies of reciprocity, extended time horizons, and reduced verification and sanctioning costs.

Neoliberals find that one way states manage verification and sanction-

Table 1. Liberal Institutionalism, Neoliberal Institutionalism, and Realism: Summary of Major Propositions

Proposition	Liberal Institutionalism	Neoliberal Institutionalism	Realism
States are the only major actors in world politics	No; other actors include: specialized international agencies supranational authorities interest groups transgovernmental policy networks transnational actors (MNCs, etc.)	Yes (but international institutions play a major role)	Yes
States are unitary–rational actors	No; state is fragmented	Yes	Yes
Anarchy is a major shaping force for state preferences and actions	No; forces such as technology, knowledge, welfare-orientation of domestic interests are also salient	Yes (apparently)	Yes
International institutions are an independent force facilitating cooperation	Yes	Yes	No
Optimistic/pessimistic about prospects for cooperation	Optimistic	Optimistic	Pessimistic

ing problems is to restrict the number of partners in a cooperative arrangement. However, neoliberals place much greater emphasis on a second factor—international institutions. In particular, neoliberals argue that institutions reduce verification costs, create iterativeness, and make it easier to punish cheaters. As Keohane suggests, "in general, regimes make it more sensible to cooperate by lowering the likelihood of being double-crossed."[8] Similarly, Keohane and Axelrod assert that "international regimes do not substitute for reciprocity; rather, they reinforce and institutionalize it. Regimes incorporating the norm of reciprocity delegitimize defection and thereby make it more costly."[9] In addition, finding that "coordination conventions" are often an element of conditional cooperation in Prisoner's Dilemma, Charles Lipson suggests that "in international relations, such conventions, which are typically grounded in ongoing reciprocal exchange, range from international law to regime rules."[10] Finally, Arthur Stein argues that, just as societies "create" states to resolve collective action problems among individuals, so too "regimes in the international arena are also created to deal with the collective suboptimality that can emerge from individual [state] behavior."[11] Hegemonic power may be necessary to establish cooperation among states, neoliberals argue, but it may endure after hegemony with the aid of institutions. As Keohane concludes, "When we think about cooperation after hegemony, we need to think about institutions."[12]

3. Realism and the Failure of the New Liberal Institutionalism

The new liberals assert that they can accept key realist views about states and anarchy and still sustain classic liberal arguments about institutions and international cooperation. Yet, in fact, realist and neoliberal perspectives on states and anarchy differ profoundly, and the former provides a more complete understanding of the problem of cooperation than the latter.

Neoliberals assume that states have only one goal in mixed-interest interactions: to achieve the greatest possible individual gain. For example, Axelrod suggests that the key issue in selecting a "best strategy" in Prisoner's Dilemma—offered by neoliberals as a powerful model of the problem of state cooperation in the face of anarchy and mixed interests—is to determine "what strategy will yield a player the highest possible score."[13] Similarly, Lipson observes that cheating is attractive in a single play of Prisoner's Dilemma because each player believes that defecting "can maximize his own reward," and, in turning to iterated plays, Lipson retains the assumption that players seek to maximize individual payoffs over the long run.[14] Indeed, reliance upon conventional Prisoner's Dilemma to depict international relationships and upon iteration to solve the dilemma unambiguously requires neoliberalism to adhere to an individualistic payoff maximization assumption, for a player responds to an iterated conventional Prisoner's Dilemma with conditional cooperation *solely out of a desire to maximize its individual long-term total payoffs.*

Moreover, neoliberal institutionalists assume that states define their interests in strictly individualistic terms. Axelrod, for example, indicates that his objective is to show how actors "who pursue their own interests" may nevertheless work together.[15] He also notes that Prisoner's Dilemma is useful to study states in anarchy because it is assumed in the game that "the object is to do as well as possible, regardless of how well the other player does."[16] Similarly, Lipson suggests that Prisoner's Dilemma "clearly parallels the Realist conception of sovereign states in world politics" because each player in the game "is assumed to be a self-interested, self-reliant maximizer of his own utility."[17]

Finally, Keohane bases his analysis of international cooperation on the assumption that states are basically atomistic actors. He suggests that states in an anarchical context are, as microeconomic theory assumes with respect to business firms, "rational egoists." Rationality means that states possess "consistent, ordered preferences, and. . . calculate costs and benefits of alternative courses of action in order to maximize their utility in view of these preferences." In turn, he defines utility maximization atomistically; egoism, according to Keohane, "means that their [i.e., state] utility functions are independent of one another: they do not gain or lose utility simply because of the gains or losses of others."[18]

Neoliberalism finds that states attain greater utility—that is, a higher level of satisfaction—as they achieve higher individual payoffs. Also, in keeping with the concept of rational egoism, a utility function specified by the new theory for one state would not be "linked" to the utility functions of others. Hence, if a state enjoys utility, U, in direct proportion to its payoff, V, then the neoliberal institutionalist specification of that state's utility function would be $U = V$.

Overall, "rational egoist" states care only about their own gains. They do not care whether partners achieve or do not achieve gains, or whether those gains are large or small, or whether such gains are greater or less than the gains they themselves achieve. The major constraint on their cooperation in mixed interest international situations is the problem of cheating.

And yet, realist theory rejects neoliberalism's exclusive focus on cheating. Differences in the realist and neoliberal understanding of the problem of cooperation result from a fundamental divergence in their interpretations of the basic meaning of international anarchy. Neoliberal institutionalism offers a well-established definition of anarchy, specifying that it means "the lack of common government in world politics."[19] Neoliberalism then proceeds to identify one major effect of international anarchy. Because of anarchy, according to neoliberals, individuals or states believe that no agency is available to "enforce rules," or to "enact or enforce rules of behavior," or to "force them to cooperate with each other."[20] As a result, according to neoliberal theory, "cheating and deception are endemic" in international relations.[21] Anarchy, then, means that states may wish to cooperate, but, aware that cheating is both possible and profitable, *lack a central agency to enforce promises.* Given this understanding of anarchy, neoliberal institutional theory correctly identifies the problem of cheating and then proceeds to investigate how institutions can ameliorate that particular problem.

For realists, as for neoliberals, international anarchy means the absence of a common inter-state government. Yet, according to realists, states do not believe that the lack of a common government only means that no agency can reliably enforce promises. Instead, realists stress, states recognize that, in anarchy, *there is no overarching authority to prevent others from using violence, or the threat of violence, to destroy or enslave them.* As Kenneth Waltz suggests, in anarchy, wars can occur "because there is nothing to prevent them," and therefore "in international politics force serves, not only as the *ultima ratio,* but indeed as the first and constant one."[22] Thus, some states may sometimes be driven by greed or ambition, but anarchy and the danger of war cause all states always to be motivated in some measure by fear and distrust.

Given its understanding of anarchy, realism argues that individual well-being is not the key interest of states; instead, it finds that *survival* is their core interest. Raymond Aron, for example, suggested that "politics, insofar as it concerns relations among states, seems to signify—in both ideal and objective terms—simply the survival of states confronting the potential threat created by the existence of other states."[23] Similarly, Robert Gilpin observes that individuals and groups may seek truth, beauty, and justice, but he emphasizes that "all these more noble goals will be lost unless one makes provision for one's security in the power struggle among groups."[24]

Driven by an interest in survival, states are acutely sensitive to any erosion of their relative capabilities, which are the ultimate basis for their security and independence in an anarchical, self-help international context. Thus, realists find that the major goal of states in any relationship is not to attain the highest possible individual gain or payoff. Instead, *the fundamental goal of states in any relationship is to prevent others from achieving advances in their relative capabilities.* For example, E. H. Carr suggested that "the most serious wars are fought in order to make one's own country militarily stronger or, *more often,* to prevent another from becoming militarily stronger."[25] Along the same lines, Gilpin finds that the international system "stimulates, and may compel, a state to increase its power; at the least, it necessitates that the prudent state prevent relative increases in the power of competitor states."[26] Indeed, states may even forgo increases in their absolute capabilities if doing so prevents others from achieving even greater gains. This is because, as Waltz suggests, "the first concern of states is not to maximize power but to maintain their position in the system."[27]

States seek to prevent increases in others' relative capabilities. As a result, states always assess their performance in any relationship in terms of the performance of others. Thus, I suggest that states are positional, not atomistic, in character. Most significantly, *state positionality may constrain the willingness of states to cooperate.* States fear that their partners will achieve relatively greater gains; that, as a result, the partners will surge ahead of them in relative capabilities; and, finally, that their increasingly powerful partners in the present could become all the more formidable foes at some point in the future.

State positionality, then, engenders a "relative gains problem" for cooperation. That is, a state will decline to join, will leave, or will sharply limit its commitment to a cooperative arrangement if it believes that partners are achieving, or are likely to achieve, relatively greater gains. It will eschew cooperation even though participation in the arrangement was providing it, or would have provided it, with large absolute gains. Moreover, a state concerned about relative gains may decline to cooperate even if it is confident that partners will keep their commitments to a joint arrangement. Indeed, if a state believed that a proposed arrangement would provide all parties absolute gains, but would also generate gains favoring partners, then greater certainty that partners would adhere to the terms of the arrangement would only accentuate its relative gains concerns. Thus, a state worried about relative gains might respond to greater certainty that partners would keep their promises with a lower, rather than a higher, willingness to cooperate.

I must stress that realists do not argue that positionality causes all states to possess an offensively oriented desire to maximize the difference in gains arising from cooperation to their own advantage. They do not, in other words, attribute to states what Stein correctly calls a mercantilist definition of self-interest. Instead, realists argue that states are more likely to concentrate on the danger that relative gains may advantage partners and thus may foster the emergence of a more powerful potential adversary. Realism, then, finds that states are positional, but it also finds that state positionality is more defensive than offensive in nature.

In addition, realists find that defensive state positionality and the relative gains problem for cooperation essentially reflect the persistence of uncertainty in international relations. States are uncertain about one another's future *intentions;* thus, they pay close attention to how cooperation might affect relative *capabilities* in the future. This uncertainty results from the inability of states to predict or readily to control the future leadership or interests of partners. As Robert Jervis notes, "Minds can be changed, new leaders can come to power, values can shift, new opportunities and dangers can arise."[28]

Thus, realism expects a state's utility function to incorporate *two distinct terms.* It needs to include the state's individual payoff, V, reflecting the realist view that states are motivated by absolute gains. Yet it must also include a term integrating both the state's individual payoff and the partner's payoff, W, in such a way that gaps favoring the state add to its utility while, more importantly, gaps favoring the partner detract from it. One function that depicts this realist understanding of state utility is

U = V − k (W − V), with k representing the state's coefficient of sensitivity to gaps in payoffs either to its advantage or disadvantage.

This realist specification of state utility can be contrasted with that
inferred from neoliberal theory, namely, U = V. In both cases, the state
obtains utility from the receipt of absolute payoffs. However, while neoliberal institutional theory assumes that state utility functions are independent of one another and that states are indifferent to the payoffs of others,
realist theory argues that state utility functions are at least partially interdependent and that one state's utility can affect another's. We may also
observe that this realist-specified function does not suggest that any payoff
achieved by a partner detracts from the state's utility. Rather, *only gaps in
payoffs to the advantage of a partner do so.*

The coefficient for a state's sensitivity to gaps in payoffs—k—will
vary, but it will always be greater than zero. In general, k will increase as a
state transits from relationships in what Karl Deutsch termed a "pluralistic
security community" to those approximating a state of war.[29] The level of
k will be greater if a state's partner is a long-term adversary rather than a
long-time ally; if the issue involves security rather than economic well-
being; if the state's relative power has been on the decline rather than on
the rise; if payoffs in the particular issue-area are more rather than less
easily converted into capabilities within that issue-area; or if these capabilities and the influence associated with them are more rather than less
readily transferred to other issue-areas. Yet, given the uncertainties of
international politics, a state's level of k will be greater than zero even in
interactions with allies, for gaps in payoffs favoring partners will always
detract from a state's utility to some degree.

Faced with both problems—cheating and relative gains—states seek to
ensure that partners in common endeavors comply with their promises and
that their collaboration produces "balanced" or "equitable" achievements
of gains. According to realists, states define balance and equity as distributions of gains that roughly maintain pre-cooperation balances of capabilities. To attain this balanced relative achievement of gains, according to
Hans Morgenthau, states offer their partners "concessions"; in exchange,
they expect to receive approximately equal "compensations." As an example of this balancing tendency, Morgenthau offers the particular case of
"cooperation" among Prussia, Austria, and Russia in their partitions of
Poland in 1772, 1793, and 1795. He indicates that in each case, "the
three nations agreed to divide Polish territory in such a way that the
distribution of power among themselves would be approximately the same
after the partitions as it had been before."[30] For Morgenthau, state balancing of joint gains is a universal characteristic of the diplomacy of cooperation. He attributes this to the firmly grounded practice of states to
balance power, and argues that "given such a system, no nation will agree
to concede political advantages to another nation without the expectation,
which may or may not be well founded, of receiving *proportionate* advantages in return."[31]

Table 2. Anarchy, State Properties, and State Inhibitions about Cooperation: Summary of Neoliberal and Realist Views

Basis of Comparison	Neoliberal Institutionalism	Political Realism
Meaning of anarchy	No central agency is available to enforce promises	No central agency is available to enforce promises *or* to provide protection
State properties		
Core interest	To advance in utility defined individualistically	To enhance prospects for survival
Main goal	To achieve greatest possible absolute gains	To achieve greatest gains *and* smallest gap in gains favoring partners
Basic character	Atomistic ("rational egoist")	Defensively positional
Utility function	Independent: $U = V$	Partially interdependent: $U = V - k(W - V)$
State inhibitions concerning cooperation		
Range of uncertainties associated with cooperation	Partners' compliance	Compliance *and* relative achievement of gains *and* uses to which gaps favoring partners may be employed
Range of risks associated with cooperation	To be cheated and to receive a low payoff	To be cheated *or* to experience decline in relative power if others achieve greater gains
Barriers to cooperation	State concerns about partners' compliance	State concerns about partners' compliance *and* partners' relative gains

In sum, neoliberals find that anarchy impedes cooperation through its generation of uncertainty in states about the compliance of partners. For neoliberals, the outcome a state most fears in mixed interest situations is to be cheated. Yet, successful unilateral cheating is highly unlikely, and the more probable neoliberal "worst case" is for all states to defect and to find themselves less well off than if they had all cooperated. For neoliberal institutionalists, then, anarchy and mixed interests often cause states to suffer the opportunity costs of not achieving an outcome that is mutually more beneficial. Keohane and Axelrod argue that games like Prisoner's Dilemma, Stag Hunt, Chicken, and Deadlock illustrate how many international relationships offer both the danger that "the myopic pursuit of self-interest can be disastrous" and the prospect that "both sides can potentially benefit from cooperation—if they can only achieve it."[32]

Realists identify even greater uncertainties for states considering cooperation: which among them could achieve the greatest gains, and would imbalanced achievements of gains affect relative capabilities? In addition, a state that knows it will not be cheated still confronts another risk that is at least as formidable: perhaps a partner will achieve disproportionate gains, and, thus strengthened, might someday be a more dangerous enemy than if they had never worked together. For neoliberal theory, the problem of cooperation in anarchy is that states may fail to achieve it; in the final analysis, the worst possible outcome is a lost opportunity. For realist theory, state efforts to cooperate entail these dangers plus the much greater risk, for some states, that cooperation might someday result in lost independence or security.

Realism and neoliberal institutionalism offer markedly different views concerning the effects of international anarchy on states. These differences are summarized in Table 2. Compared to realist theory, neoliberal institutionalism understates the range of uncertainties and risks states believe they must overcome to cooperate with others. Hence, realism provides a more comprehensive theory of the problem of cooperation than does neoliberal institutionalism.

4. Conclusion

Neoliberal institutionalism is not based on realist theory; in fact, realism specifies a wider range of systemic-level constraints on cooperation than does neoliberalism. Thus, the next scholarly task is to conduct empirical tests of the two approaches. It is widely accepted—even by neoliberals— that realism has great explanatory power in national security affairs. However, international political economy would appear to be neoliberalism's preserve. Indeed, economic relationships among the advanced democracies would provide opportunities to design "crucial experiments" for the two theories. That is, they would provide the opportunity to observe behavior confirming realist expectations in circumstances least likely to have generated such observations unless realism is truly potent, while at the same time they might disconfirm neoliberal claims in circumstances most likely to have produced observations validating neoliberal theory.

According to neoliberal theory, two factors enhance prospects for the achievement and maintenance of political-economic cooperation among the advanced democracies. First, these states have the broadest range of common political, military, and economic interests. Thus, they have the greatest hopes for large absolute gains through joint action. This should work against realism and its specification of the relative gains problem for cooperation. That is, states which have many common interests should have the fewest worries that they might become embroiled in extreme conflicts in the future and, as a result, they should have the fewest concerns about relative achievements of gains arising from their common endeavors. Neoliberal theory emphasizes another background condition: the economic arrangements of advanced democracies are "nested" in larger political-strategic alliances. Nesting, according to the theory, accentuates iterativeness and so promotes compliance. This condition should also place realist theory at a disadvantage. If states are allies, they should be unconcerned that possible gaps in economic gains might advantage partners. Indeed, they should take comfort in the latter's success, for in attaining greater economic gains these partners become stronger military allies.

We can identify a number of efforts by advanced democracies to cooperate in economic issue-areas that were characterized by high common interests and nesting. In the trade field, such efforts would include the Tokyo Round codes on non-tariff barriers and efforts by the Nordic states to construct regional free-trade arrangements. In the monetary field, there are the experiences of the European Community with exchange-rate coordination—the Economic and Monetary Union and the European Monetary System. Finally, in the field of high technology, one might examine European collaboration in commercial aviation (Airbus Industrie) or data processing (the Unidata computer consortium). If these cooperative arrangements varied in terms of their success (and indeed such variance can be observed), and the less successful or failed arrangements were characterized not by a higher incidence of cheating but by a greater severity of relative gains problems, then one could conclude that realist theory explains variation in the success or failure of international cooperation more effectively than neoliberal institutional theory. Moreover, one could have great confidence in this assessment, for it would be based on cases which were most hospitable to neoliberalism and most hostile to realism.

However, additional tests of the two theories can and should be undertaken. For example, one might investigate realist and neoliberal expectations as to the *durability* of arrangements states prefer when they engage in joint action. Neoliberal theory argues that cheating is less likely to occur in a mixed interest situation that is iterated; hence, it suggests that "the most direct way to encourage cooperation is to make the relationship more durable."[33] If, then, two states that are interested in cooperation could choose between two institutional arrangements that offered comparable absolute gains but that differed in their expected durability—one arrangement might, for example, have higher exit costs than the other— neoliberalism would expect the states to prefer the former over the latter, for each state could then be more confident that the other would remain in the arrangement. Realism generates a markedly different hypothesis. If two states are worried or uncertain about relative achievements of gains, then each will prefer a less durable cooperative arrangement, for each would want to be more readily able to exit from the arrangement if gaps in gains did come to favor the other.

A second pair of competing hypotheses concerns the *number of partners* states prefer to include in a cooperative arrangement. Advocates of neoliberalism find that a small number of participants facilitates verification of compliance and sanctioning of cheaters. Hence, they would predict that states with a choice would tend to prefer a smaller number of partners. Realism would offer a very different hypothesis. A state may believe that it might do better than some partners in a proposed arrangement but not as well as others. If it is uncertain about which partners would do relatively better, the state will prefer more partners, for larger numbers would enhance the likelihood that the relative achievements of gains advantaging (what turn out to be) better-positioned partners could be offset by more favorable sharings arising from interactions with (as matters develop) weaker partners.

A third pair of competing empirical statements concerns the effects of *issue linkages* on cooperation. Neoliberalism's proponents find that tightly knit linkages within and across issue-areas accentuate iterativeness and thus facilitate cooperation. Realism, again, offers a very different proposition. Assume that a state believes that two issue-areas are linked, and that it believes that one element of this linkage is that changes in relative capabilities in one domain affect relative capabilities in the other. Assume also that the state believes that relative achievements of jointly produced gains in one issue-area would advantage the partner. This state would then believe that cooperation would provide additional capabilities to the partner not only in the domain in which joint action is undertaken, but also in the linked issue-area. Cooperation would therefore be unattractive to this state in direct proportion to its belief that the two issue-areas were interrelated. Thus, issue linkages may impede rather than facilitate cooperation.

These tests are likely to demonstrate that realism offers the most effective understanding of the problem of international cooperation. In addition, further analysis of defensive state positionality may help pinpoint policy strategies that facilitate cooperation. If relative gains concerns do act as a constraint on cooperation, then we should identify methods by which states have been able to address such concerns through unilateral bargaining strategies or through the mechanisms and operations of international institutions. For example, we might investigate states' use of side-payments to mitigate the relative gains concerns of disadvantaged partners. Thus, with its understanding of defensive state positionality and the relative gains problem for collaboration, realism may provide guidance to states as they seek security, independence, and mutually beneficial forms of international cooperation.

Notes

1. Major realist works include: E. H. Carr, *The Twenty Years Crisis, 1919–1939: An Introduction to the Study of International Relations* (London and New York: Harper Torchbooks, 1964); Hans J. Morgenthau, *Politics Among Nations: The Struggle for Power and Peace,* 5th ed. (New York: Knopf, 1973); Raymond Aron, *International Relations: A Theory of Peace and War,* trans. Richard Howard and Annette Baker Fox (Garden City, N.J.: Doubleday, 1973); Kenneth N. Waltz, *Man, the State, and War: A Theoretical Analysis* (New York: Columbia University Press, 1959); Waltz, *Theory of International Politics* (Reading, Mass.: Addison-Wesley, 1979); Robert Gilpin, *U.S. Power and the Multinational Corporation: The*

Political Economy of Foreign Direct Investment (New York: Basic Books, 1975); and Gilpin, *War and Change in World Politics* (Cambridge: Cambridge University Press, 1981). This essay does not distinguish between realism and "neorealism," because on crucial issues—the meaning of international anarchy, its effects on states, and the problem of cooperation—modern realists like Waltz and Gilpin are very much in accord with classical realists like Carr, Aron, and Morgenthau. For an alternative view, see Richard Ashley, "The Poverty of Neorealism," in Robert O. Keohane, ed., *Neorealism and Its Critics* (New York: Columbia University Press, 1986), pp. 255–300.

2. For functionalist international theory, see David Mitrany, *A Working Peace System* (Chicago: Quandrangle Press, 1966); see also Ernst B. Haas, *Beyond the Nation-State: Functionalism and International Organization* (Stanford, Calif.: Stanford University Press, 1964). On neofunctionalism, see Haas, *The Uniting of Europe: Political, Economic, and Social Forces, 1950–1957* (Stanford, Calif.: Stanford University Press, 1958); Haas, "Technology, Pluralism, and the New Europe," in Joseph S. Nye, Jr., ed., *International Regionalism* (Boston: Little, Brown, 1968), pp. 149–76; and Joseph S. Nye, Jr., "Comparing Common Markets: A Revised Neo-Functional Model," in Leon N. Lindberg and Stuart A. Scheingold, eds., *Regional Integration: Theory and Research* (Cambridge: Harvard University Press, 1971), pp. 192–231. On interdependence theory, see Richard C. Cooper, "Economic Interdependence and Foreign Policies in the 1970's," *World Politics* 24 (January 1972), pp. 158–81; Edward S. Morse, "The Transformation of Foreign Policies: Modernization, Interdependence, and Externalization," *World Politics* 22 (April 1970), pp. 371–92; and Robert O. Keohane and Joseph S. Nye, Jr., *Power and Interdependence: World Politics in Transition* (Boston: Little, Brown, 1977).

3. See Robert Axelrod, *The Evolution of Cooperation* (New York: Basic Books, 1984); Axelrod and Robert O. Keohane, "Achieving Cooperation Under Anarchy: Strategies and Institutions," *World Politics* 38 (October 1985), pp. 226–54; Keohane, *After Hegemony: Cooperation and Discord in the World Political Economy* (Princeton, N.J.: Princeton University Press, 1984); Charles Lipson, "International Cooperation in Economic and Security Affairs," *World Politics* 37 (October 1984), pp. 1–23; and Arthur Stein, "Coordination and Collaboration: Regimes in an Anarchic World," in Stephen D. Krasner, ed., *International Regimes* (Ithaca, N.Y.: Cornell University Press, 1983), pp. 115–40.

4. Haas, "The New Europe," p. 159.

5. Keohane and Nye, *Power and Interdependence*, p. 35; see also pp. 36, 232–34, 240–42.

6. Axelrod, *Evolution of Cooperation*, p. 3; also see pp. 4, 6.

7. Axelrod and Keohane, "Achieving Cooperation," p. 226.

8. Keohane, *After Hegemony*, p. 97.

9. Axelrod and Keohane, "Achieving Cooperation," p. 250.

10. Lipson, "International Cooperation," p. 6.

11. Stein, "Coordination and Collaboration," p. 123.

12. Keohane, *After Hegemony*, p. 246.

13. Axelrod, *Evolution of Cooperation*, pp. 6, 14.

14. Lipson, "International Cooperation," pp. 2, 5.

15. Axelrod, *Evolution of Cooperation*, p. 9.

16. Ibid., p. 22.

17. Lipson, "International Cooperation," p. 2.

18. Keohane, *After Hegemony,* p. 27.

19. Axelrod and Keohane, "Achieving Cooperation," p. 226.

20. Ibid.; Keohane, *After Hegemony,* p. 7; and Axelrod, *Evolution of Cooperation,* p. 6.

21. Axelrod and Keohane, "Achieving Cooperation," p. 226.

22. See Waltz, *Man, the State, and War,* p. 232; and Waltz, *Theory of International Politics,* p. 113.

23. Aron, *Peace and War,* p. 7; also see pp. 64–65.

24. Robert Gilpin, "The Richness of the Tradition of Political Realism," in Keohane, ed., *Neorealism and Its Critics,* p. 305.

25. Carr, *Twenty-Years Crisis,* p. 111, emphasis added.

26. Gilpin, *War and Change,* pp. 87–88.

27. Waltz, *Theory of International Politics,* p. 126.

28. Robert Jervis, "Cooperation Under the Security Dilemma," *World Politics* 30 (January 1978), p. 168.

29. Karl Deutsch et al., *Political Community and the North Atlantic Area* (Princeton, N.J.: Princeton University Press, 1957), pp. 5–7.

30. Morgenthau, *Politics Among Nations,* p. 179.

31. Ibid., p. 180, emphasis added.

32. Axelrod and Keohane, "Achieving Cooperation," p. 231.

33. Axelrod, *Evolution of Cooperation,* p. 129.

Selected Bibliography

Works by Kenneth Waltz

Waltz, Kenneth N. "The Origins of War in Neorealist Theory," *Journal of Interdisciplinary History* 18 (1988): 615–28.

———. "Realist Thought and Neorealist Theory," *Journal of International Affairs* 44 (1990): 21–37.

———. "Reflections on *Theory of International Politics*," in Robert O. Keohane, *Neorealism and Its Critics*, (1986), pp. 322–45.

———. "The Richness of the Tradition of Political Realism," *International Organization* 38 (1984): 287–304.

———. *Theory of International Politics* (1979).

Important Articles or Collections Addressing the Role of Rules/Institutions

Baldwin, David A., ed., *Neorealism and Neoliberalism: The Contemporary Debate* (1993).

Grieco, Joseph M. "Understanding the Problem of International Cooperation," in David Baldwin, ed., *Neorealism and Neoliberalism* (1993), pp. 301–338.

Keohane, Robert O., ed., *Neorealism and Its Critics* (1986).

Mearsheimer, John. "The False Promise of International Institutions," *International Security* 19 (1994–95): 1–49.

Strange, Susan. "Cave! Hic Dragones: A Critique of Regime Analysis," in Stephen D. Krasner, ed., *International Regimes* (1983), pp. 337–54.

Gilpin, Robert. *The Political Economy of International Relations* (1987).

———. *War and Change in World Politics* (1981).

Grieco, Joseph. *Cooperation Among Nations* (1990).

Reviews of Literature

Ashley, Richard. "The Poverty of Neorealism," in Robert O. Keohane, ed., *Neorealism and Its Critics* (1986), pp. 255–300.

Keohane, Robert O. "Theory of World Politics: Structural Realism and Beyond," in A. Finifter, ed., *Political Science: The State of the Discipline* (1983), pp. 503–40.

Milner, Helen. "International Theories of Cooperation Among Nations: Strengths and Weaknesses," *World Politics* 44 (1992): 466–96.

Powell, Robert. "Anarchy in International Relations Theory: The Neorealist–Neoliberal Debate," *International Organization* 48 (1994): 313–44.

7

Institutionalist Approaches

Dissatisfied with the Realist account of international cooperation, a number of International Relations scholars have begun to examine the institutional structures within which international cooperation occurs. The rise of this Institutionalist approach can be viewed as a response to Realism that has largely retained certain core Realist assumptions about the significance of power, anarchy, and state-centrism, while seeking to reinvigorate an Idealist appreciation for law, rules, and institutions. The focus of these Institutionalists is broader than formal international organizations but narrower than the structure of the international system.[1]

One of the early contributions of the Institutionalists was the development of "regime" analysis. In one of the first uses of this concept within International Relations, John Ruggie described a regime as "a set of mutual expectations, rules and regulations, plans, organizational energies and financial commitments, which have been accepted by a group of states."[2] In his introduction to a 1982 special issue of *International Organization* (reprinted here), Stephen Krasner described a regime as a "set of implicit or explicit principles, norms, rules, and decision-making procedures around which actors' expectations converge in a given area of international relations." Still the hallmark of much Institutionalist writing, regime analysis has evolved significantly in the last twenty years. As Andrew Hurrell notes in his essay in this chapter, many Institutionalists now focus more narrowly on "explicit, persistent, and connected sets of rules." The study of regimes, however defined, has yielded a vast new literature that seeks to explain the emergence and persistence of cooperation and the sources of state identity and interests.

Not all Institutionalists use the same set of tools or reach the same conclusions, however. In fact, two general camps have emerged within the

Institutionalist approach. Rationalistic Institutionalists draw their tools primarily from economics, applying, for example, game theory to the study of international behavior. Many Sociological Institutionalists, by contrast, utilize critical methods.

Rationalist Institutionalists typically accept Realist assumptions that states exist in an anarchic environment and act in an essentially self-interested manner. But rather than dismissing cooperation as a marginal phenomenon in international relations, as many Realists do, Rationalist Institutionalists seek to explain the emergence of cooperation by discussing the functional benefits that rules and institutions provide to states. Rationalistic Institutionalists have extensively explored the formation of international regimes and institutions, increasingly turning their attention to the implementation of regimes and institutionalized rules. For these scholars, the primary concern is the role of institutions in affecting state behavior.

Sociological Institutionalists concentrate on cultural practices, norms, values, and the discourse of international politics. As Keohane notes in this chapter, for Sociological Institutionalists, "understanding how people think about institutional norms and rules and the discourse they engage in, is as important in evaluating the significance of these norms as measuring the behavior that changes in response to their invocation." They emphasize the "intersubjective meanings" of international norms, rules, and institutions, and the extent to which such institutions constitute, as well as reflect, the power relationships of states.[3] Postmodern Sociological Institutionalists tend to reject the assumptions of Realism altogether. While modernist Sociological Institutionalists accept certain Realist assumptions, they typically question (or "problematize") social phenomena that Realists take for granted, including state identities and interests.

In spite of the differences in assumptions and methodology separating Institutionalists, what unites scholars from these two camps is their acceptance of the fundamental proposition that rules and institutions "matter." For Institutionalists, the norms, rules, and decision-making procedures that constitute international institutions exert a significant influence—at least under certain circumstances. The challenge to discover and to describe these circumstances undoubtedly will continue to animate Institutionalist scholarship for some time to come.

Notes

1. Stephan Haggard and Beth A. Simmons, "Theories of International Regimes," *International Organization* 41 (1987): 492.

2. John G. Ruggie, "International Response to Technology: Concepts and Trends," *International Organization* 29 (1975): 570.

3. Robert O. Keohane, "International Institutions: Two Approaches," *International Studies Quarterly* 32 (1988): 381, 382.

STEPHEN KRASNER

Structural Causes and Regime Consequences: Regimes as Intervening Variables

This volume explores the concept of international regimes. International regimes are defined as principles, norms, rules, and decision-making procedures around which actor expectations converge in a given issue-area. As a starting point, regimes have been conceptualized as intervening variables standing between basic causal factors on the one hand and outcomes and behavior on the other. This formulation raises two basic questions: first, what is the relationship between basic causal factors such as power, interest, and values, and regimes? Second, what is the relationship between regimes and related outcomes and behavior? The first question is related to a number of basic paradigmatic debates about the nature of international relations. But for the purposes of this volume the second is equally or more important. It raises the issue of whether regimes make any difference.

The articles in this volume offer three approaches to the issue of regime significance. The essays of Oran Young, and Raymond Hopkins and Donald Puchala see regimes as a pervasive characteristic of the international system. No patterned behavior can sustain itself for any length of time without generating a congruent regime. Regimes and behavior are inextricably linked. In contrast, Susan Strange argues that regime is a misleading concept that obscures basic economic and power relationships. Strange, representing what is probably the modal position for international relations scholars, elaborates a conventional structural critique that rejects any significant role for principles, norms, rules, and decision-making procedures. Most of the authors in this volume adopt a third position, which can be labeled "modified structural." They accept the basic analytic assumptions of structural realist approaches, which posit an international system of functionally symmetrical, power-maximizing states acting in an anarchic environment. But they maintain that under certain restrictive conditions involving the failure of individual action to secure Pareto-optimal outcomes, international regimes may have a significant impact even in an anarchic world. This orientation is most explicitly elaborated in the essays of Arthur Stein, Robert Keohane, and Robert Jervis; it also informs the analyses presented by John Ruggie, Charles Lipson, and Benjamin Cohen.

From *International Organization* 36 (1982), edited by Stephen Krasner. Reprinted by permission of the MIT Press, Cambridge, Mass.

The first section of this introduction develops definitions of regime and regime change. The following section investigates various approaches to the relationship between regimes, and behavior and outcomes. The third section examines five basic causal factors—egoistic self-interest, political power, diffuse norms and principles, usage and custom, and knowledge—that have been used to explain the development of regimes.

Defining Regimes and Regime Change

Regimes can be defined as sets of implicit or explicit principles, norms, rules, and decision-making procedures around which actors' expectations converge in a given area of international relations. Principles are beliefs of fact, causation, and rectitude. Norms are standards of behavior defined in terms of rights and obligations. Rules are specific prescriptions or proscriptions for action. Decision-making procedures are prevailing practices for making and implementing collective choice.

This usage is consistent with other recent formulations. Keohane and Nye, for instance, define regimes as "sets of governing arrangements" that include "networks of rules, norms, and procedures that regularize behavior and control its effects."[1] Haas argues that a regime encompasses a mutually coherent set of procedures, rules, and norms.[2] Hedley Bull, using a somewhat different terminology, refers to the importance of rules and institutions in international society where rules refer to "general imperative principles which require or authorize prescribed classes of persons or groups to behave in prescribed ways."[3] Institutions for Bull help to secure adherence to rules by formulating, communicating, administering, enforcing, interpreting, legitimating, and adapting them.

Regimes must be understood as something more than temporary arrangements that change with every shift in power or interests. Keohane notes that a basic analytic distinction must be made between regimes and agreements. Agreements are *ad hoc,* often "one-shot," arrangements. The purpose of regimes is to facilitate agreements. Similarly, Jervis argues that the concept of regimes "implies not only norms and expectations that facilitate cooperation, but a form of cooperation that is more than the following of short-run self-interest."[4] For instance, he contends that the restraints that have applied in Korea and other limited wars should not be considered a regime. These rules, such as "do not bomb sanctuaries," were based purely on short-term calculations of interest. As interest and power changed, behavior changed. Waltz's conception of the balance of power, in which states are driven by systemic pressures to repetitive balancing behavior, is not a regime; Kaplan's conception, in which equilibrium requires commitment to rules that constrain immediate, short-term power maximization (especially not destroying an essential actor), is a regime.[5]

Similarly, regime-governed behavior must not be based solely on short-term calculations of interest. Since regimes encompass principles and norms, the utility function that is being maximized must embody some sense of general obligation. One such principle, reciprocity, is emphasized in Jervis's analysis of security regimes. When states accept reciprocity they will sacrifice short-term interests with the expectation that other actors will reciprocate in the future, even if they are not under a specific obligation to do so. This formulation is similar to Fred Hirsch's brilliant discussion of friendship, in which he states: "Friendship contains an element of direct mutual exchange and to this extent is akin to private economic good. But it is often much more than that. Over time, the friendship 'transaction' can be presumed, by its permanence, to be a net benefit on both sides. At any moment of time, though, the exchange is very unlikely to be reciprocally balanced."[6] It is the infusion of behavior with principles and norms that distinguishes regime-governed activity in the international system from more conventional activity, guided exclusively by narrow calculations of interest.

A fundamental distinction must be made between principles and norms on the one hand, and rules and procedures on the other. Principles and norms provide the basic defining characteristics of a regime. There may be many rules and decision-making procedures that are consistent with the same principles and norms. *Changes in rules and decision-making procedures are changes within regimes,* provided that principles and norms are unaltered. For instance, Benjamin Cohen points out that there has been a substantial increase in private bank financing during the 1970s. This has meant a change in the rules governing balance-of-payments adjustment, but it does not mean that there has been a fundamental change in the regime. The basic norm of the regime remains the same: access to balance-of-payments financing should be controlled, and conditioned on the behavior of borrowing countries. John Ruggie argues that in general the changes in international economic regimes that took place in the 1970s were norm-governed changes. They did not alter the basic principles and norms of the embedded liberal regime that has been in place since the 1940s.

Changes in principles and norms are changes of the regime itself. When norms and principles are abandoned, there is either a change to a new regime or a disappearance of regimes from a given issue-area. For instance, Ruggie contends that the distinction between orthodox and embedded liberalism involves differences over norms and principles. Orthodox liberalism endorses increasing the scope of the market. Embedded liberalism prescribes state action to contain domestic social and economic dislocations generated by markets. Orthodox and embedded liberalism define different regimes. The change from orthodox liberal principles and norms before World War II to embedded liberal principles and norms after World War II was, in Ruggie's terms, a "revolutionary" change.

Fundamental political arguments are more concerned with norms and principles than with rules and procedures. Changes in the latter may be interpreted in different ways. For instance, in the area of international trade, recent revisions in the Articles of Agreement of the General Agreement on Tariffs and Trade (GATT) provide for special and differential treatment for less developed countries (LDCs). All industrialized countries have instituted generalized systems of preferences for LDCs. Such rules violate one of the basic norms of the liberal postwar order, the most-favored-nation treatment of all parties. However, the industrialized nations have treated these alterations in the rules as temporary departures necessitated by the peculiar circumstances of poorer areas. At American insistence the concept of graduation was formally introduced into the GATT Articles after the Tokyo Round. Graduation holds that as countries become more developed they will accept rules consistent with liberal principles. Hence, Northern representatives have chosen to interpret special and differential treatment of developing countries as a change within the regime.

Speakers for the Third World, on the other hand, have argued that the basic norms of the international economic order should be redistribution and equity, not nondiscrimination and efficiency. They see the changes in rules as changes of the regime because they identify these changes with basic changes in principle. There is a fundamental difference between viewing changes in rules as indications of change within the regime and viewing these changes as indications of change between regimes. The difference hinges on assessments of whether principles and norms have changed as well. Such assessments are never easy because they cannot be based on objective behavioral observations. "We know deviations from regimes," Ruggie avers, "not simply by acts that are undertaken, but by the intentionality and acceptability attributed to those acts in the context of an intersubjective framework of meaning."[7]

Finally, it is necessary to distinguish the weakening of a regime from changes within or between regimes. *If the principles, norms, rules, and decision-making procedures of a regime become less coherent, or if actual practice is increasingly inconsistent with principles, norms, rules, and procedures, then a regime has weakened.* Special and differential treatment for developing countries is an indication that the liberal regime has weakened, even if it has not been replaced by something else. The use of diplomatic cover by spies, the bugging of embassies, the assassination of diplomats by terrorists, and the failure to provide adequate local police protection are all indications that the classic regime protecting foreign envoys has weakened. However, the furtive nature of these activities indicates that basic principles and norms are not being directly challenged. In contrast, the seizure of American diplomats by groups sanctioned by the Iranian government is a basic challenge to the regime itself. Iran violated principles and norms, not just rules and procedures.[8]

In sum, change within a regime involves alterations of rules and decision-making procedures, but not of norms or principles; change of a regime involves alteration of norms and principles; and weakening of a regime involves incoherence among the components of the regime or inconsistency between the regime and related behavior.

Do Regimes Matter?

It would take some courage, perhaps more courage than this editor possesses, to answer this question in the negative. This project began with a simple causal schematic. It assumed that regimes could be conceived of as intervening variables standing between basic causal variables (most prominently, power and interests) and outcomes and behavior. The first attempt to analyze regimes thus assumed the following set of causal relationships (see Figure 1). Regimes do not arise of their own accord. They are not regarded as ends in themselves. Once in place they do affect related behavior and outcomes. They are not merely epiphenomenal.

The independent impact of regimes is a central analytic issue. The second causal arrow implies that regimes do matter. However, there is no general agreement on this point, and three basic orientations can be distinguished. The conventional structural views the regime concept as useless, if not misleading. Modified structural suggests that regimes may matter, but only under fairly restrictive conditions. And Grotian sees regimes as much more pervasive, as inherent attributes of any complex, persistent pattern of human behavior.

In this volume Susan Strange represents the first orientation. She has grave reservations about the value of the notion of regimes. Strange argues that the concept is pernicious because it obfuscates and obscures the interests and power relationships that are the proximate, not just the ultimate, cause of behavior in the international system. "All those international arrangements dignified by the label regime are only too easily upset when either the balance of bargaining power or the perception of national interest (or both together) change among those states who negotiate them."[9] Regimes, if they can be said to exist at all, have little or no impact. They are merely epiphenomenal. The underlying causal schematic is one that sees a direct connection between changes in basic causal factors (whether economic or political) and changes in behavior and outcomes. Regimes are excluded completely, or their impact on outcomes and related behavior is regarded as trivial.

Strange's position is consistent with prevailing intellectual orientations for analyzing social phenomena. These structural orientations conceptualize a world of rational self-seeking actors. The actors may be individuals, or firms, or groups, or classes, or states. They function in a system or environment that is defined by their own interests, power, and interaction. These orientations are resistant to the contention that principles, norms, rules, and decision-making procedures have a significant impact on outcomes and behavior.

Nowhere is this more evident than in the image of the market, the reigning analytic conceptualization for economics, the most successful of the social sciences. A market is characterized by impersonality between buyers and sellers, specialization in buying and selling, and exchange based

Basic causal variables → Regimes → Related behavior and outcomes

Figure 1.

upon prices set in terms of a common medium of exchange.[10] Max Weber states that in the market "social actions are not determined by orientation to any sort of norm which is held to be valid, nor do they rest on custom, but entirely on the fact that the corresponding type of social action is in the nature of the case best adapted to the normal interests of the actors as they themselves are aware of them."[11] The market is a world of atomized, self-seeking egoistic individuals.

The market is a powerful metaphor for many arguments in the literature of political science, not least international relations. The recent work of Kenneth Waltz exemplifies this orientation. For Waltz, the defining characteristic of the international system is that its component parts (states) are functionally similar and interact in an anarchic environment. International systems are distinguished only by differing distributions of relative capabilities among actors. States are assumed to act in their own self-interest. At a minimum they "seek their own preservation and, at a maximum, drive for universal domination."[12] They are constrained only by their interaction with other states in the system. Behavior is, therefore, a function of the distribution of power among states and the position of each particular state. When power distributions change, behavior will also change. Regimes, for Waltz, can only be one small step removed from the underlying power capabilities that sustain them.[13]

The second orientation to regimes, modified structural, is most clearly reflected in the essays of Keohane and Stein. Both of these authors start from a conventional structural realist perspective, a world of sovereign states seeking to maximize their interest and power. Keohane posits that in the international system regimes derive from voluntary agreements among juridically equal actors. Stein states that the "conceptualization of regimes developed here is rooted in the classic characterization of international politics as relations between sovereign entities dedicated to their own self-preservation, ultimately able to depend only on themselves, and prepared to resort to force."[14]

In a world of sovereign states the basic function of regimes is to coordinate state behavior to achieve desired outcomes in particular issue-areas.[15] Such coordination is attractive under several circumstances. Stein and Keohane posit that regimes can have an impact when Pareto-optimal outcomes could not be achieved through uncoordinated individual calculations of self-interest. The prisoners' dilemma is the classic game-theoretic example. Stein also argues that regimes may have an autonomous effect on outcomes when purely autonomous behavior could lead to disastrous results for both parties. The game of chicken is the game-theoretic analog. Haas and others in this volume suggest that regimes may have significant impact in a highly complex world in which *ad hoc*, individualistic calculations of interest could not possibly provide the necessary level of coordination. If, as many have argued, there is a general movement toward a world of complex interdependence, then the number of areas in which regimes can matter is growing.

However, regimes cannot be relevant for zero-sum situations in which states act to maximize the difference between their utilities and those of others. Jervis points to the paucity of regimes in the security area, which more closely approximates zero-sum games than do most economic issue-areas. Pure power motivations preclude regimes. Thus, the second orientation, modified structuralism, sees regimes emerging and having a significant impact, but only under restrictive conditions. It suggests that the first cut should be amended as in Figure 2. For most situations there is a direct link between basic causal variables and related behavior (path a); but under circumstances that are not purely conflictual, where individual decision making leads to suboptimal outcomes, regimes may be significant (path b).[16]

The third approach to regimes, most clearly elaborated in the essays of Raymond Hopkins and Donald Puchala, and Oran Young, reflects a fundamentally different view of international relations than the two structural arguments just described. These two essays are strongly informed by the Grotian tradition, which sees regimes as a pervasive phenomenon of all political systems. Hopkins and Puchala conclude that "regimes exist in all areas of international relations, even those, such as major power rivalry, that are traditionally looked upon as clear-cut examples of anarchy. Statesmen nearly always perceive themselves as constrained by principles, norms, and rules that prescribe and proscribe varieties of behavior."[17] The concept of regime, they argue, moves beyond a realist perspective, which is "too limited for explaining an increasingly complex, interdependent, and dangerous world."[18] Hopkins and Puchala apply their argument not only to an issue-area where one might expect communalities of interest (food) but also to one generally thought of as being much more unambiguously conflictual (colonialism).

Oran Young argues that patterned behavior inevitably generates convergent expectations. This leads to conventionalized behavior in which there is some expectation of rebuke for deviating from ongoing practices. Conventionalized behavior generates recognized norms. If the observer finds a pattern of interrelated activity, and the connections in the pattern are understood, then there must be some form of norms and procedures.

While the modified structural approach does not view the perfect market as a regime, because action there is based purely upon individual calculation without regard to the behavior of others, the third orientation does regard the market as a regime. Patterns of behavior that persist over

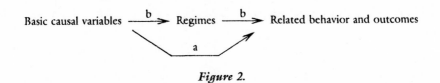

Figure 2.

Basic causal variables $\Bigg\langle$ Regimes
     ↓↑
   Related patterned behavior

Figure 3.

extended periods are infused with normative significance. A market cannot be sustained by calculations of self-interest alone. It must be, in Ruggie's terms, *embedded* in a broader social environment that nurtures and sustains the conditions necessary for its functioning. Even the balance of power, regarded by conventional structural realist analysts as a purely conflictual situation, can be treated as a regime.[19] The causal schema suggested by a Grotian orientation either closely parallels the first cut shown in Figure 1, or can be depicted as in Figure 3. Patterned behavior reflecting calculations of interest tends to lead to the creation of regimes, and regimes reinforce patterned behavior.

The Grotian tradition that Hopkins and Puchala, and Young draw upon, offers a counter to structural realism of either the conventional or the modified form. It rejects the assumption that the international system is composed of sovereign states limited only by the balance of power. Rather, Hopkins and Puchala suggest that elites are the practical actors in international relations. States are rarified abstractions. Elites have transnational as well as national ties. Sovereignty is a behavioral variable, not an analytic assumption. The ability of states to control movements across their borders and to maintain dominance over all aspects of the international system is limited. Security and state survival are not the only objectives. Force does not occupy a singularly important place in international politics. Elites act within a communications net, embodying rules, norms, and principles, which transcends national boundaries.

This minimalist Grotian orientation has informed a number of theoretical postulates developed during the postwar period. Functionalism saw the possibility of eroding sovereignty through the multiplication of particularistic interests across national boundaries. Karl Deutsch's 1957 study of integration, with its emphasis on societal communication, made a distinction between security communities and anarchy.[20] Some authors associated with the concept of transnationalism have posited a web of interdependence that makes any emphasis on sovereignty analytically misleading and normatively questionable. Keohane and Nye's discussion of complex interdependence rejects the assumptions of the primacy of force and issue hierarchy assumed by a realist perspective.[21] Ernst Haas points out that what he calls organic theories—eco-environmentalism, eco-reformism, and egalitarianism—deny conventional power-oriented assumptions.

Regimes are much more easily encompassed by a Grotian worldview. But, as the arguments made by Jervis, Keohane, Stein, Lipson, and Cohen indicate, the concept is not precluded by a realist perspective. The issue is not so much whether one accepts the possibility of principles, norms, rules, and decision-making procedures affecting outcomes and behavior, as what one's basic assumption is about the normal state of international affairs. Adherents of a Grotian perspective accept regimes as a pervasive and significant phenomenon in the international system. Adherents of a structural realist orientation see regimes as a phenomenon whose presence cannot be assumed and whose existence requires careful explanation. The two "standard cases" are fundamentally different, and it is the definition of the standard case that identifies the basic theoretical orientation. Stephen Toulmin writes that "any dynamical theory involves some explicit or implicit reference to a standard case or 'paradigm.' This paradigm specifies the manner in which, in the course of events, bodies may be expected to move." It is deviation from that movement which needs to be explained.[22] From a realist perspective, regimes are phenomena that need to be explained; from a Grotian perspective, they are data to be described.

In sum, conventional structural arguments do not take regimes seriously; if basic causal variables change, regimes will also change. Regimes have no independent impact on behavior. Modified structural arguments, represented here by a number of adherents of a realist approach to international relations, see regimes as mattering only when independent decision making leads to undesired outcomes. Finally, Grotian perspectives accept regimes as a fundamental part of all patterned human interaction, including behavior in the international system.

Explanations for Regime Development

For those authors who see regimes as something more than epiphenomena, the second major issue posed by a schematic that sees regimes as intervening variables between basic causal factors and related outcomes and behavior becomes relevant. What is the relationship between basic causal factors and regimes? What are the conditions that lead to regime creation, persistence, and dissipation? Here regimes are treated as the dependent variable.

A wide variety of basic causal variables have been offered to explain the development of regimes. The most prominent in this volume are egoistic self-interest, political power, norms and principles, habit and custom, and knowledge. The last two are seen as supplementary, augmenting more basic forces related to interest, power, and values.

1. Egoistic Self-Interest

The prevailing explanation for the existence of international regimes is egoistic self-interest. By egoistic self-interest I refer to the desire to maximize one's own utility function where that function does not include the utility of another party. The egoist is concerned with the behavior of others only insofar as that behavior can affect the egoist's utility. All contractarian political theories from Hobbes to Rawls are based on egoistic self-interest. In contrast, pure power seekers are interested in maximizing the difference between their power capabilities and those of their opponent.

In this volume the essays by Keohane and especially Stein most fully adopt and elaborate an interest-oriented perspective. Stein avers that "the same forces of autonomously calculated self-interest that lie at the root of the anarchic international system also lay the foundation for international regimes as a form of international order. . . . [T]here are times when rational self-interested calculation leads actors to abandon independent decision making in favor of joint decision making."[23]

Stein elaborates two circumstances under which unconstrained individual choice provides incentives for cooperation. The first occurs when such choice leads to Pareto-suboptimal outcomes: prisoner's dilemma and the provision of collective goods are well-known examples. Stein refers to this as the dilemma of common interests. Its resolution requires "collaboration," the active construction of a regime that guides individual decision making. Unconstrained individual decision making may also be eschewed when it would lead to mutually undesired outcomes and where the choice of one actor is contingent on the choice made by the other: the game of chicken is a prominent example. Stein refers to this as the dilemma of common aversions; it can be resolved through "coordination." Coordination need not be formalized or institutionalized. So long as everyone agrees to drive on the right side of the road, little more is needed. (Stein's concept of collaboration conforms with the definition of regimes used here. It is not so clear that coordination involves regimes. Coordination may only require the construction of rules. If these rules are not informed by any proximate principles or norms, they will not conform to the definition of regimes set forth earlier.)

While Stein employs a game-theoretic orientation, Keohane utilizes insights from microeconomic theories of market failure to examine dilemmas of common interests. He is primarily concerned with the demand for regimes, the conditions under which *ad hoc* agreements fail to provide Pareto-optimal outcomes. He maintains that "Regimes can make agreement easier if they provide frameworks for establishing legal liability (even if these are not perfect); improve the quantity and quality of information available to actors; or reduce other transactions costs, such as costs of organization or of making side-payments."[24] These benefits provided by regimes are likely to outweigh the costs of regime formation and maintenance when there is asymmetric information, moral hazard, potential dishonesty, or high issue density. In addition, the costs of forming regimes will be lower when there is a high level of formal and informal communication among states, a condition more likely to be found in open political systems operating under conditions of complex interdependence.

Egoistic self-interest is also regarded as an important determinant of regimes by several other authors. Young argues that there are three paths to regime formation: spontaneous, in which regimes emerge from the converging expectations of many individual actions; negotiated, in which regimes are formed by explicit agreements; and imposed, in which regimes are initially forced upon actors by external imposition. The first two are based on egoistic calculations. Lipson argues that the differential pattern of acceptance of liberal rules in the international trading regime is a function of differential costs of adjustment across industrial sectors; where costs are low, continued adherence to liberal principles, norms, and rules is high. Cohen maintains that the rules of the balance-of-payments financing regime changed in the 1970s because higher oil prices and the petrodollar market altered calculations of interest. Jervis posits that regimes in the security arena will only be formed when states accept the status quo, the cost of war is high, and the spillover into other arenas is substantial. This last point, which echoes Keohane's argument about the importance of issue density, is similar to arguments made by Haas and by Puchala and Hopkins. Haas makes interconnectedness a central element of his analysis: regimes are designed to manage complexity and complexity increases with interconnectedness. Similarly, Puchala and Hopkins maintain that regimes are more likely to arise under conditions of complex interdependence. Hence calculations of egoistic self-interest emerge as central elements in most of the articles in this volume.

2. Political Power

The second major basic causal variable used to explain regime development is political power. Two different orientations toward power can be distinguished. The first is cosmopolitan and instrumental: power is used to secure optimal outcomes for the system as a whole. In game-theoretic terms power is used to promote joint maximization. It is power in the service of the common good. The second approach is particularistic and potentially consummatory. Power is used to enhance the values of specific actors within the system. These values may include increasing power capabilities as well as promoting economic or other objectives. In game-theoretic terms power is used to maximize individual payoffs. It is power in the service of particular interests.

a. Power in the Service of the Common Good

The first position is represented by a long tradition in classical and neo-classical economics associated with the provision of public goods. The hidden hand was Adam Smith's most compelling construct: the good of all from the selfishness of each; there could be no more powerful defense of egoism. But Smith recognized that it was necessary for the state to provide certain collective goods. These included defense, the maintenance of order, minimum levels of welfare, public works, the protection of infant industries, and standards for commodities.[25] Economists have pointed to the importance of the state for establishing property rights and enforcing contracts; that is, creating conditions that prevent predatory as opposed to market behavior. The state must create institutions that equate public and private rates of return.[26] Keynesian analysis gives the state a prominent role in managing macroeconomic variables. For all of these arguments the purpose of state action is to further general societal interests.

The contemporary economist who has become most clearly associated with arguments emphasizing the instrumental role of power for cosmopolitan interests in the international system is Charles Kindleberger. In *The World in Depression,* Kindleberger argues that the depression of the 1930s could have been prevented by effective state leadership. An effective leader would have acted as a lender of last resort and provided a market for surplus commodities. In the interwar period the United States was able but unwilling to assume these burdens, and Great Britain was willing but unable. The result was economic chaos. In a more recent statement Kindleberger has listed the following functions that states perform for the international trading system:

1. Protecting economic actors from force.
2. Cushioning the undesirable effects of an open system by, for instance, providing adjustment assistance for import-competing industries.
3. Establishing standards for products. In the absence of such standards inordinate energy may be wasted finding information about products.
4. Providing a national currency that can be used as an international reserve and transactions currency.
5. Constructing public works such as docks and domestic transportation systems.
6. Compensating for market imperfections by, for instance, becoming a lender of last resort when private financial institutions become so cautious that their conservatism could destroy global liquidity.[27]

Despite its emphasis on political action, Kindleberger's perspective is still profoundly liberal. The purpose of state intervention is to facilitate the creation and maintenance of an environment within which a market based on individual calculations of self-interest can flourish. The market, like the human body, is basically healthy, but occasionally the intervention of some external agent (the state, a doctor) may be necessary.[28] A market economy will maximize the utility of society as a whole. Political power is put at the service of the common good.

b. Power in the Service of Particular Interests

The articles in this volume are less oriented toward cosmopolitan ends; rather, they focus on power as an instrument that can be used to enhance the utility of particular actors, usually states. A game-theoretic analogy makes it easier to distinguish between two important variants of the viewpoint of power in the service of particular interests. The first assumes that pay-offs are fixed and that an actor's choice of strategy is autonomously determined solely by these pay-offs. The second assumes that power can be used to alter pay-offs and influence actor strategy.

The first approach closely follows the analysis that applies when purely cosmopolitan objectives are at stake, except that political power is used to maximize individual, not joint, pay-offs. Under certain configurations of interest, there is an incentive to create regimes and the provision of these regimes is a function of the distribution of power. While Keohane focuses on the demand for regimes in his article in this volume, he has elsewhere argued that hegemons play a critical role in supplying the collective goods that are needed for regimes to function effectively.[29] Hegemons provide these goods not because they are interested in the well-being of the system as a whole, but because regimes enhance their own national values.

This emphasis on the need for asymmetric power distributions (supply-side considerations) should be contrasted with Stein's assertions concerning the efficacy of demand. The theory of hegemonic leadership suggests that under conditions of declining hegemony there will be a weakening of regimes. Without leadership, principles, norms, rules, and decision-making procedures cannot easily be upheld. No one actor will be willing to provide the collective goods needed to make the regime work smoothly and effectively. Stein's analysis, on the other hand, suggests that as hegemony declines there will be greater incentives for collaboration because collective goods are no longer being provided by the hegemon. The international system more closely resembles an oligopoly than a perfect market. Actors are aware of how their behavior affects others. When smaller states perceive that a hegemon is no longer willing to offer a free ride, they are likely to become paying customers. For Stein, interests alone can effectively sustain order. Hegemonic decline can lead to stronger regimes.

The second line of argument associated with power in the service of specific interests investigates the possibility that powerful actors may be able to alter the pay-offs that confront other actors or influence the strategies they choose. Here power becomes a much more central concept—the element of compulsion is close at hand. Weaker actors may not be able to make autonomous choices. The values assigned to a particular cell may be changed.

In this volume Oran Young develops the notion of imposed regimes. Dominant actors may explicitly use a combination of sanctions and incentives to compel other actors to act in conformity with a particular set of principles, norms, rules, and decision-making procedures. Alternatively, dominant actors may secure de facto compliance by manipulating opportunity sets so that weaker actors are compelled to behave in a desired way. Keohane posits that in the international system choices will be constrained in ways that give greater weight to the preferences of more powerful actors. Benjamin Cohen notes that the specific rules and institutional arrangements for the Bretton Woods institutions reflected the preferences of the United States much more than those of Great Britain. Jervis points out that weaker states had little option but to follow the balance of power regime of the 19th century with its emphasis on the special role of the great powers. In all of these cases more powerful actors created regimes that served their particular purpose, and other[s] were compelled to accept them because their pay-offs were manipulated or their options were limited.

When a hegemonic state acts to influence the strategy of other actors the regime is held hostage to the persistence of the existing distribution of power in the international system. If the hegemon's relative capabilities decline, the regime will collapse. Young argues that imposed orders are likely to disintegrate when there are major shifts in underlying power capabilities. Hopkins and Puchala suggest that regimes that are highly politicized, diffuse, and biased in their distribution of values are likely to undergo radical transformation when power distributions change. For instance, the norms of the colonial regime collapsed because the power of its supporter[s], the major European states, eroded. This set of arguments about regime change and hegemonic decline differs from the analysis emerging from a focus on the provision of collective goods for either cosmopolitan or particularistic reasons. Here a decline in power leads to a change in regime because the hegemon is no longer able to control the pay-off matrix or influence the strategies of the weak, not because there is no actor to provide the collective goods needed for efficient regime functioning.

3. Norms and Principles

To this point in the discussion, norms and principles have been treated as endogenous: they are the critical defining characteristics of any given regime. However, norms and principles that influence the regime in a particular issue-area but are not directly related to that issue-area can also be regarded as explanations for the creation, persistence, and dissipation of regimes. The most famous example of such a formulation is Max Weber's *Protestant Ethic and the Spirit of Capitalism*. Weber argues that the rise of capitalism is intimately associated with the evolution of a Calvinist religious doctrine that fosters hard work while enjoining profligacy and uses worldly success as an indication of predestined fate.[30] Fred Hirsch has argued that without precapitalist values such as hard work, self-sacrifice, loyalty, and honor, capitalist systems would fall apart. Such values are critical constraints on self-interested calculations that would too often lead to untrustworthy and dishonest behavior.[31]

Financing by various pariah groups around the world offers a clear example of the way in which noneconomic norms have facilitated market activity. For instance, bills of exchange were devised by Jewish bankers during the late Middle Ages to avoid violence and extortion from the nobility: safer to carry a piece of paper than to carry specie. However, the piece of paper had to be honored by the recipient. This implied a high level of trust and such trust was enhanced by conventions: established practices were reinforced by the exclusionary nature of the group, which facilitated surveillance and the application of sanctions. The importance of conventions for the use of bills of exchange is reflected in the fact that they were frequently used in the Mediterranean basin in the 16th century but they were not used at the interface with the non-Mediterranean world in Syria where, according to Braudel, "two mutually suspicious worlds met face to face." Here all dealings were in barter, or gold and silver.[32]

In this volume, Hopkins and Puchala make a distinction between the superstructure and the substructure. The superstructure refers to general and diffuse principles and norms that condition the principles and norms operative in a specific issue-area. They note, for example, that balance of power in 19th century Europe was a diffuse norm that influenced the nature of the regime for colonialism. Jervis argues that for regimes to develop in the security area the great powers "must believe that others share the value they place on mutual security and cooperation."[33] John Ruggie's highly original analysis of the postwar economic regime argues that it was founded upon principles of embedded rather than orthodox liberalism. The domestic lesson of the 1930s was that societies could not tolerate the consequences of an untrammeled market. This set of diffuse values, which permeated the capitalist world, was extended from the domestic to the international sphere in the Bretton Woods agreements.

This discussion suggests that there is a hierarchy of regimes. Diffuse principles and norms, such as hard work as a service to God, condition behavior in specific issue-areas. In international relations, the most important diffuse principle is sovereignty. Hedley Bull refers to sovereignty as the constitutive principle of the present international system. The concept of exclusive control within a delimited geographic area and the untrammeled right to self-help internationally, which emerged out of late medieval Europe, have come to pervade the modern international system.[34]

In this usage sovereignty is not an analytic assumption, it is a principle that influences the behavior of actors. With a few exceptions, such as Antarctica, Namibia, and the West Bank, sovereignty prevails. Those areas where sovereignty is not applied are governed by vulnerable regimes or lack regimes altogether. Sovereignty designates states as the only actors with unlimited rights to act in the international system. Assertions by other agencies are subject to challenge. If the constitutive principle of sovereignty were altered, it is difficult to imagine that any other international regime would remain unchanged.

4. Usage and Custom

The last two sets of causal variables affecting regime development are usage and custom, and knowledge. Usage and custom will be discussed in this section, knowledge in the next. Usage and custom, and knowledge, are not treated in this volume as exogenous variables capable of generating a regime on their own. Rather, they supplement and reinforce pressures associated with egoistic self-interest, political power, and diffuse values.

Usage refers to regular patterns of behavior based on actual practice; custom, to long-standing practice.[35] The importance of routinized behavior is particularly significant in the position taken by Hopkins and Puchala and by Young. For these authors, patterned behavior, originally generated purely by considerations of interest or power, has a strong tendency to lead to shared expectations. Patterned behavior accompanied by shared expectations is likely to become infused with normative significance: actions based purely on instrumental calculations can come to be regarded as rule-like or principled behavior. They assume legitimacy. A great deal of western commercial law, in fact, developed out of custom and usage initially generated by self-interest. Practices that began as *ad hoc* private arrangements later became the basis for official commercial law.[36]

In Oran Young's discussion of both spontaneous and imposed regimes, habits and usage play a significant role. Young does not make any strong claims for the specific conditions that lead to spontaneous regimes. However, the literature to which he refers—Schelling, Lewis, and Hayek —is oriented toward a microeconomic perspective focusing on egoistic self-interest. Certain patterns of behavior are first adopted because they promote individual utility. Once established, such practices are reinforced by the growth of regimes. Most American drivers (outside New York City) would feel at least a twinge of discomfort at driving illegally through a red light at an empty intersection. Behavior that was originally only a matter of egoistic self-interest is now buttressed by widely shared norms. Similarly, Young argues that successful imposed orders are bolstered eventually by habits of obedience. (It is not clear that, without these habits, Young's concept of imposed orders conforms with the definition of regime used here.) A pattern of behavior initially established by economic coercion or force may come to be regarded as legitimate by those on whom it has been imposed. Usage leads to shared expectations, which become infused with principles and norms.

5. Knowledge

The final variable used to explain the development of regimes is knowledge. Like usage and custom, knowledge is usually treated as an intervening, not an exogenous, variable. In an earlier study Ernst Haas, in this volume the most prominent exponent of the importance of knowledge, defined knowledge as "the sum of technical information and of theories about that information which commands sufficient consensus at a given time among interested actors to serve as a guide to public policy designed to achieve some social goal."[37] In his essay in this volume Haas points to the potentialities inherent in a stance of "cognitive evolutionism," which emphasizes sensitivity to the consequences of the generation of new knowledge. Knowledge creates a basis for cooperation by illuminating complex interconnections that were not previously understood. Knowledge can not only enhance the prospects for convergent state behavior, it can also transcend "prevailing lines of ideological cleavage."[38] It can provide a common ground for both what Haas calls mechanical approaches (most conventional social science theories) and organic approaches (egalitarianism and various environmentally oriented arguments).

For knowledge to have an independent impact in the international system, it must be widely accepted by policy makers. Stein points out that rules concerning health, such as quarantine regulations, were radically altered by new scientific knowledge such as the discovery of the microbe that causes cholera, the transmission of yellow fever by mosquitoes, and the use of preventive vaccines. Prior to developments such as these, national health regulations were primarily determined by political concerns. After these discoveries, however, national behavior was determined by an international regime, or at least a set of rules, dictated by accepted scientific knowledge. Jervis argues that in the present security arena the possibilities for an arms control regime may depend on whether the Soviet Union and the United States view strategy in the same way. In particular, mutual acceptance of Mutual Assured Destruction (MAD) can provide the basis for a regime. Without consensus, knowledge can have little impact on regime development in a world of sovereign states. If only some parties hold a particular set of beliefs, their significance is completely mediated by the power of their adherents.

New knowledge can provide the basis for what Hopkins and Puchala call evolutionary change, which usually involves altering rules and procedures within the context of a given set of principles and norms. In contrast, revolutionary change, which generates new principles and norms, is associated with shifts in power. As an example of evolutionary change, Benjamin Cohen points out that the fixed exchange rate system agreed to at Bretton Woods was based upon understandings derived from the interwar experience and then-current knowledge about domestic monetary institutions and structures. States were extremely sensitive to competitive devaluation and were not confident that domestic monetary policy could provide insulation from external disturbances. It was much easier to accept a floating exchange rate regime in the 1970s because the knowledge and related institutional capacity for controlling monetary aggregates had substantially increased. In a highly complex world, where goals are often ill-defined and many links are possible, consensual knowledge can greatly facilitate agreement on the development of an international regime. Such knowledge can light a clear path in a landscape that would otherwise be murky and undifferentiated.

In sum, the essays in this volume and the literature in general offer a variety of explanations for the development of regimes. The two most prominent exogenous variables are egoistic self-interest, usually economic, and political power. In addition, diffuse values and norms such as sovereignty and private property may condition behavior within specific issue-areas. Finally, usage and custom and knowledge may contribute to the development of regimes.

Conclusion

In approaching the two basic questions that guided this exercise—the impact of regimes on related behavior and outcomes, and the relationship between basic causal variables and regimes—the essays in this volume reflect two different orientations to international relations. The Grotian perspective, which informs the essays of Hopkins and Puchala and of Young, sees regimes as a pervasive facet of social interaction. It is catholic in its description of the underlying causes of regimes. Interests, power, diffuse norms, customs, and knowledge may all play a role in regime formation. These causal factors may be manifest through the behavior of individuals, particular bureaucracies, and international organizations, as well as states.

The structural realist orientation, which infuses the other essays in this volume, is more circumspect. The exemplar or standard case for the realist perspective does not include international regimes. Regimes arise only under restrictive conditions characterized by the failure of individual decision making to secure desired outcomes. The basic causal variables that lead to the creation of regimes are power and interest. The basic actors are states.

The arguments presented by Stein, Keohane, Jervis, Ruggie, Lipson, and Cohen do press beyond conventional realist orientations. They reject a narrow structural analysis that posits a direct relationship between changes in basic causal variables and related behavior and outcomes, and denies the utility of the regime concept. For this they are taken to task in Susan Strange's critique. However, the basic parametric constraints for these analyses are identical with those applied by more conventional structural arguments. The basic analytic assumptions are the same. Arguments that treat regimes as intervening variables, and regard state interests and state power as basic causal variables, fall unambiguously within the structural realist paradigm. A more serious departure from structural reasoning occurs when regimes are seen as autonomous variables independently affecting not only related behavior and outcomes, but also the basic causal variables that led to their creation in the first place. This line of reasoning is examined in the conclusion to this volume.

Notes

1. Robert O. Keohane and Joseph S. Nye, *Power and Interdependence* (Boston: Little, Brown, 1977), p. 19.

2. Ernst Haas, "Technological Self-Reliance for Latin America: the OAS Contribution," *International Organization* 34, 4 (Autumn 1980), p. 553.

3. Hedley Bull, *The Anarchical Society: A Study of Order in World Politics* (New York: Columbia University Press, 1977), p. 54.

4. Robert Jervis, in *International Organization* 36 (1982), p. 173.

5. Kenneth Waltz, *Theory of International Relations* (Reading, Mass.: Addison-Wesley, 1979); Morton Kaplan, *Systems and Process in International Poli-*

tics (New York: Wiley, 1957), p. 23; Kaplan, *Towards Professionalism in International Theory* (New York: Free Press, 1979), pp. 66–69, 73.

6. Fred Hirsch, *The Social Limits to Growth* (Cambridge: Harvard University Press, 1976), p. 78.

7. John Ruggie, in *International Organization* 36 (1982), p. 196.

8. Iran's behavior may be rooted in an Islamic view of international relations that rejects the prevailing, European-derived regime. See Richard Rosecrance, "International Theory Revisited," *International Organization* 35, 4 (Autumn 1981) for a similar point.

9. Susan Strange, in *International Organization* 36 (1982), p. 345.

10. Cyril Belshaw, *Traditional Exchange and Modern Markets* (Englewood Cliffs, N.J.: Prentice-Hall, 1965), pp. 8–9.

11. Max Weber, *Economy and Society* (Berkeley: University of California Press, 1977), p. 30.

12. Waltz, *Theory of International Relations*, p. 118.

13. Ibid., especially chapters 5 and 6. This conventional structuralist view for the realist school has its analog in Marxist analysis to studies that focus exclusively on technology and economic structure.

14. Robert O. Keohane and Arthur A. Stein, in *International Organization* 36 (1982), pp. 146 and 116.

15. Vinod K. Aggarwal emphasizes this point. See his "Hanging by a Thread: International Regime Change in the Textile/Apparel System, 1950–1979, " Ph.D. diss., Stanford University, 1981, chap. 1.

16. The modified structural arguments presented in this volume are based upon a realist analysis of international relations. In the Marxist tradition this position has its analog in many structural Marxist writings, which emphasize the importance of the state and ideology as institutions that act to rationalize and legitimate fundamental economic structures.

17. Raymond Hopkins and Donald Puchala, in *International Organization* 36 (1982), p. 86.

18. Ibid., p. 61.

19. Bull, *The Anarchical Society*, chap. 5.

20. See Arend Lijphart, "The Structure of the Theoretical Revolution in International Relations," *International Studies Quarterly* 18, 1 (March 1974), pp. 64–65, for the development of this argument.

21. Keohane and Nye, *Power and Interdependence*, especially chap. 8.

22. Stephen Toulmin, *Foresight and Understanding: An Enquiry into the Aims of Science* (New York: Harper Torchbooks, 1961), pp. 56–57. Toulmin's use of the term paradigm is similar to Kuhn's notion of an exemplar. See Thomas Kuhn, *The Structure of Specific [Scientific] Revolutions*, 2nd ed. (Chicago: University of Chicago Press, 1970), p. 187.

23. Stein, in *International Organization* 36 (1982), p. 132.

24. Keohane, in *International Organization* 36 (1982), p. 154.

25. There is a lively debate over precisely how much of a role Smith accords to the state. Some (see for instance Albert Hirschman, *The Passions and the Interests* [Princeton: Princeton University Press, 1977], pp. 103–104) maintain that Smith wanted to limit the folly of government by having it do as little as possible. Others (see for instance Colin Holmes, "Laissez-faire in Theory and Practice: Britain 1800–1875," *Journal of European Economic History* 5, 3 [1976], p. 673; and Carlos Diaz-Alejandro, "Delinking North and South: Unshackled or Un-

hinged," in Albert Fishlow et al., *Rich and Poor Nations in the World Economy* [New York: McGraw-Hill, 1978], pp. 124–25) have taken the intermediate position endorsed here. Others see Smith trying to establish conditions for a moral society that must be based on individual choice, for which a materialistically oriented, egoistically maintained economic system is only instrumental. See, for instance, Leonard Billet, "The Just Economy: The Moral Basis of the Wealth of Nations," *Review of Social Economy* 34 (December 1974).

26. Jack Hirschleifer, "Economics from a Biological Viewpoint," *Journal of Law and Economics* 20 (April 1977); Weber, *Economy and Society,* pp. 336–37; Douglass C. North and Robert Paul Thomas, *The Rise of the Western World: A New Economic History* (Cambridge: Cambridge University Press, 1973), chap. 1.

27. Charles P. Kindleberger, "Government and International Trade," *Princeton Essays in International Finance* (International Finance Section, Princeton University, July 1978). Adam Smith was less enamoured with leadership. He felt that reasonable intercourse could only take place in the international system if there was a balance of power. Without such a balance the strong would dominate and exploit the weak. See Diaz-Alejandro, "Delinking North and South," p. 92.

28. Charles P. Kindleberger, *Manias, Panics, and Crashes: A History of Financial Crises* (New York: Basic Books, 1978).

29. Robert O. Keohane, "The Theory of Hegemonic Stability and Changes in International Economic Regimes, 1967–77," in Ole R. Holsti et al., *Changes in the International System* (Boulder, Col.: Westview, 1980).

30. For a recent discussion see David Laitin, "Religion, Political Culture, and the Weberian Tradition," *World Politics* 30, 4 (July 1978), especially pp. 568–69. For another discussion of noneconomic values in the rise of capitalism see Hirschman, *The Passions and the Interests.*

31. Hirsch, *The Social Limits to Growth,* chap. 11. See also Michael Walzer, "The Future of Intellectuals and the Rise of the New Class," *New York Review of Books* 27 (20 March 1980).

32. Fernand Braudel, *The Mediterranean and the Mediterranean World in the Age of Philip II* (New York: Harper, 1975), p. 370. For the tie between bills of exchange and Jewish bankers see Hirschman, *The Passions and the Interests,* p. 72, and Immanuel Wallerstein, *The Modern World-System* (New York: Academic Press, 1974), p. 147.

33. Jervis, in *International Organization* 36 (1982), p. 177.

34. Bull, *The Anarchical Society,* pp. 8–9, 70.

35. Weber, *Economy and Society,* p. 29.

36. Leon E. Trakman, "The Evolution of the Law Merchant: Our Commercial Heritage," Part I, *Journal of Maritime Law and Commerce* 12, 1 (October 1980) and Part II, ibid., 12, 2 (January 1981); Harold Berman and Colin Kaufman, "The Law of International Commercial Transactions (*Lex Mercatoria*)," *Harvard International Law Journal* 19, 1 (Winter 1978).

37. Ernst Haas, "Why Collaborate? Issue-Linkage and International Regimes," *World Politics* 32, 3 (April 1980), pp. 367–68.

38. Ibid., p. 368.

ROBERT O. KEOHANE

International Institutions: Two Approaches

Contemporary world politics is a matter of wealth and poverty, life and death. The members of this Association have chosen to study it because it is so important to our lives and those of other people—not because it is either aesthetically attractive or amenable to successful theory-formulation and testing. Indeed, we would be foolish if we studied world politics in search of beauty or lasting truth. Beauty is absent because much that we observe is horrible, and many of the issues that we study involve dilemmas whose contemplation no sane person would find pleasing. Deterministic laws elude us, since we are studying the purposive behavior of relatively small numbers of actors engaged in strategic bargaining. In situations involving strategic bargaining, even formal theories, with highly restrictive assumptions, fail to specify which of many possible equilibrium outcomes will emerge. This suggests that no general theory of international politics may be feasible. It makes sense to seek to develop cumulative verifiable knowledge, but we must understand that we can aspire only to formulate conditional, context-specific generalizations rather than to discover universal laws, and that our understanding of world politics will always be incomplete.

The ways in which members of this Association study international relations are profoundly affected by their values. Most of us are children of the Enlightenment, insofar as we believe that human life can be improved through human action guided by knowledge. We therefore seek knowledge in order to improve the quality of human action. Many of us, myself included, begin with a commitment to promote human progress, defined in terms of the welfare, liberty, and security of individuals, with special attention to principles of justice. With this commitment in mind, we seek to analyze how the legal concept of state sovereignty and the practical fact of substantial state autonomy coexist with the realities of strategic and economic interdependence.

These value commitments help to account for the topic of this essay: the study of international institutions. I focus on institutions because I share K. J. Holsti's desire to "open intellectual doors to peer in on international collaboration, cooperation, and welfare" (Holsti, 1986:356). To understand the conditions under which international cooperation can take place, it is necessary to understand how international institutions operate

From *International Studies Quarterly* 32 (1988): 379–96. Reprinted by permission of Blackwell Publishers. Some notes have been altered.

and the conditions under which they come into being. This is not to say
that international institutions always facilitate cooperation on a global
basis: on the contrary, a variety of international institutions, including
most obviously military alliances, are designed as means for prevailing in
military and political conflict. Conversely, instances of cooperation can
take place with only minimal institutional structures to support them. But
all efforts at international cooperation take place within an institutional
context of some kind, which may or may not facilitate cooperative endeavors. To understand cooperation and discord better, we need to investigate
the sources and nature of international institutions, and how institutional
change takes place.

   "Cooperation" is a contested term. As I use it, it is sharply distinguished from both harmony and discord. When harmony prevails, actors'
policies *automatically* facilitate the attainment of others' goals. When
there is discord, actors' policies hinder the realization of others' goals, and
are not adjusted to make them more compatible. In both harmony and
discord, neither actor has an incentive to change his or her behavior.
Cooperation, however, "requires that the actions of separate individuals or
organizations—which are not in pre-existent harmony—be brought into
conformity with one another through a process of policy coordination"
(Keohane, 1984:51). This means that when cooperation takes place, each
party changes his or her behavior *contingent on* changes in the other's
behavior. We can evaluate the impact of cooperation by measuring the
difference between the actual outcome and the situation that would have
obtained in the absence of coordination: that is, the myopic self-enforcing
equilibrium of the game. Genuine cooperation improves the rewards of
both players.

   International cooperation does not necessarily depend on altruism,
idealism, personal honor, common purposes, internalized norms, or a
shared belief in a set of values embedded in a culture. At various times and
places any of these features of human motivation may indeed play an
important role in processes of international cooperation; but cooperation
can be understood without reference to any of them. This is not surprising, since international cooperation is not necessarily benign from an ethical standpoint. Rich countries can devise joint actions to extract resources
from poor ones, predatory governments can form aggressive alliances, and
privileged industries can induce their governments to protect them against
competition from more efficient producers abroad. The analysis of international cooperation should not be confused with its celebration. As Hedley Bull said about order, "while order in world politics is something
valuable, . . . it should not be taken to be a commanding value, and to
show that a particular institution or course of action is conducive of order
is not to have established a presumption that that institution is desirable or
that that course of action should be carried out" (Bull, 1977:98).

   Cooperation is in a dialectical relationship with discord, and they must
be understood together. Thus to understand cooperation, one must also

understand the frequent absence of, or failure of, cooperation, so incessantly stressed by realist writers. But our awareness of cooperation's fragility does not require us to accept dogmatic forms of realism, which see international relations as inherently doomed to persistent zero-sum conflict and warfare. As Stanley Hoffmann has put it, realism "does not, and cannot, prove that one is doomed to repeat the past and that there is no middle ground, however narrow, between the limited and fragile moderation of the past and the impossible abolition of the game" (Hoffmann, 1987:74).

Realist and neorealist theories are avowedly rationalistic, accepting what Herbert Simon has referred to as a "substantive" conception of rationality, characterizing "behavior that can be adjudged objectively to be optimally adapted to the situation" (Simon, 1985:294). But adopting the assumption of substantive rationality does not commit the analyst to gloomy deterministic conclusions about the inevitability of warfare. On the contrary, rationalistic theory can be used to explore the conditions under which cooperation takes place, and it seeks to explain why international institutions are constructed by states.

That rationalistic theory can lead to many different conclusions in international relations reflects a wider indeterminacy of the rationality principle as such. As Simon has argued, the principle of substantive rationality generates hypotheses about actual human behavior only when it is combined with auxiliary assumptions about the structure of utility functions and the formation of expectations. Furthermore, rationality is always contextual, so a great deal depends on the situation posited at the beginning of the analysis. Considerable variation in outcomes is therefore consistent with the assumption of substantive rationality. When limitations on the cognitive capacities of decision-makers are also taken into account—as in the concept of bounded rationality—the range of possible variation expands even further.

Even though the assumption of substantive rationality does not compel a particular set of conclusions about the nature or evolution of international institutions, it has been used in fruitful ways to explain behavior, including institutionalized behavior, in international relations. Its adherents are often highly self-conscious about their analytical perspective, and they have been highly successful in gaining legitimacy for their arguments.

Traditionally counterposed to rationalistic theory is the sociological approach to the study of institutions, which stresses the role of impersonal social forces as well as the impact of cultural practices, norms, and values that are not derived from calculations of interests. Yet the sociological approach has recently been in some disarray, at least in international relations: its adherents have neither the coherence nor the self-confidence of the rationalists. Rather than try in this essay to discuss this diffuse set of views about international relations, I will focus on the work of several scholars with a distinctive and similar point of view who have recently directly challenged the predominant rationalistic analysis of international politics. These authors, of whom the best-known include Hayward Alker, Richard Ashley, Friedrich Kratochwil, and John Ruggie, emphasize the importance of the "intersubjective meanings" of international institutional activity. In their view, understanding how people think about institutional norms and rules, and the discourse they engage in, is as important in evaluating the significance of these norms as measuring the behavior that changes in response to their invocation.

These writers emphasize that individuals, local organizations, and even states develop within the context of more encompassing institutions. Institutions do not merely reflect the preferences and power of the units constituting them: the institutions themselves shape those preferences and that power. Institutions are therefore *constitutive* of actors as well as vice versa. It is therefore not sufficient in this view to treat the preferences of individuals as given exogenously: they are affected by institutional arrangements, by prevailing norms, and by historically contingent discourse among people seeking to pursue their purposes and solve their self-defined problems.

In order to emphasize the importance of this perspective, and to focus a dialogue with rationalistic theory, I will treat the writers on world politics who have stressed these themes as members of a school of thought. I recognize, of course, that regarding them as members of a group or school obscures the many differences of view among them, and the substantial evolution that has taken place in the thought of each of them. Yet to make my point, I will even give them a label. In choosing such a label, it would be fair to refer to them as "interpretive" scholars, since they all emphasize the importance of historical and textual interpretation and the limitations of scientific models in studying world politics. But other approaches, such as strongly materialist historical-sociological approaches indebted to Marxism, or political-theoretical arguments emphasizing classical political philosophy or international law, also have a right to be considered interpretive. I have therefore coined a phrase for these writers, calling them "reflective," since all of them emphasize the importance of human reflection for the nature of institutions and ultimately for the character of world politics.

My chief argument in this essay is that students of international institutions should direct their attention to the relative merits of two approaches, the rationalistic and the reflective. Until we understand the strengths and weaknesses of each, we will be unable to design research strategies that are sufficiently multifaceted to encompass our subject-matter, and our empirical work will suffer accordingly.

The next section of this essay will define what I mean by "institutions," and introduce some distinctions that I hope will help us to understand international institutions better. Defining institutions entails drawing a distinction between specific institutions and the underlying practices within which they are embedded, of which the most fundamental in world politics are those associated with the concept of sovereignty. I will then attempt to evaluate the strengths and weaknesses of the rationalistic approach, taking into account the criticisms put forward by scholars who emphasize how actors are constituted by institutions and how subjective self-awareness of actors, and the ideas at their disposal, shape their activities. Throughout the essay I will emphasize the critical importance, for the further advance of knowledge, of undertaking empirical research, guided by these theoretical ideas. It will not be fruitful, in my view, indefinitely to conduct a debate at the purely theoretical level, much less simply to argue about epistemological and ontological issues in the abstract. Such an argument would take us away from the study of our subject matter, world politics, toward what would probably become an intellectually derivative and programmatically diversionary philosophical discussion.

International Institutions: Definitions and Distinctions

"Institution" is an even fuzzier concept than cooperation. Institutions are often discussed without being defined at all, or after having been defined only casually. Yet it sometimes seems, as a sociologist lamented half a century ago, that "the only idea common to all usages of the term 'institution' is that of some sort of establishment of relative permanence of a distinctly social sort" (Hughes, 1936:180, quoted in Zucker, 1977:726). In the international relations literature, this vagueness persists. We speak of the United Nations and the World Bank (part of the "United Nations System"), IBM and Exxon, as institutions; but we also consider "the international monetary regime" and "the international trade regime" to be institutions. Hedley Bull refers to "the balance of power, international law, the diplomatic mechanism, the managerial system of the great powers, and war" as "the institutions of international society" (Bull, 1977:74). John Ruggie discusses "the institutional framework of sovereignty" (Ruggie, 1986:147), and Stephen Krasner writes about "the particular institutional structures of sovereignty" (Krasner, 1987:11).

It may help in sorting out some of these troubling confusions to point out that "institution" may refer to a *general pattern or categorization* of activity or to a *particular* human-constructed arrangement, formally or informally organized. Examples of institutions as general patterns include Bull's "institutions of international society," as well as such varied patterns of behavior as marriage and religion, sovereign statehood, diplomacy, and neutrality. Sometimes norms such as that of reciprocity, which can apply to a variety of situations, are referred to as institutions. When we speak of patterns or categorizations of activity as institutions, the particular instances are often not regarded themselves as institutions: we do not speak of the marriage of the Duke and Duchess of Windsor, international negotiations over the status of the Panama Canal, or the neutrality of Sweden in World War II as institutions. What these general patterns of activity have in common with specific institutions is that they both meet the criteria for a broad definition of institutions: both involve persistent and connected sets of rules (formal or informal) that prescribe behavioral roles, constrain activity, and shape expectations.

Specific institutions, such as the French state, the Roman Catholic church, the international nonproliferation regime, or the General Agreement on Tariffs and Trade, are discrete entities, identifiable in space and time. Specific institutions may be exemplars of general patterns of activity —the United Nations exemplifies multilateral diplomacy; the French state, sovereign statehood; the Roman Catholic church, organized religion. But unlike general patterns of activity, specific institutions have unique life-histories, which depend on the decisions of particular individuals.

General patterns of "institutionalized" activity are more heterogeneous. Some of these institutions are only sets of entities, with each member of the set being an institution. Bull's institution of international law, for instance, can be seen as including a variety of institutions codified in legal form. In this sense, all formal international regimes are parts of international law, as are formal bilateral treaties and conventions. Likewise, the institution of religion includes a variety of quite different specific institutions, including the Roman Catholic church, Islam, and Congregationalism. Other general patterns of activity can be seen as norms that are applicable to a wide variety of situations, such as the norm of reciprocity.

It is difficult to work analytically with the broad ordinary-language definition of institutions with which I have started, since it includes such a variety of different entities and activities. In the rest of this essay, therefore, I will focus on institutions that can be identified as related complexes of rules and norms, identifiable in space and time. This conception of the scope of my analytical enterprise deliberately omits institutions that are merely categories of activity, as well as general norms that can be attached to any of a number of rule-complexes. It allows me to focus on *specific institutions* and on *practices*. As explained below, it is the mark of a practice that the behavior of those engaged in it can be corrected by an appeal to its own rules. This means that practices are deeply embedded—highly institutionalized in the sociological sense of being taken for granted by participants as social facts that are not to be challenged although their implications for behavior can be explicated.

Specific institutions can be defined in terms of their rules. Douglass North (1987:6) defines institutions as "rules, enforcement characteristics of rules, and norms of behavior that structure repeated human interaction." Institutions can be seen as "frozen decisions," or "history encoded into rules" (March and Olson, 1984:741). These rules may be informal or implicit rather than codified; in fact, some very strong institutions, such as the British constitution, rely principally on unwritten rules. To be institutionalized in the sense in which I will use the term, the rules must be durable, and must prescribe behavioral roles for actors, besides constraining activity and shaping expectations. That is, institutions differentiate among actors according to the roles that they are expected to perform, and institutions can be identified by asking whether patterns of behavior are indeed differentiated by role. When we ask whether X is an institution, we ask whether we can identify persistent sets of rules that constrain activity, shape expectations, and prescribe roles. In international relations, some of these institutions are formal organizations, with prescribed hierarchies and the capacity for purposive action. Others, such as the international regimes for money and trade, are complexes of rules and organizations, the core elements of which have been negotiated and explicitly agreed upon by states.

This definition of specific institutions incorporates what John Rawls has called the "summary view" of rules, in which "rules are pictured as summaries of past decisions," which allow the observer to predict future behavior (Rawls, 1955:19). Rules such as these can be changed by participants on utilitarian grounds without engaging in self-contradictory behavior. This definition is useful as far as it goes, but it does not capture what Rawls calls "the practice conception" of rules. A practice in the sense used by Rawls is analogous to a game such as baseball or chess: "It is the mark of a practice that being taught how to engage in it involves being instructed in the rules that define it, and that appeal is made to those rules to correct the behavior of those engaged in it. Those engaged in a practice recognize the rules as defining it" (Rawls, 1955:24). Were the rules of a practice to change, so would the fundamental nature of the activity in question.

Someone engaged in a practice has to explain her action by showing that it is in accord with the practice. Otherwise, the behavior itself is self-contradictory. As Oran Young points out, "It just does not make sense for a chess player to refuse to accept the concept of checkmate, for a speaker of English to assert that it makes no difference whether subjects and predicates agree, or for an actor in the existing international society to disregard the rules regarding the nationality of citizens." In international relations, the "menu of available practices" is limited: "a 'new' state, for example, has little choice but to join the basic institutional arrangements of the states system" (1986:120).

The concept of a practice is particularly applicable to certain general patterns of activity such as sovereignty and multilateral diplomacy. Their rules, many of which are not codified, define what it means to be sovereign or to engage in multilateral diplomacy. Like the rules of chess and the grammar of the English language, respect for state sovereignty and multilateral diplomacy are taken for granted by most of those who participate in them. When fundamental practices are violated, as in the seizure of the American Embassy in Teheran in 1979, disapproval is virtually universal. This is not surprising, because such practices are based on what Hans J. Morgenthau referred to as "the permanent interests of states to put their normal relations on a stable basis by providing for predictable and enforceable conduct with respect to these relations" (Morgenthau, 1940:279).

Rawls['] distinction helps us to see the specific institutions of world politics, with their challengeable rules, as embedded in more fundamental practices. Just as the actors in world politics are constrained by existing institutions, so are institutions, and prospects for institutional change, constrained by the practices taken for granted by their members. For each set of entities that we investigate, we can identify institutionalized constraints at a more fundamental and enduring level.

Consider, for instance, the practice of sovereign statehood, which has been fundamental to world politics for over three hundred years. At its core is the principle of sovereignty; that the state "is subject to no other state and has full and exclusive powers within its jurisdiction without prejudice to the limits set by applicable law" (*Wimbledon* case, Permanent Court of International Justice, series A, no. 1, 1923; cited in Hoffmann, 1987:172–73). Sovereignty is thus a relatively precise legal concept: a question of law, not of fact, of authority, not sheer power. As a legal concept, the principle of sovereignty should not be confused with the empirical claim that a given state in fact makes its decisions autonomously. Sovereignty refers to a legal status, a property of an organized entity in world politics. It does not imply that the sovereign entity possesses de facto independence, although as a political matter, the fact that an entity is sovereign can be expected to have implications for its power and its autonomy.

Sovereign statehood is a practice in Rawls' sense because it contains a set of rules that define it and that can be used to correct states' behavior. These rules are fundamental to the conduct of modern international relations. Extraterritorial jurisdiction for embassies is such a central rule, implied by the modern conception of sovereignty; immunity from ordinary criminal prosecution for a state's accredited diplomats is a corollary of this principle. More generally, as Martin Wight has argued, the norm of reciprocity is implied by that of sovereignty, and respect for reciprocity is therefore part of the practice of sovereign statehood: "It would be impossible to have a society of sovereign states unless each state, while claiming sovereignty for itself, recognized that every other state had the right to claim and enjoy its own sovereignty as well. This reciprocity was inherent in the Western conception of sovereignty" (Wight, 1977:135).

Treating sovereign statehood as a practice does not imply that the process of recognizing entities as sovereign is automatic: on the contrary, states follow political convenience as well as law in deciding which entities to regard as sovereign. But once an entity has been generally accepted by states as sovereign, certain rights and responsibilities are entailed. Furthermore, acceptance of the principle of sovereignty creates well-defined roles. Only sovereign states or entities such as international organizations created by states can make treaties and enforce them on subjects within their jurisdictions, declare and wage wars recognized by international law, and join international organizations that are part of the United Nations System.

Definitions are not interesting in themselves, but they may be more or less clear, and lead to the identification of more or less tractable problems. I have begun with a broad definition of institutions as persistent and connected sets of rules that prescribe behavioral roles, constrain activity, and shape expectations. I have focused my attention, however, on specific institutions and practices. Specific institutions can be defined in the first instance in terms of rules; but we must recognize that specific institutions are embedded in practices. In modern world politics, the most important practice is that of sovereignty. To understand institutions and institutional change in world politics, it is necessary to understand not only how specific institutions are formulated, change, and die, but how their evolution is affected by the practice of sovereignty.

The Rationalistic Study of International Institutions

Rationalistic research on international institutions focuses almost entirely on specific institutions. It emphasizes international regimes and formal international organizations. Since this research program is rooted in exchange theory, it assumes scarcity and competition as well as rationality on the part of the actors. It therefore begins with the premise that if there were no potential gains from agreements to be captured in world politics—that is, if no agreements among actors could be mutually beneficial—there would be no need for specific international institutions. But there are evidently considerable benefits to be secured from mutual agreement—as evidenced for millennia by trade agreements, rules of war, and peace treaties, and for the last century by international organizations. Conversely, if cooperation were easy—that is, if all mutually beneficial bargains could be made without cost—there would be no need for institutions to facilitate cooperation. Yet such an assumption would be equally as false as the assumption that no potential gains from agreements exist. It is the combination of the potential *value* of agreements and the *difficulty* of making them that renders international regimes significant. In order to cooperate in world politics on more than a sporadic basis, human beings have to use institutions.

Rationalistic theories of institutions view institutions as affecting patterns of costs. Specifically, institutions reduce certain forms of uncertainty and alter transaction costs: that is, the "costs of specifying and enforcing the contracts that underlie exchange" (North, 1984:256). Even in the absence of hierarchical authority, institutions provide information (through monitoring) and stabilize expectations. They may also make decentralized enforcement feasible, for example by creating conditions under which reciprocity can operate. At any point in time, transaction costs are to a substantial degree the result of the institutional context. Dynamically, the relationship between these institutionally affected transaction costs and the formation of new institutions will, according to the theory, be curvilinear. If transaction costs are negligible, it will not be necessary to create new institutions to facilitate mutually beneficial exchange; if transaction costs are extremely high, it will not be feasible to build institutions—which may even be unimaginable.

In world politics, sovereignty and state autonomy mean that transaction costs are never negligible, since it is always difficult to communicate, to monitor performance, and especially to enforce compliance with rules. Therefore, according to this theory, one should expect international institutions to appear whenever the costs of communication, monitoring, and enforcement are relatively low compared to the benefits to be derived from political exchange. Institutions should persist as long as, but only so long as, their members have incentives to maintain them. But the effects of these institutions will not be politically neutral: they can be expected to confer advantages on those to whom their rules grant access and a share in political authority; and insofar as the transaction costs of making agreements outside of an established institution are high, governments disadvantaged within an institution will find themselves at a disadvantage in the issue area as a whole. More generally, the rules of any institution will reflect the relative power positions of its actual and potential members, which constrain the feasible bargaining space and affect transaction costs.

These transaction-cost arguments have been applied in qualitative terms to international relations. As anticipated by the theory, effective international regimes include arrangements to share information and to monitor compliance, according to standards established by the regime; and they adapt to shifts in capabilities among their members. Furthermore, the access rules of different international regimes affect the success of governments in the related issue areas. As a general descriptive model, therefore, this approach seems to do quite well: international regimes work as we expect them to.

However, the rationalistic theory has not been used to explain why international institutions exist in some issue areas rather than in others. Nor has this theory been employed systematically to account for the creation or demise of such institutions. Yet the theory implies hypotheses about these questions: hypotheses that could be submitted to systematic, even quantitative, examination. For instance, this theory predicts that the incidence of specific international institutions should be related to the ratio of benefits anticipated from exchange to the transaction costs of establishing the institutions necessary to facilitate the negotiation, monitoring, and enforcement costs of agreements specifying the terms of exchange. It also predicts that in the absence of anticipated gains from agreements, specific institutions will not be created, and that most specific institutions in world politics will in fact perform the function of reducing transaction costs. Since the theory acknowledges the significance of sunk costs in perpetuating extant institutions, and since its advocates recognize that organizational processes modify the pure dictates of rationality, its predictions about the demise of specific institutions are less clear.

The rationalistic theory could also help us develop a theory of compliance or noncompliance with commitments. For international regimes to be effective, their injunctions must be obeyed; yet sovereignty precludes hierarchical enforcement. The game-theoretic literature suggests that reputation may provide a strong incentive for compliance. But we do not know how strong the reputational basis for enforcement of agreements is in world politics, since we have not done the necessary empirical work. What Oliver Williamson calls "opportunism" is still possible: reputations can be differentiated among partners and violations of agreements can often be concealed. Historically, it is not entirely clear to what extent governments that renege on their commitments are in fact punished for such actions. Indeed, governments that have defaulted on their debts have, it appears, not been punished via higher interest rates in subsequent periods for their defections.

Rationalistic theory can often help us understand the direction of change in world politics, if not always its precise extent or the form that it takes. For instance, there are good reasons to believe that a diffusion of power away from a hegemonic state, which sponsored extant international regimes, will create pressures on these regimes and weaken their rules— even though it is dubious that hegemony is either a necessary or a sufficient condition for the maintenance of a pattern of order in international relations. That is, if we are able to specify the characteristics of a given institutional situation, rationalistic theory may help us anticipate the path that change will take. As Alexander Wendt points out, rationalistic theory has "proved useful in generating insights into the emergence of and reproduction of social institutions as the unintended consequences of strategic interactions" (Wendt, 1987:368).

Yet even on its own terms, rationalistic theory encounters some inherent limitations. The so-called Folk Theorem of game theory states that for a class of games that includes 2 × 2 repeated Prisoner's Dilemma, there are many feasible equilibria above the maximin points of both players. We cannot predict which one will emerge without knowing more about the structure of a situation—that is, about the prior institutional context in which the situation is embedded. This means that the conclusions of formal models of cooperation are often highly dependent on the assumptions with which the investigations begin—that they are context-dependent. To be sure, once we understand the context, it may be possible to model strategies used by players to devise equilibrium-inducing institutions. The literatures on bureaucratic politics and agency theory complicate matters further by suggesting that the organizational "actor" will not necessarily act as "its" interests specify, if people within it have different interests. Thus even on its own terms rationalistic theory seems to leave open the issue of what kinds of institutions will develop, to whose benefit, and how effective they will be.

Even within the confines of the rationalistic research program, therefore, formal theory alone is unlikely to yield answers to our explanatory puzzles. Rationalistic theory is good at posing questions and suggesting lines of inquiry, but it does not furnish us with answers. Creative uses of simulation, as in Robert Axelrod's work are helpful; but most of all we need more empirical research, guided by theory. Such research could begin to delineate the specific conditions under which cooperation takes place. It should seek to map out patterns of interests, information flows and barriers, and anticipated long-term relationships in order to understand more specifically under what conditions cooperation will or will not take place. Brent Sutton and Mark Zacher have illustrated the value of such research in their recent analysis of the international shipping regime. They explore in depth six issue-areas within shipping, on the basis of a hypothesis that cooperation will be greatest where market imperfections and failures, hence possibilities for global welfare gains, exist. Unfortunately, there has so far been relatively little of this type of work done; but I hope and expect that we will see more during the next few years.

Rationalistic theory also needs to extend its vision back into history. To do so in a sophisticated way entails a departure from the equilibrium models emphasized by neoclassical economic theory. It requires intellectual contortions to view the evolution of institutions over time as the product of a deterministic equilibrium logic in which rational adaptation to the environment plays the key role. Institutional development is affected by particular leaders and by exogenous shocks—chance events from the perspective of a systemic theory. Theories of "path-dependence" in economics demonstrate that under specified conditions, accumulated random variations can lead an institution into a state that could not have been predicted in advance. From a technological standpoint, path-dependence occurs under conditions of increasing rather than decreasing returns—resulting for instance from positive externalities that give established networks advantages over their competitors, from learning effects, and from the convergence of expectations around an established standard. Examples include the development of the typewriter keyboard, competition between different railroad gauges or between Betamax and VHS types of video recorders, and between gasoline and steam-powered cars. Viewed from a more strictly institutional perspective, path-dependence can be a result of sunk costs. Arthur Stinchcombe (1968:120–21) points out that if "sunk costs make a traditional pattern of action cheaper, and if new patterns are not enough more profitable to justify throwing away the resource, the sunk costs tend to preserve a pattern of action from one year to the next."

Surely the General Agreement on Tariffs and Trade (GATT), the International Monetary Fund (IMF) and the United Nations are not optimally efficient, and they would not be invented in their present forms today; but they persist. In some cases, this may be a matter of sunk costs making it rational to continue involvement with an old institution. Sometimes the increasing returns pointed to by path-dependence theorists may account for this persistence. Or considerations of power and status may be more important than the functions performed by the institutions. In politics, where institutional innovators may be punished, existing institutions may have an additional advantage. Even in Congress, "it is risky to try to change institutional arrangements in a manner adverse to the interests of those currently in control" (Schepsle 1986:69). At the very least, theories of path-dependence demonstrate once again that history not only matters, but that historical investigation is consistent with a rationalistic research program.

Reflective Approaches

Scholars imbued with a sociological perspective on institutions emphasize that institutions are often not created consciously by human beings but rather emerge slowly through a less deliberative process, and that they are frequently taken for granted by the people who are affected by them. In this view the assumption of utility maximization often does not tell us much about the origins of institutions; and it also does not take us very far in understanding the variations in institutional arrangements in different cultures and political systems. Ronald Dore, for instance, suggests that Oliver Williamson's attempt to construct "timeless generalizations" perhaps "merely reflects the tendency of American economists to write as if all the world were America. Or perhaps [Williamson] does not have much evidence about America either, and just assumes that 'Man' is a hard-nosed short-run profit maximizer suspicious of everyone he deals with" (Dore, 1983:469).

Values, norms and practices vary across cultures, and such variations will affect the efficacy of institutional arrangements. This point can be put into the language of rationalistic theory: institutions that are consistent with culturally accepted practices are likely to entail lower transaction costs than those that conflict with those practices. But such a statement merely begs the question of where the practices, or the preferences that they reflect, came from in the first place. The most ambitious form of rationalistic theory, which takes fundamental preferences as uniform and constant, is contradicted by cultural variation if preferences are meaningfully operationalized. The more modest form of this theory, which treats variations in preferences as exogenous, thereby avoids seeking to explain them.

Similar problems arise with explanations of changes in institutions over time. Rationalistic theories of specific institutions can be applied historically, as we have seen. Each set of institutions to be explained is viewed within an institutional as well as material context: prior institutions create incentives and constraints that affect the emergence or evolution of later ones. Change is then explained by changes in opportunity costs at the margin, as a result of environmental changes.

Such an approach has been highly revealing, as the literature on institutional change in economics demonstrates. However, these rationalistic theories of specific institutions have to be contextualized before they are empirically useful: that is, they must be put into a prior framework of institutions and practices. Only with this prior knowledge of the situation at one point in time to guide us, can we use this theory effectively to improve our knowledge of what is likely to happen next. We can then work our way back through the various levels of analysis—explaining actor behavior by reference to institutional constraints and opportunities, explaining specific institutions by reference to prior institutions, explaining those institutions by reference to fundamental practices. Up to a point, rationalistic theory can pursue its analysis backwards in time; and it can only gain by becoming more historically sensitive. But as Field pointed out and as North has recognized in the field of economic history, at some point one must embed the analysis in institutions that are not plausibly viewed as the product of human calculation and bargaining. And ultimately, the analysis has to come to grips with the structures of social interaction that "constitute or empower those agents in the first place" (Wendt, 1987:369).

International institutions are not created *de novo* any more than are economic institutions. On the contrary, they emerge from prior institutionalized contexts, the most fundamental of which cannot be explained as if they were contracts among rational individuals maximizing some utility function. These fundamental practices seem to reflect historically distinctive combinations of material circumstances, social patterns of thought, and individual initiative—combinations which reflect "conjunctures" rather than deterministic outcomes, and which are themselves shaped over time by path-dependent processes. Rationalistic theory can help to illuminate these practices, but it cannot stand alone. Despite the ambitions of some of its enthusiasts, it has little prospect of becoming a comprehensive deductive explanation of international institutions.

Quite apart from this limitation, the writers whom I have labeled "reflective" have emphasized that rationalistic theories of institutions contain no *endogenous* dynamic. Individual and social reflection leading to changes in preferences or in views of causality—what Hayward Alker refers to as *historicity* and what Ernst Haas discusses under the rubric of *learning* is ignored. That is, preferences are assumed to be fixed. But this assumption of fixed preferences seems to preclude understanding of some major changes in human institutions. For example, as Douglass North points out, "the demise of slavery, one of the landmarks in the history of freedom, is simply not explicable in an interest group model" (North, 1987:12). Nor, in the view of Robert Cox, is American hegemony explicable simply in power terms: on the contrary, it implies a "coherent conjunction or fit between a configuration of material power, a prevalent collective image of world order (including certain norms) and a set of institutions which administer the order with a certain semblance of universality" (Cox, 1986:223).

From this perspective, rationalistic theories seem only to deal with one dimension of a multidimensional reality: they are incomplete, since they ignore changes taking place in consciousness. They do not enable us to understand how interests change as a result of changes in belief systems. They obscure rather than illuminate the sources of states' policy preferences. The result, according to Richard Ashley, has been a fundamentally unhistorical approach to world politics, which has reified contemporary political arrangements by denying "history as process" and "the historical significance of practice" (Ashley, 1986:290).

Some analysts in the reflective camp have sought to correct this lack of attention to historicity and learning. In analyzing Prisoner's Dilemma, Alker emphasizes not merely the structure of payoff matrices but the sequential patterns of learning taking place between actors over the course of a sequence of games. And Ruggie has argued that only by understanding how individuals think about their world can we understand changes in how the world is organized—for instance, the shift from medieval to modern international politics. Socially influenced patterns of learning are crucial, as Karl Deutsch and Ernst Haas—the teachers, respectively, of Alker and Ruggie—have always emphasized.

Reflective critics of the rationalistic research program have emphasized the inadequacies of rationalism in analyzing the fundamental practice of sovereign statehood, which has been instituted not by agreement but as a result of the elaboration over time of the principle of sovereignty. Sovereignty seems to be *prior* to the kinds of calculations on which rationalistic theory focuses: governments' strategies assume the principle of sovereignty, and the practice of sovereign statehood, as givens. Indeed, according to some critics of rationalistic thinking, sovereignty is of even more far-reaching significance, since it defines the very nature of the actors in world politics. Ruggie conceptualizes sovereignty as a "form of legitimation" that "differentiates units in terms of juridically mutually exclusive and morally self-entailed domains." Like private property rights, it divides space in terms of exclusive rights and establishes patterns of social relationships among the resulting "possessive individualists," whose character as agents is fundamentally shaped by sovereignty itself (Ruggie, 1986:144–47).

Ruggie's critical analysis of sovereignty calls our attention once again to the significance of practices such as sovereign statehood for our understanding of the specific institutions of world politics. The international monetary or nonproliferation regimes of the 1980s, for example, can be understood only against the background of the constraints and opportunities provided by the practice of sovereign statehood. We are reminded again of the partial nature of rationalistic theory and the need to contextualize if we are to derive meaningful insights from its analytical techniques.

The criticisms of rationalistic theory, both from within the framework of its assumptions and outside of them, are extensive and telling. The assumption of equilibrium is often misleading, and can lead to mechanical or contorted analysis. Rationalistic theory accounts better for shifts in the strength of institutions than in the values that they serve to promote. Cultural variations create anomalies for the theory. It does not take into account the impact of social processes of reflection or learning on the preferences of individuals or on the organizations that they direct. Finally, rationalistic theory has had little to say about the origins and evolution of practices, and it has often overlooked the impact of such practices as sovereignty on the specific institutions that it studies.

Yet the critics have by no means demolished the rationalistic research program on institutions, although taking their argument seriously requires us to doubt the legitimacy of rationalism's intellectual hegemony. To show that rationalistic theory cannot account for changes in preferences because it has omitted important potential explanatory factors is important, but it is not devastating, since no social science theory is complete. Limiting the number of variables that a theory considers can increase both its explanatory content and its capacity to concentrate the scholarly mind. Indeed, the rationalistic program is heuristically so powerful precisely because it does not easily accept accounts based on post hoc observation of values or ideology: regarding states as rational actors with specified utility functions forces the analyst to look below the surface for interests that provide incentives to behave in apparently anomalous ways. In quite a short time, research stimulated by rationalistic theory has posed new questions and proposed new hypotheses about why governments create and join international regimes, and the conditions under which these institutions wax or wane. A research program with such a record of accomplishment, and a considerable number of interesting but still untested hypotheses about reasons for persistence, change, and compliance, cannot be readily dismissed.

Indeed, the greatest weakness of the reflective school lies not in deficiencies in their critical arguments but in the lack of a clear reflective research program that could be employed by students of world politics. Waltzian neorealism has such a research program; so does neoliberal institutionalism, which has focused on the evolution and impact of international regimes. Until the reflective scholars or others sympathetic to their arguments have delineated such a research program and shown in particular studies that it can illuminate important issues in world politics, they will remain on the margins of the field, largely invisible to the preponderance of empirical researchers, most of whom explicitly or implicitly accept one or another version of rationalistic premises. Such invisibility would be a shame, since the reflective perspective has much to contribute.

As formulated to date, both rationalistic and what I have called reflective approaches share a common blind spot: neither pays sufficient attention to domestic politics. It is all too obvious that domestic politics is neglected by much game-theoretic strategic analysis and by structural explanations of international regime change. However, this deficiency is not inherent in the nature of rationalistic analysis: it is quite possible to use game theory heuristically to analyze the "two-level games" linking domestic and international politics, as Robert Putnam has done. At one level reflective theory questions, in its discussion of sovereignty, the existence of a clear boundary between domestic and international politics. But at another level it critiques the reification of the state in neorealist theory and contemporary practice, and should therefore be driven to an analysis of how such reification has taken place historically and how it is reproduced within the confines of the domestic-international dichotomy. Such an analysis could lead to a fruitful reexamination of shifts in preferences that emerge from complex interactions between the operation of international institutions and the processes of domestic politics. Both Kenneth Waltz's "second image"—the impact of domestic politics on international relations—and Peter Gourevitch's "second image reversed" need to be taken account of, in their different ways, by the rationalist and reflective approaches.

Conclusion

I believe that international institutions are worth studying because they are pervasive and important in world politics and because their operation and evolution are difficult to understand. But I also urge attention to them on normative grounds. International institutions have the *potential* to facilitate cooperation, and without international cooperation, I believe that the prospects for our species would be very poor indeed. Cooperation is not always benign; but without cooperation, we will be lost. Without institutions there will be little cooperation. And without a knowledge of how institutions work—and what makes them work well—there are likely to be fewer, and worse, institutions than if such knowledge is widespread.

A major challenge for students of international relations is to obtain such knowledge of institutions, through theory and the application of theory to practice, but especially through empirical research. Neither pure rationalistic theory nor pure criticism is likely to provide such knowledge. We should demand that advocates of both rationalistic and reflective theory create genuine research programs: not dogmatic assertions of epistemological or ontological superiority, but ways of discovering new facts and developing insightful interpretations of international institutions.

Both rationalistic and reflective approaches need further work if they are to become well-developed research programs. Rationalistic theories of institutions need to be historically contextualized: we need to see specific institutions as embedded in practices that are not entirely explicable through rationalistic analysis. And the many hypotheses generated by rationalistic theory need to be tested empirically. Reflective approaches are less well specified as theories: their advocates have been more adept at pointing out what is omitted in rationalistic theory than in developing theories of their own with *a prior* content. Supporters of this research program need to develop testable theories, and to be explicit about their scope. Are these theories confined to practices or do they also illuminate the operations of specific institutions? Above all, students of world politics who are sympathetic to this position need to carry out systematic empirical investigations, guided by their ideas. Without such detailed studies, it will be impossible to evaluate their research program.

Eventually, we may hope for a synthesis between the rationalistic and reflective approaches—a synthesis that will help us to understand both practices and specific institutions and the relationships between them. Such a synthesis, however, will not emerge full-blown, like Athena from the head of Zeus. On the contrary, it will require constructive competition and dialogue between these two research programs—and the theoretically informed investigation of facts. Thus equipped with our new knowledge, we can intervene more persuasively in the policy process, by drawing connections between institutional choices and those practices of cooperation that will be essential to human survival, and progress, in the twenty-first century.

References

Ashley, R. K. (1986) The Poverty of Neorealism. In *Neorealism and Its Critics,* edited by R. O. Keohane. New York: Columbia University Press.

Bull, H. (1977) *The Anarchical Society.* New York: Columbia University Press.

Cox, R. W. (1986) Social Forces, States and World Orders: Beyond International Relations Theory. In *Neorealism and Its Critics,* edited by R. O. Keohane, pp. 204–55. New York: Columbia University Press.

Dore, R. (1983) Goodwill and the Spirit of Market Capitalism. *British Journal of Sociology* 34:459–82.

Hoffman, S. (1987) Hans Morgenthau: The Limits and Influence of "Realism." In *Janus and Minerva: Essays in the Theory and Practice of International Politics,* edited by S. Hoffmann, pp. 70–81. Boulder: Westview.

Holsti, K. J. (1986) The Horsemen of the Apocalypse: At the Gate, Detoured, or Retreating? *International Studies Quarterly* 30:355–72.

Hughes, E. C. (1936) The Ecological Aspect of Institutions. *American Sociological Review* 1:180–89.

Keohane, R. O. (1984) *After Hegemony: Cooperation and Discord in the World Political Economy.* Princeton: Princeton University Press.

Krasner, S. D. (1987) Sovereignty: An Institutional Perspective. Manuscript. Stanford, Calif.: Center for Advanced Study in the Behavioral Sciences, October.

March, J., and J. Olson (1984) The New Institutionalism: Organizational Factors in Political Life. *American Political Science Review* 79:734–49.

Morgenthau, H. J. (1940) Positivism, Functionalism and International Law. *American Journal of International Law* 34:260–84.

North, D. C. (1984) Government and the Cost of Exchange in History. *Journal of Economic History* 44:255–64.

North, D. C. (1987) Institutions and Economic Growth: An Historical Introduction. Paper prepared for the Conference on Knowledge and Institutional Change sponsored by the University of Minnesota, Minneapolis, November.

Rawls, J. (1955) Two Concepts of Rules. *Philosophical Review* 64:3–32.

Ruggie, J. G. (1986) Continuity and Transformation in the World Polity: Toward a Neorealist Synthesis. In *Neorealism and Its Critics,* edited by R. O. Keohane, pp. 131–57. New York: Columbia University Press.

Shepsle, K. (1986) Institutional Equilibrium and Equilibrium Institutions. In *Political Science: The Science of Politics,* edited by H. F. Weisberg, pp. 51–81. New York: Agathon Press.

Simon, H. A. (1985) Human Nature in Politics: The Dialogue of Psychology with Political Science. *American Political Science Review* 79:293–304.

Stinchcombe, A. L. (1968) *Constructing Social Theories.* New York: Harcourt, Brace and World.

Wendt, A. E. (1987) The Agent-Structure Problem in International Relations Theory. *International Organization* 41:335–70.

Wright, M. (1977) *Systems of States,* edited with an introduction by H. Bull. Leicester: Leicester University Press.

Young, O. R. (1986) International Regimes: Toward a New Theory of Institutions. *World Politics* 39:104–22.

Zucker, L. G. (1977) The Role of Institutionalization in Cultural Persistence. *American Sociological Review* 42:726–43.

ANDREW HURRELL

International Society and the Study of Regimes: A Reflective Approach

1. Introduction

This chapter seeks to place the growth of the undoubtedly US-dominated literature on regime theory within the broader tradition of thought on the existence of international society. This tradition was in many ways a distinctively European one whose central expression lay in the emergence of ideas about the role and function of international law. More recently it has come to be associated with the work of such writers as Martin Wight and Hedley Bull. This chapter addresses three questions: First, what does regime theory tell us about co-operation in international life that theories of international society do not? Second, to what extent can ideas about international law and society illuminate some of the weaknesses of regime theory? And third, to what extent, if at all, does this analysis suggest areas for further research?

2. The Core Problem

Regime theory cannot be described as a fad, as is sometimes alleged by its critics, because its central question is one which has been fundamental to the evolution of western thought about international relations: how is co-operation possible between states claiming sovereignty but competing for power and influence in a situation of anarchy? Equally the search for origins is not about finding earlier uses of the term "regimes," but rather about tracing similarities and differences between the multiple answers that have been given to this basic question. The idea that co-operation between states was indeed possible and that some form of international society could indeed exist has been a persistent theme of European thought and is extremely deep-rooted. The academic study of international relations is often presented as being founded on the fundamental difference between domestic "society" and international "anarchy." Yet one of the most striking features of European thought before 1914 was just how few theorists actually accepted such a dichotomy. Indeed the distortions produced by such a rigid dichotomy and by the parallel bifurcation of theorists into realist or idealist camps have become a theme of much recent writing. It was perhaps only the extreme

From Volker Rittberger, ed., *Regime Theory and International Relations* (Oxford, 1993), pp. 49–72. ©Andrew Hurrell 1993. Reprinted by permission of Oxford University Press. Some notes have been altered.

nature of post-war US realism that produced a situation in which co-operation came to be seen as an "anomaly" in need of explanation.

But confusion has also arisen in the writings of those who have attempted to derive and explore an international society tradition. Thus, for example, Bull's use of the term "Grotian" was applied in two quite distinct senses and (except in an early paper first written in the 1950s and published in 1966) he never systematically explored the differences between various conceptions of international society.[1] His central purpose was to contrast the Grotian tradition with a Hobbesian, or realist, tradition on one side, and with a Kantian, or cosmopolitan, tradition on the other. Yet the positions with which the Grotian tradition is contrasted turn out on closer inspection to be concerned with many of the same themes and, at times, to be making many similar arguments. Thus the past decade has seen the recasting of Hobbes, picking up the argument made nearly thirty years ago by Stanley Hoffmann (1965: 61) that Hobbes should as "the founder of utilitarian theories of international law and relations." Increasingly Hobbes has been viewed as a precursor of precisely those theorists who seek to construct models of co-operation, and indeed of justice, based on rational prudence. Indeed, for both Bull himself, just as for earlier theorists such as Pufendorf, Wolff, and Vattel, the first stage in the argument in favour of international society consists in the application of Hobbes's own arguments about the differences between domestic and international life: that states are less vulnerable than individuals and have less fear of sudden death; that they are unequal in power and resources; and that, if they are rational, they will be less tempted to destroy each other than will individuals in a state of nature and will be able to develop at least minimal rules of coexistence based on self-interest and rational prudence. On the other side, there is a good deal to justify the view of Kant not as a cosmopolitan intent on fostering a global society of mankind, but as a "statist," deeply committed to the creation of a law-governed international society between sovereign states.

It is also the case that modern discussions of regime theory and older ideas about international society have to come to terms with the same essential problematic: what is the relationship between law and norms on the one hand and power and interests on the other? The difficulties here are twofold. On one side, there have always been those who claim that the rules and norms of international life are purely reflective of the power and interests of states: they are just power politics translated into a different idiom, "a record of the methods and results of power politics" (Donelan 1990:36). Classical international law was always susceptible to this line of attack because of the role of custom and practice in the creation of legal rules and because of the extent to which it accepted almost all of what states actually did: thus treaties under duress were valid; there was no restraint on the right to wage war; successful conquest was accepted as legitimate; and the definition of state sovereignty gave no place to self-determination or the rights of citizens.

This line of criticism has been very common and unites liberals, realists, and Marxists. Thus, liberals from Kant onwards have bemoaned the role of the "sorry comforters" such as Grotius, Pufendorf, and Vattel in legitimizing the immoral and aggressive actions of states. For realists such as E. H. Carr, the fine language of law and morality was merely a rationalization and a cloak for the particular interests of a particular group of states who happened to have a vested interest in protecting the status quo. For Carr (1981: 87, 88), supposedly abstract and universal legal and moral norms were merely "the unconscious reflexions of national policy based on a particular interpretation of national interests at a particular time," or the "transparent disguises of selfish vested interests." Such a position follows very closely the traditional Marxist view of law, including international law, as reflecting the class interests of a particular group or group of states.[2] These kinds of arguments are reflected in many of the most common criticisms of regime theory. On the one hand, the perspective of critical theory that it is inherently conservative, statist, and technocratic. On the other, the general structuralist position that rules and norms are a direct reflection of power and interest. Crudely put, one is better off studying underlying power structures than wasting time on surface phenomena.

Yet, if one danger arose from the possibility that norms and rules might be purely reflective of state interests and might therefore have no independent compliance pull in themselves, then there has always been an equal and opposite danger: that the norms and rules of international life are so far away from the power political "realities" that their study becomes an empty and formalistic exercise, well captured by the derogatory force of the term "legalistic." There was certainly a clear need to get away from two of the central preoccupations of progressivist international lawyers: first, the idea that constitution-making would in itself enable states to live together in a more harmonious and peaceful manner—Clark and Sohn's (1958) *World Peace through World Law* being a clear exemplar; and second, the preoccupation with enforcement or with finding some functional equivalent for enforcement (hence the idealist obsession with collective security). It was of course precisely against this tendency that the regime theorists were reacting. On the one hand, there was the need to achieve maximum distance from such perceived formalism and from anything tainted by the sins of idealism. On the other, to be academically credible, ideas of co-operation had to take into account the harsher and more Hobbesian world of the early 1980s, the structuralist turn in the overall direction of international relations theory, and the need to achieve as much theoretical rigour as the other social sciences had purportedly been able to do. Whilst the nature of this reaction is understandable within the context of the evolution of the discipline, it is hard to avoid the conclusion that the rejection of international law was too absolute and all-encompassing.

The central problem, then, for regime theorists and international lawyers is to establish that laws and norms exercise a compliance pull of their own, at least partially independent of the power and interests which underpinned them and which were often responsible for their creation. To avoid empty tautology it is necessary to show not only that rules exist and that they are created and obeyed primarily out of self-interest or expediency, but also that they are followed even in cases when a state's self-interest seems to suggest otherwise. Whilst arguments about regime creation are important, it is this fundamental question that lies at the heart of the matter: do regimes make a difference? If so, how, why, and to what degree? On the one hand, the rules of a system that depends on self-enforcement must be sufficiently close to the power and interests of states if they are to have any meaningful political impact. Thus Oscar Schachter (1982: 26, 25) argues that international law is "a product of political and social forces, that it is dependent on behaviour and that it is an instrument to meet changing needs and values." But on the other side, it "is in essence a system based on a set of rules and obligations. They must in some degree be binding, that is, the rules must be accepted as a means of independent control that effectively limits the conduct of the entities subject to law." If their political impact is to be significant, international norms cannot be the automatic and immediate reflection of self-interest. There has to be some notion of being bound by a particular rule despite countervailing self-interest.

Despite their lack of interaction, this central question is one which unites regime theorists and international lawyers.[3] Indeed their mutual concerns have in many ways grown closer. On the one hand, many lawyers have come to view international treaties and conventions over such matters as the environment, not as a definitive and unchanging set of rules, but rather as a means of creating law-making frameworks. Their purpose is to provide a framework for negotiation in which the techniques and general principles of international law can be employed, first to negotiate and formalize accepted but very general principles, and second to create a means of facilitating ongoing negotiations from which more specific, "harder" rules may subsequently emerge. On the other, regime theorists such as Robert Keohane appear to have become less interested in the rather generalized definitions of regimes and more concerned with the need to focus on specific sets of rules. Take, for instance, the definition of regimes given by Stephen Krasner in 1983: "implicit or explicit principles, norms, rules, and decision-making procedures around which actors' expectations converge in a given area of international relations" (Krasner 1983: 2). And compare this with Keohane's 1989 definition: "institutions with explicit rules, agreed upon by governments, which pertain to particular sets of issues in international relations" (Keohane 1989: 4). The apparently growing stress on explicit, persistent, and connected sets of rules brings regime theory and international law much closer together.

3. The Differences Between Regime Theory and International Law

Perhaps the most important difference that marks regime theory from international law and older notions of international society concerns the reasons why states obey rules that are usually unenforced and mostly unenforceable. There have been many answers to this question: power and coercion, self-interest and reciprocal benefits, institutionalized habit or inertia, the existence of a sense of community, procedural legitimacy of the process of rule creation, or the moral suasion that derives from a shared sense of justice. Previous explanations of co-operation have often tended to produce an aggregate list of these kinds of factors without providing any precise guide as to their interrelationship. This was one of the most common criticisms of Bull's work.

Regime theory seeks above all to be far more discriminating and to try and derive testable hypotheses about which factors explain co-operation under which conditions and in what circumstances. Regime theory has certainly examined the role of power and there has, of course, been a heated debate over the role of power and, in particular, hegemonic power in the creation and maintenance of regimes. Leaning towards realism, regime theorists stress the close connections that exist between the emergence of institutions and the distribution of power. But it is a cardinal feature of rationalist regime theory that power alone cannot explain the emergence or impact of institutions. Whilst the steam may be running out of the hegemonic stability debate, the role of power and coercion in the *implementation* of rules remains fundamental. For international lawyers the idea of decentralized sanctions, whether in the form of direct retaliation or actions by third parties, has always been one way of maintaining the belief that all legal systems need to be backed by some coercive power (an idea particularly associated with Hans Kelsen). And, for all the undoubted importance of functional benefits and "learning," sanctions and coercion continue to play a major role: think of the role played by the "carrot" of aid and technology transfer and of the "stick" of trade sanctions in the recent negotiations of the ozone regime. Regime theory has also considered the role of habit or inertia, for instance in explaining why regimes persist after the conditions that underpinned their emergence have long since changed.

But it remains the case that regime theory's most distinctive contribution is to have developed the idea of self-interest and reciprocal benefits and, in general, to have downplayed the traditional emphasis placed on the role of community and a sense of justice. The central challenge was to explain the emergence of co-operation on the basis of realist assumptions—that states are self-interested actors competing in a world of anarchy, that co-operation need not depend on altruism, that it can develop from the calculations of instrumentally rational actors.

> International cooperation does not necessarily depend on altruism, personal honor, common purposes, internalized norms, or a shared belief in a set of values embodied in a culture. At various times and places any of these features of human motivation may indeed play an important role in processes of international cooperation; *but cooperation can be*

understood without reference to any of them[.] [my emphasis] (Keohane 1988: 380)

The core claim is that regimes are created and that states obey the rules embodied in them because of the functional benefits that they provide. The understanding of co-operation on realist assumptions also explains why labelling becomes tricky and why it is often hard—at least for a European—to separate the "neorealist" from the "neo-liberal institutionalist."

Functional benefits have always formed one part of explanations for the existence of co-operation between states. They lie at the heart of Vattel's conception of the "voluntary law of nations," as that law is "deducible from the natural liberty of nations, from the attention due to their common safety, from the nature of their mutual correspondence, [and] from their reciprocal duties." Hume's description of the emergence of convention and co-operation within domestic society also provides a powerful statement of this idea:

> I observe, that it will be for my interest to leave another in the possession of his goods, provided he will act in the same manner with regard to me. He is sensible of a like interest in the regulation of his conduct. When this common sense of interest is mutually expressed, and is known to both, it produces a suitable resolution and behaviour. And this may properly enough be called a convention or agreement betwixt us, though without the imposition of a promise; since the actions of each of us have a reference to those of the other, and are performed upon the supposition that something is to be performed on the other part . . . repeated experience of the inconveniences of transgressing [the convention] . . . assures us still more that the sense of interest has become common to all our fellows, and gives us confidence of the future regularity of their conduct; and it is only on the expectation of this that our moderation and abstinence are founded[.] (Hume (1739) in Cohen 1981: 15)

In addition, many international law textbooks have described the role of international law in predominantly functionalist or purposive terms. Almost all accounts of the role of law describe its political impact in terms of the benefits of order, the costs of violation, and the extent to which it provides an order based on the co-ordination of interests and of patterned expectations. What regimes theorists have done is to give this general idea a much greater degree of specificity and coherence. In the first place regime theory seeks to specify far more precisely what the functional benefits provided by rules and institutions actually are. It stresses their impact in overcoming the assurance problem and affecting the pattern of costs by means of the reduction of uncertainty; the facilitation of communication; the promotion of learning; and the transmission of knowledge and information. Secondly, regime theory seeks to demonstrate in far tighter and more rigorous terms how co-operative behaviour can arise between self-interested actors and thereby to specify the conditions which facilitate the emergence of rules and institutions (for instance the impact of different numbers of players, the importance of issue density and linkage strategies, the critical role of knowledge and information). Its objective has been to move down from generalized discussion of international society to the detailed understanding of the conditions applicable to specific institutions.

4. The Weaknesses of Regime Theory

But the gains have also involved losses and doubts remain whether a sufficiently wide range of factors that explain the dynamics of co-operation can be captured within the terms of rationalist models. Indeed it is interesting to note how many of the criticisms of regime theory that have appeared during the 1980s have involved the re-emergence of older ideas or, at least, the picking up of older, if often unresolved, arguments.

4.1. Specific Legal Rules and the Broader Structure of the International System

The first issue concerns the relationship of specific bargains and bargaining processes to the broader international context and to the broader structures of the international system. Now, from one perspective, moves in this direction open up problems for neo-institutionalist approaches to co-operation built on explicitly rationalist foundations. The problem here is that inter-state bargaining is notoriously concerned with relative gains and with the distribution of the costs and benefits of co-operation. It may be true that states have an interest in co-operation in order to maximize their absolute gains. But the competitive and anarchical structure of the state system reinforces concern with the impact of co-operation on a state's relative power political and economic position. States are positional rather than atomistic actors and are often deterred from entering into co-operative arrangements if these entail negative implications for their relative power position.

This argument has been revived recently by Joseph Grieco but echoes a deep-rooted tradition in realist and mercantilist thought. To quote Rousseau:

> Let us add finally that, though the advantages resulting to commerce from a great and lasting peace are in themselves certain and indisputable, still, being common to all States, they will be appreciated by none. For such advantages make themselves felt only by contrast, and he who wishes to increase his relative power is bound to seek only such gains as are exclusive.

The neo-institutionalist response is to argue that their theories take relative gains into account and indeed are based on competitive behaviour between states keenly interested in the distribution of the pie. On this view, states bargain fiercely over the distribution of the costs and benefits of co-operation, but will ultimately accept a settlement which advances their own individual utility. The critics, however, argue more than this, namely that utility is always fundamentally interdependent and that the high degree of "envy" that exists between states will undermine rationalist models of co-operation.

In an important sense the realist critics overreach themselves. States are not inherently and immutably positional actors obsessed with relative gains under all circumstances. The point here, however, is to highlight the way in which the broader structure of the international system, and in particular of the international legal system, can work to overcome this problem. A good deal of the compliance pull of international rules derives from the relationship between individual rules and the broader pattern of international relations: states follow specific rules, even when inconvenient, because they have a longer-term interest in the maintenance of law-impregnated international community. It is within this broader context that ideas about reputation are most powerful and most critical. This can, to a certain extent, be captured by ideas of "lengthening the shadow of the future," by broadening notions of self-interest and reciprocity, and by trying to trace precisely the processes by which reputation matters. But, as the concern for reputation becomes more generalized and diffuse, it also becomes harder to measure and assess. More importantly, rationalist models of co-operation miss the crucial link between the costs and benefits of specific legal rules and the role of international law as constitutive of the structure of the state system itself—and, one might add, its role as provider of the legal underpinnings of the capitalist world economy, in terms of both detailed rules and fundamental assumptions.

Individual legal rules are important because of their relationship to the legal structure of the state system. As Tom Franck (1990: 196) has put it: "Nations, or those who govern them, recognize that the obligation to comply is owed by them to the community of states as the reciprocal of that community's validation of their nation's statehood." The functional benefits of specific rules are, therefore, only one part of the picture. An essential element is the legitimacy of rules which derives from the common sense of being part of a legal community and which serves as the crucial link between the procedural rules of state behaviour and the structural principles which define the character of the system and the identity of the players. Of course the "power of legitimacy" varies enormously according to the rule and issue involved and such considerations are only one element in decision-making. But they can be an important element. For weak states the achievement of external legal recognition and acceptance as a member of the "club" is very often a crucial determinant of who holds power domestically: think of the direct political impact of international recognition in cases of civil war or secession. Equally, restraints on intervention and the use of force provide weak states with some measure of external protection. For weak states, then, the legal conventions of sovereignty and the fabric of the international legal order bolster their very ability to maintain themselves as "states" and provide a powerful incentive to take legal rules seriously, although not always to follow them. Just as the structural realists argue that states are "socialized" into the game of power politics whatever their domestic systems or the inclinations of their leaders, so a parallel process is in operation in the workings of the international legal order. As the newly independent states of the developing world discovered, the acceptance of the basic structures of international law was a necessary corollary of their assertion of independence and their claim to be treated as a sovereign state.

On the other side, rich and powerful states have a double reason for accepting the principles of the legal order. First, such states have a disproportionate stake in maintaining the stability of the status quo, from which they clearly benefit. Second, they have a disproportionate influence over the content and application of international legal rules. As Oscar Schachter (1982: 28) puts it:

> International law must also be seen as the product of historical experience in which power and the "relation of forces" are determinants. Those States with power (i.e. the ability to control outcomes contested by others) will have a disproportionate and often decisive influence in determining the content of rules and their application in practice. Because this is the case, international law, in a broad sense, both reflects and sustains the existing political order and distribution of power.

Once states see themselves as having a long-term interest in participating in an international legal system, then the idea of obligation and the normativity of rules can be given concrete form and can acquire a degree of distance from the immediate interests or preferences of states. Within this society, law exists but is no longer seen to depend on the command of the sovereign. Law is rather the symbol of the idea of being bound and voluntarily accepting a sense of obligation. It is not based on external sanctions or the threat of them but is based rather on the existence of shared interests, of shared values, and of patterned expectations. It is a law of co-ordination rather than subordination. The nature of obligation and the validity and applicability of specific rules can be adduced within the context of the legal system and with reference to the relevant principles, treaties, etc. Being a political system, states will seek to interpret obligations to their own advantage. But being a legal system that is built on the consent of other parties, they will be constrained by the necessity of justifying their actions in legal terms. It is for these reasons that it is important to make a clearer distinction than is common in regime theory between specifically legal rules and the workings of the legal system within which they operate on the one hand, and the wide variety of other formal and informal norms and rules and the processes of negotiation, bargaining, or imposition that underpin them on the other.

4.2. Sense of Community and the Emergence of Co-operation

The second issue also concerns the importance of a sense of community, but stresses the moral rather than legal dimension. Rationalist models of co-operation may indeed explain how co-operation is possible once the parties have come to believe that they form part of a shared project or community in which there is a common interest that can be furthered by co-operative behaviour. But they neglect the potential barriers that can block the emergence of such a shared project—perhaps because regime theory has been so dominated by understanding co-operation between liberal developed states that enjoy a compatibility of major values and a common conceptualization of such basic concepts as "order," "justice," "state," "law," "contract," etc. Robert Axelrod (1984: ch. 4), for example, takes the example of the "spontaneous" co-operation that arose between the trenches in the First World War. This does indeed show how informal co-operation can emerge in an unpromising situation on the basis of a tit-for-tat strategy. But to what extent did such co-operation not rest upon a prior mutual acceptance of some minimal sense of community and of the other side as legitimate players? Where no such sense of community exists and where one side is convinced that the other has no moral status (or a heavily unequal one), then formal and informal co-operation is unlikely to emerge. The pursuit of holy wars against the infidel, the barbarous behaviour of the imperialist powers in their treatment of indigenous peoples, and the savagery of the fighting on the Eastern Front in the Second World War provide striking examples of where the absence of any shared sense of community has worked to undermine co-operative limitations on conflict based on reciprocity and self-interest.

Once there is a common identification of, and commitment to, some kind of moral community (however minimalist in character) within which perceptions of potential common interest can emerge, then there may indeed be prudential reasons for the players collectively to co-operate. But rational prudence alone cannot explain the initiation of the game, why each player individually might choose to begin to co-operate. This problem might be solved by coercion or the role of a hegemonic power. Or it might be solved by some pre-existing sense of community embodying some common moral purpose.

For many of the classical theorists of international society, this problem was overcome by reliance on the obligations of natural law. For Grotius both the sources and obligatory force of law rested heavily on its natural law foundations. By the time of Vattel, the balance had altered. For Vattel positive law had become the central means of regulating international life in a manner consistent with the realities of the age of *raison d'état*. At the same time, however, the untrammeled freedom of states continued to be balanced by a belief in the residual obligations and restraints derived from natural law. Indeed it is this ultimately unconvincing balance between the voluntary and necessary law of nations that lies at the heart of Vattel's system of law.

For the modern theorists of international society, the problem is recognized but the solution remains ambiguous. The stress on forming part of society or community was one of the most characteristic features of

Bull's and Wight's work. Thus for Martin Wight (1966: 96–7), international society

> is manifest in the diplomatic system; in the conscious maintenance of the balance of power to preserve the independence of the member communities; in the regular operations of international law whose binding force is accepted over a wide though politically unimportant range of subjects; in economic, social and technical interdependence and the functional international institutions established latterly to regulate it. *All these presuppose an international social consciousness, a world wide community sentiment.* [my emphasis]

For Bull (1977: 13) the subjective sense of being bound by a community was the cornerstone of his definition of international society:

> A *society of states* (or international society) exists when a group of states, conscious of certain common interests and common values, form a society in the sense that they conceive themselves to be bound by a common set of rules in their relations with one another and share in the workings of common institutions.

Bull wants to reject any natural law foundations, or, at least, to develop some empirical equivalent to natural law, some set of general principles without which no society could be said to exist—the influence of H.L.A. Hart is important here. The aim is to identify a conception of international society consistent with self-interest and with the realities of power. Yet, at the same time, there was the awareness that international society could not be understood solely in these terms and had to be rooted within the cultural and historical forces that had helped shape the consciousness of society and had moulded perceptions of common values and common purposes. In other words the dominant line of Bull's thought was to follow Wight (1966: 96): "International society, then, on this view, can be properly described only in historical and sociological depth." Great stress was therefore laid on culture and the sense of common interest that developed historically within and across different societies. According to Bull, a common cultural tradition contributes to international society in three ways. First, the existence of a common epistemology, a common language, and a common cultural tradition will facilitate communication between the members of international society. Second, the existence of such a common culture reinforces the bonds of common interest by adding a sense of moral obligation. Third, the existence of a common value system will help ensure that states place the same relative valuation on such objectives as order, justice, peace, etc.

This conception of international co-operation can be related to the arguments of Kratochwil and Ruggie that international regimes are necessarily intersubjective phenomena whose existence and validity is created and sustained in the interrelationship of their subjects. As they have suggested, the problem is that such a view is at odds with the epistemological positivism of mainstream rationalist regime analysis. It suggests the need for a hermeneutic or interpretivist methodology that seeks to re-create the historical and social processes by which rules and norms are constituted and a sense of obligation engendered. But whilst it may not be easy to measure the normativity of rules in exact terms, we can still try to understand exactly what this sense of obligation consists of, not in general terms but on a specific case-by-case basis: what it is, how it determines the precise nature of the law, and how state practice is to be measured and assessed against it. In other words, precisely what international lawyers spend most of their time doing. In this respect it is the continued *practice* of international law and of the "invisible college of international lawyers" which is both indicative of this sense of being bound and which gives specific content to legal rules. The role of practice has been usefully stressed by Kratochwil (1989: 61):

> Actors are not only programmed by rules and norms, but they reproduce and change by their practice the normative structures by which they are able to act, share meanings, communicate intentions, criticize claims and justify choices. Thus, one of the most important sources of change, neglected in the present regime literature, is the *practice of the actors* themselves and its concomitant process of interstitial law-making in the international arena.

The importance of a shared sense of cultural or moral community in the creation and maintenance of regimes will depend on their scope. If the regimes are primarily intended to secure some minimum degree of coexistence, then common values and a common culture will be of marginal relevance (unless, as argued earlier, one of the players espouses an exclusivist conception of international life based on notions of its own inherent superiority). Thus states of many different ideologies and cultures have come to see the benefits provided by such basic legal principles as the mutual recognition of sovereignty, the norm of non-intervention, the need to observe treaties, the need to maintain a functioning diplomatic system, etc. A further example might be the non-legal and often informal network of rules and understandings that developed through the course of the Cold War. (But even this was a fitful process in which the idea of a common interest in avoiding nuclear war had to struggle against the exclusivist ideologies of cold warriors in both East and West.) Minimum rules of coexistence of this kind reflect the inherent necessities of a pluralist system of autonomous states: a practical association in Terry Nardin's terms that is not built around a common vision of the good life.

But as regimes become increasingly global, as the hard shell of the state is increasingly eroded, and as the scope of co-operation is expanded, the picture changes. As co-operation comes increasingly to involve the creation of rules that affect very deeply the domestic structures and organization of states, that invest individuals and groups within states with rights and duties, and that seek to embody some notion of a common good (human rights, democratization, the environment, the construction of more elaborate and intrusive inter-state security orders), then these questions of society and community re-emerge and the validity of models of co-operation that exclude them needs at least to be questioned.

4.3. Justice and Order

This leads to the third issue, which also concerns the adequacy of regime theory's discussion of the normative dimension of international co-operation. Clearly there are many international norms that derive their compliance pull from a shared sense of justice: human rights most notably, but also, for example, norms against armed conquest and the annexation of territory. Rules and norms of this kind do not develop as a result of the direct interplay of state interests or because of the functional benefits which they provide. Rather they depend on a common moral awareness that works directly, if still in fragile and uneven ways, on the minds and emotions of individuals within states. In some cases such ideas can work to disrupt or complicate the functioning of other inter-state regimes (this has always been the realist argument against the promotion of human rights). In other cases, a sense of common moral purpose can work to reinforce inter-state co-operation. The sense in which global ecological interdependence has given greater plausibility to a Beitzian vision of a global moral community may, for example, increase the weight given to aggregate global utility and lead policy-makers to act against narrow, short-term definitions of national self-interest.

This is not at all to say that the creation of such regimes owes nothing to considerations of power and interest. The creation of the post-war human rights regime depended fundamentally on the particular values and interests of the United States and other western states. Equally, the desire to promote the spread of human rights and democracy has always interacted with, and often been dominated by, baser and less noble sentiments. Finally, there is much to be said for Hume's argument that the *origins* of many moral sentiments depended in the first instance on pragmatic and self-interested calculation (for instance that formal empire no longer paid) but that, over time, the prohibition of conquest and empire came to assume a moral quality.

Once again the importance of specifically legal rules should be stressed. If shared moral concerns are important in the emergence of co-operative behaviour, it is through legal rules that they are predominantly expressed. Indeed one of the virtues of international law is its flexibility and the extent to which it allows new norms and principles to be introduced (often by weak states and sometimes even by individuals or pressure groups), to be given formal expression, and gradually to be hardened into binding rules that are capable of giving rise to specific duties and obligations. The emergence of human rights law is one example, the current process of groping from general principles of environmental management to specific regulatory regimes is another. Of course, this process is in some sense determined by the power and interests of dominant states. But the workings of the legal system provide a degree of autonomy within which the changing normative climate can be given concrete expression. Thus at one end of the spectrum there is a constant and unstable balance between raw power-political behaviour and law-governed behaviour. At the other there is an equally unstable relationship between legal rules as reflective of the actual political interests of states and legal rules as embodying evolving notions of how the international community *should* be organized.

It is certainly the case that many regime theorists have recognized the force of moral obligations—for example Keohane in chapter 7 of *After Hegemony*. But this raises an important difficulty. Can one relax the basic assumption of rational egoism and accept the role of empathetic interdependence, without the overall force of the rationalist project being undermined? Is one not in danger of slipping back into the kinds of older explanations that see co-operation as resulting from a changing mixture of various factors that cannot be encapsulated in a tight and rigorous theory?

There is a further very interesting aspect to the normative question. For a European at least, there is a striking contrast between the concerns of US international relations scholars of the 1940s and those of the 1980s. For all their claims to be uncovering timeless and objective laws of politics, the early post-war realists were passionately committed to a moral project: to uncovering and exposing the dangers of utopianism, and to prescribing the guidelines of rational statecraft, which, although they could never allow states to escape from the dilemmas of the international anarchy, could at least mitigate its worst effects (hence the charge that they were in fact peddling a conservative utopia). But whatever their conclusions, their explicit concern with the deeply problematic relationship between power and morality remains one of the most noteworthy features of their work. The picture of the 1980s is very different. In one sense, there is an implicit moral concern in the work of regime theorists, centred around the assumption that the understanding and promotion of co-operation has an intrinsic value. There is in fact a good deal of clear prescription: if we understand the conditions under which co-operation is possible, we will be able to promote greater co-operation. At the same time, however, there is also the recognition that not all regimes are benign: "Since the point is often missed, it should be underlined: although international regimes may be valuable to their creators, *they do not necessarily improve world welfare*. They are not *ipso facto* 'good'" (Keohane 1984: 73). Indeed, as the conclusion to *After Hegemony* makes clear, the order created by regimes needs to be subjected to relevant moral standards.

Order and justice are thus seen as separate tracks. First you understand how order is created and then you assess it against some outside normative standards. (The direction of the argument is similar here to that of Bull (1977: ch. 4).) Order is the product of norms whose emergence can be understood in sociological terms and whose impact derives from the functional benefits which they provide. Indeed the term "norm" is mostly used in regime theory to describe generalized rules of co-operative social behaviour.

The basic question is whether order and justice can in fact be separated in this way. First, is there not a good deal of evidence to suggest that questions of justice and perceptions of equity play a major role in the formation of actors' preferences and in the determination of actors' behaviour? Second, is there not also a good deal of evidence to suggest that successful bargaining outcomes do not depend on the achievement of some notion of optimum allocative efficiency, but rather on the perception that the outcome meets some criterion of justice and equity? As Robert Jervis (1988: 348) puts it: "Considerations of morality, fairness, and obligation are almost surely large parts of the explanation for the fact that individuals in society co-operate much more than the Prisoners' Dilemma would lead us to expect." And finally, the status of the norm of reciprocity raises serious difficulties. It is seen within rationalist and game-theoretic approaches as a given, an ahistorical and acultural norm that is naturally occurring *dans la nature des choses.* But there is a powerful argument that its functioning depends on a pre-existing sense of community, or at least that it is itself reflective of that community. And the more that reciprocity becomes generalized and diffuse, the more it tends to become synonymous with fairness. If this is so, then the validity of separating order from justice is as problematic for the neo-liberal institutionalists as it was for the theorists of international society.

On the one hand, then, notions of justice need to be seen as intrinsic to the process by which order is produced. On the other, the order that is produced tends naturally to reflect the dominant interests of the most powerful states. In terms of future research this suggests two things: first, there is a pressing need to understand a good deal more about how conceptions of a just international order vary between states. The radically divergent perceptions on the nature of order and legitimacy thrown up in the wake of the Gulf War (and in post-Cold War Europe) attest to the complexity and centrality of this question. Second, it is surely important to try and bridge the gap that has opened up between theorists of international co-operation and the increasing number of political theorists who have become more aware of the need to develop theories of justice within an inter-state and global context. In part this involves the creation of appropriate principles of justice. But in part—and this is surely the distinctive task for international relations as a discipline—it means the critical analysis of how such principles can be applied within the political dynamics of the international system, in other words returning once more to the interaction between politics and morality.

4.4. The Domestic Dimension

The fourth and final issue concerns the domestic dimension. Although regime theory grew out of theories of interdependence and transnationalism that stressed the multiple linkages between the domestic and the international, it sought essentially to explain co-operation in third image terms. The need to address the domestic dimension has become a common theme. Clearly, the way in which states bargain and co-operate cannot be understood except with reference to the changing nature of the state and the domestic political system. State interests are not fixed but vary according to the institutional context, to the degree of organization of the contending political forces within the state and wider political system, and to the leadership capacities of the major actors.

Domestic factors are also central to the issues raised in this chapter. Notions of society and community cannot be easily separated from the character of domestic political systems. This was one of the central problems with the Bull-Wight approach to international society. On the one hand, they sought to develop a conception of international society that was focused at the inter-state level, to locate a set of common rules applicable to the workings of a society of states (along lines not so very different from Kissinger's conception of legitimacy). But on the other, the reliance on the role of common values and a common culture almost inevitably opens up questions about the impact of domestic social, cultural, and political factors. In addition, conceptions of fairness and equity are closely related to distinct histories and to specific cultures. This is particularly true when the idea of costs and benefits is extended beyond the purely economic, when, for example, the safeguarding of political autonomy or cultural heritage is seen as having a fundamental value that must be built into co-operative inter-state regimes.

As the primary focus of research shifts from regime creation to implementation, domestic factors become, if anything, even more critical. Various issues and possibilities can be noted. First, there is the role of international rules, and especially international law, in the policy-making process. If the focus is on the subjective sense of being bound, then we need to look in far more detail at how this sense of obligation plays out within the policy-making process. It is, after all, only individual policy-makers who are capable of feeling a sense of obligation. Despite the methodological difficulties there is much that can be done. We can, for instance, build on the work of Louis Henkin and reconstruct the ways in which international law shaped the policy options that were considered by governments and the extent to which these options reflected the internalization of legal rules. Indeed by looking on the basis of detailed documentary work at the options that were considered but ultimately rejected, we can go some way towards overcoming the dilemma of counterfactuals.

Second, there are specific and often technical linkages between international law and domestic legal systems and the complex processes that underpin the national implementation of international rules. As Antonio Cassese (1986: 15) has observed: "It is therefore apparent that international law cannot work without the constant help, co-operation, and support of national legal systems." If regime theory is seriously interested in questions of compliance and implementation (and in explanations of differing patterns of compliance between different types of states), then it is essential that these technical linkages should be understood and assessed by political scientists.

Third, many of the political costs of violating international rules are domestic. One of the most powerful reasons for complying with international legal rules, even in "hard cases" in which national security interests are involved, lies in the degree to which the creation of a convincing legal case is essential for ensuring domestic political support. Conversely, it is often the violation of specific international norms and laws that provides the focal point around which domestic opposition is able to mobilize. For all the alleged weakness of international law, it is striking just how often international rules form the basis of claims and political action within states. Equally, given that governments are often not good at blowing the whistle on each other, a good deal of the monitoring of international regimes is carried out by domestic groups acting either within one country or transnationally.

5. Conclusions

The purpose of this chapter has been to place regime theory within a broader tradition of thought on the possibilities and problems of co-operation in international life that focused on the concept of international society and gave a key role to international law. Seen in this light the charge of faddishness falls away and the way in which the concerns of regime theorists have built on the ideas and concepts of earlier theorists becomes apparent. Moreover, the reformulation of the problem of co-operation within more rigorous rationalist models has brought clear benefits, above all in terms of giving greater precision to the functional benefits of norms, the concept of reciprocity, and the ways in which co-operation can develop between self-interested actors. But this rigour has been bought at a significant cost. First, the centrality and complexity of the normative dimension has been neglected or downplayed: above all in terms of the importance of a shared sense of community in understanding how the co-operative enterprise can get off the ground, and in terms of the necessity of viewing ethics as intrinsic to the processes by which order is produced. And second, the quest for rigour (and perhaps an excessive desire to avoid the sins of idealism) has led to far too wholesale a dismissal of the need to understand both the specific character and the technical features of the international legal system. It is international law that provides the essential bridge between the procedural rules of the game and the structural principles that specify how the game of power and interests is defined and how the identity of the players is established. It provides a framework for understanding the processes by which rules and norms are constituted and a sense of obligation engendered in the minds of policy-makers. And it provides one way of analysing the linkages that exist between the rules that facilitate order internationally and the domestic political and legal systems of states.

Notes

1. Bull (1977: 322) used the term "Grotian" in two senses: first, to describe the doctrine that there is such a thing as international society; and, second, to contrast the solidarist conception of international society from the more pluralist Vattelian conception. The distinction between the solidarist and pluralist conceptions is laid out in his "The Grotian Conception of International Society" (Bull 1966). One important feature of Bull's later work is the move away from the pluralist/realist positions dominant in *The Anarchical Society* and towards a more genuinely "Grotian" position. For a thorough discussion of the Grotian tradition and the problems raised by it see Bull, Kingsbury, and Roberts (1990).

2. Nevertheless, it is important to stress the extent to which Soviet policy came to accept the positive role of international law as providing an essential framework for coexistence and the "co-ordination of wills."

3. It is worth recalling, however, that one of the claims to originality and innovation of regime theory was precisely that it included patterns of co-operation that were embodied neither in formal international organizations nor in specific sets of legal rules.

References

Axelrod, Robert. (1984) *The Evolution of Cooperation*. New York: Basic Books.

Bull, Hedley. (1977) *The Anarchical Society*. New York: Columbia University Press.

———. (1966) "The Grotian Conception of International Society," in Martin Wight and Herbert Butterfield, eds. *Diplomatic Investigations*. London: Allen & Unwin.

———, Benedict Kingsbury, and Adam Roberts, eds. (1990) *Hugo Grotius and International Relations*. Oxford: Oxford University Press.

Carr, E. H. (1981) *The Twenty Years' Crisis, 1919–1939*. London: Macmillan.

Cassese, Antonio. (1986) *International Law in a Divided World*. Oxford: Oxford University Press.

Cohen, Raymond. (1981) *International Politics: The Rules of the Game*. London: Longman.

Donelan, Michael D. (1990) *Elements of International Political Theory*. Oxford: Clarendon.

Franck, Thomas M. (1990) *The Power of Legitimacy Among Nations*. New York: Oxford University Press.

Hoffmann, Stanley. (1965) "Rousseau on War and Peace," in Hoffmann, *The State of War: Essays in the Theory and Practice of International Politics*. New York: Praeger.

Jervis, Robert. (1988) "Realism, Game Theory, and Cooperation," *World Politics* 40 (April): 317–49.

Keohane, Robert O. (1984) *After Hegemony: Cooperation and Discord in the World Political Economy*. Princeton, N.J.: Princeton University Press.

———. (1988) "International Institutions: Two Approaches," *International Studies Quarterly* 32:379–96.

———. (1989) "Neoliberal Institutionalism: A Perspective on World Politics," in Keohane, *International Institutions and State Power: Essays in International Relations Theory*. Boulder, Colo: Westview.

Krasner, Stephen D. (1983) "Structural Cause and Regime Consequences," in

Stephen D. Krasner, ed., *International Regimes.* Ithaca, N.Y.: Cornell University Press.

Kratochwil, Friedrich. (1989) *Rules, Norms, and Decisions.* Cambridge: Cambridge University Press.

Schachter, Oscar. (1982) "General Course in Public International Law," *Recueil des Cours* 5: 1–395.

Wight, Martin. (1966) "Western Values in International Relations," in Martin Wight and Herbert Butterfield, eds., *Diplomatic Investigations.* London: Allen & Unwin.

Selected Bibliography

Prominent Books and Articles on Institutionalism

Adler, Emanuel, and Peter M. Haas. "Conclusion: Epistemic Communities, World Order, and the Creation of a Reflective Research Program," *International Organization* 46 (1992): 367–90.

Aggarwal, Vinod. *Liberal Protectionism: The International Politics of Organized Textile Trade* (1985).

Baldwin, David A., ed. *Neorealism and Neoliberalism: The Contemporary Debate* (1993).

Cox, Robert. "Social Forces, States, and World Orders," in Robert O. Keohane, ed., *Neorealism and Its Critics* (1986), pp. 204–54.

Dessler, David. "What's at Stake in the Agent-Structure Debate?" *International Organization* (1989): 441–74.

Duffield, John S. *Power Rules: The Evolution of NATO's Conventional Force Structure* (1995).

Haas, Ernst B. "Is There a Whole in the Whole? Knowledge, Technology, Interdependence and the Construction of International Regimes," *International Organization* 29 (1975): 827–76.

———. *When Knowledge Is Power: Three Models of Change in International Organizations* (1990).

———. "Why Collaborate?" Issue Linkage and International Regimes," *World Politics* 32 (1980): 357–405.

———. "Worlds Can Hurt You; or, Who Said What to Whom?" *International Organization* 36 (1982): 207–43.

Haas, Peter, ed. "Knowledge, Power, and International Policy Coordination." Special issue of *International Organization* 46 (1992).

Jepperson, Ronald, Alexander Wendt, and Peter J. Katzenstein. "Norms, Identity, and State Security in the Contemporary World System." 1994 Annual APSA paper.

Keohane, Robert O. *After Hegemony: Cooperation and Discord in the World Political Economy* (1984).

———. *International Institutions and State Power* (1989). (a collection of Keohane essays on institutions)

Klotz, Audie. *Protesting Prejudice: Apartheid and the Politics of Norms in International Relations* (1995).

Krasner, Stephen D., ed. *International Regimes* (1983).

Kratochwil, Friedrich. *Rules, Norms and Decisions: On the Conditions of Practical and Legal Reasoning in International Relations and Domestic Affairs* (1989).

———, and Edward D. Mansfield. *International Organization: A Reader* (1994).

Nadelmann, Ethan. "Global Prohibition Regimes: The Evolution of Norms in International Society," *International Organization* 44 (1990): 479–526.

Onuf, Nicholas G. *World of Our Making: Rules and Rule in Social Theory and International Relations* (1989).

Rittberger, Volker, ed. *Regime Theory and International Relations* (1993).

Ruggie, John G. "Continuity and Transformation in World Polity," in Robert O. Keohane, ed., *Neorealism and Its Critics* (1986), pp. 131–157.

———. "Territoriality and Beyond," *International Organization* 46 (1993): 139–74.

Wendt, Alexander. "The Agent-Structure Problem in International Relations Theory," *International Organization* 41 (1987): 335–70.

———. "Anarchy Is What States Make of It," *International Organization* 46 (1992): 391–425.

———. "Constructing International Politics," *International Security* 20 (1995), pp. 71–81.

———. "Collective Identity Formation and the International State," *American Political Science Review* 88 (1994): 384–96.

———. *Social Theory of International Politics* (forthcoming).

Young, Oran R. *International Cooperation: Building Regimes for Natural Resources and the Environment* (1989).

Reviews of the Institutionalist Literature

Abbott, Kenneth W. "Modern International Relations Theory: A Prospectus for International Lawyers," *Yale Journal of International Law* 14 (1989): 335–411.

Haggard, Stephan, and Beth A. Simmons. "Theories of International Regimes," *International Organization* 41 (1987): 491–517.

Keohane, Robert O. "International Institutions: Two Approaches," *International Studies Quarterly* 32 (1988): 379–96.

Kratochwil, Friedrich, and John G. Ruggie. "International Organization: A State of the Art on the Art of the State," *International Organization* 40 (1986): 753–75.

Powell, Robert. "Anarchy in International Relations Theory: The Neorealist-Neoliberal Debate," *International Organization* 48 (1994): 313–44.

Young, Oran R. "International Regimes: The Problem of Concept Formation," *World Politics* 32 (1980): 331–56.

———. "International Regimes: Toward a New Theory of Institutions," *World Politics* 39 (1986): 104–22.

8

The New Stream

The New Stream of international legal scholarship has its roots in the Critical Legal Studies approach that became popular among American legal scholars focusing on domestic law during the 1980s. The application of this critical approach to international law was pioneered by David Kennedy, now a law professor at Harvard University. Like Critical Legal Studies, much of the New Stream scholarship utilizes the linguistic methodology of the French structuralists and draws its theoretic inspiration from the neo-Marxist Frankfurt school. New Stream scholars reject Positivism and Naturalism. In fact, they reject the very notion that law is an objective enterprise. The self-described project of the New Stream scholarship is to unite the theory and practice of international law in a manner that will restructure international social life.

According to David Kennedy, the "key to developing a style of legal analysis which could aid in elaborating the connections between practice and theory" is "concentration upon discourse and upon the hidden ideologies, attitudes and structures which lie behind discourse, rather than upon the subject matter of legal talk."[1] It is this attempt to transcend the substantive debates of international law by assuming a critical posture that defines and unites the New Stream scholarship.

The assumptions of the New Stream critical method are strongly reminiscent of the assumptions of Marxist theory. Just as Marxists view politics as a superstructure, built on and disguising the economic base of society, New Stream scholars consider ideology to be the base upon which all law and politics are constructed. Ideology is disguised and strengthened by the structure of international legal discourse. By focusing on the structure of theoretical and doctrinal arguments within the system, New Stream scholars seek to disclose the inherent contradictions, antinomies, dichotomies, and the essentially oppositional nature of international law.

227

Ultimately, the New Stream scholars trace the oppositional structure of international law to a single fundamental contradiction—the contradiction inherent in the notion of sovereignty. This Janus-faced concept has both a "positive" aspect—which is the source of state independence, autonomy, and authority—and a "negative" aspect—which limits states by asserting their juridical equality, interdependence, and community responsibilities.

The essential contradiction between these two faces of sovereignty pervades international law discourse and results in the essential paradox that international law both confirms and constrains state authority. According to Kennedy, "individual nations find in socialization both the source of their identity and a threat to their existence."[2] The repetition of this essential contradiction at all levels of legal discourse results in what Kennedy calls the "binary and transformational structure" of international law. By this he means that the various manifestations of the contradiction are all metamorphoses of the same essential antinomy, and that their opposition is not permanent and irreconcilable—it can be mediated by internal transformations.

The essential opposition of international law takes on different forms at different levels of the discourse. At the doctrinal level, it manifests itself as an antinomy between sovereign immunity and sovereign equality. At the theoretical level, it manifests itself in the conflicting conceptions of law as "separate from and critical of state behavior," or alternatively, as "grounded in and fused with state behavior." By switching back and forth between these inconsistent foundations of international law, a decision-maker can manipulate the legal discourse to arrive at any desired outcome, according to Kennedy. For the New Stream scholars, then, not only do rules not control decisions, the rules themselves are indeterminate. In Kennedy's words, "international law discourse is a conversation without content."[3]

The New Stream critical methodology, according to its adherents, is a noncontentious, value-free form of analysis. It is, according to Kennedy, akin to reading hieroglyphics. The method is intended to allow the examiner to absent himself or herself from the text and to see the argument primarily in terms of the symbols it uses. It is "self-referential" and seeks only "critical knowledge" through critical reflection. To understand the structure of international law, New Stream scholars focus on the "discourse" or "rhetoric" as reflected in the texts and materials of international law.

New Stream scholars view the long-standing debate between Naturalists' and Positivists' approaches as a largely futile exercise, and note that much of the debate has now been replicated within the confines of the Positivist project. The failure of international law theory to *explain* existing rules is mirrored, according to New Stream scholars, by the failure of international law doctrines to *persuade*.

New Stream scholars acknowledge that legal practitioners and government officials may believe themselves to have been "convinced" by doctrinal arguments. In fact, however, these arguments have no logical force independent of their ideological context. They are hollow, indeterminate, and manipulable. New Stream scholars believe that because doctrinal arguments merely mask ideological forces, international law is incapable of playing the neutral role traditional approaches prescribe for it. It cannot resolve dilemmas. Instead, it mirrors and reinforces them through its rhetorical structure. Law, according to Kennedy, "is nothing but an attempt to project a stable relationship between spheres it creates to divide."

The New Stream has been criticized by Positivists and others as an intellectual dead end. They suggest that the critical project can offer no alternatives to the theory and doctrine it deconstructs. It offers no affirmative vision of international social life, for it holds that no such vision can justify itself. To some critics of the New Stream, it appears that the critical project degenerates rapidly into cynicism. Nonetheless, New Stream scholarship continues to flourish and exerts a significant influence on other approaches to the study of international rules, including Feminist approaches.

Notes

1. David Kennedy, "Theses about International Law Discourse," *German Yearbook of International Law* 23 (1980): 355.
2. Ibid., p. 361.
3. Ibid., p. 376.

DAVID KENNEDY

A New Stream of International Law Scholarship

1. Discipline and Method

A. *Introduction*

Over the past nine years, I have pursued a number of criticisms of public international law as it is understood in the United States. I am grateful to the Institute of International Public Law and International Relations, not only for the invitation to deliver these lectures, but also for the opportunity to reflect on this collection of critical projects. Although I am glad for the encouragement to speak of my own work, I should say at the outset that this has hardly been a solitary effort. Indeed, my international law work has been supported and influenced by much recent critical legal scholarship in the United States, as well as by the variety of critical projects being pursued in the field of international law by scholars such as David Bederman, Nathan Berman, Jamie Boyle, Tony Carty, Paula Escarameia, Gter Frankenberg, Veijo Heiskanen, Martti Koskenniemi, Matt Kramer, Mohammed Lalia, Ed Morgan, Joel Paul, Manuel Rodriguez-Orellana, Phillipe Sands, Surakiart Sathirathai, Leo Specht, and Dan Tarullo.

Taken together, my own projects have been animated by a single interlocutory—the tragic voice of post-war public law liberalism. By the end of the Vietnam War, this voice exercised a stranglehold over the discipline of public international law in the United States as practiced by lawyers and scholars of most every political conviction. In this lecture series, I will explore the voice of contemporary public international law along four dimensions. Today, I will quite briefly sketch the recent history of the field of public international law in the United States and outline the ideas, methods and images of legal and political culture which are now coming to the field. Over the coming days, I will speak about the historiography of public international law, about doctrinal analysis in the field, and about the discipline of international institutions.

Let me say something about my argument's thesis and structure at the outset. Much of my work has been directed to demonstrating and criticizing international public law's obsessive repetition of a rather simple narrative structure. Succinctly stated, the discipline of international public law, narratives of public law history and public law doctrine, and even international institutions, seem structured as movements from imagined origins

Lectures I and III from *Wisconsin International Law Journal* 7 (1988): 1–12, 28–39. Reprinted by permission.

through an expansive process towards a desired substantive goal. My claim is that international public law exists uneasily in the relations among these imagined points—constantly remembering a stable origin, foreshadowing a substantive resolution, but living in an interminable procedural present.

Moreover, the single most important aspect of contemporary public international law seems to be its preoccupation—doctrinally, institutionally and methodologically—with process, and in particular with a process which might convince us of international law's *being* by imagining it in relationship to something else—often thought of as "political authority." My contention is that this relationship to history or politics, far from being some pre-existing chasm international law must bridge, is produced by relations among pieces of the discipline's own self-image. Given this thesis about international law scholarship as a whole, it is perhaps appropriate that I have structured these lectures to illustrate and propose a move to process—to the process of rhetoric—in three major steps: by thinking about international law's disciplinary and historical origins, the rhetorical fabric of doctrinal elaboration, and the promise of international institutions.

Let me begin today with a brief look at the academic discipline of public international law in the United States, and at the influence of tragic liberalism over the work of the last generation. In a way, taking on public international law after the Vietnam War was kicking a discipline while it was down. The conceptual, even theoretical, self-confidence which had animated the field before the Second World War had long since been eroded by post-war "pragmatism." And the enthusiastic world-building ethos of the immediate post-war era—in both its economic functionalist and ideological idealist modes—had long since floundered on the limits of the American empire.

B. Public International Law—Some Generations

American public international lawyers active between the two world wars defined the field in the United States, produced the first comprehensive modern treatises of a distinct public international law in the United States, founded many of what were to become the large international law practices and fueled the two great waves of international institution building in this century. They were public lawyers with an independent intellectual vision and an effective international practice. Indeed, for these men it was possible to aspire to an individual practice of international public law, even if this ambition was often simply an international extension of the elite bar's traditional "public service" orientation. Imperialists and humanitarians, these men developed the private practice of statecraft and set in motion the international bureaucracy. They were largely establishment figures, usually Republicans, who had rebuilt the field after the debacle of America's absence from that quintessentially progressive institution, the League of Nations.

Intellectually, they consummated the nineteenth century struggle between naturalism and positivism in an uneasy positivist truce. These were the years of the Harvard Research Project, a massive effort of intellectual systematization. The field was largely untouched by the scholarly revolution wrought in American jurisprudence by the realist critique of private law doctrine. And it participated only vaguely in the transformation of public law thought brought about by New Deal federalism. Instead, public international law scholars in the United States before the Second World War reinforced what was taken to be the high road of European doctrinal formalism, insisting that only a carefully delimited and predictable doctrinal corpus could sustain the positivist image of international compliance with law. This strong resistance to any blurring of doctrinal categories fit with these scholars['] resistance to the developing administrative state— and seemed confirmed by the increasingly apparent failure of the League.

The post World War II generation was different. Public law, and perhaps particularly international public law, came to be dominated— intellectually and politically—by Democrats eager to rebuild in the name of democracy and decolonization. The Republicans migrated into private law and practice. Many in this next generation received their first professional experience in the post-war reconstruction effort or in the United States business and investment boom in Europe that followed. These men increased the scope of doctrinal systematization and expanded the international bureaucracy. If their predecessors had laid down the doctrinal contours of the field, these men gave it institutional shape, not only in the United Nations system and in the new international economic institutions, but also in the United States State Department, in the law firms and in the multinational corporations.

Although these men were enthusiasts about international law and institutions, they slowly abandoned the doctrinal purity and institutional isolation characteristic of the pre-war generation. Self-described pragmatists and functionalists, sneaking up on sovereignty in numerous ingenious ways, they self-consciously blurred the boundaries between national and international, public and private law. They imported into public international law precisely the realist attack on doctrinal formalism which the pre-war generation has resisted. They rejoiced as the discipline lost its coherence—renaming it "transnational" law. These men were also successors to the progressive faith in international administration—and they brought to the United Nations their faith in New Deal federal reform.

In short, the post-war generation expanded the practice of international law by sacrificing its distinctive intellectual self-image and coherence. Not surprisingly, these changes reopened the philosophical debate about international law's distinctiveness and binding force. Consequently, this generation resurrected the intellectual struggle between norm and deed which had been settled before the War in a timid doctrinal positivism. At first, they pursued their idealism in the language of valuative sociology or administrative gamesmenship. By the end of the Kennedy administration, their scholarship grew timid. Eventually, they responded to the question "why international law?" with a simple anecdotal description of its apparent presence and a confusion of partial explanations among which the student was invited to choose like a debutante at a smorgasbord.

By the end, as their shiny new bureaucracies failed to produce the reform which they had prophecied, this generation's erosion of doctrinal and intellectual purity overwhelmed their enthusiasm. Although they had expanded the international bureaucracy and increased the scope of doctrinal systematization—developing a distinct international administrative law and fleshing out the constitutional processes of the post-war institutions—their scholarship became increasingly uncertain and fragmented. Their intellectual problem was to account for the simultaneous distinctiveness of public international law and its now quite strongly asserted connection to private national economic structures and political processes.

On the one hand, the doctrinal and theoretical world of the pre-war generation had not been abandoned. Quite the contrary, the post-war cohort had self-consciously engaged in its "reconstruction." On the other hand, however, public international law scholars of the fifties and sixties had devoted their careers to escaping the confines of those earlier doctrinal categories—subverting them at every turn with qualification and inter-disciplinary reflection in a tragically incomplete Oedipal challenge. This dilemma produced a proliferation of interdisciplinary musings about the neo-positivism and neo-naturalism of their immediate predecessors—a proliferation which took on a manic tone during the Vietnam War as one scholar after another sought to weave the political and social anguish of that struggle into their image of public lawfulness. Either they needed a new theory of law which could account for its violation or a new theory of violation which could account for America's activity. Neither was forthcoming.

Coming to the academy after the Vietnam War, I found a rather large group of imaginative and renowned scholars reaching retirement. Rarely does the generation that defines a field depart from the scene as gracefully—even sheepishly—or with so few successors as has the generation that reached its apogee directly after the Second World War. As they did so, the elaborate edifice they had honored was succumbing to the erosion and fragmentation they had encouraged. Attacked from the left and right, theoretically weak, jurisprudentially behind the times, the old edifice they had so lovingly sheltered seemed hopelessly ill-equipped to the broad functions they had encouraged us to think it might perform.

As a result, public international law was characterized by a defensive enthusiasm and a corrosive scepticism. Despite the "special dignity" public international law still claimed—tracing its origins to the interwar public statecraft of a Republican establishment—no one seemed to "specialize" in public international law anymore. Indeed, most courses "in the field" presented international law as either the specialized continuation of some domestic subject such as taxation or investment, or as an esoteric, quasi-

historical or philosophical by-way. This classroom marginalization of public law, when coupled with the municipal focus of private law specialities,
reflected America's foreign policy determination to remake international
society as a democratic market. In a way, it is not too much to say that
international law in the United States simply disappeared during this period, as *public* became marginal and private became *municipal* legal study.

Intellectually, there were more rules, more often observed, covering a
wider variety of subjects than ever before. But this optimistic façade was a
delicate one. We were given too many reasons to believe in international
law—as our teachers struggled to make good their enthusiasm after having pawned their idealism. Public international law was to be viewed
alternatively as an infant industry and a frail dowager, too weak to with-
stand sustained criticism, in need of enrichment, protection, and an obser-
vant fealty. If there were weaknesses in the international legal system,
scholars and practitioners should tolerate and explain them. If international law seemed rather simple, it was, of course, still primitive. If it seemed
unenforceable, it was simply a different *sort* of law ("horizontal" perhaps),
like some eccentric cousin who still belonged at family celebrations.

The origins and goals of international law's optimistic façade seemed
to have been taken out of discussion—displaced by an endless intellectual
and bureaucratic process. Neither the elite confidence of the pre-war establishment nor the enthusiastic optimism of the post-war reformers had
survived. The vision associated with the large-scale post-war reordering
projects had disappeared—transformed into the details of bureaucratic
pragmatism and policy formulation familiar from American public law.

By 1970, it was just no longer possible to speak of an American
inspired world democracy, or to view decolonization as an administrative
matter of peaceful adjustment. When public international lawyers addressed substantive issues, they presented their work as marginal theoretical or utopian speculation. At best they produced hortatory denunciations
of state policy in a "letters to the editor" format. The American Society of
International Law had become simply one more pretentious and dis-
affected intellectual lobby—precisely the sort of folk former Vice President Agnew would attack as "nattering nabobs of negativism."

In short, when I entered the field in the late seventies, it was clear I
was being asked to be a bureaucrat, a laborer in an institutional plant that
no one believed was able to respond to international racism, inequality or
violence. No one seemed to think that international law was intellectually
rich. No one seemed to think that international institutional structures
looked forward or provided socially and culturally engaged lives for their
inhabitants. No one seemed to think international legal theory could offer
more than an easy patois of lazy justification and arrogance for a discipline
which had lost its way and kept its jobs.

My own rather idiosyncratic doctrinal and historical projects fit together as an effort to dislodge the discipline of international law from its
stagnation in post-war realism. I have sought to dislodge this resignation

and rejuvenate the field as an arena of meaningful intellectual inquiry in part by recapturing its history and substantive aspiration, and in part by heightening the move to process—by reimagining the field rhetorically. Before going on to that work, we need to look for a moment at a few ideas, images, and constellations of belief which needed to be set aside, or questioned, or supplemented by recent theoretical work from other disciplines, in order that the project of the discipline of public international law as it existed in the seventies and eighties might be drawn into question. We need, in other words, to develop some account, some common story or stories about a field which presents itself in hopeless fragmentation.

C. Public International Law—Some Ideas

Let me begin with ideas about the relationship between public international law on the one hand, and something called "society" or "political economy" or "state behavior" on the other. Images of such a relationship have preoccupied public international law scholarship. Everyone has seemed convinced that these two things were, or should be, or purported to be, or struggled to be, different from one another. Indeed, they seemed to feel public international law could only *be* law if it were independent and "normative," a word which, somewhat oddly, has been read to mean "against the state." At the same time, and equally fervently, everyone has seemed convinced that the goal, or achievement, or aspiration or project of public international law is to link law with international "society." This could be done descriptively, or theoretically, or by enacting resolutions, or signing treaties or allocating rights—but it had to be done. Otherwise public international law would seem hopelessly irrelevant to what really mattered, out of touch with the sovereign, in danger of losing touch with the source of power, glory and employment.

This conviction—that international law was not politics but struggled to be politics—has accounted for much of the discipline's eclectic insecurity. It explains the pressure to regularize international law institutionally, and to analogize international law to more familiar domestic constitutional configurations. It explains the historic preoccupation with the relationship between norm and deed, and the mountain of theory—be it naturalist or positivist—explaining how law might both emanate from and control the state. It undergirds the oscillation between Republican formalism and Democratic enthusiasm and explains the doctrinal preoccupation with rights—be they rights to food, to self-determination or to asylum—which could link legislative determination to political enactment and ensure respect for public law.

Displacing—and I mean "displacing," setting aside, neither proving nor disproving but simply avoiding—such an entrenched constellation of imagery has been difficult. Doing so has meant borrowing from recent linguistic and literary theory and from the work of contemporary critical legal scholarship—which has itself drawn on the European philosophical

traditions or structuralism and post-structuralism—in order to reformu-
late the relationship between law and politics in *rhetorical* terms.

Rather than concentrating on the relationship between a law and a
society which actually *are* separate, joined or related only through the
prism of the state or sovereign, I have tried to extend what has been the
single most telling and controversial insight of much recent critical legal
scholarship in the United States: namely, that law is nothing but a repetition of the relationship it posits between law and society. Rather than a
stable domain which *relates* in some complicated way *to* society or political
economy or class structure, law is simply the practice and argument about
the relationship between something posited as law and something posited
as society.

Mine is a relational and rhetorical image of a "law" and a "society"—
invoked by a language which establishes them by positing their originality,
their priority, their presence. My sense is that this rhetorical project—in
many ways *the* rhetorical project of public international law scholarship—
accounts for the doctrinal structures of "public" and "private" or "objective" and "subjective" which we find recurring throughout international
public law doctrine and for the recurrent scholarly contrasts we find between theory and practice.

In this alternative picture, law is nothing but an attempt to project a
stable relationship between spheres it creates to divide. As a result, the
relationship between these zones is much looser than we usually think.
This has led much recent critical scholarship to flaunt both an anti-Marxist
tone and a certain opposition to rights. And my own work has shared these
tendencies. Indeed, my own position often seems to fade quite easily into
neo-conservatism.

Let me go on, then, to a set of ideas about politics or about the
relationship between the intellectual and the state which seem equally
imbedded in public international law scholarship. The mainstream legal
academic in the United States has an ambivalent relationship to politics.
Law purports to be *both* above, removed, or neutral with respect to political life *and* the procedural rules, the instrumental expression, the forum
and historical embodiment of political culture. The mainstream legal
academic—and the public international legal scholar is no exception—has
a similar ambition. He wants to retain his distance and independence from
the state, to retain his status as an intellectual, for this independence
underwrites the value of his wisdom and gives him confidence in his class
position.

At the same time, he wants to deploy the state, guide it, instruct it,
manage it, work for it. He wants his opinions to be transformed into state
policy, and for this they must be redolent with political savvy. In short, if
the public international law scholar wanted his scholarship to separate and
then join "law" with "society" through the mechanisms of the state, he
also wants both to separate and join himself as a citizen, as an intellectual,
to the state through the medium of the law.

A common fantasy about "politics" sustains this double image. Public international legal scholars generally equate politics with the state. It is the state which provides the arena for political action and makes political choices. It is the state which recognizes people as citizens and employs people as politicians. In this arena, in the struggle of interests and commitments, the political remains resolutely a matter of the conscious, of the public, the visible, the overt. For all the legal academic might consume his politics in private, he does so as a matter of conscious decision. For the state, there is nothing beneath the surface, just as the legal academic knows no unconscious.

Political commitment, whether by the state or citizen, is known publicly, in writing, in action. We know a person's politics by his statements and his associations. We might ask a lawyer whom he represents. And we know the politics of the state by its statements, by whom it recognizes and represents. And the most central vocabulary of mutual recognition is that of rights. Within the discipline of public international law, it is a commonplace, for example, that individuals are known to the legal system as subjects only to the extent it can be said that they have rights.

My own work, like that of many other contemporary legal scholars, aims to displace this set of ideas about politics and the state. Doing so has meant borrowing a bit from the traditions of contemporary philosophy and social theory critical of a state-centered image of political culture. The fragmentation of political culture and the turn inward, to the self, even to the unconscious self, has also been supported by interdisciplinary borrowings from the literatures of psychiatry and feminism. And I have relied upon popular images from the sixties—the state displaced by meditation, alienated citizenship by direct political engagement, representational efforts for the client by pedagogic encouragements of self help, disempowerment by empowerment, the surface style of interest group pluralism by the psychobabble of encounter group analysis. Of course, such an approach retains the image of the intellectual as custodian of correct theory for a political culture.

At their best, these literatures have heightened criticism of the vision of the state as a "center of power" or a "sovereignty" which actually exists, is factual and is the site of either law or politics or both, which is developed independent of the narrative of law's history, alongside it, before or ancillary to law's image of sovereignty. The goal seems an image of the state as an imaginary relationship between law and politics, as a site for their rhetorical awareness of one another. And this image, in turn, of a more rhetorical, interactive, dispersed sense of power and thought, has suggested an alternative *topos* for political engagement.

Gone is the privileged realm of the clientele, and the privileged zone of their "representation." The fantasy that one might someday serve the state gives way to a turn inward, to the local, private, even unconscious politics riddling civil society. This shifted sense of the state is thus accompanied by scepticism about both the discourse of "rights" and the practice

of representation—by lawyers of clients and the government of constituents or interests—which supports it.

D. Some Preliminary Methodological Notes

My project over the next few days will be, quite literally, to redraw some
rather familiar territory, returning to some of the most basic materials of
public international law to describe them in a somewhat novel way. Overall, my aspiration is to begin releasing the discipline of public international
law from a constellation of images of law, politics and the state which
seemed characteristic of the field as late as 1980.

My sense is that some aspects of my method may seem strange at first.
Let me finish today with a few precautions and clarifications which may be
helpful as we go along. Think of a traditional piece of contemporary
international law scholarship. It might contain one or more of three types
of argument: theoretical or historical justification, doctrinal description or
elaboration, and programmatic or institutional recommendations.

The theoretical and historical work, whether developed to support or
criticize particular doctrinal and institutional analyses, works to support
the project of the field as a whole—indeed, takes that project for granted
to resolve the problems it sets forth for the scholar. In seeking to displace
this set of problems, I have taken a somewhat different approach to questions in history and theory. I have not looked to them as sources for the
authority or wisdom or content for international law doctrine. Rather, I
have looked at the discipline's history, and its sense of history, for clues to
its general argumentative practice. In other words, I have treated stories
about history and theories about "international law" and "sovereignty" as
if they were simply doctrines.

Doctrinal work, moreover, whether supportive or critical of particular
doctrinal interpretations, generally begins with a sense both of doctrine's
independent coherence and of doctrine's authoritative origin in history or
theory and normative bite in the culture of sovereign behavior. Doctrine,
as normally considered in international law scholarship, gets its energy and
motivation from its origin in sovereign accord, in history, or in theory.
And it has its effects outside the realm of law, in practice or thought. I have
not considered doctrine in this way. I do not analyze the relationship
between international legal materials and their political and interpr[e]tive
milieu. I am not concerned about the context within which arguments are
made and doctrines developed.

I focus rather upon the relationships among doctrines and arguments
and upon their recurring rhetorical structure. I trace the references which
one doctrine makes to another and the repetitions which characterize
doctrinal materials widely dispersed through the field as a whole. Setting
aside issues of origin and meaning to discuss international law internally, as
a self-sufficient rhetoric, encourages an often implausible attribution of
moods, desires and affect to the rhetoric of law. I often will speak as if

one doctrine "sought independence" from another or "seemed uneasy" about its coherence. It might be useful to think of this project as a look at public international law from the *inside*.

Programmatic and institutional scholarship in the international field is generally preoccupied either with establishing an institutional form—with the doctrinal pragmatics of constitutional structure—or with implementing the resolution of doctrine and the wisdom of theory in the terrain of inter-sovereign activity. Scholars worry about capturing the functional relationship between institutions and states and the details of institutional design on paper. The discipline considers problems of situated and practical management rather than normative authority and application. But I do not follow this invitation to harness modernity's tone to the realm of institutional life. My work on international institutions treats the patterns of constitutional establishment and implementation as histories and doctrines. I am concerned to understand institutional life, even the professional life of the international legal scholar, as the enactment of a set of rhetorical maneuvers, as the living forth of doctrine and historiography.

Taken together, this methodological reformulation seeks to unify the historical, theoretical, doctrinal and institutional projects of the discipline. My method is to begin by focusing on argumentative patterns—patterns of contradiction and resolution, of difference and homology—which are reasserted in the materials of international law history, doctrine, and institutional structure. The project thus begins with a certain unsettling of the stability of differences both within and among the materials about international legal history, doctrine and institutions. Within the legal world I describe, stability—between what are now simply terms in a debate—needs to be explained solely *within* the debate itself.

This means, for example, that sociological explanations of doctrine will be set aside in favor of accounts anchored solely within the materials of doctrine. It also means that the sociological contexts of international law—its institutions and history—need be reconceptualized in rhetorical terms. To do so, I have sought to develop close, anthropology-like accounts of the relations in particular bureaucratic settings of doctrine and institutional structure.

Over the next days, I will seek a single optic—a single structural pattern which could be followed throughout the discipline. In this sense perhaps my effort will be too linear, too logical, and indeed, I am somewhat dissatisfied with the structural repetitiveness, the flat logical demeanor of my results. Perhaps it is only a way to begin the project of redrawing the discipline.

Later in the week, it may be useful to think more systematically about ways to reinvigorate the project's specificity—by discussing its relationship to the margins of legal culture, to women, to the religious, to the impoverished, to the violent, to the sexual. One way of understanding this critical move to substance is as an attempt to reawaken—or capture, or, less kindly, exploit—the exotic margins of establishment culture. Indeed, the central contemporary reorientation of the relationship between law and politics—the claim that law is a restatement of its imaginary relationship to society—has been developed by bringing the margin (society) into the core of law, rather than trying to stabilize and relate one to the other.

I want to question the stability of both, and I think this desire might be responsible for political difficulties much contemporary critical legal scholarship has encountered with the left, the right and the center of legal academia. Without anchor, my vision might be pursued equally well by pushing law to the limit ("completing" the project of liberalism, finally enforcing rights, etc.) or by pushing society to the limit ("deconstructing" and historicizing liberalism, disaggregating rights, completing the project of the market). In this, of course, it refers us back to our image of law's origin and to the procedures of social transaction.

Nevertheless, most recently, I have been working to anchor this effort in a broader margin, for it seems that the entire rhetorical apparatus I have been contemplating—all of law and society—however fuzzy and uncertain, exists within and against another set of margins—a margin composed of things thought of as perversion, faith, eros, terror, chaos, tyranny, war, etc. These things are excluded from, distanced from international public culture exactly as society or political economy seemed to be distanced from law. They are treated as at once frightening and fascinating. And most importantly, they are treated as *real* things, capable of signification within public culture. If time permits, I will reach out to these margins along what might be thought of as a rhetorical final frontier.

III. Doctrine: The Rhetoric of International Law

The strange voice of the tragic modern scholar appears as vividly in contemporary international law doctrine as it did in the theory and historiography of the discipline. In today's lecture, I will trace patterns and strategies of rhetoric which recur in different doctrinal areas of public international law, seeking a sense for the mechanisms of their coherence. As I indicated in the first lecture, I have not analyzed the relationship between international legal materials and their political and interpretive milieu, nor am I concerned about the context within which arguments are made and doctrines developed. I have focused on the relationships among doctrines and arguments and upon their recurring rhetorical structure. I have been particularly keen to trace the references one doctrine makes to another and the repetitions which characterize doctrinal materials widely dispersed through the field as a whole—to look at the doctrinal corpus our discipline nourishes from the inside out.

In a way, thinking of things this way reflects the discipline's self image. When it thinks historically, modern public international law locates its origin in a series of ideas and texts about sovereignty and law—and in their movement away from historical or political constellation. Although these ideas are thought particularly to characterize modern western European statecraft, they are treated as if they remained somewhat—and one must stress this quite complex "somewhat"—independent of the particular facts of Western European diplomatic history.

Although public international law presents itself as concerned with issues of politics and statecraft, it seeks to transcend particular political alignments. It moves away from its political origins and towards its substantive—even aspirational—achievement, but remains itself firmly in the procedural between. It participates in war and peace but is itself neither war nor peace. Public international law presents itself much more as the language in which international affairs is written. I have tried to follow the logic of this presentation, emphasizing the veil which separates the discursive materials of the field from their origins and referents to understand public international law precisely *as* a language.

I will take up public international legal materials in three familiar categories—which I have labeled "sources," "process" and "substance." To a certain extent, this organizational structure follows that of more traditional casebooks and treatises, and indeed, these three doctrinal areas seem anxious to differentiate themselves from one another. Sources doctrine is concerned with the origin and authority of international law—a concern it resolves by referring the reader to authorities constituted elsewhere. Process doctrine—the bulk of modern international public law—considers the participants and jurisdictional framework for international law independent of both the process by which international law is generated and the substance of its normative order. Substance doctrine seems to address issues of sovereign cooperation and conflict more directly. Like sources doctrine, it does so largely by referring to the boundaries and authorities established in other doctrinal fields. After reviewing briefly some of the rhetorical strategies characteristic of doctrines of each sort, I will reflect on the doctrinal system as a whole.

A. Sources of International Law

International legal scholars have produced a large body of work about the conditions under which treaties, custom or general principles of law bind actors and the hierarchy among the various doctrinal forms which might apply in a given instance. This body of doctrine provides a good introduction to the rhetorical patterns of public international law as a whole. Contemporary analyses generally work from the sources enumerated in Article 38 of the Statute of the International Court of Justice, proceeding to examine the conditions under which norms of these types will be binding, the hierarchical relationships among them, and the extent to which potential sources not included in the list (such as U.N. resolutions) might be assimilated to one of these classic forms.

Several aspects of this literature might seem odd to a man from the moon. For one thing, the literature proceeds quite abstractly, attempting to delimit boundary conditions for each category independent of the particular content of the norms whose source is being considered. There seems a shared sense that the abstract categories will control the content of the norms, rather than merely register them. Argument about sources doctrine is similarly abstracted from the content of the norm under consideration.

Much of this argument, moreover, seems to repeat a rather simple and familiar debate between the authoritative power of sovereign consent on the one hand, and some extraconsensual norm on the other. Argument about the relative authority of various sources, about their boundaries and effects, seems to be carried out as a debate about sovereign consent. It is an odd debate. At one level, it seems that the choice between a preference for consensual and non-consensual norms will answer all questions. Either a consensual treaty beats a non-consensual custom or it does not. But somehow this question is never squarely faced in doctrinal argument—somebody always seems to muddy the waters.

The bindingness of treaties, after all, seems more than consent, prior to consent, the very condition for a consensual system. And custom might also be the product of consent. Although arguments about the authority of international norms appeal either to consent or to some norm beyond consent as if these were exclusive and definitive possibilities, in the end, each always seems to invoke the other somehow—in a subordinate interpretation, or secondary doctrine.

The basic debate about consent suggests that the discourse of sources will address a basic theoretical dilemma for international law: how can it be simultaneously independent of and enmeshed with sovereign will? The autonomy of sovereigns ensures the attractiveness of consensual sources, while their participation in a pre-existing normative order encourages a non-consensual rhetorical line. In order to fulfill the desire for an autonomous system of normative law, argument about the sources of international law simply included strands associated with both visions. Sources rhetoric is interesting not because it resolves the issue, but because it transforms it into a debate between abstract legal forms—a debate which can manage the conflict between them interminably.

For all its abstraction, sources rhetoric is a distinctly doctrinal affair, neither theoretical nor political. Norms are legally binding which fit within one of a series of doctrinally elaborated categories, not when a persuasive argument about political interest or theoretical coherence can be made for their observance. The distinction between consensual and non-consensual sources—used to distinguish treaties from custom, to contrast various schools of thought about the nature of custom, to divide arguments for and against the application of specific norms in various situations, and in dozens of other ways throughout the materials on sources—opposes themes whose fluidity encourages a proliferation of rhetorical possibilities and strategies more than decisive identifications and differentiations.

The play between these themes gives sources discourse a doctrinal feel without ever presenting the clash between two norms—or two sovereigns—in substantive or political terms. A sources discourse which operated completely within the rhetoric of either consent or systemic considerations would seem doctrinal, but it would not be able to avoid a more substantive face. A consensual rhetoric could certainly differentiate and prioritize norms in an abstract way, but in choosing among two norms, one would need to choose between the claims of two sovereigns about their autonomous consents. A purely extra-consensual rhetoric, while it would obviously avoid this problem, would have a difficult time avoiding a more substantive choice among various systemically grounded norms. By combining those two rhetorics, sources discourse can defend its independence from sovereign autonomy and from substantive legal regulation.

The question, obviously, is how do they do it? My own examination of various sources doctrines and cases suggested a number of rather obvious rhetorical strategies. The most obvious is simply repetition: differentiating various doctrines from one another as consensual and non-consensual and then repeating the distinction in distinguishing each doctrine from its exception or interpreting doctrinal strands which have once been characterized and perhaps adopted as consensual in non-consensual terms. Thus, custom might seem non-consensual when contrasted with treaty, but be measured in consensual terms, or subjected to a consent based exception—say, for persistent opposers.

Taken as a whole, however, sources doctrine seems tilted in favor [of] a consensual rhetoric. Consensual doctrines seem to dominate and consensual interpretations of non-consensual doctrines seem most compelling. The doctrinal hierarchy seems to favor the rhetoric of consent. At the same time, however, sources discourse seems tilted towards the systemic authority of legal norms—towards the normative force of the legal order and away from sovereign autonomy. A certain systemic authority seems to be taken for granted in the rhetoric which is most emphatic about its consensual foundation.

This combination suggests something about the project of sources doctrine as a whole. Sources discourse, so long as it seems consensual, guarantees that the legal order will not derogate from—will indeed express—sovereign authority and autonomy. So long as it seems extra-consensual, sources rhetoric guarantees that the international legal order will not be hostage to sovereign whim. The important thing is the co-existence of these two rhetorics—and the relationship between them. Each must temper the other and the discourse as a whole must seem to move forward from autonomy to community. The hesitancy to adopt either extreme position, and the continual oscillation between them, prevents sources doctrine from disappearing into a theory of state power or a catalog of substantive norms—and, most significantly, transforms a variety of theoretical concerns into a doctrinal proliferation.

B. The International Legal Process

However central theoretically, however paradigmatic of public international law rhetoric, however crucial as secondary—even last resort—persuasive strategies in doctrinal argument, sources doctrines are of only marginal importance. Were it not for their central and exemplary theoretical function, it would be hard to understand why scholars would waste any energy on their elaboration. Discourse about process, by contrast, dominates the field of public international law. If process rules supreme, moreover, it also rules alone. Doctrines about problems of participation and authority in international legal life—doctrines which address actors and their jurisdictions—proceed relatively free of consideration of either substantive standards of behavior or sources of law.

This independence and domination are hard won. After all, determining the source of law to be applied by a court often seems indistinguishable from establishing the court's jurisdiction, and a "process" rule about the jurisdictional limits of sovereign power may not seem any more different from a "substance" rule about the prohibited acts of sovereign power than a jurisdictional authorization would feel different from a substantive empowerment. One way of understanding process doctrine is to think of its central mission as the struggle to maintain this independent centrality to public international law as a whole.

Take the two great areas of process doctrine: doctrines which abstractly delimit the actors whose interests and nature will be constitutive of international law and whose substantive behavior will be controlled by international law on the one hand, and doctrines which abstractly delimit the avenues of legitimate interchange out of which authoritative norms grow and the spheres of activity which will be governed by substantive law. We might term these doctrines of participation and jurisdiction. Between them, they divide the role of establishing and limiting sovereign identity without reference to sources or substance.

The aim of participation doctrines—of statehood, recognition, etc.—is to open the system to qualified actors and ratify their powers. The aim of jurisdiction doctrines, by contrast, is to structure international life by defining the boundaries of various authorities. Where participation is open ended, ratifying, registering sovereign authority, jurisdiction is closed, delimiting sovereign powers. Between them they respond to the modern scholar's sense that the international legal process must be elaborated so as to remain simultaneously independent of and engaged with sovereignty. Between them, precisely in the relation between them, there is nothing they cannot do.

But there is more. Participation doctrine must do its job without reference to legal sources. If the job of sources had been to establish law, the job of participation doctrines is to establish sovereignty. Just as sources needed to do so without reference to the substance of the law, by thinking only of consent, so participation doctrine must refer only to facts and practices, precisely not to the consensual authority of legal sources. That which poses as open must remain closed to the whims of consent—must preexist the canvassing of consent.

Similarly, jurisdiction doctrine must limit sovereign authority without reference to substantive law—must remain procedural. That which poses as closed must do so without abridging the sovereign's ability to act— must indeed be the ground, the basis, the preexisting supposition of sovereign autonomy. In short, to be open-ended is to remain free of substance while complementing sources, while to be regulatory is to remain free of sources while complementing substance.

To retain their collective independence from both sources and substance, process doctrines treat issues of participation and jurisdiction in a number of familiar ways. Again we find abstraction—typical treaties consider the "subjectivity" of individuals, trust territories, colonies, multinationals so as neither simply to register their essence nor to elaborate the substantive doctrines which implicate them. And again we find repetition: the division of responsibility between participation and jurisdiction for open and closed responses to sovereign power is replayed in the relationship between formal (recognition) and material (territory) bases for participation. Again we find argumentative equivocation, managing the tension between the rhetorical invocations—of substantive and formal bases for participation and jurisdictional authority—which seem incompatible and unworkable when considered separately.

The dominance of process doctrine is a strange one, its mastery achieved through elision, hyperbole and equivocation. But if process doctrines work hard at their independence, they also rely heavily on sources and substance doctrine to succeed—or at least upon an image of sources and substance. In the rhetorical division of labor between participation and jurisdiction, much depends on a stable image of substance and sources. Jurisdiction doctrine, seeking independence from substance, asserts its objectivity and elides reliance upon substantive notions of territory and statehood. Participation doctrine, seeking independence from sources, asserts its subjectivity, and understates its reliance upon formal or consensual criteria.

By seeming objective, jurisdiction doctrine, the doctrine responsible for limiting sovereign authority, can seem differential to state power. It is not, after all substantive. By seeming subjective, participation doctrine, the doctrine responsible for registering and recognizing sovereign authority can appear to establish a communal, legal control over the membership process. It is not, after all, a consensual source. In this way, process establishes itself, sustains its independence, by projecting that which it would achieve elsewhere—back to sources or onward towards substance. As a result, process is able to refer to, even subtly determine, both sources and substance by a continual reference towards them—a reference which leaves them always at a distance. In this sense, the domination of process might be understood as a self-effacement.

But these ideas, these arguments, these images of jurisdiction and participation doctrine, depend upon extremely monochromatic images of sources and substance. Sources doctrine, after all, is hardly consensual. Indeed, when looked at directly its most striking feature is its equivocal oscillation between consensual and non-consensual rhetorics. Substance, as we shall see, is hardly communal—indeed, its most salient feature is its equivocation and reference back to sources and process for the resolution of difficult questions.

C. *The Memory and Dream of Substance*

Unlike the international legal process, the regime of substantive public international norms is fragmented and incomplete. Although process and sources doctrine seem more doctrinally complete, they present themselves as the servants of a substantive order which will be achieved and protected. We expect little of process—and less of sources—because we expect so much of substance. Here, in the laws of war and peace, we hope to find a social fabric, the wise constraints which keep us free. Yet these expectations are quickly disappointed, for the substantive doctrines of international law remain largely promises—promises that eventually, in a world of good states, or enlightened statesmen, or after the next codification, we might achieve world peace through world law. Process we might have today—it seems real, enmeshed in the conflicted world of contemporary international life. For substance we will need to wait.

And this double presentation—partial and yet completing, extending the international legal order forward into the future—is repeated in the rhetoric of substantive doctrine and argument. Take the two large categories of substantive doctrine: the law of peace and the law of force. Between them, they share the labor of completing the entire substantive agenda for international law—to address the conflicts of sovereign autonomy and the cooperation of sovereign equality. Either alone seems impossible. A fully integrated international order seems impossible, naive, utopian or quaint. An order responsive only to state interests seems dangerously anarchistic. Like the demands for a process which is both open and closed—or for a legal regime which is both normative and independent of social life—these narrative constraints shape the rhetoric of substantive doctrine.

Again we find the rhetorical management of alternative images—of interventionist regulation and simple, almost architectural, communal structures. The rhetoric of the law of peace stresses the necessity or inevitability of cooperation while preserving national autonomy. The rhetoric of force law stresses the inevitability of sovereign autonomy while struggling to accommodate cooperation. Again we find repetition: the distinction between cooperative regulation and deferential proceduralism which distinguished peace law from the law of force is responsible as well for the division within the law of force between the laws of war and the law in war. And again we find the reference elsewhere—to sources for consensual authority to ground images of peace, to process for boundaries to the use of force which do not impinge on sovereign freedom to act.

In its strange comprehensivity, then, substantive doctrines seem, for all their fragmentation, to fulfill the ambition for a law which grapples directly with both sovereign autonomy and community. But not quite. The law of peace shrinks back from substantive enactment to a process of regulation, a reference to institutions, or a reliance upon a set of procedurally established boundaries. Close examination of even so substantive appearing a regime as the Law of the Sea Treaty reveals a series of rhetorical references and uncertainties—references forward to future process and back to an earlier sovereign agreement. We seem unable to locate the moment of law's substance. Similarly, the law of force shrinks back from enforcement to a rhetoric of procedurally established jurisdictional boundaries and a reference to the violence at the core of sovereign authority.

And indeed, violence comes to seem ever more central to the project of substantive legal doctrine. Together, the law in war and the law of war are situated between a promise and a fear—the promise that violence will be displaced by law and the fear that it will not. Beneath, around the rhetorical maneuvers of substantive doctrine, floats the memory and practice of violence—in the constitution of the state, the definition of autonomy. Rather than a regulation we find a vocabulary of force. Whether we think of substantive international law as the establishment of an institutional system—as a return to process—or as a ratification of force, the law seems to have devoured its other—to have ingested the politics of sovereign force and become a language, a grammar, a logic, for violence.

D. Reflections on a Doctrinal System

I have looked at these doctrinal materials in this way in order to think about the overall coherence of public international law as a set of relationships among the discursive fields of sources, process and substance. It is striking how effectively these distinctive fields, each with its own characteristic doctrinal structure and argumentative style, work with and against one another to generate and sustain an international legal system. Moreover, the rhetorical practices of contemporary doctrinal discussion in each area—practices of elision, avoidance, deferral and projection—are remarkably similar.

Each group of doctrines seems to invoke—and promises to resolve—a particular set of social or historical problems. Sources discourse seems to consider law's origin and authority—and hence its distinctiveness—in a social order of which it is a part. Sources doctrine thus seems closest to the concerns of international public law theory. Substantive discourse, by contrast, seems to consider law's participation in formulating a social order between freedom and coercion. It thus seems closest to institutional life and political implementation. Process discourse seems to consider international law's ability both to remain distinct from the social order as demanded by sources and to relate to it as demanded by substance.

Several interesting points emerge from exploration of this classification. To begin with, none of these doctrinal areas actually do what they say—or rather they do so only obliquely. Sources discourse, for example, transforms an aspiration to consider origins and authority into a rhetoric of deference to or departure from already constituted authority; speaking of overriding or deferring to the *consent* of sovereigns. Thus it recapitulates the philosophical debate between norm and deed while deferring either to politics or to process for the very authority it purports to establish.

Process discourse transforms its aspiration for a simultaneously open and closed legal system into a rhetorical fabric of objective and subjective doctrine and argument. It talks about the neutrality of formal standards and the reality in immersion of the facts. Thus it also recapitulates the forgotten struggle between positive and natural law, while referring either to a formality of sources or the content of substance for the structure it purports to establish.

Finally, substance pulls back from its claim to order freedom and coercion to develop a system of rhetorical references to the constraints and deferences of process and sources. It develops schemes of architecture which reinforce the boundaries established by process and of regulation which refer to the process of dispute resolution and to the codification of regulatory purpose through the mechanisms of sources.

In pursuing their varied projects, these three doctrinal practices echo themes and references familiar to one another. The return of the law of force to doctrines about sources demonstrates this quite strikingly. Although these two fields seemed very distinct—sources a very doctrinal, logical field, the law of force a very substantively engaged field—both seem to be concerned with invoking and then muffling the sovereign authority behind its most basic principles.

Moreover, in many cases, the same issue arose for consideration in one area after another, each time taking on a slightly different tone. Take the constitution of the sovereign subject for example. Although sources seemed to rely upon a category of sovereign subjects whose consent might be canvassed—seemed indeed to depend upon process definitions of statehood—it also traced patterns of legitimate authority in its catalogs of authoritative norms. Statehood doctrine seemed able to determine participation, but depended upon both authoritative sources and legitimate monopolies of force to do so. The law of peace and war harnessed their prohibitions to the boundaries established by statehood while seeming to regulate the construction of sovereign authority.

All of these similarities and repetitions seemed interesting in part because they seemed likely to provide a way of understanding the practice of international legal argumentation. If, as it seems, a rather small set of argumentative maneuvers and doctrinal distinctions repeat themselves in a wide variety of different contexts throughout public international law, it might be possible to unite the field around these patterns rather than to be forced to think of them each time anew in response to different situations or in different doctrinal areas. Further study might indeed substantiate such a claim.

The most interesting result of this effort to identify repeating rhetorical technique, however, was a new sense of the relationship among the three doctrinal areas which I had chosen for examination. For all their structural similarity, the discourses of source, process and substance seemed both to distinguish themselves and to relate to their brother discourses in a series of quite distinctive rhetorical maneuvers. Quite paradoxically, each discourse seemed to distinguish itself by referring to its brothers for the completion and continuation of its project.

This was most apparent in the projections of process onto both source and substance of authority and order. Process seemed to sustain its self-image as open to authority and productive of order by alternating in its references to the authority of consensual sources which it implemented and the order of an international substantive regime which it facilitated. It also seemed that process led us to substance with a promise of some resolution to the problem of sovereign autonomy and cooperation—which the law of peace repeated and which the laws of force only fulfilled by grounding us in violence while referring us back to the boundaries of process and the authority of sources.

Despite the difficulty of saying with any certainty that references from any one of these areas generates doctrine in any other, it does seem that these various projections and references as a whole constitute public international law as a single rhetorical fabric. These rhetorical areas work together to sustain the independent purport of each—and to reinforce the general purport of public international law as a whole to be a system of normative authority and practice among sovereigns.

The general purport of public international law is reinforced in three ways. First, it seems that the rhetorical system is able to assert itself quite firmly as an international regime while sustaining a very humble and deferential tone. Public international law seems a quite well articulated and complete legal order even though it is difficult to locate the authoritative origin or substantive voice of the system in any particular area. Each doctrine seems to free ride somewhat on this overall systemic image—an image which is sustained by a continual reference elsewhere for authority or decisiveness.

Sources refers us to the states constituted by process and grounded in the violence defined and limited by substance. Process refers us to its origin in sources and its determination in substance. Substance refers us to the boundaries of process, its origins in sources and its resolution in an institutional system of application and interpretation. Thus, the variety of references among these discursive areas always shrewdly locates the moment of authority and of application in practice elsewhere—perhaps behind us in process or before us in the institutions of dispute resolution.

Second, this system of references among discursive areas seems to substantiate the overall claims of public international law by generating a sense of progress or momentum. The momentum developed through reference from sources to process and substance reinforces the image of public international law on the move from theory to practice, from differentiation to regulation, and, consequently, from the deference to state autonomy characteristic of sources to the constitution of an international cooperative regime characteristic of substance.

The momentum is generated through a series of promises and repetitions. Individual doctrines position themselves between an openness past and a closure future—exactly as the Covenant of the League situated us between war and parliament. By situating themselves between stasis and motion in this way—by relying upon an image of the determination of discourses past and the indeterminacy of discourses future—the rhetorical system is able both to claim to be becoming an international order and to be experienced as fulfilling that promise.

Yet these various rhetorics are not logically either indeterminate or determinate. I began my investigation interested in the structural contradictions of doctrine—hoping to dislodge the arrogance of modernity by uncovering its loose and contradictory logic. But this is only half the story. Indeed, every story about indeterminacy only works by a projection elsewhere—onto the facts or wherever—of an equally determinate image. These rhetorics only seem closed when the possibilities for association are not fully utilized. They only seem open and indeterminate when their object is thought to be closure. In fact, they are most interesting when they are neither—when the pattern of repetition, association and referral produces a practice of interminable discourse.

Indeed, modern public international law discourse is significant, in my view because it subtly transforms social difficulties into rhetorical alternatives which invoke social choices and fears in only the most hyperbolic fashion. The resulting field of rhetorical maneuver can extend itself virtually to infinity, so long as the specters of social power and aspiration can be kept safely, tamely, at bay. In short, my doctrinal investigations have convinced me that the interminability of international law is the subtle secret of its success.

Selected Bibliography

Prominent Book-Length Works

Carty, Anthony. *The Decay of International Law? A Reappraisal of the Limits of Legal Imagination in International Affairs* (1986).
Kennedy, David. *International Legal Structures* (1987).
Koskenniemi, Martti. *From Apology to Utopia: The Structure of International Legal Argument* (1989).

Prominent Articles from the David Kennedy Corpus

Kennedy, David. "Critical Theory, Structuralism and Contemporary Legal Scholarship," *New England Law Review* 21 (1985–86): 209–89.
———. "International Legal Education," *Harvard International Law Journal* 26 (1985): 361–84.
———. "The Move to Institutions," *Cardozo Law Review* 8 (1987): 841–988.
———. "Primitive Legal Scholarship," *Harvard International Law Journal* 27 (1986): 1–98.
———. "The Sources of International Law," *American University Journal of International Law and Policy* 2 (1987): 1–96.
———. "Spring Break," *Texas Law Review* 63 (1985): 1377–1423.
———. "Theses About International Law Discourse," *German Yearbook of International Law* 23 (1980): 353–91.
———, and Chris Tennant. "New Approaches to International Law: A Bibliography," *Harvard Journal of International Law* 35 (1994): 417–60.

Other Prominent Articles and Books

Altman, Andrew. *Critical Legal Studies: A Liberal Critique* (1990).
Berman, Nathaniel. "Modernism, Nationalism and the Rhetoric of Reconstruction," *Yale Journal of Law and the Humanities* 4 (1992): 351–80.
———. "Sovereignty in Abeyance: Self-determination in International Law," *Wisconsin International Law Journal* 7 (1988): 51–105.
Binder, Guyora. *Treaty Conflict and Political Contradiction* (1989).
Boyle, James. "Ideals and Things: International Legal Scholarship and the Prisonhouse of Language," *Harvard International Law Journal* 26 (1985): 327–59.
Carty, Anthony. "Critical International Law: Recent Trends in the Theory of International Law," *European Journal of International Law* 2 (1991): 66–96.
Koskenniemi, Martti. "The Future of Statehood," *Harvard International Law Journal* 32 (1991): 397–410.
O'Meara, Richard L. "Applying the Critical Jurisprudence of International Law to the Case Concerning Military and Paramilitary Activities in Nicaragua," *Virginia Law Review* 7 (1985): 1183–1210.
Purvis, Nigel. "Critical Legal Studies in Public International Law," *Harvard International Law Journal* 32 (1991): 81–127.

Sathirathai, Surakiart. "An Understanding of the Relationship Between International Legal Discourse and Third World Nations," *Harvard International Law Journal* 25 (1984): 395–419.

Scobbie, Iain. "Towards the Elimination of International Law," *British Yearbook of International Law* (1990): 339–62.

Tarullo, Daniel K. "Logic, Myth, and the International Economic Order," *Harvard International Law Journal* 26 (1985): 533–52.

Book Reviews

Alvarez, Jose E. "The Quest for Legitimacy: An Examination of *The Power of Legitimacy Among Nations,*" *New York University Journal of International Law and Politics* 24 (1991): 199–267.

Kennedy, David. "Review of Anthony Carty's *The Decay of International Law?*" in *American Journal of International Law* 81 (1987): 451–55.

———. "Review of Louis Henkin's *How Nations Behave,*" in *Harvard International Law Journal* 21 (1980): 301–31.

———. "Review of Martti Koskenniemi's *From Apology to Utopia,*" in *Harvard International Law Journal* 31 (1990): 385–91.

Onuf, Nicholas. "Review of David Kennedy's *International Legal Structure,*" in *American Journal of International Law* 83 (1989): 630–40.

———. "Review of Martti Koskenniemi's *From Apology to Utopia,*" in *American Journal of International Law* 84 (1990): 771–75.

Trimble, Phillip R. "International Law, World Order, and Critical Legal Studies," *Stanford Law Review* 42 (1990): 811–45.

9

Feminist Voices

Hilary Charlesworth, Christine Chinkin, and Shelley Wright, in the following essay on "Feminist Approaches to International Law," suggest that the essential insight of feminist legal scholarship generally has been that it "exposed the gender bias of apparently neutral systems of rules." They seek to explore and extend the implications of this insight into the sphere of international law.

Charlesworth, Chinkin, and Wright acknowledge the debt of feminist legal theory to the Critical Legal Studies movement. Feminist and Critical Legal Studies approaches are also united in their criticism of liberal ideology and their use of linguistic tools of analysis. Like the New Stream approach, which applies Critical Legal Studies methods to international law, the Feminist approach to international law views law as an essentially ideological enterprise, though one that often masquerades as a system of neutral principles.

Even so, Charlesworth, Chinkin, and Wright also note that their project differs from that of the Critical Legal scholars, being "more focused and concrete" than the work of the New Stream scholars, for instance. Certainly the nascent feminist approach of international law is more concerned with the content of the law than is the New Stream scholarship. Feminist scholars attempt to look behind the abstract entities of states to "the actual impact of rules on women within states." In so doing, Feminist legal scholars believe they can develop a distinctive mode of analysis and methodology, though they recognize that a single Feminist methodology for studying international rules is unlikely to develop. Feminist approaches to international rules are diverse, eclectic, and interdisciplinary, drawing on the work of Feminists who have already developed distinctive scholarships in a number of other social sciences. Feminists express explicit policy preferences and are concerned with real politics and the substantive content of the law.

The Feminist approach "derives its theoretical force from the immediate experience of the role of the legal system in creating and perpetuating the unequal position of women." Though the approach seeks to define a genuinely feminine "voice" in the process, its adherents often recognize that no single "voice" may ultimately be able to speak for all women. Women in the First and Third Worlds, for instance, have very different experiences of international law. Ultimately, it is the focus on the *common* experiences women have of international law that unifies Feminist approaches to international law.

Feminist scholars suggest that both the organization and the normative structure of international law are essentially male-dominated and patriarchical. Some Feminists argue that a truly "feminine" mode of reasoning about international rules, based on factors excluded from the male-dominated legal discourse, might be developed. This approach would be less litigious, more nonconfrontational, and disposed to negotiated solutions. Other Feminists criticize this view as too close to the "sociobiologism" from which women have struggled to escape. Charlesworth, Chinkin, and Wright are ambivalent about the existence of a feminine morality that might inform international law. They are primarily concerned, they note, not with feminine moral principles, but with women's experiences that have been systematically excluded from the international legal process.

Authors Charlesworth, Chinkin, and Wright offer two basic explanations for this exclusion of women from the international legal process. First, they contend that the organizational structure of international law has operated to the detriment of women. In the international legal system, two of the primary actors are states and international organizations. Yet the decision-making elites in both consist overwhelmingly of men. As a consequence, women's voices are rarely part of the power structure of the system. It is therefore no wonder that the rules created in this process do not adequately address the concerns of women.

A second reason for the gender bias of the international legal system lies in what Charlesworth, Chinkin, and Wright call the "normative structure" of international law. In the "masculine world" of contemporary international law, legal rules seek to regulate the "public" sphere—"the work place, the law, economics, politics," and so on. But legal rules do not address the so-called private sphere—"the home, the hearth and children." By attaching greater value to the public, "male," world over the private, "female," world, international law privileges the male worldview and reinforces male domination of the international legal order. An example of this problem can be seen in international legal rules prohibiting torture. By excluding "private" violence—that is, domestic violence— from the sphere regulated by international human rights law, international law fails to address a form of inhumane behavior just as cruel as state-inflicted torture.

By exposing these and other problems of the international legal system, Charlesworth, Chinkin, and Wright have set the stage for further research from a Feminist perspective. As the bibliography at the end of this chapter indicates, Feminist scholars have already begun examining a host of specific international legal issues—including human rights, the use of force, and development. Inasmuch as their project draws upon Feminist legal theory generally and Feminist approaches to International Relations, the potential for interdisciplinary research is promising. As Feminist research into international rules continues, it seems likely that more bridges can be built between the International Law and International Relations communities.

HILARY CHARLESWORTH, CHRISTINE CHINKIN,
AND SHELLEY WRIGHT

Feminist Approaches to International Law

I. Introduction

The development of feminist jurisprudence in recent years has made a rich
and fruitful contribution to legal theory. Few areas of domestic law have
avoided the scrutiny of feminist writers, who have exposed the gender bias
of apparently neutral systems of rules.[1] A central feature of many western
theories about law is that the law is an autonomous entity, distinct from
the society it regulates. A legal system is regarded as different from a
political or economic system, for example, because it operates on the basis
of abstract rationality, and is thus universally applicable and capable of
achieving neutrality and objectivity.[2] These attributes are held to give the
law its special authority. More radical theories have challenged this abstract
rationalism, arguing that legal analysis cannot be separated from the political, economic, historical and cultural context in which people live. Some
theorists argue that the law functions as a system of beliefs that make
social, political and economic inequalities appear natural.[3] Feminist jurisprudence builds on certain aspects of this critical strain in legal thought.[4]
It is much more focused and concrete, however, and derives its theoretical
force from immediate experience of the role of the legal system in creating
and perpetuating the unequal position of women.

There is no single school of feminist jurisprudence. Most feminists
would agree that a diversity of voices is not only valuable, but essential,
and that the search for, or belief in, one view, one voice is unlikely to
capture the reality of women's experience or gender inequality. "One true
story" cannot be told, and the promise is of "the permanent partiality of
feminist inquiry."[5] As Nancy Hartsock has said, "At bottom, feminism is a
mode of analysis, a method of approaching life and politics, a way of asking
questions and searching for answers, rather than a set of political conclusions about the oppression of women."[6]

International law has thus far largely resisted feminist analysis. The
concerns of public international law do not, at first sight, have any particular impact on women: issues of sovereignty, territory, use of force and state
responsibility, for example, appear gender free in their application to the
abstract entities of states. Only where international law is considered directly relevant to individuals, as with human rights law, have some specifically feminist perspectives on international law begun to be developed.[7]

From the *American Journal of International Law* 85 (1991): 613–45. The American Society
of International Law. Reprinted by permission. Some notes have been altered.

In this article we question the immunity of international law to feminist analysis—why has gender not been an issue in this discipline?—and indicate the possibilities of feminist scholarship in international law. In the first section, we examine the problems of developing an *international* feminist perspective. We then outline the male organizational and normative structure of the international legal system. We go on to apply feminist analyses developed in the context of domestic law to various international legal principles. Our approach requires looking behind the abstract entities of states to the actual impact of rules on women within states. We argue that both the structures of international lawmaking and the content of the rules of international law privilege men; if women's interests are acknowledged at all, they are marginalized. International law is a thoroughly gendered system.

By challenging the nature and operation of international law and its context, feminist legal theory can contribute to the progressive development of international law. A feminist account of international law suggests that we inhabit a world in which men of all nations have used the statist system to establish economic and nationalist priorities to serve male elites, while basic human, social and economic needs are not met. International institutions currently echo these same priorities. By taking women seriously and describing the silences and fundamentally skewed nature of international law, feminist theory can identify possibilities for change.

II. Different Voices in International Law

In this section we examine the notion of a "different voice" in the international context: first, the relationship between feminist and Third World challenges to international law; and second, whether the voices of women from the developed and developing worlds have anything in common.

Much feminist scholarship has been concerned with the identification of a distinctive women's voice that has been overwhelmed and underestimated in traditional epistemologies. Rehabilitation of this voice challenges the objectivity and authority of male-designed disciplines. Feminist legal scholars have drawn in particular on the work of psychologist Carol Gilligan[8] to investigate whether there is a distinctively feminine way of thinking or solving problems: do women have a "different voice," a different way of reasoning, from that of men?

Gilligan's research into childhood development indicates that young girls, when asked to solve a moral dilemma set in a hypothetical problem, typically think about, and react to, the problem differently than boys.[9] Girls tend to invoke an "ethic of care"[10] and see things in terms of relationships, responsibility, caring, context, communication; boys rely on an "ethic of rights" or "justice"[11] and analyze problems in abstract terms of right and wrong, fairness, logic, rationality, winners and losers, ignoring context and relationships. Traditional psychological theory has regarded the male type of reasoning as more "advanced" than the female pattern.

Gilligan's work has been useful to a critical analysis of legal reasoning, which lays claim to abstract, objective decision making. If legal reasoning simply reproduced a masculine type of reasoning, its objectivity and authority are reduced. Feminists have been able to describe the possibility of an equally valid "feminine" reasoning based on factors usually considered irrelevant to legal thinking. Alternative, nonlitigious, dispute resolution and nonconfrontational negotiation techniques are sometimes proposed as examples of such an approach.

The notion of women's "different voice" has been criticized by some feminist scholars. Although Gilligan attributes the difference in masculine and feminine voices primarily to gendered child-rearing practices, the identification of women with caring, conciliation and concern with personal relationships, writes Carol Smart, "slides uncomfortably and exceedingly quickly into socio-biologism which merely puts women back in their place."[12] And Catharine MacKinnon argues: "For women to affirm difference, when difference means dominance, as it does with gender, means to affirm the qualities and characteristics of powerlessness."[13] Our concern here with women's voices, however, is to identify not so much a distinctive feminine morality as distinctive women's experiences, which are factored out of the international legal process and thus prevent this discipline from having universal validity.

Feminist and Third World Challenges to International Law

Are women's voices and values already present in international law through the medium of the Third World? The divisions between developed and developing nations (and between socialist and nonsocialist states) have generated a lively debate over the universality of principles of international law.[14] One consequence of decolonization has been the great increase in the number of independent states, particularly in Africa and Asia. These states have challenged both substantive norms of international law and the traditional lawmaking processes as either disadvantageous to them or inadequate to their needs. The impact of this challenge to assumptions about the objective neutrality of norms by showing them to support western values and interests has been substantial. Developing states have also emphasized decision making through negotiation and consensus, and through the use of nontraditional methods of lawmaking such as the "soft law" of General Assembly resolutions. These techniques find some parallel in the types of dispute resolution sometimes associated with the "different voice" of women. In his study of American diplomacy in the first half of this century, George Kennan implied that nonwestern views of international relations and the feminine were linked:

> If . . . instead of making ourselves slaves of the concepts of international law and morality, we would confine these concepts to the unobtrusive, almost feminine function of the gentle civilizer of national self-interest in which they find their true value—if we were able to do these things in our dealings with the peoples of the East, then, I think, posterity might look back upon our efforts with fewer and less troubled questions.[15]

This apparent similarity between the perspective culturally identified with women and that of developing nations has been studied in a different context. In *The Science Question in Feminism,* Sandra Harding notes the "curious coincidence of African and feminine 'world views'"[16] and examines them to determine whether they could be the basis of a "successor," alternative view of science and epistemology. Harding observes the association of the feminine with the second half of the set of conceptual dichotomies that provide the essential framework for traditional, Enlightenment science and epistemology: "Reason vs. emotion and social value, mind vs. body, culture vs. nature, self vs. others, objectivity vs. subjectivity, knowing vs. being."[17] In the generation of scientific truth, the "feminine" parts of these dichotomies are considered subordinate. Harding then notes the similarity of this pattern and the description of the "African world view" identified by scholars in other disciplines. This world view is characterized by "a conception of the self as intrinsically connected with, as part of, both the community and nature."[18] The attribution to women and Africans of "a concept of the self as dependent on others, as defined through relationships to others, as perceiving self-interest to lie in the welfare on the relational complex," permits the ascription to these groups of an ethic based on preservation of relationships and an epistemology uniting "hand, brain and heart." These perceptions contrast with the "European" and male view of the self as autonomous, separate from nature and from others, and with its associated ethics of "rule-governed adjudication of competing rights between self-interested, autonomous others" and its view of knowledge as an entity with a separate, "objective" existence.[19]

There are problems in identifying these subordinate voices. For example: How far are these world views the product of colonial and patriarchal conceptual schemes? Are they in fact generally held by the groups they are ascribed to? How accurate are contrasting schemata in capturing reality? Harding argues that the linkage of the two discourses may nevertheless be useful as providing "categories of challenge"—that is, naming "what is absent in the thinking and social activities of men and Europeans" and stimulating analysis of how social orders based on gender and race can come into being.[20]

More general analogies have been drawn between the position of Third World states and that of women. Both groups are said to encounter the paternalist attitude that they must be properly trained to fit into the world of developed countries and men, respectively.[21] Both feminists and developing nations have also resisted assimilation to prevailing standards and have argued for radical change; emphasizing cooperation rather than individual self-advancement. Both groups have identified unilinear structures that allow their systematic domination and the development of apparently generally applicable theories from very narrow perspectives.

Thus far, however, the "different voice" of developing nations in international law has shown little concern for feminist perspectives. The power structures and decision-making processes in these societies are ev-

ery bit as exclusive of women as in western societies and the rhetoric of
domination and subjugation has not encompassed women, who remain
the poorest and least privileged.[22] Thus, at the United Nations Mid-
Decade for Women Conference in Copenhagen in 1985, an Indian dele-
gate could argue that since he had experienced colonialism, he knew that it
could not be equated with sexism. Although the developing nations' challenge to international law has been fundamental, it has focused on disparities in economic position and has not questioned the silence of half the
world's population in the creation of international law or the unequal
impact of rules of international law on women. Indeed, this challenge to
the European origins of international law and many of its assumptions may
have had an adverse effect on the development of a gender-based analysis
of international law precisely because of the further level of confrontation
it is assumed such an analysis would cause.

Feminism in the First and Third Worlds

An alternative, feminist analysis of international law must take account of
the differing perspectives of First and Third World feminists. Third World
feminists operate in particularly difficult contexts. Not only does the dominant European, male discourse of law, politics and science exclude the
kind of discourse characterized by the phrase "a different voice," both
female *and* non-European, but also feminist concerns in the Third World
are largely ignored or misunderstood by western feminists. Western feminism began as a demand for the right of women to be treated as men.
Whether in campaigns for equal rights or for special rights such as the right
to abortion, western feminists have sought guarantees from the state that,
as far as is physically possible, they will be placed in the same position as
men. This quest does not always have the same attraction for nonwestern
women. For example, the western feminist preoccupation with a woman's
right to abortion is of less significance to many Third World women
because population-control programs often deny them the chance to have
children. Moreover, "nonpositivist" cultures, such as those of Asia and
Africa, are just as masculinist, or even more so, than the western cultures in
which the language of law and science developed. In the context of international law (and, indeed, domestic law), then, Third World feminists are
obliged to communicate in the western rationalist language of the law, in
addition to challenging the intensely patriarchal "different voice" discourse of traditional non-European societies. In this sense, feminism in the
Third World is doubly at odds with the dominant male discourse of its
societies.

The legacy of colonial rule has been particularly problematic for many
women in the Third World. Local women were seen as constituting a pool
of cheap labor for industries, agriculture and domestic service, and local
men were often recruited to work away from their families. Local women
also provided sex to the colonizers, especially where there was a shortage

of women from home. To local men, the position of their women was symbolic of and mirrored their own domination: while colonialism meant allowing the colonial power to abuse colonized women, resistance to colonialism encompassed reasserting the colonized males' power over their women.

Nationalist movements typically pursued wider objectives than merely to transfer power from white colonial rulers to indigenous people: they were concerned with restructuring the hierarchies of power and control, reallocating wealth within society, and creating nothing less than a new society based on equality and nonexploitation. It was inevitable that feminist objectives, including the restructuring of society across gender lines, would cause tension when set beside nationalist objectives that sounded similar but so frequently discounted the feminist perspective.

Nevertheless, local women were needed in the fight against colonialism, which imposed numerous restrictions on them. The Sri Lankan feminist Kumari Jayawardena has shown that for many nationalists the objective of overthrowing colonial rule required both the creation of a national identity around which people could rally and the institution of internal reforms designed to present themselves as western and "civilized," and therefore worthy of self-rule.[23] Thus, both the colonizers and the local men demanded that local women be modeled on western women. On the one hand, "ladylike" (western) behavior was regarded as a "mainstay of imperialist behavior," as "feminine respectability" taught the colonized and colonists alike that "foreign conquest was right and necessary."[24] On the other hand, many local males believed that "women needed to be adequately Westernized and educated in order to enhance the modern and 'civilized' image of their country."[25] Of course, the model handed down by western civilization embraced all the restrictions imposed on western women.

The need to rally around a national identity, however, required that local women, even while being groomed on the western model, also take it upon themselves to be "the guardians of national culture, indigenous religion and family traditions."[26] These institutions in many instances repressed women. Halliday points out that, despite the belief that the spread of nationalism and nationalist ideas is beneficial to women, "nationalist movements subordinate women in a particular definition of their role and place in society, [and] enforce conformity to values that are often male-defined."[27] Women could find themselves dominated by foreign rule, economic exploitation and aggression, as well as by local entrenched patriarchies, religious structures and traditional rulers.

These conflicting historical perspectives highlight a significant problem for many feminists in the developing world. Feminist and women's movements have been active in numerous developing countries since at least the late nineteenth and early twentieth centuries, but too often women in nationalist movements have had to choose between pressing their own concerns and seeing those concerns crushed by the weight of the overall struggle against colonial rule. Feminists in nonwestern countries and, before independence, in the nationalist movements, were open to attack from their own people for accepting decadent western capitalism, embracing the neocolonialism of a foreign culture, and turning away from their own culture, ideology and religion. The explicit or implicit addition was that their acceptance of western feminist values was diverting them from the revolutionary struggle against the colonial power. In other contexts, the emancipation of women has been regarded as a Communist tactic to be resisted by resort to traditional values. Problems of loyalty and priorities arise in this context that do not exist for western feminists. Many Third World feminist movements either were begun in cooperation with nationalistic, anticolonial movements or operate in solidarity with the process of nation building. Overt political repression is a further problem for feminism in the Third World. In nonwestern cultures there may be a much greater fear and hatred of the feminine, especially when it is not strictly confined to the domestic sphere, than is apparent or expressed in western society.

Despite differences in history and culture, feminists from all worlds share a central concern: their domination by men. Birgit Brock-Utne writes: "Though patriarchy is hierarchical and men of different classes, races or ethnic groups have different places in the patriarchy, they are united in their shared relationship of dominance over their women. And, despite their unequal resources, they are dependent on each other to maintain that domination."[28] Issues raised by Third World feminists, however, require a reorientation of feminism to deal with the problems of the most oppressed women, rather than those of the most privileged. Nevertheless, the constant theme in both western and Third World feminism is the challenge to structures that permit male domination, although the form of the challenge and the male structures may differ from society to society. An international feminist perspective on international law will have as its goal the rethinking and revision of those structures and principles which exclude most women's voices.

III. The Masculine World of International Law

In this section we argue that the international legal order is virtually impervious to the voices of women and propose two related explanations for this: the organizational and normative structures of international law.

The Organizational Structure of International Law

The structure of the international legal order reflects a male perspective and ensures its continued dominance. The primary subjects of international law are states and, increasingly, international organizations. In both states and international organizations the invisibility of women is striking. Power structures within governments are overwhelmingly masculine:

women have significant positions of power in very few states, and in those where they do, their numbers are min[i]scule. Women are either unrepresented or underrepresented in the national and global decision-making processes.

States are patriarchal structures not only because they exclude women from elite positions and decision-making roles, but also because they are based on the concentration of power in, and control by, an elite and the domestic legitimation of a monopoly over the use of force to maintain that control. This foundation is reinforced by international legal principles of sovereign equality, political independence and territorial integrity and the legitimation of force to defend those attributes.

International organizations are functional extensions of states that allow them to act collectively to achieve their objectives. Not surprisingly, their structures replicate those of states, restricting women to insignificant and subordinate roles. Thus, in the United Nations itself, where the achievement of nearly universal membership is regarded as a major success of the international community, this universality does not apply to women.

Article 8 was included in the United Nations Charter to ensure the legitimacy of women as permanent staff members of international organizations. Article 8 states: "The United Nations shall place no restrictions on the eligibility of men and women to participate in any capacity and under conditions of equality in its principal and subsidiary organs." While there was no overt opposition to the concept of gender equality at the 1945 San Francisco Conference, which drafted the Charter, some delegates considered the provision superfluous and said that it would be "absurd" to put anything so "self-evident" into the Charter. However, at the insistence of the Committee of Women's Organizations, Article 8 was included. It was phrased in the negative, rather than as an affirmative obligation to include women, as the right to choose delegates and representatives to international organizations was thought to belong to nation-states, whose freedom of choice was not to be impeded in any way. In reality, women's appointments within the United Nations have not attained even the limited promise of Article 8. The Group on Equal Rights for Women in the United Nations has observed that "gender racism" is practiced in UN personnel policies "every week, every month, every year."[29]

Women are excluded from all major decision making by international institutions on global policies and guidelines, despite the often disparate impact of those decisions on women. Since 1985, there has been some improvement in the representation of women in the United Nations and its specialized agencies. It has been estimated, however, that "at the present rate of change it will take almost 4 more decades (until 2021) to reach equality (i.e.: 50% of professional jobs held by women)."[30] This situation was recently described as "grotesque."[31]

The silence and invisibility of women also characterizes those bodies with special functions regarding the creation and progressive development of international law. Only one woman has sat as a judge on the International Court of Justice[32] and no woman has ever been a member of the International Law Commission. Critics have frequently pointed out that the distribution of judges on the Court does not reflect the makeup of the international community, a concern that peaked after the decision in the *South West Africa* cases in 1966. Steps have since been taken to improve "the representation of the main forms of civilization and of the principal legal systems of the world"[33] on the Court, but not in the direction of representing women, half of the world's population.

Despite the common acceptance of human rights as an area in which attention can be directed toward women, they are still vastly underrepresented on UN human rights bodies. The one committee that has all women members, the Committee on the Elimination of Discrimination against Women (CEDAW Committee), the monitoring body for the Convention on the Elimination of All Forms of Discrimination against Women (Women's Convention), has been criticized for its "disproportionate" representation of women by the United Nations Economic and Social Council (ECOSOC). When it considered the CEDAW Committee's sixth report, ECOSOC called upon the state parties to nominate both female and male experts for election to the committee. Thus, as regards the one committee dedicated to women's interests, where women *are* well represented, efforts have been made to decrease female participation, while the much more common dominance of men in other United Nations bodies goes unremarked. The CEDAW Committee in fact rejected ECOSOC's recommendation on various grounds, including the fear that it might open the gates to a flood of men, diluting the women's majority and undermining the committee's effectiveness. The representatives believed that the state parties and ECOSOC should direct their attention to equality of representation elsewhere before seeking to interfere with the membership of this committee.

Why is it significant that all the major institutions of the international legal order are peopled by men? Long-term domination of all bodies wielding political power nationally and internationally means that issues traditionally of concern to men become seen as general human concerns, while "women's concerns" are relegated to a special, limited category. Because men generally are not the victims of sex discrimination, domestic violence, and sexual degradation and violence, for example, these matters can be consigned to a separate sphere and tend to be ignored. The orthodox face of international law and politics would change dramatically if their institutions were truly human in composition: their horizons would widen to include issues previously regarded as domestic—in the two senses of the word. Balanced representation in international organizations of nations of differing economic structures and power has been a prominent theme in the United Nations since the era of decolonization in the 1960s. The importance of accommodating interests of developed, developing and socialist nations and of various regional and ideological groups is recognized in all aspects of the UN structure and work. This sensitivity

should be extended much further to include the gender of chosen representatives.

The Normative Structure of International Law

Since the primary subjects of international law are states, it is sometimes
assumed that the impact of international law falls on the state and not
directly on individuals. In fact, the application of international law does
affect individuals, which has been recognized by the International Court
in several cases. International jurisprudence assumes that international law
norms directed at individuals within states are universally applicable and
neutral. It is not recognized, however, that such principles may impinge
differently on men and women; consequently, women's experiences of the
operation of these laws tend to be silenced or discounted.

The normative structure of international law has allowed issues of
particular concern to women to be either ignored or undermined. For
example, modern international law rests on and reproduces various dichotomies between the public and private spheres, and the "public"
sphere is regarded as the province of international law. One such distinction is between public international law, the law governing the relations
between nation-states, and private international law, the rules about conflicts between national legal systems. Another is the distinction between
matters of international "public" concern and matters "private" to states
that are considered within their domestic jurisdiction, in which the international community has no recognized legal interest. Yet another is the
line drawn between law and other forms of "private" knowledge such as
morality.

At a deeper level one finds a public/private dichotomy based on
gender. One explanation feminist scholars offer for the dominance of men
and the male voice in all areas of power and authority in the western liberal
tradition is that a dichotomy is drawn between the public sphere and the
private or domestic one. The public realm of the work place, the law,
economics, politics and intellectual and cultural life, where power and
authority are exercised, is regarded as the natural province of men; while
the private world of the home, the hearth and children is seen as the
appropriate domain of women. The public/private distinction has a normative, as well as a descriptive, dimension. Traditionally, the two spheres
are accorded asymmetrical value: greater significance is attached to the
public, male world than to the private, female one. The distinction drawn
between the public and the private thus vindicates and makes natural the
division of labor and allocation of rewards between the sexes. Its reproduction and acceptance in all areas of knowledge have conferred primacy on
the male world and supported the dominance of men.

Feminist concern with the public/private distinction derives from its
centrality to liberal theory. Explanations for the universal attribution of
lesser value to women and their activities have sometimes proposed a

variation of the public/private dichotomy: women are identified with nature, which is regarded as lower in status than culture—the province of men. As Carole Pateman has pointed out, however, this universal explanation for the male domination of women does not recognize that the concept of "nature" may vary widely among different societies. Such an analysis can be reduced easily to a simple biological explanation and does not explain particular social, historical or cultural situations. Women are not always opposed to men in the same ways: what is considered "public" in one society may well be seen as "private" in another. But a universal pattern of identifying women's activities as private, and thus of lesser value, can be detected.

How is the western liberal version of the public/private distinction maintained? Its naturalness rests on deeply held beliefs about gender. Traditional social psychology taught that the bench marks of "normal" behavior for men, on the one hand, and women, on the other, were entirely different. For men, normal and natural behavior was essentially active: it involved tenacity, aggression, curiosity, ambition, responsibility and competition—all attributes suited to participation in the public world. "Normal" behavior for women, by contrast, was reactive and passive: affectionate, emotional, obedient and responsive to approval.

Although the scientific basis of the public/private distinction has been thoroughly attacked and exposed as a culturally constructed ideology, it continues to have a strong grip on legal thinking. The language of the public/private distinction is built into the language of the law itself: law lays claim to rationality, culture, power, objectivity—all terms associated with the public or male realm. It is defined in opposition to the attributes associated with the domestic, private, female sphere: feeling, emotion, passivity, subjectivity.[34] Moreover, the law has always operated primarily within the public domain; it is considered appropriate to regulate the work place, the economy and the distribution of political power, while direct state intervention in the family and the home has long been regarded as inappropriate. Violence within the home, for example, has generally been given different legal significance from violence outside it; the injuries recognized as legally compensable are those which occur outside the home. Damages in civil actions are typically assessed in terms of ability to participate in the public sphere. Women have difficulty convincing law enforcement officials that violent acts within the home are criminal.

In one sense, the public/private distinction is the fundamental basis of the modern state's function of separating and concentrating juridical forms of power that emanate from the state. The distinction implies that the private world is uncontrolled. In fact, the regulation of taxation, social security, education, health and welfare has immediate effects on the private sphere. The myth that state power is not exercised in the "private" realm allocated to women masks its control.

What force does the feminist critique of the public/private dichotomy in the foundation of domestic legal systems have for the international legal order? Traditionally, of course, international law was regarded as operating only in the most public of public spheres: the relations between nation-states. We argue, however, that the definition of certain principles of international law rests on and reproduces the public/private distinction. It thus privileges the male world view and supports male dominance in the international legal order.

The grip that the public/private distinction has on international law, and the consequent banishment of women's voices and concerns from the discipline, can be seen in the international prohibition on torture. The right to freedom from torture and other forms of cruel, inhuman or degrading treatment is generally accepted as a paradigmatic civil and political right. It is included in all international catalogs of civil and political rights and is the focus of specialized United Nations and regional treaties.[35] The right to be free from torture is also regarded as a norm of customary international law—indeed, like the prohibition on slavery, as a norm of *jus cogens.*

The basis for the right is traced to "the inherent dignity of the human person."[36] Behavior constituting torture is defined in the Convention against Torture as

> any act by which severe pain or suffering, whether physical or mental, is intentionally inflicted on a person for such purposes as obtaining from him or a third person information or a confession, punishing him for an act he or a third person has committed or is suspected of having committed, or intimidating or coercing him or a third person, or for any reason based on discrimination of any kind, when such pain or suffering is inflicted by or at the instigation of or with the consent or acquiescence of a public official or other person acting in an official capacity.[37]

This definition has been considered broad because it covers mental suffering and behavior "at the instigation of" a public official. However, despite the use of the term "human person" in the Preamble, the use of the masculine pronoun alone in the definition of the proscribed behavior immediately gives the definition a male, rather than a truly human, context. More importantly, the description of the prohibited conduct relies on a distinction between public and private actions that obscures injuries to their dignity typically sustained by women. The traditional canon of human rights law does not deal in categories that fit the experiences of women. It is cast in terms of discrete violations of rights and offers little redress in cases where there is a pervasive, structural denial of rights.

The international definition of torture requires not only the intention to inflict suffering, but also the secondary intention that the infliction of suffering will fulfill a purpose. Recent evidence suggests that women and children, in particular, are victims of widespread and apparently random terror campaigns by both governmental and guerrilla groups in times of civil unrest or armed conflict. Such suffering is not clearly included in the international definition of torture.

A crucial aspect of torture and cruel, inhuman or degrading conduct, as defined, is that they take place in the public realm: a public official or a person acting officially must be implicated in the pain and suffering. The rationale for this limitation is that "private acts (of brutality) would usually be ordinary criminal offenses which national law enforcement is expected to repress. *International* concern with torture arises only when the State itself abandons its function of protecting its citizenry by sanctioning criminal action by law enforcement personnel."[38]

Many women suffer from torture in this limited sense. The international jurisprudence on the notion of torture arguably extends to sexual violence and psychological coercion if the perpetrator has official standing. However, severe pain and suffering that is inflicted outside the most public context of the state—for example, within the home or by private persons, which is the most pervasive and significant violence sustained by women— does not qualify as torture despite its impact on the inherent dignity of the human person. Indeed, some forms of violence are attributed to cultural tradition. The message of violence against women, argues Charlotte Bunch, is domination:

> [S]tay in your place or be afraid. Contrary to the argument that such violence is only personal or cultural, it is profoundly political. It results from the structural relationships of power, domination, and privilege between men and women in society. Violence against women is central to maintaining those political relations at home, at work, and in all public spheres.[39]

States are held responsible for torture only when their designated agents have direct responsibility for such acts and that responsibility is imputed to the state. States are not considered responsible if they have maintained a legal and social system in which violations of physical and mental integrity are endemic. In its draft articles on state responsibility, the International Law Commission did not widen the concept of imputability to incorporate such acts. A feminist perspective on human rights would require a rethinking of the notions of imputability and state responsibility and in this sense would challenge the most basic assumptions of international law. If violence against women were considered by the international legal system to be as shocking as violence against people for their political ideas, women would have considerable support in their struggle.

The assumption that underlies all law, including international human rights law, is that the public/private distinction is real: human society, human lives can be separated into two distinct spheres. This division, however, is an ideological construct rationalizing the exclusion of women from the sources of power. It also makes it possible to maintain repressive systems of control over women without interference from human rights guarantees, which operate in the public sphere. By extending our vision beyond the public/private ideologies that rationalize limiting our analysis of power, human rights language as it currently exists can be used to describe serious forms of repression that go far beyond the juridically narrow vision of international law. For example, coercive population control techniques, such as forced sterilization, may amount to punishment or coercion by the state to achieve national goals.

Another example of the failure of the normative structure of international law to accommodate the realities of women's lives can be seen in its response to trafficking in women. Trafficking in women through prostitution, pornography and mail-order-bride networks is a pervasive and serious problem in both the developed and the developing worlds. These practices do not simply fall under national jurisdiction, as the ramifications of the trafficking and exploitative relationships cross international boundaries. They involve the subordination and exploitation of women, not on the simple basis of inequality or differences among individuals, but as a result of deeply engrained constructs of power and dominance based on gender. Catharine MacKinnon's observation that women's "material desperation" is connected to violence against women[40] is even more powerful in the international context. To a large extent, the increase in trafficking in women in the Third World stems from growing economic disparities on the national and international levels.[41] Once caught up in the trafficking networks, penniless women in foreign countries are at the mercy of those who arrange and profit from the trade.

Existing norms of international law could be invoked to prohibit at least some of the international exploitation of women and children. The international law on this issue, however, is incomplete and limited in scope. Just as the prohibition of the slave trade, and subsequently of slavery itself, did not occur until economic considerations supported its abolition,[42] so a real commitment to the prevention of sexual trafficking in women is unlikely to be made unless it does not adversely affect other economic interests. As Georges Scelle has written:

> The struggle against slavery, the protection of the bodily freedom of individuals only begin in international law when it is clearly demonstrated that slave labour has *economic* drawbacks and that the progress of modern technology allows it to be *replaced*. Whenever human manpower has not been replaced, slave labour and forced labour still exist, despite all efforts made to proscribe it. This proves that a *moral conviction,* even if of a general character, does not override the necessities of economic life in the formation of legal rules.[43]

No technological advances have succeeded in replacing the many services of women, and the economic benefits of pornography and trafficking are immense. The role and stake of the media "in sensationalizing, exploiting and commercializing women's bodies" also cannot be ignored as contributing factors.[44]

Some branches of international law have recognized and addressed issues relating to women. Various International Labour Organisation Conventions focus on women. A growing literature on these conventions examines the assumptions they make about the role of women, the topics they cover, and their approach to the position of women.

The Women's Convention is the most prominent international normative instrument recognizing the special concerns of women. But the terms of the Convention and the way it has been accepted by states prompt us to ask whether it offers a real or chimerical possibility of change.

The Women's Convention has been ratified or acceded to by almost two-thirds of the members of the United Nations. Article 1 defines "discrimination against women" as

> any distinction, exclusion or restriction made on the basis of sex which has the effect or purpose of impairing or nullifying the recognition, enjoyment or exercise by women, irrespective of their marital status, on a basis of equality of men and women, of human rights and fundamental freedoms in the political, economic, social, cultural, civil or any other field.

Although the Convention goes further than simply requiring equality of opportunity and covers the more contentious concept of equality of result, which justifies affirmative action programs and protection against indirect discrimination, the underlying assumption of its definition of discrimination is that women and men are the same. Most international commentators treat this model of equality as uncontroversial. But the notions of both equality of opportunity and equality of result accept the general applicability of a male standard (except in special circumstances such as pregnancy) and promise a very limited form of equality: equality is defined as being like a man. "[M]an," writes Catharine MacKinnon, "has become the measure of all things."[45] On this analysis, equality can be achieved in a relatively straightforward way by legally requiring the removal of identifiable barriers to the rise of women to the same status as men: equality is achievable within the social and legal structures as they are now. This assumption ignores the many real differences and inequities between the sexes and the significant barriers to their removal.

The phenomenon of male dominance over women is above all one of power. Sexism is not a legal aberration but a pervasive, structural problem. MacKinnon says, "[Gender] is [a question] of hierarchy. The top and the bottom of the hierarchy are different all right, but that is hardly all."[46] On this basis, the most productive analysis of inequality is in terms of domination and subordination. Thus, equality is not freedom to be treated without regard to sex but freedom from systematic subordination because of sex.

Certainly, the separate focus on women in the Women's Convention is beneficial in some respects. Attention is drawn to issues of distinct concern to women (for example, trafficking in women and prostitution) and to the fact that not all women have the same problems (for example, rural women have special needs). The reporting provisions require that state parties focus on the steps they have taken to implement the goals of the Convention so that discrimination against women does not become submerged in general human rights issues. The Convention also provides an important mix of civil, political, economic and social rights.

The Women's Convention, however, establishes much weaker implementation procedures than those of other human rights instruments of apparently universal applicability such as the International Convention on the Elimination of All Forms of Racial Discrimination and the Covenant on Civil and Political Rights. More generally, the specialized nature of the Women's Convention has been used by "mainstream" human rights bodies to justify ignoring or minimizing women's perspectives. They can assure themselves that, since these problems are scrutinized elsewhere, their organizations are relieved from the task. Yet the impact on women and men of many provisions of, for example, the Covenant on Civil and Political Rights may not be the same.

States have made a significant number of reservations and declarations of understanding when becoming parties to the Women's Convention. Article 28(1) permits ratification subject to reservations, provided the reservations are not "incompatible with the object and purpose of the present Convention" (Article 28(2)). No criteria are given for the determination of incompatibility. Over 40 of the 105 parties to the Convention have made a total of almost a hundred reservations to its terms. Many of these reservations were motivated by the conflict between some interpretations of Islam and the notion of sexual equality. They take the form of limiting the reserving state's obligations under the Convention to the taking of steps compatible with Islamic law and customs. Both general reservations and reservations to specific provisions have been made that are regarded by other state parties as incompatible with the overall object and purpose of the Convention. Other reservations concern national religious or customary laws that restrict women's inheritance and property rights; nationality laws that do not accord women the same rights as men to acquire, change or retain their nationality upon marriage; and laws limiting women's economic opportunities, freedom of movement and choice of residence.

The pattern of reservations to the Women's Convention underlines the inadequacy of the present normative structure of international law. The international community is prepared to formally acknowledge the considerable problems of inequality faced by women, but only, it seems, if individual states are not required as a result to alter patriarchal practices that subordinate women. Members of the CEDAW Committee, which monitors the implementation of the Convention but does not have jurisdiction to determine the compatibility of reservations with it, have questioned representatives of state parties about their reservations. The biennial meetings of the state parties, however, have not taken action to obtain an authoritative determination on the compatibility of the reservations with the object and purpose of the Convention. The numerous reservations made to the Women's Convention stand in stark contrast to the four substantive reservations made to the Convention on the Elimination of All Forms of Racial Discrimination and suggest that discrimination against women is somehow regarded as more "natural" and acceptable than racial discrimination.

In sum, the Women's Convention, the international legal flagship with respect to women, is an ambiguous offering. It recognizes discrimination against women as a legal issue but is premised on the notion of progress through good will, education and changing attitudes and does not promise any form of structural, social or economic change for women. The limited scope of the Convention is further restricted by the international community's general tolerance of reservations to it by the state parties.

IV. Toward a Feminist Analysis of International Law

How can feminist accounts of law be applied in international law? Feminist legal theory can promote a variety of activities. The term signifies an interest (gender as an issue of primary importance); a focus of attention (women as individuals and as members of groups); a political agenda (real social, political, economic and cultural equality regardless of gender); a critical stance (an analysis of "masculinism" and male hierarchical power or "patriarchy"); a means of reinterpreting and reformulating substantive law so that it more adequately reflects the experiences of all people; and an alternative method of practicing, talking about and learning the law.[47] Feminist method must be concerned with examining the fundamentals of the legal persuasion: the language it uses; the organization of legal materials in predetermined, watertight categories; the acceptance of abstract concepts as somehow valid or "pure"; the reliance in practice on confrontational, adversarial techniques; and the commitment to male, hierarchical structures in all legal and political organizations.

Christine Littleton has said, "Feminist method starts with the very radical act of taking women seriously, believing that what we say about ourselves and our experience is important and valid, even when (or perhaps especially when) it has little or no relationship to what has been or is being said *about* us."[48] No single approach can deal with the complexity of international legal organizations, processes and rules, or with the diversity of women's experiences within and outside those structures. In this section we look at two interconnected themes developed in feminist accounts of the law that suggest new ways of analyzing international law.

Critique of Rights

The feminist critique of rights questions whether the acquisition of legal rights advances women's equality. Feminist scholars have argued that, although the search for formal legal equality through the formulation of rights may have been politically appropriate in the early stages of the feminist movement, continuing to focus on the acquisition of rights may not be beneficial to women. Quite apart from problems such as the form in which rights are drafted, their interpretation by tribunals, and women's access to their enforcement, the rhetoric of rights, according to some feminist legal scholars, is exhausted.

Rights discourse is taxed with reducing intricate power relations in a simplistic way. The formal acquisition of a right, such as the right to equal treatment, is often assumed to have solved an imbalance of power. In practice, however, the promise of rights is thwarted by the inequalities of power: the economic and social dependence of women on men may discourage the invocation of legal rights that are premised on an adversarial relationship between the rights holder and the infringer. More complex still are rights designed to apply to women only such as the rights to reproductive freedom and to choose abortion.

In addition, although they respond to general societal imbalances, formulations of rights are generally cast in individual terms. The invocation of rights to sexual equality may therefore solve an occasional case of inequality for individual women but will leave the position of women generally unchanged. Moreover, international law accords priority to civil and political rights, rights that may have very little to offer women generally. The major forms of oppression of women operate within the economic, social and cultural realms. Economic, social and cultural rights are traditionally regarded as a lesser form of international right and as much more difficult to implement.

A second major criticism of the assumption that the granting of rights inevitably spells progress for women is that it ignores competing rights: the right of women and children not to be subjected to violence in the home may be balanced against the property rights of men in the home or their right to family life. Furthermore, certain rights may be appropriated by more powerful groups: Carol Smart relates that provisions in the European Convention on Human Rights on family life were used by fathers to assert their authority over ex nuptial children. One solution may be to design rights to apply only to particular groups. However, apart from the serious political difficulties this tactic would raise, the formulation of rights that apply only to women, as we have seen in the international sphere, may result in marginalizing these rights.

A third feminist concern about the "rights" approach to achieve equality is that some rights can operate to the detriment of women. The right to freedom of religion, for example, can have differing impacts on women and men. Freedom to exercise all aspects of religious belief does not always benefit women because many accepted religious practices entail reduced social positions and status for women. Yet attempts to set priorities and to discuss the issue have been met with hostility and blocking techniques. Thus, at its 1987 meeting the CEDAW Committee adopted a decision requesting that the United Nations and the specialized agencies promote or undertake studies on the status of women under Islamic laws and customs and in particular on the status and equality of women in the family on issues such as marriage, divorce, custody and property rights and their participation in public life of the society, taking into consideration the principle of El Ijtihad in Islam.[49]

The representatives of Islamic nations criticized this decision in ECOSOC and in the Third Committee of the General Assembly as a threat to their freedom of religion. The CEDAW Committee's recommendation was ultimately rejected. The General Assembly passed a resolution in which it decided that "no action shall be taken on decision 4 adopted by the Committee and request[ed that] the Committee. . . review that decision, taking ccount the views expressed by delegations at the first regular session of the Economic and Social Council of 1987 and in the Third Committee of the General Assembly."[49a] CEDAW later justified its action by stating that the study was necessary for it to carry out its duties under the Women's Convention and that no disrespect was intended to Islam.

Another example of internationally recognized rights that might affect women and men differently are those relating to the protection of the family. The major human rights instruments all have provisions applicable to the family. Thus, the Universal Declaration proclaims that the family is the "natural and fundamental group unit of society and is entitled to protection by society and the State." These provisions ignore that to many women the family is a unit for abuse and violence; hence, protection of the family also preserves the power structure within the family, which can lead to subjugation and dominance by men over women and children.

The development of rights may be particularly problematic for women in the Third World, where women's rights to equality with men and traditional values may clash. An example of the ambivalence of Third World states toward women's concerns is the Banjul Charter, the human rights instrument of the Organization of African Unity.

The Charter, unlike "western" instruments preoccupied with the rights of individuals, emphasizes the need to recognize communities and peoples as entities entitled to rights, and it provides that people within the group owe duties and obligations to the group. "Peoples'" rights in the Banjul Charter include the right to self-determination, the right to exploit natural resources and wealth, the right to development, the right to international peace and security, and the right to a generally satisfactory environment.

The creation of communal or "peoples'" rights, however, does not take into account the often severe limitations on the rights of women within these groups, communities or "peoples." The Preamble to the Charter makes specific reference to the elimination of "all forms of discrimination, particularly those based on race, ethnic group, colour, sex, language, religion or political opinion." Article 2 enshrines the enjoyment of all rights contained within the Charter without discrimination of any kind. But after Article 2, the Charter refers exclusively to "his" rights, the "rights of man." Articles 3–17 set out basic political, civil, economic and social rights similar to those contained in other instruments, in particular the International Covenants, the Universal Declaration of Human Rights (which is cited in the Preamble) and European instruments. Article 15 is significant in that it guarantees that the right to work includes the right to "receive equal pay for equal work." This right might be useful to women who are employed in jobs that men also do. The difficulty is that most African women, like women elsewhere, generally do not perform the same jobs as men.

Articles 17 and 18 and the list of duties contained in Articles 27–29 present obstacles to African women's enjoyment of rights set out elsewhere in the Charter. Article 17(3) states that "[t]he promotion and protection of morals and traditional values recognized by the community shall be the duty of the State." Article 18 entrusts the family with custody of those morals and values, describing it as "the natural unit and basis of society." The same article requires that discrimination against women be eliminated, but the conjunction of the notion of equality with the protection of the family and "traditional" values poses serious problems. It has been noted in relation to Zimbabwe and Mozambique that

> [t]he official political rhetoric relating to women in these southern African societies may be rooted in a model derived from Engels, via the Soviet Union, but the actual situation they face today bears little resemblance to that of the USSR. In Zimbabwe particularly, policy-makers are caught between several ideological and material contradictions, which are especially pertinent to women-oriented policies. The dominant ideology has been shaped by two belief-systems, opposed in their conceptions of women. Marxism vies with a model deriving from pre-colonial society, in which women's capacity to reproduce the lineage, socially, economically and biologically, was crucial and in which lineage males controlled women's labour power.[50]

This contradiction between the emancipation of women and adherence to traditional values lies at the heart of and complicates discussion about human rights in relation to many Third World women. The rhetoric of human rights, on both the national and the international levels, regards women as equal citizens, as "individuals" subject to the same level of treatment and the same protection as men. But the discourse of "traditional values" may prevent women from enjoying any human rights, however they may be described.

Despite all these problems, the assertion of rights can exude great symbolic force for oppressed groups within a society and it constitutes an organizing principle in the struggle against inequality. Patricia Williams has pointed out that for blacks in the United States, "the prospect of attaining full rights under the law has always been a fiercely motivational, almost religious, source of hope."[51] She writes:

> "Rights" feels so new in the mouths of most black people. It is still so

> deliciously empowering to say. It is a sign for and a gift of selfhood that is
> very hard to contemplate restructuring . . . at this point in history. It is
> the magic wand of visibility and invisibility, of inclusion and exclusion, of
> power and no power. . . .[52]

The discourse of rights may have greater significance at the international level than in many national systems. It provides an accepted means to challenge the traditional legal order and to develop alternative principles. While the acquisition of rights must not be identified with automatic and immediate advances for women, and the limitations of the rights model must be recognized, the notion of women's rights remains a source of potential power for women in international law. The challenge is to rethink that notion so that rights correspond to women's experiences and needs.

The Public/Private Distinction

The gender implications of the public/private distinction were outlined above. Here we show how the dichotomy between public and private worlds has undermined the operation of international law, giving two examples.

The Right to Development

The right to development was formulated in legal terms only recently and its status in international law is still controversial. Its proponents present it as a collective or solidarity right that responds to the phenomenon of global interdependence, while its critics argue that it is an aspiration rather than a right. The 1986 United Nations Declaration on the Right to Development describes the content of the right as the entitlement "to participate in, contribute to, and enjoy economic, social, cultural and political development, in which all human rights and fundamental freedoms can be fully realized."[53] Primary responsibility for the creation of conditions favorable to the right is placed on states:

> States have the right and the duty to formulate appropriate national
> development policies that aim at the constant improvement of the well-
> being of the entire population and of all individuals, on the basis of their
> active, free and meaningful participation in development and in the fair
> distribution of the benefits resulting therefrom.[54]

The right is apparently designed to apply to all individuals within a state and is assumed to benefit women and men equally: the preamble to the declaration twice refers to the Charter exhortation to promote and encourage respect for human rights for all without distinction of any kind such as of race or sex. Moreover, Article 8 of the declaration obliges states to ensure equality of opportunity for all regarding access to basic resources and fair distribution of income. It provides that "effective measures should be undertaken to ensure that women have an active role in the development process."

Other provisions of the declaration, however, indicate that discrimination against women is not seen as a major obstacle to development or to the fair distribution of its benefits. For example, one aspect of the right to development is the obligation of states to take "resolute steps" to eliminate "massive and flagrant violations of the human rights of peoples and human beings." The examples given of such violations include apartheid and racial discrimination but not sex discrimination.

Three theories about the causes of underdevelopment dominate its analysis: shortages of capital, technology, skilled labor and entrepreneurship; exploitation of the wealth of developing nations by richer nations; and economic dependence of developing nations on developed nations. The subordination of women to men does not enter this traditional calculus. Moreover, "development" as economic growth above all takes no notice of the lack of benefits or disadvantageous effects this growth may have on half of the society it purports to benefit.

One aspect of the international right to development is the provision of development assistance and aid. The UN General Assembly has called for international and national efforts to be aimed at eliminating "economic deprivation, hunger and disease in all parts of the world without discrimination" and for international cooperation to be aimed, inter alia, at maintaining "stable and sustained economic growth," increasing concessional assistance to developing countries, building world food security and resolving the debt burden.[55]

Women and children are more often the victims of poverty and malnutrition than men.[56] Women should therefore have much to gain from an international right to development. Yet the position of many women in developing countries has deteriorated over the last two decades: their access to economic resources has been reduced, their health and educational status has declined, and their work burdens have increased. The generality and apparent universal applicability of the right to development, as formulated in the UN declaration, is undermined by the fundamentally androcentric nature of the international economic system and its reinforcement of the public/private distinction. Of course, the problematic nature of current development practice for Third World women cannot be attributed simply to the international legal formulation of the right to development. But the rhetoric of international law both reflects and reinforces a system that contributes to the subordination of women.

Over the last twenty years, considerable research has been done on women and Third World development. This research has documented the crucial role of women in the economies of developing nations, particularly in agriculture. It has also pointed to the lack of impact, or the adverse impact, of "development" on many Third World women's lives. The international legal order, like most development policies, has not taken this research into account in formulating any aspect of the right to development.

The distinction between the public and private spheres operates to make the work and needs of women invisible. Economic visibility depends on working in the public sphere and unpaid work in the home or community is categorized as "unproductive, unoccupied, and economically inactive."[57] Marilyn Waring has recently argued that this division, which is institutionalized in developed nations, has been exported to the developing world, in part through the United Nations System of National Accounts (UNSNA).

The UNSNA, developed largely by Sir Richard Stone in the 1950s, enables experts to monitor the financial position of states and trends in their national development and to compare one nation's economy with that of another. It will thus influence the categorization of nations as developed or developing and the style and magnitude of the required international aid. The UNSNA measures the value of all goods and services that actually enter the market and of other nonmarket production such as government services provided free of charge. Some activities, however, are designated as outside the "production boundary" and are not measured. Economic reality is constructed by the UNSNA's "production boundaries" in such a way that reproduction, child care, domestic work and subsistence production are excluded from the measurement of economic productivity and growth. This view of women's work as nonwork was nicely summed up in 1985 in a report by the Secretary-General to the General Assembly, "Overall socio-economic perspective of the world economy to the year 2000." It said: "Women's productive and reproductive roles tend to be compatible in rural areas of low-income countries, since family agriculture and cottage industries keep women close to the home, permit flexibility in working conditions *and require low investment of the mother's time.*"[58]

The assignment of the work of women and men to different spheres, and the consequent categorization of women as "nonproducers," are detrimental to women in developing countries in many ways and make their rights to development considerably less attainable than men's. For example, the operation of the public/private distinction in international economic measurement excludes women from many aid programs because they are not considered to be workers or are regarded as less productive than men. If aid is provided to women, it is often to marginalize them: foreign aid may be available to women only in their role as mothers, although at least since 1967 it has been recognized that women are responsible for as much as 80 percent of the food production in developing countries. The failure to acknowledge women's significant role in agriculture and the lack of concern about the impact of development on women mean that the potential of any right to development is jeopardized from the start.

Although the increased industrialization of the Third World has brought greater employment opportunities for women, this seeming improvement has not increased their economic independence or social standing and has had little impact on women's equality. Women are found in the lowest-paid and lowest-status jobs, without career paths; their working conditions are often discriminatory and insecure. Moreover, there is little difference in the position of women who live in developing nations with a socialist political order. The dominant model of development assumes that any paid employment is better than none and fails to take into account the potential for increasing the inequality of women and lowering their economic position.

As we have seen, the international statement of the right to development draws no distinction between the economic position of men and of women. In using the neutral language of development and economics, it does not challenge the pervasive and detrimental assumption that women's work is of a different—and lesser—order than men's. It therefore cannot enhance the development of the group within developing nations that is most in need. More recent UN deliberations on development have paid greater attention to the situation of women. Their concerns, however, are presented as quite distinct, solvable by the application of special protective measures, rather than as crucial to development.

The Right to Self-determination

The public/private dichotomy operates to reduce the effectiveness of the right to self-determination at international law. The notion of self-determination as meaning the right of "all peoples" to "freely determine their political status and freely pursue their economic, social and cultural development"[59] is flatly contradicted by the continued domination and marginalization of one sector of the population of a nation-state by another. The treatment of women within groups claiming a right to self-determination should be relevant to those claims. But the international community's response to the claims to self-determination of the Afghan and Sahrawi people, for example, indicates little concern for the position of women within those groups.

The violation of the territorial integrity and political independence of Afghanistan by the Soviet Union when it invaded that country in 1979, and other strategic, economic, and geopolitical concerns, persuaded the United States of the legality and morality of its support for the Afghan insurgents. In deciding to support the rebels, the United States did not regard the policies of the *mujahidin* with respect to women as relevant. The mujahidin are committed to an oppressive, rural, unambiguously patriarchal form of society quite different from that espoused by the socialist Soviet-backed regime. Indeed, Cynthia Enloe notes that "[o]ne of the policies the Soviet-backed government in Kabul pursued that so alienated male clan leaders was expanding economic and educational opportunities for Afghanistan's women."[60] A consequence of the continued support for the insurgents was the creation of a vast refugee flow into Pakistan. Of these refugees, 30 percent were women and 40 percent were children under thirteen. The mullahs imposed a strict fundamentalist regime in the refugee camps, which confined women to the premises, isolated them, and even deprived them of their traditional rural tasks. There is no indication

that any different policy would be followed if the mujahidin were successful and able to form a government in Afghanistan. Indeed, this marginalization and isolation of Afghan women is being projected into the future, as
the educational services provided by the UN High Commissioner for
Refugees are overwhelmingly for boys. The vital impact of education on
women and its effect in undermining male domination have been well
documented.

Morocco's claims to Western Sahara and the Polisario resistance to
those claims have led to the establishment of Sahrawi refugee camps in
Algeria that are mainly occupied by women and children. In these camps,
however, women have been able to assert themselves: they have built
hospitals and schools, achieved high rates of literacy, and supported "the
right of the woman and the mother," as well as the "fight for independence."[61] The international community, through the International Court
of Justice and the General Assembly, has reiterated the right of the people
of Western Sahara to self-determination. Despite this legal support, the
Sahrawis' only backing comes from Algeria, while Morocco is backed,
inter alia, by France and the United States. The determination of these
women to keep alive a "democracy, based on proportional representation,
with centralised and equal distribution, full employment, [and] social and
political parity between the sexes" in the adverse conditions of refugee
camps has received little international support.[62]

The international community recognizes only the right of "peoples"
to self-determination, which in practice is most frequently linked to the
notion of the independent state. Women have never been viewed as a
"people" for the purposes of the right to self-determination. In most
instances, the pursuit of self-determination as a political response to colonial rule has not resulted in terminating the oppression and domination of
one section of society by another.

States often show complete indifference to the position of women
when determining their response to claims of self-determination; the international invisibility of women persists. Thus, after the Soviet Union vetoed
a Security Council resolution on the invasion of Afghanistan, the General
Assembly reaffirmed "the inalienable right of all peoples . . . to choose
their own form of government free from outside interference" and stated
that the Afghan people should be able to "choose their economic, political
and social systems free from outside intervention, subversion, coercion or
constraint of any kind whatsoever."[63] The General Assembly's concern
was with "outside" intervention alone. Women arguably suffer more from
"internal" intervention: women are not free to choose their role in society
without the constraints of masculine domination inside the state and are
constantly subject to male coercion. The high-sounding ideals of noninter-
ference do not apply to them, for their self-determination is subsumed by
that of the group. The denial to women of the freedom to determine their
own economic, social and cultural development should be taken into
consideration by states in assessing the legitimacy of requests for assistance
in achieving self-determination and of claims regarding the use of force.

V. Conclusion

The feminist project, it has been said, has the "twin aims of challenging the existing norms and of devising a new agenda for theory."[64] This paper emphasizes the need for further study of traditional areas of international law from a perspective that regards gender as important. In a review of two Canadian legal textbooks on remedies, Christine Boyle points out that they simply do not address the concerns and interests of women. She criticizes this great silence and concludes: "Men and Law" is tolerable as an area of intellectual activity, but not if it is masquerading as "People and Law." International legal structures and principles masquerade as "human"—universally applicable sets of standards. They are more accurately described as international men's law.

Modern international law is not only androcentric, but also Euro-centered in its origins, and has assimilated many assumptions about law and the place of law in society from western legal thinking. These include essentially patriarchal legal institutions, the assumption that law is objective, gender neutral and universally applicable, and the societal division into public and private spheres, which relegates many matters of concern to women to the private area regarded as inappropriate for legal regulation. Research is needed to question the assumptions of neutrality and universal applicability of norms of international law and to expose the invisibility of women and their experiences in discussions about the law. A feminist perspective, with its concern for gender as a category of analysis and its commitment to genuine equality between the sexes, could illuminate many areas of international law; for example, state responsibility, refugee law, use of force and the humanitarian law of war, human rights, population control and international environmental law. Feminist research holds the promise of a fundamental restructuring of traditional international law discourse and methodology to accommodate alternative world views. As Elizabeth Gross points out, this restructuring will not amount to the replacement of one set of "truths" with another: "[feminist theory] aims to render patriarchal systems, methods and presumptions unable to function, unable to retain their dominance and power. It aims to make clear how such a dominance has been possible; and to make it no longer viable."[65]

The centrality of the state in international law means that many of the structures of international law reflect its patriarchal forms. Paradoxically, however, international law may be more open to feminist analysis than other areas of law. The distinction between law and politics, so central to the preservation of the neutrality and objectivity of law in the domestic sphere, does not have quite the same force in international law. So, too, the western domestic model of legal process as ultimately coercive is not echoed in the international sphere: the process of international law is consensual and peaceful coexistence is its goal. Finally, the sustained Third World critique of international law and insistence on diversity may well have prepared the philosophical ground for feminist critiques.

A feminist transformation of international law would involve more

than simply refining or reforming existing law. It could lead to the creation
of international regimes that focus on structural abuse and the revision of
our notions of state responsibility. It could also lead to a challenge to the
centrality of the state in international law and to the traditional sources of
international law.

The mechanisms for achieving some of these aims already exist. The
Covenant on Economic, Social and Cultural Rights and the Women's
Convention could be used as a basis for promoting structural economic
and social reform to reduce some of the causes of sexual and other abuse of
women. The notion of state responsibility, however, both under these
Conventions and generally, will have to be expanded to incorporate responsibility for systemic abuse based on sexual discrimination (broadly
defined) and imputability to the state will have to be extended to include
acts committed by private individuals. An international mechanism to hear
complaints of individuals or groups, such as a protocol to the Women's
Convention allowing for individual or representative petitions to the
CEDAW Committee, could give women's voices a direct audience in the
international community.

Is a reorientation of international law likely to have any real impact on
women? Feminists have questioned the utility of attempts at legal reform
in domestic law and warn against attributing too much power to law to
alter basic political and economic inequalities based on sex. Could this
reservation be made a fortiori with respect to international law, whose
enforcement and efficacy are in any event much more controversial?
Would an altered, humanized international law have any capacity to
achieve social change in a world where most forms of power continue to
be controlled by men?

Like all legal systems, international law plays an important part in
constructing reality. The areas it does not touch seem naturally to belong
within the domestic jurisdiction of states. International law defines the
boundaries of agreement by the international community on the matters that
states are prepared to yield to supranational regulation and scrutiny. Its
authority is derived from the claim of international acceptance. International
legal concerns have a particular status; those concerns outside the ambit of
international law do not seem susceptible to development and change in the
same way. To redefine the traditional scope of international law so as to
acknowledge the interests of women can open the way to reimagining
possibilities for change and may permit international law's promise of
peaceful coexistence and respect for the dignity of all persons to become a
reality.

Notes

1. *See e.g.*, Olsen, *The Family and the Market*, 96 HARV. L. REV. 1497
(1983); Karst, *Women's Constitution*, 1984 DUKE L.J. 447; Lahey & Salter, *Corpo-
rate Law in Legal Theory and Legal Scholarship: From Classicism to Feminism*, 23

OSGOODE HALL L.J. 543 (1985); Scales, *The Emergence of Feminist Jurisprudence: An Essay*, 95 YALE L.J. 1373 (1986); Minow, *The Supreme Court October 1986 Term—Justice Engendered*, 101 HARV. L. REV. 47 (1987); Grbich, *The Position of Women in Family Dealing: the Australian Case*, 15 INT'L J. SOC. L. 309 (1987); Bender, *A Lawyer's Primer on Feminist Theory and Tort*, 38 J. LEGAL EDUC. 3, 29–30 (1988); Bartlett, *Feminist Legal Methods*, 103 HARV. L. REV. 831 (1990); R. GRAYCAR & J. MORGAN, THE HIDDEN GENDER OF LAW (1990).

    2. *See generally* D. N. MACCORMICK, LEGAL REASONING AND LEGAL THEORY (1978); J. W. HARRIS, LEGAL PHILOSOPHIES (1980).

    3. *E.g.*, Gordon, *New Developments in Legal Theory*, in THE POLITICS OF LAW 281 (D. KAIRYS ED. 1982).

    4. For a discussion of the major differences between feminist jurisprudence and the "liberal" and "critical" schools of jurisprudence, see West, *Jurisprudence and Gender*, 55 U. CHI. L. REV. 1 (1988); *see also* West, *Feminism, Critical Social Theory and Law*, 1989 U. CHI. LEGAL F. 59; Polan, *Towards a Theory of Law and Patriarchy*, in THE POLITICS OF LAW, *supra* note 3, at 294, 295–96.

    5. S. HARDING, THE SCIENCE QUESTION IN FEMINISM 194 (1986); *see also* Bartlett, *supra* note 1, at 880–87.

    6. Hartsock, *Feminist Theory and the Development of Revolutionary Strategy*, in CAPITALIST PATRIARCHY AND THE CASE FOR SOCIALIST FEMINISM 56, 58 (Z. R. Eisenstein ed. 1979); *see also* Rhode, *Gender and Jurisprudence: An Agenda for Research*, 56 U. CINN. L. REV. 521, 522 (1987); Gross, *What is Feminist Theory?*, in FEMINIST CHALLENGES: SOCIAL AND POLITICAL THEORY 190, 196–97 (C. Pateman & E. Gross eds. 1986). Some feminists dispute this description of feminism. Catharine MacKinnon, for example, has argued:

> Inequality on the basis of sex, women share. It is women's collective condition. The first task of a movement for social change is to face one's condition and name it. The failure to face and criticize the reality of women's condition, a failure of idealism and denial, is a failure of feminism in its liberal forms. The failure to move beyond criticism, a failure of determinism and radical paralysis, is a failure of feminism in its left forms. . . . As sexual inequality is gendered as man and woman, gender inequality is sexualized as dominance and subordination. . . . The next step is to recognize that male forms of power over women are affirmatively embodied as individual rights in law.

C. MACKINNON, TOWARD A FEMINIST THEORY OF THE STATE 241–44 (1989).

    Some continental European, particularly French, feminists have pursued a different set of concerns from those of Anglo-American feminists. They have undertaken the task of deconstructing the dominant masculine modes of speech and writing. "We must reinterpret the whole relationship between the subject and discourse, the subject and the world, the subject and the cosmic, the microcosmic and the macrocosmic," writes Luce Irigaray. "And the first thing to say is that, even when aspiring to a universal or neutral state, this subject has always been written in the masculine form. . . ." Irigaray, *Sexual Difference*, in FRENCH FEMINIST THOUGHT: A READER 118, 119 (T. Moi ed. 1987). Although male language and social structures have also concerned Anglo-American feminists, they have generally not approached the issue by focusing on a wholly new type of discourse in which new feminine meanings, associated with the undiscovered potential of the female body, are seen as the potential source of a reconstructed world. *Id.* at 129. A brief introduction to French feminist thought can be found in Dallery, *The Politics of Writing (The) Body: Ecriture Feminine*, in GENDER/BODY/KNOWLEDGE 52 (A. M. Jaggar & S. R. Bordo eds. 1989).

7. *E.g.*, Holmes, *A Feminist Analysis of the Universal Declaration of Human Rights*, in BEYOND DOMINATION: NEW PERSPECTIVES ON WOMEN AND PHILOSOPHY 250 (C. Gould ed. 1983): A. Byrnes, Can the Categories Fit the Crimes? The Possibilities for a Feminist Transformation of International Human Rights Law (paper delivered at Conference on International Human Rights and Feminism, New York, Nov. 18, 1988); Neuwirth, *Towards a Gender-Based Approach to Human Rights Violations*, 9 WHITTIER L. REV. 399 (1987); Bunch, *Women's Rights as Human Rights: Toward a Re-vision of Human Rights*, 12 HUM. RTS. Q. 486 (1990).

8. C. GILLIGAN, *In a Different Voice: Psychological Theory and Women's Development* (1982).

9. *Id.* at 25–51.

10. *Id.* at 164.

11. *Id.* at 164, 174.

12. C. SMART, FEMINISM AND THE POWER OF LAW 75 (1989).

13. C. MACKINNON, FEMINISM UNMODIFIED: DISCOURSES ON LIFE AND LAW 38–39 (1987). *Compare* Gilligan, *Reply [to Critics]*, 11 SIGNS 324 (1986).

14. *See, e.g.*, A. CASSESE, INTERNATIONAL LAW IN A DIVIDED WORLD 105–25 (1986).

15. G. KENNAN, AMERICAN DIPLOMACY, 1900–1950, at 53–54 (1953).

16. S. HARDING, *supra* note 5, at 165.

17. *Id.*

18. *Id.* at 170.

19. *Id.* at 171.

20. *Id.* at 186.

21. Brock-Utne, *Women and Third World Countries—What Do We Have in Common?*, 12 WOMEN'S STUD. INT'L F. 495, 496–97 (1989).

22. K. JAYAWARDENA, FEMINISM AND NATIONALISM IN THE THIRD WORLD *passim* (1986); C. ENLOE, MAKING FEMINIST SENSE OF INTERNATIONAL POLITICS: BANANAS, BEACHES AND BASES 42–64 (1989).

23. "Western secular thought is a crucial factor in fashioning a consciousness and devising structures that would make possible an escape from the domination of Western political power." K. JAYAWARDENA, *supra* note 22, at 6.

24. C. ENLOE, *supra* note 22, at 48.

25. K. JAYAWARDENA, *supra* note 22, at 8.

26. *Id.* at 14.

27. Halliday, *Hidden from International Relations: Women and the International Arena*, 17 MILLENNIUM 419, 424 (1988).

28. Brock-Utne, *supra* note 21, at 500.

29. EQUAL TIME, March 1986, at 8–9.

30. EQUAL TIME, July 1985, at 5.

31. B. URQUHART & E. CHILDERS, A WORLD IN NEED OF LEADERSHIP: TOMORROW'S UNITED NATIONS 29 (1990); *see also id.* at 61.

32. Mme. Suzanne Bastid was a judge *ad hoc* in Application for Revision and Interpretation of the Judgment of 24 February 1982 in the Case concerning the Continental Shelf (Tunisia/Libyan Arab Jamahiriya) (Tunisia v. Libya), 1985 ICJ REP. 192 (Judgment of Dec. 10).

33. Statute of the International Court of Justice, Art. 9.

34. Olsen, *Feminism and Critical Legal Theory: An American Perspective,* 18 INT'L J. SOC. L. 199 (1990); Thornton, *Feminist Jurisprudence: Illusion or Reality?* 3 AUSTL. J. L. & SOC'Y 3, 6–7 (1986).

35. United Nations Convention against Torture and Other Cruel, Inhuman or Degrading Treatment or Punishment, GA Res. 39/46 (Dec. 10, 1984), *draft reprinted in* 23 ILM 1027 (1984), *substantive changes noted in* 24 ILM 535 (1985) [hereinafter Torture Convention].

36. *Id.,* Preamble.

37. *Id.,* Art. I(1).

38. Rodley, *The Evolution of the International Prohibition of Torture,* in AMNESTY INTERNATIONAL, THE UNIVERSAL DECLARATION OF HUMAN RIGHTS 1948–1988: HUMAN RIGHTS, THE UNITED NATIONS AND AMNESTY INTERNATIONAL 55, 63 (1988).

39. Bunch, *supra* note 7, at 490–91.

40. C. MACKINNON, *supra* note 13, at 40–41.

41. *See* EQUAL TIME, March 1989, at 22–23 (report on UNESCO Conference on the Elimination of Trafficking in Women and Children, New York, 1988).

42. For a brief history of the international prohibition of slavery, see A. CASSESE, *supra* note 14, at 52–54.

43. 2 G. SCELLE, PRÉCIS DE DROIT DES GENS 55 (1934), *translated and quoted in id.* at 53.

44. EQUAL TIME, *supra* note 41, at 22.

45. C. MACKINNON, *supra* note 13, at 34.

46. MacKinnon, *Feminism, Marxism, Method and the State: Toward Feminist Jurisprudence,* 8 SIGNS 635 (1983).

47. Wishik, *To Question Everything: The Inquiries of Feminist Jurisprudence,* 1 BERKELEY WOMEN'S L.J. 64 (1985).

48. Littleton, *Feminist Jurisprudence: The Difference Method Makes* (Book Review), 41 STAN. L. REV. 751, 764 (1989).

49. UN Doc. E/1987/SR.11, at 13.

49a. GA Res. 42/60, para. 9 (Nov. 30, 1987).

50. Jacobs & Tracy, *Women in Zimbabwe: Stated Policies and State Action,* in WOMEN, STATE IDEOLOGY: STUDIES FROM AFRICA AND ASIA 28, 29–30 (H. Afshar ed. 1988).

51. Williams, *Alchemical Notes: Reconstructing Ideals from Deconstructed Rights,* 22 HARV. C.R.-C.L. L. REV. 401, 417 (1987).

52. *Id.* at 431. *See also* Schneider, *The Dialectic of Rights and Politics: Perspectives from the Women's Movement,* 61 N.Y.U. L. REV. 589 (1986).

53. GA Res. 41/128, Art. 1(1) (Dec. 4, 1986).

54. *Id.,* Art. 2(3).

55. GA Res. 41/133 (Dec. 4, 1986).

56. *See* M. WARING, COUNTING FOR NOTHING 134 (1988).

57. M. WARING, *supra* note 56, at 13.

58. UN Doc. A/40/519, para. 210, at 99 (1985) (emphasis added).

59. International Covenant on Civil and Political Rights, Art. 1; International Covenant on Economic, Social and Cultural Rights, Art. 1.

60. C. ENLOE, *supra* note 22, at 57.

61. As demonstrated by the objectives of The Women's Union, founded in 1974. Cumming, *Forgotten Struggle for the Western Sahara,* NEW STATESMAN,

May 20, 1988, at 14 ("Women are at the heart of the revolution; their own struggle for rights doesn't have to wait until the war is over, the two are indivisible").

62. *Id.*, at 15.
63. GA Res. ES-6/2 (Jan. 14, 1980).
64. Thornton, *supra* note 34, at 23.
65. Gross, *supra* note 6, at 197.

Selected Bibliography

Feminist Approaches to International Law

Charlesworth, Hilary, and Christine Chinkin. "The Gender of *Jus Cogens*," *Human Rights Quarterly* 15 (1993): 63–76.

Cook, Rebecca J. "Reservations to the Convention on the Elimination of All Forms of Discrimination Against Women," *Virginia Journal of International Law* 30 (1990): 643–716.

———. "Women's International Human Rights: A Bibliography," *New York University Journal of International Law and Policy* 24 (1992): 857–88.

———, ed. *Women's International Human Rights* (1992).

Dallmeyer, Dorinda G., ed. *Reconceiving Reality: Women's Perspectives on International Law and Governance* (ASIL Studies in Transnational Legal Policy, No. 25, 1993).

Elshtain, Jean. "Reflections on War and Political Discourse: Realism, Just War and Feminism in a Nuclear Age," *Political Theory* 13 (1985): 39–57.

Gunning, Isabelle. "Arrogant Perception, World Travelling and Multicultural Feminism: The Case of Female Genital Surgeries," *Columbia Human Rights Law Review* 23 (1992): 189–248.

Morsink, Johannes. "Women's Rights in the Universal Declaration," *Human Rights Quarterly* 13 (1991): 229–56.

Peters, J. S., ed. *Women's Rights, Human Rights: International Feminist Perspectives* (1995).

Tully, Catherine. "A Feminist Analysis of the Prohibition Against Sex Discrimination in International Law: The Convention on the Elimination of Discrimination Against Women" (1989).

Whitford, Sandra. *Feminism and International Relations: Gender in the International Planned Parenthood Federation and the International Labour Organization*, Carleton University, Doctoral Dissertation, 1991.

Response to Charlesworth, Chinkin, and Wright

Tesón, Fernando, "Feminism and International Law: A Reply," *Virginia Journal of International Law* 33 (1993): 647–84.

Papers from Conference

In August 1990 an international conference was convened at the Australian National University. The conference focused on two themes, one of which was "feminist analysis of selected areas of international law." The papers delivered on this issue were subsequently published in the *Australian Yearbook of International Law.*

Byrnes, Andrew. "Women, Feminism and International Human Rights Law: Methodological Myopia, Fundamental Flaws or Meaningful Marginalism? Some Current Issues," *Australian Yearbook of International Law* 12 (1991): 205–41.

Charlesworth, Hilary. "The Public/Private Distinction and the Right to Development in International Law," *Australian Yearbook of International Law* 12 (1991): 190–204.

Chinkin, Christine. "A Gendered Perspective to the International Use of Force," *Australian Yearbook of International Law* 12 (1991): 279–93.

Gardam, Judith. "A Feminist Analysis of Certain Aspects of International Humanitarian Law," *Australian Yearbook of International Law* 12 (1991): 265–78.

Waring, Marilyn. "Gender and International Law: Women and the Right to Development," *Australian Yearbook of International Law* 12 (1991): 177–89.

Wright, Shelley. "Economic Rights and Social Justice: A Feminist Analysis of Some International Human Rights Conventions," *Australian Yearbook of International Law* 12 (1991): 265–78.

Two Prominent Books on the General Subject of Feminist Legal Theory

Bartlett, Katharine T., and Rosanne Kennedy, eds. *Feminist Legal Theory* (1991). See especially Elizabeth M. Schneider, "The Dialectic of Rights and Politics," and Katharine T. Bartlett, "Feminist Legal Methods."

Smith, Patricia, ed. *Feminist Jurisprudence* (1993).

Feminist Theory in International Relations

Enloe, Cynthia. *Bananas, Beaches and Bases: Making Feminist Sense of International Politics* (1989).

Grant, Rebecca, and Kathleen Newland, eds. *Gender in International Relations* (1991).

Keohane, Robert O. "International Relations Theory: Contributions of a Feminist Standpoint," in Rebecca Grant and Kathleen Newland, eds., *Gender in International Relations* (1991), pp. 41–50.

Nielsen, Joyce McCarl, ed. *Feminist Research Methods: Exemplary Readings in the Social Sciences* (1990).

Peterson, V. Spike, ed. *Gendered States: Feminist (Re)Visions of International Relations Theory* (1992).

Runyon, Anne Sisson, and V. Spike Peterson. "The Radical Future of Realism: Feminist Subversions of I.R. Theory," *Alternatives* 16 (1991).

Sylvester, Christine. *Feminist Theory and International Relations in a Postmodern Era* (1994).

Tickner, J. Ann. *Gender in International Relations: Feminist Perspectives on Achieving Global Security* (1993).

Development of American Feminist Theory

Donovan, Josephine. *Feminist Theory: The Intellectual Traditions of American Feminism*, expanded edition (1994).

Extensive Bibliography Including Feminist Works

Kennedy, David, and Chris Tennant. "New Approaches to International Law: A Bibliography," *Harvard Journal of International Law* 35 (1994): 417–60.

10

Toward an Understanding of International Legal Rules

ANTHONY CLARK AREND

In a 1990 essay on recent works on international legal rules, Professor Phillip Trimble observed that "[t]o academics and practitioners alike, international law is a peripheral enterprise."[1] He then went on to cite a report prepared by John King Gamble and Natalie S. Shields in which they argue that "many academics still regard international law as . . . a 'fringe' specialty, well meaning, even noble, but naive and largely irrelevant to the real world."[2] Similarly, many International Relations theorists have also questioned the importance of studying international rules within the discipline of International Relations. For the Classical Realists and Structural Realists, international rules—whether actually called international law, seen as an element of an "international regime," or termed international norms—are largely epiphenomenal. The rules may exist, but they do not exert an independent influence on state behavior.

Notwithstanding these rather pessimistic views on the role of international rules, however, scholarly interest in international rules has been increasing over the past several years. International Relations theorists have continued to devote serious research to the nature and role of international rules. "Regime theory," in particular, has proven not to be the fad that some of its early critics claimed it would be.[3] Moreover, there has been a growing dialogue between scholars of International Law and scholars of International Relations, with individuals such as Anne-Marie Slaughter, Kenneth Abbott, Oran Young, Friedrich Kratochwil, and Andrew Hurrell making significant contributions to this conversation. One purpose of this book is to foster this dialogue. By bringing together what we believe to be important writings from both disciplines, we seek to promote a better understanding of differing approaches to international rules and to stimulate further interdisciplinary research and discussion. As can be seen from an examination of the exemplars included in this work, there are wide-ranging views on both the nature of international rules and the roles they play in the formulation and implementation of foreign policy.

One of the most important contributions that interdisciplinary work can make to the study of international rules is to recognize the distinctiveness of international *legal* rules and the role they play in international relations. As Andrew Hurrell notes, much of the literature on regimes has ignored the distinctiveness of international legal rules and the international legal system.[4] But as Hurrell asserts, "[i]t is international law that provides the essential bridge between the procedural rules of the game and the structural principles that specify how the game of power and interests is defined and how the identity of the players is established." International law, he continues, "provides a framework for understanding the processes by which rules and norms are constituted and a sense of obligation engendered in the minds of policy-makers." As a consequence, the purpose of this concluding essay is to take the first steps toward formulating an analytical approach to international legal rules—international law—that is relevant to world politics at the end of the twentieth century. It does this by focusing on three main issues. Section 1 examines the nature of international law. What are international legal rules? Are they really "law"? Section 2 explores the sources of international law. Where do international legal rules come from? Section 3 discusses the relevance of international legal rules to international relations. Do legal rules matter? Section 4 serves as a conclusion.

1. The Nature of International Law
A Definition of International Law

Over the years, international law has been defined in a variety of ways. We believe that international law is most appropriately and accurately defined as *a set of binding rules that seek to regulate the behavior of international actors by conferring rights and duties.* To clarify this definition, we make several observations.

First, we deem international law to be a set of binding rules. Unlike the adherents of the New Haven School, we do not accept the notion that international law *is* process. Undoubtedly, law is *created* through a process, and law can be *changed* through a process. But law is not a process itself. To make law equal the process ignores that at a given point in time, certain concrete *rules* can be identified.[5] Similarly, we reject the idea advanced by David Kennedy that law is "the practice and argument about the relationship between something posited as law and something posited as society".[6] The behavior of state officials and other participants in the international systems clearly reflects the notion that these decision-makers believe there are specific legal rules that can be determined.[7] Law does not equal process, nor does it equal the rhetoric of legal argumentation.

Second, legal rules are *binding* rules. For a rule to constitute international law, it must be obligatory. It must be a rule that international actors are required to follow. This crucial point differentiates *legal* rules from other types of rules. At the international level there may be a variety of rules—informal agreements, rules of the game, rules of protocol, and so forth. There may, for example, be a rule of international protocol that the visiting head of state must be given a twenty-one-gun salute on entering the territory of a state. While this rule may generally be followed, it is not regarded as a rule of international law; it is not seen as obligatory.

This element of our definition raises an important question: What makes rules binding? A Natural Law theorist would say that some rules are binding rules—and hence *legal* rules—because they are required by natural law. Some Legal Positivists would say that they are binding because there is an ever-present sanction for their violation. We reject both of these approaches. We believe that international legal rules are binding because the constitutive agents of the international system—states—regard them as binding and believe that a sanction, while perhaps not forthcoming, would be an *appropriate* response to their violation.

The Naturalist position, while perhaps desirable, does not conform with the realities of the international system. We do not deny the existence of moral principles. We do believe, however, that the moral order and the legal order are two different spheres. As will be discussed in this chapter, a rule becomes law only through *consent*. It is certainly possible that moral principles could become legal rules, but they are not automatically so. That which is legal is not always moral; and that which is moral is not always legal. It may be legal to provide financial assistance to a dictatorial government experiencing a low level of civil strife, but not moral. Conversely, it may be moral to intervene to overthrow an oppressive regime, but not legal.

We also reject the Positivist notion that rules are only binding if backed by the certainty of sanction. Despite efforts by Hans Kelsen to find a system of sanction at the international level, there is no true sanctioning arrangement at that level.[8] As a consequence, if sanction were a requirement for an international rule to be binding, there would be no binding international rules. Sanction, we submit, is not a requirement for binding rules. Even domestic law is not ultimately dependent on the existence of sanction for it to be law. The oft cited example is the famous *Steel Seizure* case. When President Truman ordered the seizure of the steel mills during the Korean War, the U.S. Supreme Court ruled his action unconstitutional. The Court, however, had no means of enforcing the decision. The president, after all, is the individual charged by the Constitution with executing the law. Nonetheless, the Court's decision was deemed to be binding on the president despite the inability of the Court to force Truman to comply. Moreover, at a deeper level, no *domestic* law can fundamentally be dependent on a sanction. Even though there are sanctions to punish those who violate the law, the efficacy of domestic law cannot ultimately depend on those sanctions. Instead, the law is based on perceptions of legitimacy. If even a very small percentage of the population of the

United States—2 percent for example—believed that a particular law was illegitimate and refused to obey it, no amount of coercive power could enforce compliance. It is thus the perception of legitimacy that makes the rule law, not the guarantee of sanction. Similarly, we assert that a sanction is not necessary to make *international* legal rules binding. It is enough that states regard the rules as binding and, accordingly, believe that a sanction would be appropriate for a violation of such rules.[9]

Third, international law consists of both *rights* and *duties*. On the one hand, international law consists of rules that grant rights to international actors. For example, the 1982 Convention on the Law of the Sea grants the right of innocent passage through the territorial sea. On the other hand, international law also consists of rules that impose duties. These duties may take the form of either *prescriptions* or *proscriptions*. Prescriptive rules require international actors to take some positive actions. For example, legal rules require states to make efforts to rescue and return astronauts from other states.[10] Proscriptive rules require international actors to abstain from a particular action. The Vienna Convention on Diplomatic Relations, for example, prohibits host states from arresting an accredited diplomat without the consent of the sending state.[11]

Fourth, in our definition we specifically note that international legal rules apply to *international actors*. Under traditional definitions, international law is said to regulate the behavior of *states*.[12] It is clear, however, that states are only one type of international actor that may be subject to international law. Other international actors include international organizations, "peoples," and individual human beings. International organizations may have extensive rights and duties under international law. They may enter into international agreements; their representatives may be entitled to immunity from jurisdiction; they may be able to bring claims against other international actors on behalf of their agents. Similarly, "peoples" may have rights and duties under international law. While the word "people" is not extremely well defined, it seems to indicate a group that has a common ethnic, racial, religious, linguistic identity. Under contemporary international law, "peoples" have the right to self-determination.[13] Finally, individuals may also be regulated by international law. For years, individual persons have been deemed to have certain duties under international law. It is illegal for a person to engage in piracy or slave trade or to commit genocide or war crimes. More recently, individuals have been seen as having rights under international law. Numerous treaties, including the International Covenant on Civil and Political Rights, seek to codify rights for individuals.

Is International Law Really "Law"?

Much ink has been spilled over the question of whether international law is really "law." In many respects, John Austin began the debate. For Austin, what is generally called international law is simply "positive international morality." It cannot be law because it does not represent the command of a sovereign. Since Austin's time, many international legal scholars have gone to great lengths to prove that international law is law indeed. Anthony D'Amato, for example, has recently written a strong defense of the legal status of international law.[14] Other legal scholars, such as Thomas Franck, have concluded that international law is not really "law"—at least not the same way domestic law is law.[15] Franck, however, contends that there is "a system of rules which conduces to a fairly high level of perceived obligation among members of a voluntarist community. . . ."[16] But it is not "law." Most international relations scholars have avoided the question by discussing "international rules" without differentiating between legal rules and other rules.

We submit that international law is *law* and believe that it is critical to acknowledge it as such. Even though there is no centralized legislature to make the law, even though there is no guaranteed system of enforcement, international law is properly called law. Why? Following Hedley Bull, we believe that the most important reason to consider certain international rules to be law is because international actors regard them as such. As Bull notes, "[t]he activity of those who are concerned with international law, public and private—statesmen and their legal advisers, national and international courts, and international assemblies—is carried on in terms of the assumption that the rules with which they are dealing are rules of law."[17] When policymakers of a state act, when the Secretary General of the United Nations speaks, when a human rights group appeals to a state, they all refer to international "law." They all behave with the understanding that the rules about which they speak are in fact law, not rules of the game or nonbinding moral norms. As Professor Bull asserts, "[i]f the rights and duties asserted under these rules were believed to have the status merely of morality or of etiquette, this whole corpus of activity could not exist."[18] Bull explains that "[t]he fact that these rules are believed to have the status of law, whatever theoretical difficulties it might involve, makes possible a corpus of international activity that plays an important part in the working of international society." In short, international actors call these rules law, and act as though these rules are law. Thus, even though the rules might be created differently from domestic law, they still have been constituted as law by the authoritative decision makers of the international system.

2. The Sources of International Law

Assuming that international legal rules can in fact be regarded as law, a second important issue is the source of international law. Who creates international law? How is it created? And how does a scholar, court, government official, or anyone else, for that matter, determine the existence of a rule of international law?

The Constitutive Agents

States

In most domestic legal systems, the primary means of creating legal rules[19] is through the actions of a centralized legislative body—a congress, a parliament, or even an individual "lawgiver." There is no such body at the international level. As the Classical Realists and Structural Realists observe, the international system is "anarchic," there is "no common power" to make the law.[20] Accordingly, most international legal scholars have asserted that in the decentralized international system, international law is created in a decentralized fashion by *states*. This notion proceeds from the Realist assumption that states are the primary players in the international system and that they act essentially as unitary actors. "States" thus make law.

We would agree that states are indeed the primary actors in the international system. States, however, should not be thought of in a completely anthropomorphic fashion. States do not act; the decision-making elites in states act *on behalf of the state*. It is not Sierra Leone that agrees to a rule, but rather those individuals empowered to make decisions in Sierra Leone that agree to the rule. Accordingly, we believe that international law is created by the interactions of the decision-making elites of the states in the international system.

By decision-making elite, we mean those individuals who are the effective decision-makers for the state. "Effective decision-makers" would be those officials of a state who are in control of the governmental mechanisms of the state, irrespective of whether they are perceived to be legitimate.

In sum, international law is created by the interaction of the decision-making elite of states. As a useful shorthand, however, we will say that "states" create international law.

Nonstate Actors

As noted in our definition of international law, legal rules are binding not merely on the behavior of states, but also on the behavior of nonstate actors. A reasonable question to pose, therefore, is what role these nonstate actors play in the constitutive process of legal rules.

Under the present condition of the international system, we believe that nonstate actors generally do not participate *directly* in the law-creating process. Nonstate actors, with some exceptions that will be discussed, do not interact with states in an unmediated manner. Nonstate actors may be the origins of proposed legal rule, but for the proposal to become law it must be accepted by states. For example, transnational environmental groups may formulate a proposed legal rule on ozone-layer depletion. But this rule becomes international law only when *states* through their interactions make it law.

With the growing prominence of nonstate actors, it is possible that the international system may be moving toward one in which states would interact with nonstate actors directly in the law-creating process. At present, there are two notable exceptions to the notion that nonstate actors do not participate directly in the law-creating process: intergovernmental organizations and peoples.

Intergovernmental organizations are organizations whose members are states—the United Nations, the Organization of American States, the International Atomic Energy Agency, and the like. In certain cases these organizations have limited ability to enter into the law-creating process. This can be seen in two areas. First, intergovernmental organizations can in some cases conclude treaties. Thus, for example, the United States concluded the "Headquarters Agreement" with the United Nations to set forth the relationship between U.S. territorial jurisdiction and the rights of the United Nations. Second, some international organizations are empowered to enact resolutions that are binding on their members. The United Nations Security Council, for example, is authorized in certain circumstances to adopt decisions that are binding on members of the United Nations.[21] Similarly, various organs of the European Union are able to make decisions that are binding on the member states.

In both these cases, however, the law creating authority of the international organization results because states have vested this authority in the organization. International organizations can enter into international agreements because their framers intended them to be able to have that ability, and certain organizations can adopt binding decisions because the member states consented to that power. Intergovernmental organizations are not truly *independent* actors in the law-creating process.

A second type of nonstate actor that has recently been able to enter directly into the law-creating process are peoples. The decision-making elites of self-determination movements have been able to enter into international negotiations and conclude international agreements on behalf of their people. Hence, the Palestine Liberation Organization was able to conclude agreements with Israel to attempt to establish peace in the region. Various factions in Cambodia were able to conclude agreements to establish a United Nations transition authority in their country.

Once again, however, the authority to conclude these agreements can be derived from the consent of states or an organization representing states. Moreover, these agreements are very specific accords dealing with particular sets of issues. The groups are not given a broad right to enter into the international law-creating process in general. In other words, except for their right to conclude these agreements, they do not participate in the day-to-day interactions that give rise to general—global—international law.

As time passes, nonstate actors may come to play a greater role in the law-creating process. There may come a time when the international system will consist of states and many nonstate actors interacting directly in the making of global international law. At present, however, states remain the fundamental law-creating entities.

The Traditional Sources of International Law[22]

If states create international law, how do they do so? What, in other words, are the sources of international law? Even though virtually all basic international law texts begin with a discussion of the sources of international law, we believe that it is useful to discuss those sources briefly to clarify our own approach.

The traditional starting place for a discussion of the sources of international law is Article 38 of the Statue of the International Court of Justice.[23] Strictly speaking, this article is merely an enumeration of the sources that the Court is to consult when attempting to determine the existence of a rule of international law for a pending case. In practice, however, scholars and decision-making elites nearly universally regard the sources listed in Article 38 as the authoritative delineation of the sources of international law.[24]

Article 38 lists three main sources of international law and two "subsidiary means for the determination of rules of law." The three main sources are international conventions, international custom, and general principles of law. The two subsidiary means are "judicial decisions" and the "teachings of the most highly qualified publicists of the various nations."

International Conventions
Conventions—treaties—are the most obvious, and perhaps the most maligned, source of international law. Treaties are formal, written agreements. Once a treaty has been signed and ratified and has entered into force, it is binding international law on all the parties. In essence, a treaty is the international equivalent of a contract; states consent to certain rules in a written document.

In the language of the discipline of international law, many different types of instruments can be termed treaties or international agreements. At the one end of the spectrum are bilateral treaties that establish rules for regulating the behavior of two states on a very specific issue for a very limited time. An example would be a treaty between the United States and France on the exchange of a particular spy. At the other end of the spectrum are major multilateral agreements that seek to establish complete governing regimes, such as the Charter of the United Nations or the 1982 Law of the Sea Convention. What makes both these kinds of agreements similar is that the rules they create, no matter how limited or how broad, are intended by states to be obligatory. The agreements do not merely establish "gentleperson's agreements" or informal arrangements; they establish law.

Customary International Law

The second source listed in Article 38 is "international custom as evidence of a general practice accepted as law." Unlike with treaties, customary international law is not created by what states put down in writing but rather by what they do in practice. A rule of customary international law develops when states engage in a particular activity and come to regard that activity as required by law. In short, for a rule of customary international law to exist, two elements must be present. First, states must engage in an activity; there must be a practice. Second, states must believe that the practice is required by law; they must believe that the practice is obligatory. Take, for example, the notion that diplomats enjoy immunity from criminal enforcement jurisdiction in their host state. This became a rule of customary international law as states began in fact to refrain from exercising criminal enforcement jurisdiction against diplomats and came to regard this restraint as legally obligatory.

Despite the less formal nature of customary international law, it is just as much "law" as written treaties. In effect, customary international law is analogous to common law in the Anglo-American tradition. Just as common law principles develop without a formal legislative act, so customary international law develops without formal codification.[25]

General Principles of Law

The third, and probably most imprecise, source of international law is what Article 38 rather anachronistically calls "general principles of law accepted by the civilized nations." Although there is a great deal of debate among scholars about what general principles are, there seem to be at least three plausible meanings of this phrase that are not necessarily mutually exclusive.

First, "general principles of law" may refer to principles that are common to the domestic legal systems of states. In other words, if an individual were to examine the domestic law of states throughout the world, he or she would find that there are certain legal rules that are present in all or almost all of those domestic systems. One such rule might be *estoppel*—the concept that a party may not act in a way contrary to a way in which the party has previously acted.[26] A defense attorney, for example, cannot argue on the first day of a trial that the client *had* killed the victim but should be found not guilty because he or she had acted in self-defense, and then contend on the second day that the client *had not* killed the victim at all. It is possible that an examination of all the world's legal systems would reveal that each has adopted such a rule for domestic law. If this were found to be the case, it would be logical to assert that if a dispute arose between states, the principle of estoppel could also be applied. If all, or virtually all, states had adopted this principle in domestic law, it could certainly be argued that they would accept it for international disputes, even though there may not have been an actual practice *among* states creating this principle as a matter of *customary* international law. This interpretation of general principles has received wide support from decision-making elites in the international system and would seem to be an acceptable meaning of this provision of Article 38.

Second, "general principles of law" may refer to general principles about the *nature* of international law that are accepted by states. Under this interpretation, general principles would refer to first principles about the international law-making process that are accepted by states. States, it could be contended, enter the international law-creating process with certain a priori assumptions. For the process by which customary international law and treaty law are created to make sense, states must first accept these basic principles. One such principle could be the notion of *pact sunt servanda*—the notion that promises should be kept. Unless states have first accepted this principle, it would be impossible to regard any particular treaty as binding. Because these basic principles are philosophically prior to custom and treaties, they can be regarded as a separate source of international law. States cannot by treaty establish the principle that treaties are binding.

Even though few scholars have *explicitly* recognized this interpretation, we believe it is an important understanding of general principles. The other sources of international law are comprehensible only if states have first accepted certain a priori principles.

Third, some scholars would contend that "general principles of law" may refer to certain natural law principles. Two examples of such principles that are often cited are "equity" and "humanity." The difficulty with this understanding of general principles is that there do not seem to be universally accepted definitions of concepts such as equity and humanity. Rather, they seem merely to reflect subjective values espoused by certain states. From the perspective of the United States, for example, the Soviet Union may have violated the principle of humanity in shooting down the civilian Korean Airline flight 007 in 1983. The Soviets, however, probably did not believe such a principle existed, let alone that they violated it.[27]

Scholarly Writings and Judicial Decisions

Finally, Article 38 lists the writings of scholars and court decisions as "subsidiary means for the determination of rules of law." Although there may be some debate on the question,[28] we believe that these two items are not independent sources of international law. Rather, they are materials that a scholar or decision-maker can consult to determine the existence of one of the three main sources of international law. A scholar, for example, could examine court decisions and the writings of international legal scholars to assist him or her in determining the content of a particular rule of custom or a general principle, or the existence and meaning of a treaty. Courts and scholars do not "make" the law, but rather testify to its existence. Since it could be quite time consuming for each person seeking to identify a particular legal rule to undertake an independent assessment of state practice, it is often convenient to cite credible scholars and generally accepted court decisions that have already reaped the fruits of such an assessment.

Other Possible Sources of International Law

With the increased prominence of international organizations, much attention has been given to the role that resolutions of international organizations play in the development of international law.[29] As noted earlier, some bodies of international organizations, for example, the Security Council of the United Nations, have the authority to create law that is binding on its member states. Some scholars, however, have contended that resolutions of the United Nations General Assembly may also have legal significance.

Under the Charter of the United Nations, resolutions of the General Assembly are for the most part only recommendations.[30] Only resolutions dealing with such issues as financial contributions, budgetary matters,[31] and internal housekeeping are binding on member states. General Assembly resolutions are, however, often cited as evidence of state practice. This is normally done in one of two ways. Some scholars contend that if a General Assembly resolution is adopted unanimously, or nearly unanimously, it indicates a belief on the part of states that the principles enunciated in the resolution are "regarded as law."[32] These individuals would, in consequence, be willing to rely on the resolution as the main indicator of state practice. Other scholars and decision-makers would disagree with this interpretation.[38] They would argue that states vote for United Nations General Assembly resolutions for a variety of reasons—to appease a domestic audience, to gain international acceptance, to gain specific favors from other states, and so forth. These reasons may have little to do with the perception that the resolution should be regarded as indicative of state practice. Individuals supporting this interpretation would contend that generally a General Assembly resolution should be regarded as but *one* possible indicator of a customary practice that should be taken into consideration along with the more traditional indicators—daily actions of states, statements of government officials, behavior of commanders in the field, and the like. These scholars would contend that it would be possible for a resolution to constitute a codification of existing customary international law. The resolutions could thus be cited as a "shorthand" to denote the custom, much as treaties that codify customary international law are cited. To do this, however, it would be necessary to demonstrate that there was a norm of customary law that existed before the adoption of the resolution and that the states adopting the resolution intend to codify this norm.

The Test of International Law

Most social scientists are quite explicit about their disciplinary methodology. All too often, however, international legal scholars are unclear about the methodology they use to determine the existence of a legal rule. This problem may result from the training legal scholars receive, which has a domestic legal orientation and a well-established method of determining domestic law. As can be seen from the exemplars contained in this anthology, there are many different methodologies for determining the existence of international rules. Accordingly, we wish to make our methodology quite clear.

It is our belief that international legal rules are created through *authoritative state practice*.[34] Drawing on the traditional sources of international law as just discussed, we have proposed a two-prong test for the determination of a rule of international law.[35] For a putative international rule to be an international *legal* rule, it must possess two elements: authority and control. First, the rule must be controlling of state behavior. This is simply another way of saying that it must be reflected in state practice. Second, it must be perceived by states to be authoritative. That is, the decision-making elites in states must regard the rule to be law; they must regard it to be obligatory. In the language of international law, the rule must have *opinio juris*.

We believe that this test reflects a proper understanding of the traditional sources of international law. It is clear how it applies to customary law, since authority and control are simply another way of saying that a rule of customary law requires a practice (control) regarded as law (authority). We also assert that the "authority-control" test can be applied to treaties and general principles. This contention is a bit more controversial. Some international legal scholars would argue that a treaty that has been properly ratified and has entered into force remains "law" until states have formally terminated or withdrawn from the treaty.[36] We believe, however, that states have in practice effectively withdrawn their consent from a particular provision of a treaty, and hence that it is not "law," if the provision is not believed by them to be authoritative and/or there is very little compliance with the provision, even though the treaty may remain technically "in force." Similarly, we would argue that if a putative general principle is not controlling and is not perceived to be authoritative, it cannot be considered a "general principle of law *recognized* by the civilized nations." In sum, whatever the traditional source of a particular rule of law in question may be, the validity of the rule can be determined by reference to its authority and control.

This "authority-control" test raises two further questions. First, how does one measure authority and control? Unlike barometric pressure or relative humidity, authority and control do not admit of precise measurement. It is, however, reasonably clear what one looks at to determine if a putative rule has authority and control. A rule is controlling if international actors comply with the rule. To determine compliance, a scholar would examine the behavior of the international actor to whom the rule is addressed. If, for example, one were to explore the rule of diplomatic immunity, one would examine all those cases where diplomats had been implicated in a crime. If the rule were completely controlling, the investigator would expect to find no case where the diplomat, once his or her status had been established, was arrested and tried. This kind of empirical examination may be relatively easy for some putative rules because the cases would be easily observable. In other cases it might be more difficult to determine control, since it could be nearly impossible for the observer to identify clearly the cases where a decision-maker was confronted with the issue of compliance with the rule. For example, if one wished to examine whether the prohibition against aggressive force were controlling, it might be easy to find times when a decision-maker chose to commit an act of aggression; but it could be very difficult to determine those times when a decision-maker contemplated an act of aggression but chose not to undertake the act.

To determine whether a rule is authoritative one would examine official and unofficial communications by the decision-making elites about the rule. What do executive heads of government—prime ministers, presidents—say? What do domestic legislative bodies proclaim? What do domestic courts rule? Taking a previous example, if one finds that executive heads have endorsed the concept of diplomatic immunity, that domestic legislatures have enacted laws that support the immunity of diplomats, that domestic courts have upheld the notion of immunity, then the rule likely has authority.

A second question raised by the test is how much authority and control are necessary for a putative rule to be considered a *legal* rule. Here there is no simple answer. And indeed, this may be one reason there is often significant disagreement about whether a would-be rule is international law. We would contend that perceptions of authority and the existence of control can be understood in terms of a continuum. At one end there are rules that enjoy both a very high degree of authority and control. The rule that states are entitled to a 12-nautical-mile territorial sea would fall at this end of the spectrum. The decision-making elites in nearly all states would claim that this rule is law, and their flagships would behave accordingly. Hence, this rule and other rules that enjoy this level of authority and control would clearly be "law." At the other end of the continuum are putative rules that enjoy little authority and little control. An example might be a putative rule that every person has a right to holidays with pay.[37] While this provision is contained in the Universal Declaration of Human Rights, it lacks authority. Most government officials throughout the world would probably claim this might be an aspiration, not a legal right. Moreover, the provision is not truly reflected in the practice of states. A large percentage of the world's population consists of workers not guaranteed paid holidays by the state. Accordingly, there would be no *legal* right to paid holidays.

It is relatively easy to identify the legal status of putative rules at both extremes of the spectrum and proclaim them either to be law or to not be law. The preceding examples can be roughly depicted as in Figure 1. Rules

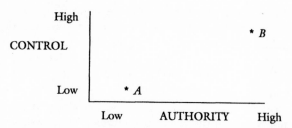

Figure 1. *B = high authority and high control = law (e.g., 12-nautical-mile territorial sea); *A = low authority and low control = not law (e.g., paid holidays)

at point *B* would be law; they possess a high degree of authority and control. Rules at point *A* would not be law; they possess a low degree of authority and control.

The question of the legal status of the rules becomes more complicated when dealing with rules located elsewhere on the graph. What about a rule at point *Y*, where there is a high degree of control but a low degree of authority (Figure 2)? Or conversely, what about a rule at point *Z*, where there is a high degree of authority but a low degree of control? Or finally, what is the legal status of a rule at point *X*, where there is but a moderate degree of both authority and control? For putative rules at points *X, Y*, and *Z*, it is impossible to set an absolute standard against which the legal status of the rule could be judged. This is in part due to the difficulty of assigning numerical values to authority and control, as well as the lack of any international consensus on such a standard. As a consequence, there will likely be disagreements among scholars and decision-making elites about putative rules in these ranges. This should not be a reason to despair. Even in domestic legal systems, there are areas where different courts and other authoritative decision-makers have very different assessments about what the law is. In a sense, this problem reflects the essence of the law-creating process. Law is dynamic; hence at any point in time some putative rules may be in this middle range—somewhere between being clearly law and being clearly not law. We would submit, however, that

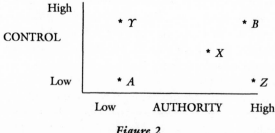

Figure 2

there is a substantial body of rules that have both a high degree of authority and a high measure of control.

3. The Relevance of International Legal Rules to International Relations

As noted earlier, one of the reasons for the estrangement that developed between international relations theorists and international legal scholars was a growing perception by adherents of the Realist School that international law did not matter, that legal rules did not play a significant, independent role in international relations. With the more recent International relations literature on international regimes, it has become more acceptable to discuss the relevance of international rules to international relations. For the regimes theorists, the question was normally posed in the new idiom—Do regimes matter? Given our specific interest in international legal rules, we would simply ask—Do international legal rules matter? Does international law matter?

Given our understanding of the nature and sources of international law discussed in this chapter, we answer this question affirmatively. International legal rules do matter in international relations. They are not merely epiphenomenal. To elaborate on this hypothesis, this section will explore three potential roles of international legal rules: (1) giving structure to the international system, (2) influencing state behavior, and (3) regulating the activity of certain nonstate actors. At the outset of this section, we would note that much empirical research needs to be done on this question. Our purpose here is to *continue* a discussion of the question, not to provide the final answer.

International Law and the Structure of the International System

When scholars explore the question of the relationship of international legal rules to international relations, they frequently focus on the specific role these rules play (or do not play) in the foreign policy decision-making processes in particular cases (the issue taken up in the next subsection). They do not often, however, examine the role that legal rules play in constituting the structure of the international system. As Andrew Hurrell observes, "Rationalist models of co-operation miss the crucial link between the costs and benefits of specific legal rules and the role of international law as constitutive of the structure of the state system itself."[38] But how does international law constitute the international system?

As many of the Sociological (Reflectivist) Institutionalists have noted, there are a number of ways in which international law constitutes the structure of the state system. We will note several. First, international law enshrines the doctrine of sovereignty.[39] The concept of sovereignty—the notion that states are independent, that they can be bound by no higher law without their consent, that they are juridically equal—is one of the fundamental assumptions underlying international relations. While we agree with the standard caveats about the notion of sovereignty—it may not be absolute, it may undergo change, it can be distinguished from empirical autonomy,[40] and so on—the concept forms a most basic operating principle of international affairs. It is ingrained in the minds of all international actors and can be considered one of the primary building blocks of the modern international system.

Second, and inextricably related to the first point, international law establishes the criteria for membership in the international system.[41] It determines when a particular international actor will enjoy certain rights and duties at the global level. International law, for example, establishes the criteria for statehood. It determines when an entity can be regarded as a state. In so doing, international law confers legitimacy on states. International legal rules also determine when nonstate actors will be endowed with rights and duties. It determines, for example, when an international organization can enter into international agreements and when the decision of such an organization can be binding on members.

Third, international law provides a language for diplomacy. Even Nigel Purvis, commenting on the New Stream of international legal scholarship, observes that "[o]n the most basic level, sovereigns seem to take for granted the propriety of engaging in international legal discourse (instead of some other type of discourse) when they seek to resolve international issues."[42] When international actors speak, they use the idiom of international law. Decision-making elites in states assert their positions in terms of legal rights. They make *legal* claims. When, for instance, a state decides to use armed force, it will invariably present its claim in terms of international law. It is rare indeed for a state to justify its actions solely on the basis of political, practical, or even moral factors.[43] Some reference to legal principles is made in virtually every case. When the United States invaded Grenada in 1983, or Argentina seized the Falkland (Malvinas) Islands in 1982, or Iraq moved into Kuwait in 1990, these states justified their actions in legal terms.

Likewise, if a state is critical of the behavior of another state, it will frequently castigate that state for failure to abide by its *legal* obligations. Many states criticized the South African system of apartheid as a violation of international human rights law; the United States accused the Soviet Union of violating the Anti-Ballistic Missile Treaty by establishing a phased-array radar at Krasnoyarsk.

Fourth, international law gives normative value to actions and claims made by international actors. As Friedrich Kratochwil has noted, the international legal order "specifies the steps necessary to insure the validity of their official acts and assigns weight and priority to different claims."[44] In other words, when states or other international actors contemplate a particular action, legal rules provide guidance about what procedure to follow for the act to be perceived as legitimate. During the Gulf War, for example, international law provided a procedure that the United States and its allies could use to ensure that the action against Iraq would receive the maximum degree of legitimacy. By using the process set forth in Chapter VII of the United Nations Charter, the United States did much to avoid the charge of unilateralism. In addition, once a state or other international actor has acted, international legal rules reflect certain normative judgments about the legitimacy of the action. Thus, when Iran denied immunity to diplomats from the United States, the act was perceived to be "wrong." Similarly, when the United Nations sent peacekeeping troops into Cambodia to supervise a transition to power, other international actors believed that action to be "right."

International Law and the Behavior of States

In playing a constitutive role in the international system, we believe that international law is extremely relevant to international relations. The Sociological (Reflectivist) Institutionalists make this useful contribution to the understanding of the role of legal rules. Other scholars from a more "rationalistic" approach might explore the question of rules a bit differently. They would ask whether any theory can be developed that will explain and predict the role that legal principles play in specific foreign policy decision. In other words, can any theoretical insights be gleaned as to what role *specific* legal rules play in *specific* cases that are decided by *specific* decision-makers?[45]

This is an area where much research needs to be done. It presents one of the most tricky theoretical questions. As can be seen from Section 2, it is clear that we follow in the tradition of Legal Positivism. We believe that international legal rules are created by the consent of states. Accordingly, we believe that the rules were created to reflect the interests of states. If this is the case, can these legal rules have an independent influence on state behavior? As Andrew Hurrell noted, "[t]he central problem . . . for regime theorists and international lawyers is to establish that laws and norms exercise a compliance pull of their own, at least partially independent of the power and interests which underpinned them and which were often responsible for their creation."[46] He explains that "[t]o avoid empty tautology it is necessary to show not only that the rules exist and that they are created and obeyed primarily out of self-interest or expediency, but that they are followed even in cases when a state's self-interest seems to suggest otherwise." It is easy to demonstrate that, in cases where international law is consistent with immediate policy goals, states will follow the law. But what about cases where there is a conflict between international legal rules and other specific policy goals? What will decision-makers do in those cases?

In an effort to stimulate further empirical research on this question, we would suggest several tentative hypotheses about the role of international legal rules in the actual decision-making process.

First, foreign policy decision-makers will almost always attempt to find out what international law says about a contemplated course of action. They may choose not to comply with the law, but they will wish to know its content. We believe that it would be rare indeed for a state to be unconcerned about what the law provided. Accordingly, the foreign ministries of virtually all states have certain individuals charged with informing decision-makers about what they believe international law is on a particular issue.

Second, the higher the degree of authority and control of a particular rule, the more likely it is to be followed, even though it may be in the immediate short-term interest of the state not to follow the rule. A state does not particularly want to be perceived as a "law breaker." The stronger the rule, the more likely the state will be seen as violating the rule.[47]

Third, the more easily the rule could be violated reciprocally to the detriment of the state in question, the more likely the state is to comply with the rule. Argentina, for example, is probably not inclined to shoot British diplomats, deny British flagships innocent passage through the territorial sea, or kill British prisoners of war, if Britain could reciprocate in kind.

It is our hope that these and other hypotheses can be tested by empirical research. Such research that examines the role of law in foreign policy decision-making is still in its formative stages. Recent research projects have tended to focus on United States foreign policy decision-making. Clearly, for any comprehensive theory to be developed, scholars must examine the behavior of a wide range of states and a variety of issue areas.

International Law and the Behavior of Nonstate Actors

Finally, another way in which legal rules matter in international relations relates to the behavior of nonstate actors. As noted previously, international law determines who the legitimate actors in the international system are and establishes that nonstate actors can play a role in international relations. The function of international law, however, goes beyond this simple acknowledgment. International law regulates the behavior of nonstate actors in the international system much as domestic law regulates the behavior of actors in the domestic legal system. Whenever a person takes an international flight or sails on the high seas, that individual's behavior is controlled by accepted legal rules. When someone mails a letter, it arrives at its destination through the operation of international legal rules dealing with international communication.[48] These kinds of rules generally operate without violation or much controversy. Accordingly, they tend to be neglected in discussions of the role of international law. They are, nonetheless, extremely important in providing order to innumerable international transactions that take place. Indeed, if the amount of private or other nonstate interaction increases, these types of legal rules will play an even more critical role in international relations.

4. Conclusion

From the discussion in this essay it is clear that we believe that an under-standing of international legal rules is critical to an understanding of con-temporary international relations. There are distinctive *legal* rules, and they do matter. Much more research needs to be done, however, about the nature of these rules and the role they play in international relations. For this research to take place, scholars must appreciate the insights from both international lawyers and International Relations theorists. Such work re-quires a knowledge of the salient writings in both fields. We hope that this anthology as a whole can serve as a starting point for accumulating this knowledge and that further interdisciplinary research can take up some of the issues presented in this concluding essay.

Notes

I am indebted to Robert J. Beck for his helpful insights in the preparation of this essay. The work draws heavily upon concepts that we have been developing in our other collaborative efforts.

1. Phillip R. Trimble, "International Law, World Order, and Critical Legal Studies," *Stanford Law Review* 42 (1990): 811–45 at 811.

2. John King Gamble, Jr., and Natalie S. Shields, "International Legal Scholarship: A Perspective on Teaching and Publishing," *Journal of Legal Education* 39 (1989): 39–46 at 40.

3. This was one of the criticisms raised by Susan Strange in her classic critique of regime theory, "*Cave! Hic Dragones:* A Critique of Regime Analysis," in Stephen D. Krasner, ed., *International Regimes* (Ithaca, N.Y.: Cornell University Press, 1983), pp. 337–42. Andrew Hurrell in his contribution to the present volume rejects the idea that the regime approach is a fad.

4. Hurrell explains that "the quest for rigour (and perhaps an excessive desire to avoid the sins of idealism) has led to far too wholesale a dismissal of the need to understand both the specific character and the technical features of the international legal system." Andrew Hurrell, "International Society and the Study of Regimes: A Reflective Approach," in Volker Rittberger, ed., *Regime Theory and International Relations* (Oxford: Oxford University Press, 1993), reprinted in this volume in chapter 7.

5. Presumably, the scholars of the New Haven School prefer to understand law as process in order to recognize the dynamic nature of law. They seem to believe that if "law" is conceived to be a set of rules, this dynamic nature is missed. We appreciate their desire to avoid thinking of law as a set of static, ossified rules. Law is dynamic. Nonetheless, law is not process itself.

6. David Kennedy, "A New Stream of International Law Scholarship," *Wisconsin International Law Journal* 7 (1988); Lectures 1 and 3 reprinted in chapter 8 of this book.

7. See Hedley Bull, *The Anarchical Society* (New York: Columbia University Press, 1977), pp. 125–36.

8. The United Nations Security Council, of course, has the authority to take measures to respond to a "threat to the peace," "breach of the peace," or an "act of aggression" U.N. Charter, arts. 39–51. The Council also has the authority to

enforce decisions of the International Court of Justice (art. 94). There is, however, no blanket right given to the Security Council to punish all violations of international law. Moreover, with each of the permanent members exercising a veto in the Council, the body's effectiveness is severely hampered.

9. See Hurrell, "International Society and the Study of Regimes," pp. 50–61, for a similar understanding.

10. Agreement on the Rescue of Astronauts, the Return of Astronauts, and the Return of Objects Launched into Outer Space, entered into force December 3, 1968, 672 UNTS 119, 19 UST 7570, TIAS 6599.

11. Vienna Convention on Diplomatic Relations, Article 29, entered into force April 24, 1964, 500 UNTS, 23 UST 3227, TIAS 7502.

12. Brierly, for example, defines international law "as the body of rules and principles of action which are binding upon civilized *states* in their relations with one another." J. L. Brierly, *The Law of Nations,* (6th Waldock ed. Oxford: Clarendon Press, 1963), p. 1.

13. The Charter of the United Nations makes reference to "self-determination of peoples." U.N. Charter, art. 1, para. 2 (1945).

14. Anthony D'Amato, "Is International Law Really Law?" in *International Law: Process and Prospect* (Irvington, N.Y.: Transnational, 1987), pp. 1–26.

15. Thomas M. Franck, *The Power of Legitimacy Among Nations* (New York: Oxford University Press, 1990).

16. Ibid., p. 40.

17. Hedley Bull, *The Anarchical Society* (New York: Columbia University Press, 1977), p. 136.

18. Ibid.

19. This is the *primary* means of creating law. In the Anglo-American legal tradition, common law, which develops through practice, is also an important means of creating law.

20. Robert J. Lieber uses this expression from Thomas Hobbes's *Leviathan* as the title for his international relations text. Robert J. Lieber, *No Common Power,* 3d ed. (New York: HarperCollins, 1995).

21. U.N. Charter, art. 25.

22. We have set forth our understanding of the sources of international law in Anthony Clark Arend and Robert J. Beck, *International Law and the Use of Force: Beyond the UN Charter Paradigm* (London: Routledge, 1993), pp. 5–10. This discussion seeks to elaborate on that previous formulation.

23. Statute of the International Court of Justice, art. 38, para. 1.

24. Almost all international law texts and case books begin with this claim about article 38. See, e.g., Malcolm N. Shaw, *International Law,* 3rd ed. (Cambridge: Grotius Publications, 1991), p. 59. ("Article 38(1) . . . is widely recognised as the most authoritative statement as to the sources of international law") (footnote omitted).

25. Frequently, rules of customary international law do receive codification. For example, the customary international law on diplomatic immunity was codified in 1961 in the Vienna Convention on Diplomatic Relations. These rules on immunity, however, were *law* long before their codification.

26. *Black's Law Dictionary* notes, in part, that "'estoppel' means that a party is prevented by his own acts from claiming a right to detriment of other party who was entitled to rely on such conduct and has acted accordingly. . . . An estoppel

arises when one is concluded and forbidden by law to speak against his own act or deed. . . . Estoppel is a bar or impediment which precludes allegation or denial of a certain fact or state of acts, in consequence of previous allegation or denial or conduct or admission, or in consequence of a final adjudication of the matter in a court of law." *Black's Law Dictionary,* 5th ed. (St. Paul: West, 1979), p. 494.

27. See John T. Phelps, "Aerial Intrusions by Civil and Military Aircraft in Time of Peace," *Military Law Review* 255 (1985): 107, for an excellent discussion of the principle of humanity in this context.

28. See Shaw, *International Law,* p. 59.

29. M. Akehurst, *A Modern Introduction to International Law,* 5th ed. (London: Allen and Unwin, 1984), p. 37.

30. U.N. Charter, art. 10.

31. Ibid., art. 17.

32. See Richard Falk, "On the Quasi-Legislative Competence of the General Assembly," *American Journal of International Law* 60 (1966): 782; Samuel Bleicher, "The Legal Significance of Re-Citation of General Assembly Resolutions," ibid., 63 (1969):444. This discussion of the legal status of General Assembly resolutions draws on L. Henkin, R. Pugh, O. Schachter, and H. Smit, *International Law,* 3rd. ed. (St. Paul: West, 1991), pp. 126–48.

33. See the comments of a former legal counsel to the United Nations in E. Suy, *Innovations in International Law-making Process* (1978), cited in Gerhard von Glahn, *Law Among Nations,* 5th ed. (New York: Macmillan, 1986), pp. 18–19.

34. In the development of our test of international law, we draw heavily on the work of the New Haven School. As will be noted, however, our conceptions of authority and control differ somewhat from those of McDougal and associates.

35. See Arend and Beck, *International Law and the Use of Force,* pp. 9–10; Anthony Clark Arend, "International Law and the Recourse to Force: A Shift in Paradigms," *Stanford Journal of International Law* 27 (1990): 1.

36. Professor Edward Gordon, for example, has made this argument with respect to provisions of the United Nations Charter dealing with the use of force. Edward Gordon, "Article 2(4) in Historical Context," *Yale Journal of International Law* 10 (1985): 271, 275.

37. I am indebted to Dr. David Little of the U.S. Institute of Peace for noting this issue.

38. Hurrell, "International Society and the Study of Regimes," p. 59. Robert O. Keohane makes a similar observation about institutions in general. He notes that adherents to what he calls the reflectivist school of international relations submit that "institutions are . . . *constitutive* of actors as well as vice versa." Robert O. Keohane, "International Institutions: Two Approaches," *International Studies Quarterly* 32 (1988): 379, 382.

39. Kratochwil makes this point. Friedrich V. Kratochwil, *Rules, Norms, and Decisions: On the Conditions of Practical and Legal Reasoning in International Relations and Domestic Affairs* (Cambridge: Cambridge University Press, 1989), pp. 251–56.

40. As Keohane explains: "As a legal concept, the principle of sovereignty should not be confused with the empirical claim that a given state in fact makes its decisions autonomously." Keohane, *International Institutions: Two Approaches,* p. 385.

41. See Hurrell, "International Society and the Study of Regimes," pp. 59–60.

42. Nigel Purvis, "Critical Legal Studies in Public International Law," *Harvard Journal of International Law* 32 (1991): 110.

43. An excellent study of such use of international law to justify a particular foreign policy action is Robert J. Beck, *The Grenada Invasion: Politics, Law, and Foreign Policy Decisionmaking* (Boulder, Colo.: Westview, 1993).

44. Kratochwil, *Rules, Norms, and Decisions,* p. 251.

45. Hurrell notes that this question is an area for further research. Hurrell, "International Society and the Study of Regimes," pp. 70–71.

46. Ibid., p. 53.

47. This hypothesis draws on the arguments of Professor Franck. See Franck, *The Power of Legitimacy Among Nations.*

48. Professor Robert J. Lieber has made this point.